SAT II Biology For Dummies®

Cheat Sheet

Tips and Tricks for SAT II Biology Questions

- Remember that easy questions are worth the same amount [...] so don't rush through the easy questions to get to the hard on[...]
- Eliminate answer choices that don't make sense.
- Guess if you can eliminate at least one answer choice.
- Don't be afraid to skip a question if you can't eliminate any answer choices.
- Take advantage of your pencil. Draw pictures, make graphs, and cross out wrong answers.

Things to take with you to the test

- **Your admission ticket:** When you register for the SAT II, the College Board sends you a form that you must bring to the test with you. It proves you're registered.
- **A photo ID:** You have to prove that you are you and not your really smart neighbor coming in to take the test for you. Any form of identification that does not have your picture on it is unacceptable.
- **Several number 2 pencils, a big eraser, and a little pencil sharpener:** Avoid anxiety by carrying a bunch of pencils with you and a pencil sharpener just in case they all break. A large eraser comes in handy, especially if you need to make clean erasures on your answer sheet.
- **A quiet watch:** Chapter 2 relates the importance of having your own watch with you during the test. Just make sure that your watch does not make any sounds at all.

Important cell biology info

- Prokaryotic cells are smaller and have no organelles. Eukaryotic cells are larger and have organelles, especially a nucleus.
- Cellular respiration is the processes of burning fuel, especially glucose, to produce ATP. The aerobic kind uses oxygen (O_2) while the anaerobic kind does not.
- Photosynthesis is the process of using light energy to produce organic molecules, especially glucose.
- Mitosis is the asexual reproduction of individual cells. Meiosis is the production of gametes (eggs or sperm) for sexual reproduction.

Important molecular biology info

- Lipids are the only kinds of organic molecules that are hydrophobic.
- A polymer is any large chain of molecules.
- Proteins are polymers of amino acids.
- Nucleic acids like DNA and RNA are polymers of nucleotides.
- Cellulose is a polymer of glucose, and is used to make cell walls.

For Dummies: Bestselling Book Series for Beginners

SAT II Biology For Dummies®

Important ecology info

- Primary producers are the things that do photosynthesis, like plants and algae. They produce food for everyone else.
- Consumers are the things that need to eat food because they cannot make their own food. This includes herbivores, carnivores, and omnivores.
- Decomposers are a special kind of consumers that eat nonliving organic material.
- Carrying capacity refers to how many individuals an ecological area can support.
- The tropical rainforest has the highest diversity and density of species of all the biomes. The desert (too dry) and the tundra (too cold) have the lowest diversity and density.

Important evolution info

- All life on earth is descended from bacteria-like organisms that first lived over 3 billion years ago.
- Darwinian natural selection happens when the organisms with the most successful characteristics in a population survive and reproduce, while the others do not survive or reproduce.
- A population is a group of individuals of the same species that live in the same area and can interbreed. This is the same as a gene pool.
- The ultimate source of diversity comes from random mutations on the DNA. Most mutations are bad for the organism, but some of them can be beneficial.

Important organismal biology information

- The nervous system uses fast electrical signals and neurotransmitters to control different parts of the body.
- The endocrine system exerts control by releasing different hormones into the blood stream.
- The digestive system breaks down food and absorbs nutrients.
- The respiratory system performs gas exchange.
- The cardiovascular system sends the nutrients and gasses where they need to go.
- Gymnosperms are trees with cones, like pine and fir. Angiosperms are plants that produce flowers.
- Monocots are grasses and grains. Dicots are all the other flowering plants, including everything that produces fruit.
- Xylem carries water and minerals up from the soil, through the roots, and then up to the leaves. Phloem carries the organic molecules made in photosynthesis from the leaves to the rest of the plant.

For Dummies: Bestselling Book Series for Beginners

*SAT II Biology
FOR
DUMMIES®

by Lisa Hatch
and Scott Hatch

WILEY

Wiley Publishing, Inc.

*SAT is a registered trademark of the College Board, which was not
involved in the production of, and does not endorse, this product.

*SAT II Biology For Dummies®

Published by
Wiley Publishing, Inc.
111 River St.
Hoboken, NJ 07030-5774
www.wiley.com

For general information on our other products and services, please contact our Customer Care Department within the U.S. at 800-762-2974, outside the U.S. at 317-572-3993, or fax 317-572-4002.

For technical support, please visit www.wiley.com/techsupport.

Wiley also publishes its books in a variety of electronic formats. Some content that appears in print may not be available in electronic books.

Library of Congress Control Number: 2005921602

ISBN-13: 978-07645-7842-7

ISBN-10: 0-7645-7842-1

Manufactured in the United States of America

10 9 8 7 6 5 4 3 2 1

1B/RX/QT/QV/IN

*SAT is a registered trademark of the College Board, which was not involved in the production of, and does not endorse, this product.

WILEY

About the Authors

Scott and Lisa Hatch have prepared students for college entrance exams for over 25 years. While in law school in the late '70s, Scott Hatch taught LSAT preparation courses throughout Southern California to pay for his education. He was so good at it that, after graduation, he went out on his own. Using materials he developed himself, he prepared thousands of anxious potential test-takers for the SAT, ACT, PSAT, LSAT, GRE, GMAT, and even the unassuming Miller's Analogy Test (MAT).

Scott and Lisa have a special place in their hearts for standardized tests; they kindled their romance in the classroom. Lisa took one of Scott's LSAT preparation courses at the University of Colorado and improved her love life as well as her LSAT score. Lisa's love for instructing and writing allowed her to fit right in with Scott's lifestyle, teaching courses, and preparing course materials. They married shortly thereafter.

Since then Scott and Lisa have taught test preparation to students worldwide. Currently over 300 universities and colleges offer their courses through live lectures and online. They have written the curriculum for both formats. The company they have built together, The Center for Legal Studies, not only provides standardized test preparation courses but also courses for those who desire careers in the field of law, including paralegals, legal secretaries, legal investigators, victim advocates, and legal nurse consultants.

Scott has presented standardized test preparation courses since 1979. He is listed in *Who's Who in California, Who's Who Among Students in American Colleges and Universities,* and has been named one of the Outstanding Young Men of America by the United States Jaycees. He was a contributing editor to *The Judicial Profiler* (McGraw-Hill) and the *Colorado Law Annotated* (West/Lawyers Co-op) series, and editor of several award-winning publications.

Lisa has been teaching legal certificate and standardized test preparation courses since 1987. She graduated with honors in English from the University of Puget Sound, and received her master's degree from California State University. She and Scott have co-authored numerous law and standardized test texts, including *Paralegal Procedures and Practices,* published by Thomson/West Publishing, and *A Paralegal Primer,* published by The Center for Legal Studies, and *Preparing for the SAT, Preparing for the ACT, Preparing for the LSAT, Preparing for the GRE,* and *Preparing for the GMAT,* all of which are available online in an interactive classroom format.

Dedication

We dedicate our *For Dummies* series books to Alison, Andrew, Zachary, and Zoe Hatch. Rather than file missing persons reports on their parents with local law enforcement agencies, they demonstrated extreme patience, understanding, and assistance while we wrote this book, which made this innovative, comprehensive, informative, and entertaining standardized test preparation series possible.

Authors' Acknowledgments

This book would not be possible without the extensive research and writing contribution of standardized test prep and biology expert, Michael J. Zerella. His efforts greatly enhanced our writing, editing, and organization, and we are deeply grateful to him.

We also need to acknowledge the input of the thousands of high school students and other college applicants who have completed our test preparation courses over the last 25 years. The classroom and online contributions offered by these eager learners have provided us with a lot of information about what areas require the greatest amount of preparation. Their input is the reason we are able to produce accurate and up-to-date test preparation. Many of our students have also taken the sample tests that we have set forth in this book and have assisted us in perfecting the questions and answer choices.

Our meticulous scholarship and attempts at wit were greatly facilitated by the editing professionals at Wiley Publishing. Our thanks go out to Jennifer Connolly for her unflagging support and encouragement and Tracy Boggier for initiating us to the process and being available whenever we had questions.

Finally, we wish to acknowledge our literary agents, Bill Gladstone and Margo Maley Hutchinson, at Waterside Productions in Cardiff for introducing us to the innovative *For Dummies* series. Wiley Publishing has to be commended for its pioneering efforts to make preparing for compulsory entrance exams fun. We thrive on positive reinforcement and feedback from our students and encourage our readers to provide comments and critiques at feedback@legalstudies.com.

Publisher's Acknowledgments

We're proud of this book; please send us your comments through our Dummies online registration form located at www.dummies.com/register/.

Some of the people who helped bring this book to market include the following:

Acquisitions, Editorial, and Media Development

Project Editor: Jennifer Connolly

Acquisitions Editor: Tracy Boggier

Copy Editor: Jennifer Connolly

Technical Editor: Scott Caldwell

Editorial Manager: Michelle Hacker

Editorial Supervisor: Carmen Krikorian

Editorial Assistant: Courtney Allen

Cartoons: Rich Tennant, www.the5thwave.com

Composition

Project Coordinator: Maridee Ennis

Layout and Graphics: Carrie A. Foster, Denny Hager, Joyce Haughey, Stephanie D. Jumper, Barry Offringa, Lynsey Osborn, Mary Gillot Virgin,

Proofreaders: Arielle Mennelle, Charles Spencer

Indexer: Lynnzee Elze

Publishing and Editorial for Consumer Dummies

Diane Graves Steele, Vice President and Publisher, Consumer Dummies

Joyce Pepple, Acquisitions Director, Consumer Dummies

Kristin A. Cocks, Product Development Director, Consumer Dummies

Michael Spring, Vice President and Publisher, Travel

Kelly Regan, Editorial Director, Travel

Publishing for Technology Dummies

Andy Cummings, Vice President and Publisher, Dummies Technology/General User

Composition Services

Gerry Fahey, Vice President of Production Services

Debbie Stailey, Director of Composition Services

Contents at a Glance

Table of Contents

Part IV: Constructing Creatures: Organismal Biology 181

Chapter 13: Going Vegetarian: Plant Structures and Functions...............183

Chapter 14: Making A Body Work: Animal Organ Systems 197

Introduction

There you are merrily skimming through the admissions requirements for your favorite college. When all of a sudden you are dealt a shocking blow. Your absolute top choice — you'll die if you don't get in — college requires not only the SAT I and the ACT but also the SAT II. Indeed there is yet another set of tests for which you will need to sharpen more number 2 pencils and for which you'll have to awaken at the crack of dawn on an otherwise sleepy Saturday.

The SAT II Biology is just one of many possible SAT II subject tests that you can take, and most students who take a subject test in science take the biology test. So you will be in good company on test day. Many of your fellow SAT II test takers will be sitting down to draw Punnet squares and trace life cycles.

You know you have to get ready for the challenge, but what are you going to do? You know you recorded the characteristics of protists somewhere. (There it is! No, wait. That was the description of the blind date your best friend tried to set you up with.) And even if you could read your handwriting, the details are concealed by your little brother's dirty handprint left when he was looking through your stuff for paper airplane material. Come to think of it, that handprint smudge may just contain a sample protist! Yuk! Maybe reading through old notes isn't such a good idea . . .

Clearly, you need a readable, more concisely structured resource. You've come to right place. *SAT II Biology For Dummies* puts at your fingertips everything you need to know to conquer the SAT II Biology test. We give you a complete review of the biology concepts it tests and provide insights into how to avoid the pitfalls that your friends who create the SAT II want you to fall into, and we try to make it as enjoyable as a book that devotes itself to biomes and photosynthesis shapes can be.

About This Book

We suspect that you aren't eagerly anticipating sitting through the SAT II, and you're probably not looking forward to studying for it either. Chances are your parents or some other well-meaning authority figure bought this book for you for your own good, and we know just how much human beings enjoy doing things that are good for them!

Therefore, we've attempted to make the study process as painless as possible by giving you clearly written advice in an easy to swallow, casual tone. We realize you have a bunch of things you'd rather be doing, so we have broken down the information in easily digested bites. If you have an extra hour before basketball practice or clarinet lessons, you can devour a chapter or even a particular section within a chapter. (If these eating metaphors are making you hungry, feel free to take a snack break.)

We pepper the biology reviews with plenty of sample questions, so you can see just how the SAT II tests a particular concept. Our sample questions read like the actual test questions, so you can get comfortable with the way the SAT II phrases questions and expresses answer choices. And to further enhance your comfort with the test questions, this book contains two practice tests. Ultimately, the best way to prepare for any standardized test is to practice on lots of test questions, and this book has over 200 of them.

This book also gives you time tested techniques for improving your score. We show you how to quickly eliminate incorrect answer choices and make educated guesses. You'll learn how to manage your time wisely. And we give you suggestions for creating a relaxation routine to employ if you start to panic during the test. We have included all kinds of information to help you do your best on the SAT II.

Conventions Used in This Book

You should find this book to be easily accessible, but there may be a few things that require explanation. You can use the following highlighting tools to focus on the most important elements of each chapter:

- **Sidebars:** A few of the chapters may contain sidebars (a paragraph or two in a shaded box). Sidebars contain quirky bits of information that we think may interest you but that aren't essential to your performance on the SAT II. If you're trying to save time, you can skip the sidebars.

- **Bulleted lists:** Lists are bulleted and marked with a solid bar to the left of the lists.

- **Italic:** Words to remember are italicized so that you can develop vocabulary lists from them if you wish.

Foolish Assumptions

Here are our assumptions about you:

- Although we guess it is possible that you have picked up this book just because you have an insatiable love for biology, we are betting it's more likely that you are reading this book particularly because you've been told you have to take the SAT II Biology test. (We have been praised for our startling ability to recognize the obvious!) And since we're pretty astute, we have figured that this means that you intend to apply to undergraduate programs that either require you take the test for admissions purposes or suggest that you take it for a variety of other considerations.

- Generally, the schools that require the SAT II are highly selective, so we're thinking that you're a pretty motivated student since you have your sights on these competitive institutions of higher learning. You probably know a lot about biology already, and you've probably taken at least a year of it in high school. Some of you may have even taken advanced biology classes in high school, like genetics. If you have, you should do very well on the SAT II.

- There are those of you for whom biology is fresh in your mind, and you just need this book to know what to expect when you arrive at the test site. This book has that information for you.

- It's also possible that you have been out of high school for a while, and your biology knowledge may have left for parts unknown. If this is you, this book provides you with all of the basics as well as advanced concepts to give you a comprehensive foundation for the more challenging concepts you'll need to know to excel on the SAT II.

How This Book Is Organized

The first part of this book introduces you to the nature of the SAT II beast and advises you on how to tame it. The comprehensive biology review follows. The first part of the review provides you with basic concepts that you may have forgotten and need to know to build a firm foundation for the concepts covered in the rest of the review. Once you feel ready, you can take the four practice tests that come after the review and find out your score.

Part I: Putting the SAT II Biology E/M Test into Perspective

Read this part if you want to know more about what information the SAT II Biology tests and how you can handle it in the best way.

Part II: Getting Up Close: Cells, Genetics, and Other Stuff on the Biology-M Section

The SAT II Biology test has two versions: the Biology-E Test and the Biology-M Test. This first part focuses on the information you will need to know if you take the Biology-M Test, but don't skip this part if you are taking the Biology-E Test. The review in this part also contains information that you'll find in the core part of the test that everybody has to take regardless of which version they pick.

Part III: Environmentally Aware: Evolution, Ecology, and Other Stuff on the Biology-E Section

This second part focuses on the information you will need to know if you take the Biology-E Test, but please don't think you can skip this part if you are taking the Biology-M Test . The review in this part also contains information that you'll find in the core part of the test that everybody has to take regardless of which version they pick.

Part IV: Constructing Creatures: Organismal Biology

If you need a review on how organisms tick, this is the part for you. These chapters give you the practical information you need to know on the SAT II Biology E/M Test about the makeup of plants and animals and how they function.

Part V: Practice Makes Perfect

Once you feel comfortable with your biology knowledge, you can practice on the two full-length tests found in this part. For your testing enjoyment, each test contains a Biology-E version and a Biology-M version, so you can take both versions to see which suits you best. Each comes complete with a scoring guide and explanatory answers. We suggest you practice on both tests and both versions even if you already know which version you want to take.

Part VI: The Part of Tens

This part finishes up the fun with a summary of the important concepts you should have down pat for the test.

Icons Used in This Book

One exciting feature of this book is the icons that highlight especially significant portions of the text. These little pictures in the margins alert you to areas where you should pay particularly close attention.

Throughout the book we will give you insights into how you can enhance your performance on the SAT II. The tips give you juicy timesavers and point out especially relevant concepts to remember for the test.

This icon points out those little tricks contained in the SAT II that the test makers use to tempt you into choosing the wrong answer.

Your world won't fall apart if you ignore our warnings, but your score may suffer. Heed these cautionary anecdotes to avoid making careless mistakes that can cost you points.

Whenever you see the Example icon in the text, you know you're going to get to practice the particular area of instruction covered in that section with a question like one you may see on the test. Our examples include detailed explanations of how to most efficiently answer SAT II questions and avoid common pitfalls.

This icon flags parts of the text that describe interesting, but technical facts about biology. They aren't essential to understanding biology, so you can skip them . . . if you want.

Whenever you see this icon in the book, be sure to take note. You won't want to forget the ideas this icon flags.

Where to Go from Here

We know that everyone who uses this book has different strengths and weaknesses, so this book is designed for you to read in the way that best suits you. If you are a biology whiz and only need to brush up on a few areas, you can go right to the chapters and sections that cover those areas.

We suggest that you take a more thorough approach, however. Familiarize yourself with the general test-taking process in the first two chapters and then work through the complete biology review. You can skim through sections that you know a lot about by just reading the Tips, Warnings, and Traps and Tricks and working through the Examples.

Some of our students like to take a diagnostic test before they study. This is a fancy way of saying that they take one of the practice tests in Part V before they read the rest of the book. Taking a preview test shows you which questions you seem to cruise through and which areas need more work. After you read through the biology review, you can take another practice test and compare your score to the one you got on the first test. This way you can see just how much you improve with practice.

Part I

Putting the SAT II Biology E/M Test into Perspective

The 5th Wave   By Rich Tennant

These evolution questions never make sense to me.

In this part . . .

The first part of this book initiates you to the wonders of the SAT II. Its chapters introduce the format of the test and explain how to take it seriously (but not too seriously). You may be tempted to skip this part and jump headlong into the biology review. If you do, we strongly suggest that you come back to this part later. We include information in here that you may not get otherwise.

Among other things, you'll learn what to expect on the test, how the test is scored, whether you should take the Biology-M or Biology-E test, and what stuff is tested on each of them. You'll also discover some helpful tips for organizing your time and relaxing if you get nervous. So, do yourself a favor and give it the 20 minutes or so that it takes to read through these two chapters.

Chapter 1

Getting the Lowdown on the SAT II

*E*ven if you're familiar with the way the general SAT I test is set up, you'll need to read this chapter. The SAT II is significantly different from the SAT I in the way that it's formatted and the way that you approach it.

Justification: How Colleges Use the SAT II

How colleges and universities evaluate your SAT II Biology E/M score really depends on the particular college. Some colleges use your SAT II score as an additional admissions tool equal in value to your other standardized test scores, like the SAT and the ACT, your GPA, and other factors, like the difficulty of your high school course load. Your SAT II test scores may allow you to test out of taking specific first year college courses at some schools.

Figuring out whether the SAT II is an admissions requirement

Before you fill out the application form, research the admissions requirements of your top school choices. The most up-to-date information is usually found on the college's website. Read the requirements carefully because there are all sorts of ways that schools apply the information they get from your SAT II score.

Most of the schools that require you to take the SAT II want you to take two or three of them. Some schools tell you exactly which subjects they expect you to take and others leave the choice up to you.

What part the SAT II plays in the admissions decision also varies from school to school. Some schools don't even consider your SAT II score when they decide whether to sign you on or not. Other colleges give your SAT II score the same weight as they do your SAT or ACT score and your GPA. And other colleges may not put the same amount of importance on your SAT II score as they other standardized tests and GPA, but they use it for additional consideration like they would your extracurricular activities.

A case study: How the University of California system uses the SAT II for admissions

The University of California requires students to take the SAT II for all of its extensions; so if you plan to attend any campus of the University of California, you'll have to take the SAT II. According to Ravi Poorsina of the UC Office of the President, the primary concern of the university is that an incoming student comes to the campus ready to handle the rigors of the college curriculum. The university needs to know what the students know about particular subjects. That's why as of the time of this book's printing, the admissions committee mandates that every prospective student take two SAT II subject tests. The SAT II is so important to the University of California that it will probably weigh it equally with the regular SAT or ACT score and your GPA.

A student in the freshman class of 2006 and beyond will have to take two SAT II subject tests. Each test has to be from a different general subject area, like one science and one history or a language test and the literature test. If you submit two scores from the same subject area, you won't meet the requirement. The university system does not require any one particular test as long as you take two from different subjects.

Because the new general SAT contains math questions that are similar in difficulty to those in the SAT II Math Level I, the University of California will no longer accept the Level I math test. Therefore, if you want to use a math test for acceptance to a University of California undergraduate program, you must take the Level II test.

Even with the advent of a new general SAT, the University of California system still values the information it gets from a student's SAT II score. We guess you'll just have to keep on taking those standardized tests!

Each SAT II subject test falls into one of five general categories. It is important to know these categories because some colleges won't accept two tests from the same category. The five categories are as follows:

- **English:** As of the spring of 2005 there is only one English test and that is the SAT II Literature exam.

- **History and Social Studies:** The two history tests make up this category, SAT II U.S. History and SAT II World History.

- **Science:** The SAT II Biology E/M, SAT II Chemistry, and SAT II Physics are all considered to be science tests. Go figure!

- **Mathematics:** The SAT II Math has two separate math tests, the Level IC and the more advanced Level IIC.

- **Languages:** The SAT II has language tests in nine languages, Chinese, French, German, Italian, Japanese, Korean, Latin, Modern Hebrew, and Spanish. Some of the languages consist of one-hour listening tests; some are one-hour written tests. The French, German, and Spanish each have two separate tests, one listening and one written. You can choose which of these you prefer.

Find out how your college choices evaluate your score, and if you are confused by their websites call their admissions offices directly. It's nice to know just what is at stake before you walk into the test.

Using the SAT II as a placement tool

Colleges that use your SAT II score as an admissions requirement, and even those that don't, *may* consider it for placement purposes. Quite a few colleges and universities allow first year students to meet a core course requirement if they do well on the SAT II in that particular subject. So, if you did really well on the SAT II Literature test, for instance, you may not have to take a 101 English class in college. Specific information about using the SAT II for placement purposes is not usually spelled out for you on the college websites, so call the admissions office directly if you need more information about whether your SAT II score can get you out of taking one of those huge freshman lectures with 500 other students.

Decisions, Decisions: Determining Which Subject Test You Should Take

Until the regular SAT changed in 2005, it used to be a little easier to decide which SAT II subject area tests you needed to take. Most of the colleges that required the SAT II made you take the SAT II Math, the SAT II Writing, and one other. The only decisions your overworked brain had to make was whether to take Level I or Level II for math and which of the other subjects would provide the least amount of torture for your third choice.

Things have changed, however. Beginning with students entering college in Fall 2006, the College Board offers a new SAT that incorporates the old SAT II Writing test and some of the elements of the Level I Math test. The result is that colleges will probably no longer mandate particular subject tests, and you will have to decide which tests are best for you.

Figuring out the right subject area tests for you

To determine which of the over 15 different subject tests are best for you, consider your strengths. Ignore what your friends are doing and choose the subjects that you do best in and that you know the most about. If you can recite the Declaration of Independence in your sleep, the SAT II U.S. History is probably a good bet. If all of your friends seek you out for help with their trigonometry homework, you'd do well taking the SAT II Math. Maybe you spend all of your free time expanding your bug collection; the SAT II Biology E/M is the test for you. Knowing what you'd like to major in can help direct you toward a particular subject test as well. If you're really conflicted, it may help you to know that you can decide which tests you're taking on test day. We highly suggest, however, that you are certain about which tests you want to take before you step into the testing room.

Harvard University, for example, requires its applicants to take three SAT II subject tests to be considered for admission. Although the requirements don't mandate that each test comes from a different general subject area (like those of the University of California) the admissions committee suggests that you show your range of understanding by taking as broad a mix of subjects as you feel comfortable with. So, it's probably best to take your SAT II tests in a variety of subjects.

Knowing which emphasis of the SAT II Biology test you should take

The SAT II Biology test allows you to choose an emphasis. You can either take the exam with the "E" emphasis or the one with the "M" emphasis. Both tests start out with a core section of 60 questions that you take regardless of whether you choose Biology-E or Biology-M. Then the test diverges into two separate parts for the last 20 questions. The Biology-E tests concentrates on things like ecology and diversity in organisms. The Biology-M test emphasizes cellular biology and genetics. You can't take the Biology-E and the Biology-M on the same day because the first 60 questions would be the same on that day, but you could take one on one test day and the other on another test day. We can't think of too many good reasons to do this, however. Unless you apply to a university that requests that you take both emphases, we suggest that you stick to one and meet your SAT II requirement with other subject tests.

Then the trick is to discover which emphasis is better for you. Some high school biology courses stress certain areas more than others. If you have questions about what emphasis fits better with the types of things you studied in high school, you can probably find the best information from your biology teacher. Another way to figure out which emphasis you're best suited for is to carefully examine the practice tests you take in this book. We suggest that you answer all of the test questions (Biology-E and Biology-M) in the practice tests. Score yourself for both parts and see which emphasis gives you the highest score. If you do better on Biology-E questions, take the Biology-E, but if your score is higher on the Biology-M questions, choose Biology-M on test day. If you score roughly the same on both parts, take the emphasis that you like more. You may as well enjoy yourself as much as possible on test day!

It's All in the Timing: When to Take Your SAT II Biology E/M Exam (and What to Bring)

You're not done making decisions yet. Once you've figured out what subject tests are best for you, you need to determine when's the best time to take them and what you should bring along with you to the test.

The best time to take the SAT II

Most of the SAT II subject tests are offered in January, May, June, October, November, and December. When in your high school career you choose to take a particular subject test really depends on what the subject test covers. SAT II subject tests that cover the material you learned in a two-semester course (like U.S. history, world history, biology, chemistry, and physics) are best taken as soon after you've taken the course as possible. This means that if you take U.S. history and biology in your sophomore year, you may be wise to take the SAT II U.S. History and SAT II Biology after you complete your sophomore year on either the May or June test date. This is much earlier than you would normally take other admissions tests. Most don't take the regular SAT or ACT until the end of their junior years.

The math, literature, and foreign language subject tests, however, cover information that you learn over the span of several years of coursework. You'll probably get a better score on these subjects if you wait until you've had at least two or three years of high school courses. You could take these subjects at the end of your junior year or even in the fall of your senior year in most cases.

You can take up to three SAT II subject tests in one day, but you can take only one or two on one day if that's what works for you. Some people like to get them over with all at once. Others like to be able to concentrate on just one subject. You're less likely to suffer burnout if you take only one or two tests on any one testing day.

When you've settled upon the date for your SAT II, you'll need to register. The deadline is usually a little over a month before the test date. Everything you need to know about registering for the SAT II is located in the *Registration Bulletin* published by the College Board. It has the test dates, instructions, registration deadlines, fees, test center codes, and other related information. You can get the bulletin from your school counselor. Or you can get the same information and register online at the College Board's website, www.collegeboard.com.

The things to take with you to the SAT II

Regardless of when you take the SAT II and how many subjects you take in one day, you will need to take certain things along with you. The absolute essentials include the following:

- ✔ **Your admission ticket:** When you register for the SAT II, the College Board sends you a form that you must bring to the test with you. It proves you're registered.

- ✔ **A photo ID:** You have to prove that you are you and not your really smart neighbor coming in to take the test for you. Any form of identification that does not have your picture on it is unacceptable, so bring along one of the following:

  - a driver's license

  - a government or state-issued identification card

  - a school identification card

  - a valid passport

  - a school identification form prepared by your school counselor if you don't have any of the other forms of ID

- ✔ **Several number 2 pencils, a big eraser, and a little pencil sharpener:** Avoid anxiety by carrying a bunch of pencils with you and a pencil sharpener just in case they all break. A large eraser comes in handy, especially if you need to make clean erasures on your answer sheet.

- ✔ **A quiet watch:** Chapter 2 relates the importance of having your own watch with you during the test. Just make sure that your watch does not make any sounds at all.

If you plan to take more than one test, you should also bring in a quick, light snack (like a power bar) to eat during the short break between tests. You'll need energy for the other tests.

Don't expect to be able to eat or drink during the test. Keep your snack in your pocket for later. And don't eat anything too heavy before a test. You want the blood pumping to your brain not your stomach.

Don't bring any scratch paper, highlighters, protractors, calculators, or books with you. Pretty much anything that isn't listed above is not allowed. As nice as it would be to tune out your neighbors hacking cough with your CD player, listening and recording devices are taboo (unless you're taking a language listening test).

First Impressions: The Format and Content of the SAT II Biology E/M

As we have mentioned earlier, the SAT II Biology E/M actually has two separate emphases: the Biology-E and the Biology-M. You choose one to take on test day. You could take each of these tests during separate administrations, but most colleges and universities will accept only one.

Each emphasis contains 80 questions that you have to answer within 1 hour. 60 of the questions are the same for both emphases; 20 are unique to either the Biology-E or the Biology-M. Unlike many other standardized tests, the SAT II Biology E/M questions do not necessarily get harder as you move along through the test. The different subjects that you could be tested on for biology vary so greatly that question difficulty is based more on how well you know a subject than where the question appears on the test. There may be questions toward the end of the test that are easier for you because they test a math subject that you are better at. For instance, if you know more about genetics than you do cell division geometry, you wouldn't want to spend a bunch of time trying to answer a mitosis question early on in the test because it may keep you from getting to a pea plant pollination question later on. (For more on managing your time wisely during the test, check out Chapter 2.)

Managing the answer sheet

The answer sheets for the SAT II have places for 100 questions, but you will only mark answers for 80 since there are only 80 questions on the math test. Managing the answer sheet for biology can be a little tricky, so you have stay alert. If you are taking the Biology-E, you'll mark your answers on the sheet in order from 1–80. Put a little pencil mark under question 80 on your answer sheet. If for some reason you mark an answer after your pencil mark, you know you've done something wrong. Be sure to erase the pencil mark before you turn in your answer sheet.

If you choose to take the Biology-M, you'll mark answers on your sheet for questions 1–60. Then you skip over questions 61–80 on the answer sheet and start marking answers from 81–100. Put a light pencil mark under question 60 on you answer sheet and another after question 80. This tells you that you should not have any answers marked for any bubbles between 61 and 80. Erase the pencil marks at the end of the test.

Keeping the question types straight

The SAT II Biology E/M present three ways of asking you questions. You'll see basic multiple-choice questions with five answer choices and classification questions (which are kind of multiple-choice questions in reverse). Included in the standard issue multiple-choice questions are data interpretation questions, which give you a bunch of information, like experiment data or charts, and then ask anywhere from three to five questions about the data. Questions that ask you to interpret data can sometimes be easier than the other types because the information you need to answer the question is right there in the question booklet. You just need to know how to analyze it.

The classification question type is pretty much unique to the biology test. It isn't all that fancy. You just get a list of answer choices first. Then you get a series of "questions" that are just descriptions. You need to choose which of the answers fits the description. We talk more about how to answer classification questions in Chapter 2.

Reveling in the subject matter

Table 1-1 provides a breakdown of the general subjects covered on the SAT II Biology E/M test and how they are specifically tested on each of the emphases.

Table 1-1	Topics Covered on the SAT II Biology				
	Organismal Biology	*Ecology*	*Genetics*	*Cells and Molecules*	*Evolution*
Explanation	These questions test what you know about how plants and animals are structured and how they function.	You'll need to know about what makes up populations and communities and how they function, how energy flows, how organisms absorb and use nutrients, and what constitutes the variety of biomes.	Genetics questions ask you about meiosis, patterns of inheritance, Mendelian genetics, molecular genetics, and population genetics.	You'll be asked about the elements of cells, how they reproduce and "breathe." For plant cells, you'll need to know about photosynthesis. Questions will test what you know about enzymes, DNA and RNA, and biological chemistry.	Evolution questions test your knowledge of origin of life theories and patterns of evolution, the concept of natural selection, and how species come about. You'll need to know how organisms are classified and some basic differences among the different classifications.
Biology-E	About 25%	About 25%	About 15%	About 15%	About 20%
Biology-M	About 25%	About 15%	About 20%	About 25%	About 15%

The SAT II Biology E/M exam covers a lot of territory, so make sure you read through the reviews in this book thoroughly.

Where You Stand: Scoring Considerations

Okay, so you know what the colleges are looking for, but when it comes down to it, the thing you're probably most concerned about is your final score, the number the colleges see when they get your report.

How the SAT II testers figure out your score

The SAT II is scored similarly to the regular SAT. Each multiple-choice question has five possible answer choices. If you pick the correct answer, you get 1 full point for that question. If you pick the wrong answer, the SAT II deducts ¼ point from your raw score. So, one right answer covers four wrong answers. If you skip a question, you don't get any points but you don't lose any points. It's still better to guess if you can eliminate at least one answer choice. For more on guessing strategies, see Chapter 2.

You determine your raw score by taking the total number of questions you answered incorrectly times 4. Then you subtract that number from the total number of questions you answered correctly. The SAT II doesn't stop there, however. To try to make every test measure students equally, the SAT II develops a scale for each test. Where your raw scores lands on the scale determines your final score, the one that the colleges get to see.

Why you should never cancel your SAT II score

The fine folks at the College Board allow you to cancel your SAT II score either on the test day itself or in writing by the Wednesday after you take the test. Here are some reasons why you should never take them up on their offer.

You can't know what your score would be if you hadn't cancelled it. It is really difficult to know how well you've done on an exam when you are in the middle of it, and you can miss a fair amount of questions and still do well on the SAT II. So you may feel like you messed up when you really shined.

If you cancel one SAT II test score, the scores for any and all other SAT II tests you take on that day will be cancelled, too.

It is highly unlikely that you will do significantly better on one administration over another. Only unusual circumstances, like getting the stomach flu in the middle of a test, will cause you to perform much differently on an SAT II test.

Most colleges and universities only consider your top scores, so if you do pretty poorly on one test, you can retake it. The yucky score will be reported with the others, but most schools will ignore it in favor of the good ones.

There are only a few circumstances where canceling a score may be a good idea. The flu scenario mentioned is one. The others involve mechanical failure. If your calculator malfunctions on the math test or your cassette player fails on a language listening test, you can cancel your score on that particular test without canceling the scores for the other tests you took that day. Be prepared, however, and have a backup calculator or cassette player with you just in case you run into this problem.

Every SAT II subject test has a final score value of 200–800 points. You get 200 points for knowing your name and recording it correctly on your answer sheet, but colleges aren't going to be satisfied with a 200, so you're going to have to work harder than that. Generally, if you answer at least 60% of the questions on the test correctly, you'll get a score of around 600. The mean score on an SAT II test is a little higher than it is on the regular SAT because most of the students who take an SAT II test take it because they think they know something about the subject.

Check with the schools you want to get into regarding acceptable SAT II scores, we think you'll find that most of the more selective schools are looking for numbers in the upper 600s and beyond. This means you can still skip about 20 questions and get a good score, as long as you are right on questions you do answer. Don't skip more than 20 questions on any SAT II test, though.

Here is a rough idea of how many questions you need to answer correctly on the SAT II Biology test to achieve a particular scaled score as long as you don't answer too many of the other questions incorrectly. Our assumption in each case is that of the remaining answer choices you skipped twenty questions and answered the rest incorrectly. The scales for the Biology-E and Biology-M tests are about the same.

To get a 500, you need to answer about 38 of the 80 questions correctly.

To get a 550, you need to answer about 43 of the 80 questions correctly.

To get a 600, you need to answer about 49 of the 80 questions correctly.

To get a 660, you need to answer about 55 of the 80 questions correctly.

To get a 710, you need to answer about 60 of the 80 questions correctly.

To get a 750, you need to skip fewer than 20 questions and answer about 69 of the 80 questions correctly.

To get an 800, you can skip about 6 questions as long as you answer all of the other 74 correctly.

How the SAT II testers report your score

Unless you choose to cancel your score within three days of taking the SAT II, your score will be reported to the colleges you choose. If you take more than one SAT II subject test, all of the scores will be reported together. The colleges get to see them all, and usually they will choose the top scores to use in their admissions calculations.

All Over Again: Retaking the SAT II

Because most colleges consider only your top scores, it may be in your best interest to retake a subject test if aren't happy with your first score. The SAT II administrators let you take a test over and over again if you want (that's pretty big of them considering you have to pay for it every time). The SAT II reports to the colleges scores for up to six administrations of the same test, but we don't suggest you take the same test as many as six times. If you do retake the test, make sure you take it seriously. You want to show improvement. A college will be much more impressed to see a rising score than a falling one. And most colleges will be turned off if they see that you have taken one particular subject test more than two or three times. The key is to prepare to do your best on the first try, and obviously that is your goal since you have chosen to read this book.

Chapter 2

Maximizing your Score on the SAT II

*Y*ou could have been sleeping, but instead you have to give up a cozy, quiet down comforter with fluffy pillows for a claustrophobic classroom, a bundle of number 2 pencils, and a neighbor with a chronic cough. If you have to endure this agony, you may as well reward yourself with the best SAT II score you can get. This chapter contains the tools you need to put together a winning strategy. Using what you know to your full advantage and avoiding common test-taking hazards can help you almost as much as brushing up on your biology.

Knowing When to Skip: Guessing Strategies

It may surprise you that we mention guessing at all given that the SAT II penalizes you at ¼ point for every wrong answer. The SAT II folks created that penalty to keep you from using your testing hour fabricating fantastic artwork on your answer sheet with random sweeps of your number 2 pencil instead of methodically reading through questions and answer choices. But don't let that punitive point deduction keep you from guessing. You only get points if you fill in your bubbles; and if you mark an answer only when you are absolutely sure you're right, you may not have enough bubbles filled in to get the score you want.

Getting the lead out

So then, how do you know when you should mark your best guess and when you should skip? It all depends on how many answer choices you can cross out. So the first thing you do is figure out how to cross out wrong answers.

One of the biggest favors you can do for yourself when you take a multiple-choice test is to use your pencil to cross out wrong answers in the test booklet. Crossing out wrong answers serves several purposes:

✔ You'll never waste time rereading a wrong answer choice. You have a limited amount of time to answer questions, so you don't want to spend time reading answers you've already decided are wrong.

✔ Crossing out answers gives you a psychological boost. When you look at the question, you don't see five possible answer choices anymore. You've made your test booklet look more manageable.

✔ It will be easier to determine whether or not you have eliminated enough choices to mark a bubble on your answer sheet.

Now, you may think that all that crossing out takes up too much precious time. Or maybe you're concerned about a shortage of pencil lead. These are lame excuses. It takes less than a second to push your pencil through a line of text. And if you're concerned about your pencil supply, take in a bundle with you. Arrive at the test with at least ten finely sharpened number 2 pencils at your service. Heck you may even take in a sharpener just in case. Just make sure it is a manual model and not some noisy battery-operated machinery to make the proctor scowl.

If crossing out answer choices doesn't come naturally to you, practice at home. Use your practice tests to not only hone your knowledge but also train yourself to mark through your question booklet.

X marks the spot

Now that you've mastered the fine art of lead spreading, you'll use it to determine whether you should go one step further with your pencil and fill in a bubble for a question on your answer sheet. Here's a little system that helps you decide when you should guess and provides a code to let you know which questions are best to return to if you have time at the end of the test. The approach outlined below will help make you a better test taker because you will think and write while most people are just thinking:

1. **Read the question carefully.**

2. **Examine each answer choice.**

3. **Use your pencil to cross out answer choices that are obviously incorrect. (We know you've heard this before, but repetition is a powerful learning tool!)**

4. **If you are able to eliminate four answer choices and therefore know the correct answer, fill in the appropriate bubble on your answer sheet, mark a big X next to the question in your test booklet, and go on to the next question.**

5. **If you are able to eliminate at least three of the five answer choices, choose one of the remaining answer choices and fill in its bubble on the answer sheet. Put a big X next to this question in your test booklet and go on to the next question.**

6. **If you are able to eliminate only two of the five answer choices, go ahead and choose one of the remaining answer choices and fill in its bubble on the answer sheet. Write a large 3 next to the question and go on.**

7. **If you can cross out only one of the five answer choices, put a big 4 next to the question in your test booklet. Leave the answer bubbles blank for this question. Go on to the next question.**

8. **If you can't cross out any of the five answer choices, put a big 5 next to the question in your test booklet. Leave the answer bubbles blank. Don't worry about the question and go on.**

9. **If you finish before the proctor calls time, you know which questions in the section are the best to take another look at. First go to the questions with 3s by them, then those with 4s, and then, only as a last resort if you have lots of time, the 5s.**

10. **When you read through a question again, you may find that you are able to eliminate more answer choices. Mark a new answer if you left the question blank or change the one you previously marked if you come up with a different answer.**

Remember that this is a technique. And just like when learning any other technique, it may be awkward for you at first. With practice, though, it can become your greatest asset.

Eliminating Choices: How to Recognize a Wrong Answer

You know what to do once you have determined an answer choice is wrong, but how do you know when an answer is incorrect? With a little know-how, you can master the art of answer elimination even if you are unsure about the information a question tests.

Using common sense

Eliminate answer choices that don't make sense. Senseless answer choices are the easiest to spot if you read carefully. For instance, consider the following question.

Which of the following is true about plants that contain no circulatory system?

(A) They are called tracheophytes.

(B) They belong to a group that includes bacteria.

(C) They don't contain seeds.

(D) They belong to a group that includes only mosses.

(E) Some of them grow to be quite large.

Even if you know nothing about plants that contain no circulatory systems, you can probably eliminate an answer choice right off the bat just using your common sense. A circulatory system provides an organism with a way to transport nutrients. It is highly unlikely that a plant with no circulatory system and no way of transporting nutrients over a vast surface would grow to be quite large. So even if you knew nothing about plants, you could eliminate (E) with very little thought.

Relying on what you do know

If you come across a subject that you don't know anything about, don't panic. Read through the answer choices to see if one deals with a subject you are familiar with. For instance, in the sample question above, you may not know a thing about plants, but you do know that bacteria are not plants. Therefore, you can eliminate (B). Using common sense and stuff you *do* know about, you can eliminate two answer choices about a topic that may be unfamiliar.

Avoiding choices with debatable words

Another way you can weed out answer choices (so to speak), is to cross out those that contain debatable words. *Debatable words* are those words that leave no room for exception and could therefore provoke debate. Some examples of debatable words are *all, always, only, complete, never, must, every,* and *none.* Take a look at the same sample question again. Choice (D) contains the word *only,* stating that the group of non-circulatory system plants only contains mosses. Now, the most common plants without circulatory systems are mosses. In fact, most humans have never encountered a type of plant that lacks a circulatory system that isn't moss. However, there do exist other plants in this category (hornworts and liverworts, specifi-cally), so saying that the category includes *only* mosses is up for debate. So, eliminating the answer choice with the debatable word leaves you with two remaining answer choices.

Don't avoid choices with debatable words indiscriminately. There are two occasions when you absolutely should not eliminate an answer choice based on the presence of a debatable word.

- ✔ If the presence of the debatable word makes the answer choice correct because the debatable word is not debatable, you can't eliminate it. Huh? For example, if the sample question contained a choice that read, "They only survive in wet climates," you couldn't eliminate the choice. That's because this *only* isn't a matter for debate. Plants without circulatory systems must live in wet areas because they have no way to pull water from the environment and transport it through their systems.

- ✔ If the question asks you to choose an answer that is *not* true, a choice that contains a debatable word may be just the ticket. For example, if the sample question asked you to choose the answer that was *not* true about plants with no circulatory systems, the choice that states that they belong to a group that includes *only* mosses very well may be the best answer.

Going for the most specific

When you have narrowed the answer choices to two seemingly reasonable options and you can't decide between them, usually the most specific choice of the two is the best answer. Take a look at the sample question one more time. Using the process of elimination, you have reduced your options to (A) and (C). Now you may have known that plants without circula-tory systems are nontracheophytes (not tracheophytes); but even if you didn't, you're prob-ably safer choosing the more specific of the two remaining choices. (C) reveals a special characteristic and is therefore more specific than is (A), which provides a general name.

Please note that choosing the more specific answer often works when you have narrowed your options to two. *It is not wise to choose the most specific answer of the all the ones pro-vided.* Also, keep in mind that these elimination techniques are ways to get you involved in the process of thinking your way through to the best answer choice. We don't guarantee that they will work in every situation, but they do provide you positive steps you can take to come closer to choosing the right answers.

Being politically correct

Though it's unlikely that the biology test will contain answer choices that violate political suitability, we'll mention the point just in case. If you ever see an answer choice that suggests racial, gender, or cultural bias on the SAT II, you can confidently eliminate it. These types of answers will never be right on the SAT II.

Classifying answers to classification questions

The biology test contains a rather unique question type that the College Board calls classifi-cation questions. This section lists the five answer choices first, and then provides you with three or more statements. For example, take a look at this group of questions about plants.

What's the difference between the SAT II, SAT I, and ACT?

Many people confuse the SAT II tests with the SAT I or the ACT. The following points can help you keep these three different tests straight.

✔ Who requires the tests?

The SAT II, or the SAT Subject Tests, isn't required by most universities (except in California). See Chapter 1 for the specifics.

The SAT I, the general SAT, is accepted as an admissions requirement by almost all colleges and universities and is generally more popular with Eastern colleges than it is with Western schools.

The ACT is accepted by most colleges and universities as an admission requirement and is generally more popular with colleges in the West than with those in the East.

Find out from the colleges and universities which exams they require. They provide this information on their application forms, in their promotional material, and on their websites.

✔ What's tested by these exams?

The SAT II tests individual subjects, ranging from literature to biology to U.S. history to Japanese.

The SAT I tests reading (in the form of sentence completion and passage-based questions), writing (through an essay and questions that ask you to identify grammar, punctuation, and construction errors), and math skills (arithmetic, geometry, and algebra).

The ACT tests reading comprehension, English grammar, science reasoning, and math (the same subjects as those on the SAT I, with a little trig thrown in).

✔ Which test is the easiest?

The SAT II can be pretty challenging depending on your level of knowledge about a specific subject, so a good study tool is crucial (but you know that; that's why you've got this book!).

The SAT I is easiest if you feel comfortable with writing and grammar, and you haven't had any trig classes. It's harder if you dread writing and grammar. Ten of the math questions on the SAT II are grid-in rather than multiple-choice questions, which means you have to work out the answer to them and write in the answer on your sheet. Some people don't like questions that aren't multiple-choice.

The ACT is easier for most people than the SAT I in the reading questions but a little harder in the math. The ACT grammar questions are a little easier than those on the SAT I, too.

✔ How are the tests scored?

The SAT II gives you a score of 200–800. You get a point for every right answer and zero points for every omitted answer. You lose 1/4 of a point for every question you answer incorrectly.

The SAT I gives you a critical reading score of 200–800, and writing score of 200–800, and a math score of 200–800. You get your overall score by adding all three scores together. Each correct answer counts one point, and each omitted question counts zero points. A wrong answer can have no penalty (grid-in math questions) or can cost you 1/4 of a point (all the multiple-choice questions).

The ACT scores range from 1–36 for all four areas, English usage, reading, math, and science reasoning. The overall score comes from an average of all four scores. The ACT doesn't subtract any points for wrong answers, so you should always guess.

✔ How long does each test take?

The SAT II takes one hour for each subject test.

The SAT I takes over three and 1/2 hours. You have six 25-minute sections (two writing, two reading, and two math), two 20-minute sections (one reading and one math), and one 10-minute writing section with just grammar questions.

The ACT takes almost three hours (45 minutes for the English test, 60 minutes for the math test, 35 minutes for the science test, and 35 minutes for the reading test).

✔ When are the tests given?

The SAT II is given six times a year, usually in October, November, December, January, May and June. The SAT I and SAT II are held on the same day at the same time, so you can't take both exams on the same administration date.

The SAT I is given seven times a year, usually in October, November, December, January, March, May and June.

The ACT is held five times a year, usually in October, December, January, March, May and June.

Questions 1–3

(A) Gymnosperms

(B) Monocots

(C) Algae

(D) Tracheophytes

(E) Nontracheophytes

1. **General category for plants that do not contain a circulatory system**

2. **Plant type that includes grasses and grains**

3. **Plant type that includes flowering plants**

Eliminating answer choices for these questions really isn't too different than it is for the other questions on the biology test. You can cross out answer choices for one statement; you just need to erase the strikethroughs for the next statement, though, because each statement is a new question.

However, if you are absolutely sure you will never choose one of the possible answer choices, you can cross it out. For instance, in the sample question you could cross out algae. Algae are not plants, so there is no way C is the right answer for any of the three statements because each statement asks about plants. You've just narrowed your choices to four possibilities instead of five.

Gymnosperms and monocots are tracheophytes and therefore possess circulatory systems. You can eliminate all three and choose E for statement 1.

For statement 2, you can eliminate E because grasses and grains have circulatory systems, so they're not nontracheophytes. Gymnosperms are cone-bearing trees, so grasses and grains wouldn't fall in this category. You can lightly cross out A, and you are left with B and D. Grasses and grains are monocots, and monocots are part of the tracheophyte group, so both choices include grasses and grains. How do you decide? Remember when you have to choose between two seemingly acceptable answer choices, go with the one that is more specific. In this case monocots consist specifically of grasses and grains, so B is the best answer.

Statement 3 doesn't make you work so hard. Flowering plants are dicots, and dicots are tracheophytes. Dicots is not a possibility, though, so D is the best answer. (If this terminology is causing your brain to perform somersaults, check out the plant chapter in this book, Chapter 13.)

Winning the Race Against the Clock: Wise Time Management

Unlike those on the SAT I and even other SAT II subjects, questions on the SAT II Biology do not necessarily increase in difficulty as you move through the test. Generally, the first ten questions are easier than the last ten, but there is not a drastic difference in difficulty. For this reason, it is even more important to manage your time wisely on the biology test than it is on other standardized tests.

Pacing yourself

Chances are you're taking three different subject tests in one morning, so you need a plan to help you stay focused throughout each test. Each subject test lasts for exactly one hour, and the biology test has 80 questions. If you do the math, you realize that you have about ¾ of a minute to spend on each question. Now, before you panic, go get your watch with the sweep second hand. Take a deep breath and hold it for 45 seconds. Unless you're an underwater distance swimmer or a tuba player, you probably had a pretty hard time holding your breath that long. Suddenly, ¾ of a minute seems like a pretty long time. Plus, some questions will be easy to answer in less than 45 seconds, so you'll have more time to spend on the others.

You'll need to keep track of your timing, but you don't want to waste precious seconds glancing at your watch continually. So go in with a plan. Check your progress at quarter intervals. With 80 questions, that means every 20 questions or so you should check your time. At question 20, you should be about 15 minutes into the section, at question 40 about a half hour, at question 60 (or when you start the E or M part of the test) you should be 45 minutes into the test. If at any time, you find yourself significantly off this pace — say by five or more questions in either direction — you need to make an adjustment. If you are behind, you're probably spending too much time on hard questions. You need to encourage yourself to move on. If you're ahead, you may be moving through questions too quickly at the risk of reading carelessly. You'll be much less likely to find yourself in either of these positions if you experiment with practice tests using the same strict timing as the test.

Using your own timepiece

One of our students took the test in a room with two clocks. The two clocks looked exactly alike except that they displayed different times. The proctor timed from the clock propped up on the table, and the other clock hung on the wall. Our student noted the time when the proctor began the test, but when she checked her pace at question 20, she couldn't remember which clock she began timing from, and she wasn't sure how much time had gone by.

You can avoid this same frustration by ignoring the clocks in the testing room. Get your hands on a watch with a sweep second hand that you can take with you to the test, and use your watch rather than the clock provided to time yourself during the test. At the beginning of the test, set your watch to the top of the hour, any hour. You don't care about the actual time, just the passing of one hour. It is much easier to remember that your test started when the big hand was at the 12 than it is to remember that it started at exactly 9:17 and 32 seconds. You have enough to remember for the SAT II without having to keep in mind what time it was when the proctor said, "Go." Set your watch for noon, and you know you need to be finished by 1:00 (even if it is really only 8:43 and 11 seconds).

Playing it Smart: A Few Things You Shouldn't Do

The majority of this chapter focuses on the things you should do to perform your best on test day. But there a few equally helpful *don'ts* you should know about to make sure you get your best score.

Don't lose track of the numbers on your answer grid

Skipping questions is normal on the SAT II. Just be really careful that if you do skip question 5, you mark the answer to question 6 in the bubble for question 6 and not those for question 5. If you do, you could mess up your answer sheet from that point forward. And if you don't notice until the end of the test . . . Yikes! All that hard work for nothing! You could cancel your score (what a waste!) or try to change your answers before the proctor calls time (make sure you have a big eraser!), but the best plan is to avoid the problem altogether.

Get in the habit of checking your answer grid every fifth question to make sure that you're marking the right answer in the proper spot. And always circle the right answer in your question booklet before you grid in the answer sheet. That way if you do discover that you've messed up your answer sheet, you won't have to reread the questions to figure out the right answers.

For those of you who are taking the M portion of the biology exam, you must skip from question 60 to question 81 on your answer grid. Don't mark the answers for the M section in the E section spot. M takers will have no answers marked on the grid for questions 61 through 80. E takers won't have any bubbles filled in for questions 81 on.

Don't lose your focus

It may surprise you to learn that one hour of biology may get a little boring. Don't use this as an excuse for your mind to wander. The test is too important to let yourself get distracted daydreaming about what it would be like to share a piece of chocolate mousse cake with the hottie sitting in front of you. Keep your perspective, focus on the task at hand, and promise yourself you'll get the cutie's number after the test is over.

Don't judge your performance by looking around at others

Sometimes in the frenzy of the exam you forget that not everyone in the room is taking the test that you are. So, it can be disconcerting if you see others put down their pencils while you're still slaving away. You can really psych yourself into thinking you're a loser if you compare yourself to those around you, and feeling like a loser doesn't do much for your test score. Keep your eyes on the test and your watch until the proctor signals that time's up.

Don't waste your time on hard questions

You've probably heard it before, but we're going to say it again. An easy question is worth the same amount of points as a hard question is. While in the classroom your teacher may reward you for knowing the answers to the hard questions, you don't get more Brownie buttons for answering a hard question on the SAT II. So, discipline yourself to know when to give it up. As tempting as it may be to ponder a question until you see the light, you can't afford that luxury. There may be a simple question at the end of the test that you don't even get to because you've been stubbornly trying to work out a hard problem. If you need to spend more than 1½ minutes on any one question, you probably won't get it right anyway. Skip it and go on.

Don't stew about how you performed on another test

Each SAT II subject test that you take on test day is a separate entity. Keep it that way. Don't let what you think may have been a poor performance on an earlier subject test affect how you do on the biology test. Every subject test has its own score, and the next test is a chance to start fresh.

Don't fail to use extra time at the end of the section

You may finish before the testing time is up. Use those last few minutes wisely. You've already marked your test booklet so that you know which questions are the best to return to double-check your answers. Go back to the questions with 3s next to them and double-check your answers. You may have learned something from the questions you answered later in the test that will help you with the questions you had trouble with earlier. Or you may have an "Aha" moment where the answer suddenly becomes clear to you. Or you catch a careless error. Use your extra time to pick up additional points.

Don't cheat

Cheating isn't the right thing to do and it's also just plain illogical. Your hand simply isn't big enough to hold all the information you need to master the biology test, and the person next to you is probably working on the Chinese language test, so peeking won't help. This book gives you everything you need to do your best on the exam, so don't take the risk.

Curbing a Case of Nerves: Relaxation Techniques

If all this talk about what you should and shouldn't do is making you nervous, relax! After you have read this book, you'll be plenty prepared for whatever the SAT II Biology exam dishes out. You may feel nervous on test day, however. That's normal and even a little beneficial. The extra shot of adrenaline keeps you alert. But too much anxiety isn't good for you or your test performance, and sometimes a frustrating question can paralyze you, so arrive at the testing site with a practiced relaxation plan at the ready in case you get caught with a major case of nerves.

It can happen. You'll be joyfully filling in answer bubbles when all of a sudden a seemingly monstrous question comes along. You know this stuff, so you're probably just missing something. But the question makes you so tense, you can't think. At the first sign of freaking, take a quick time out. The trick is to forget about that nasty question for just long enough that when you go back to it, you'll have that "Aha!" experience and suddenly see the right answer. Or you'll get enough perspective to realize that it's just one little test question and not worth your anguish, so you can merrily skip it and leave it for later if you have the time. Just don't let one or two yucky questions ruin you for the rest of the test.

Inhaling

When you stress out, you tighten up and take quick breaths, which doesn't do much for your oxygen intake. Your brain needs oxygen to think straight. Stressing out restricts the oxygen flow to the brain, and you need to do something about it. Fortunately the solution is easy. All you need to do is breathe. Deeply. Feel the air all the way down to your toes. Hold it. Then let it all out slowly and do it again, several times. (Just don't blow out your air too loudly; you don't want to attract the proctor's attention.)

Stretching

Anxiety causes tension. Your muscles get all tied up in knots, and it helps to untie them. While you're breathing deeply, focus on reducing your muscle tension. Most people feel stress in their necks and shoulders, so do a few stretches in these areas to get the blood flowing.

- Shrug your shoulders up towards your ears; hold it for a few seconds, and then release.
- Roll your head from front to back and from side to side.
- With your hands together, stretch your arms straight up over your head as high as you can. Relax. Then do it again.
- Stretch your legs out in front of you. Move your ankles up and down, but don't kick the person in front of you!
- Shake your hands vigorously as if you just washed your hands in a public restroom with no paper towels.
- Open your mouth wide as if to say "Ahhh." (Don't actually say it out loud, however.) Close your mouth quickly to avoid catching flies.

These quick stretches shouldn't take you more than ten seconds, so don't invest in a full workout. You need to get back to work!

Giving yourself a mini massage

If you still feel tense after all that stretching, play masseuse and give yourself a little rub down. Rub your right shoulder with your left hand and your left shoulder with your right hand. Use both hands to massage your neck. Then move up to your scalp.

Don't get carried away, though. This should only take about ten seconds out of your testing time. (Let's see . . . at today's going rate for a masseuse, you'll owe yourself about 30 cents.)

Taking a little vacation

Have ready a place in your imagination that makes you feel calm and comforted. Maybe it's the beach. Or perhaps a ski slope. Wherever it is, sit back in your chair, close your eyes, and visit your happy place for a few seconds to get away from the question that's bugging you. Just make sure you come back!

Don't use this technique unless you are really tense. You can stay longer in "la la" land once the test is over.

Think positive thoughts

Give yourself a break. Realize that the SAT II test is tough, and you'll probably not feel comfortable about every question. But don't beat yourself up about it. That is a sure path to disaster. If after you've tried these relaxation efforts you still feel frustrated about a particular question, fill in your best guess if you're able to eliminate a couple answer choices or just skip it if you can't eliminate any answers. Mark the question in case you have time to review it at the end, but don't think about it until then. Put your full efforts into answering the remaining questions.

Focus on the positive. Congratulate yourself for the answers you do feel confident about and force yourself to leave the others behind.

Part II

Getting Up Close: Cells, Genetics, and Other Stuff on the Biology-M Section

In this part . . .

With Part II, you can start diving into the actual biology information that you need to understand to conquer the SAT II. Part II focuses on the Biology-M section material, which includes chemistry, cells, cell processes, and genetics. Unfortunately for the ecology and evolution fans who plan on doing the Biology-E section instead the Biology-M section, you still need to know a lot of this cellular and molecular stuff because it makes up about 35 percent of the Biology E/M core section that everybody has to do. One cool thing to remember is that a lot of this is stuff is going on inside your body right now, even though you can't actually see most of it without a really awesome microscope.

Chapter 3

Packets of Life: Cells and Cell Parts

....

In This Chapter

▶ Going way back: The history and study of cells

▶ Entering and exiting: Transporting molecules across membranes

▶ Telling them apart: Prokaryotes vs. eukaryotes

▶ Understanding the parts: Cell structures

▶ Discovering organelles

▶ Cloning cells with mitosis

....

*O*rganisms come in all different shapes and sizes, from microscopic bacteria to massive blue whales. There's such a huge diversity of life forms on the planet, sometimes it seems impossible to understand biology, leading to a lot of groans and yawns from biology students. Luckily, there's a bunch of stuff that all organisms have in common, no matter what they look like on the outside. All organisms have DNA and RNA (see Chapter 7); they all use glucose as fuel (see Chapter 6); and they are all made of tiny living units called cells. And although an individual cell is really small, it still has all of the structures and functions you need to be alive: metabolism, growth, reproduction, etc. If you try to go any smaller than a cell, then something important is lost and what's left really isn't alive anymore; one cell is the smallest living organism you can have. The smallest organisms, like bacteria, are only as big as one cell. Other organisms, called multicellular organisms, are made of a large number of cells, which all work together. All plants and animals are multicellular organisms, and some of the biggest ones have bodies made of many trillions of cells.

The Biology-M section of the SAT II will focus on cells and the stuff that goes on inside of cells. To show you how to become the master of the Biology-M section, this chapter gives you basic information about cells, including cell parts and their functions. The first section goes through some of the history behind the discovery of cells and how the teeny little things can actually be seen. The next sections show you how cells transport substances in and out, lay out what kinds of cells there are and how to distinguish them, and cover all of the important cell parts and how they function.

Seeing the Light: Cell Discovery

Cells are so small that until the invention of the microscope in the early 1700s, nobody even knew they existed. Imagine being the first person to see all the little critters squirming around in your well water or on your skin! It would be like discovering a whole new world populated with all sorts of bizarre monsters! The first person to see this was the inventor of the microscope, Antoine van Leeuwenhoek, and we bet people didn't believe him until they had a chance to see for themselves — we know we would have been pretty skeptical.

Because of the invention of the microscope, scientists can actually see cells and prove that they're real, which has allowed biologists to come up with two simple conclusions that form the basis of the cell theory:

- ✔ All living things are made of cells.
- ✔ All cells arise from pre-existing cells.

Catching some rays: Light microscopes

Like regular microscopes today, the first microscope built by van Leeuwenhoek used only one strong magnifying lens to see cells. Modern microscopes send the magnified image through a second lens that magnifies it even more. Microscopes that use light and lenses are called *light microscopes* because a strong light source shines light rays on or through the cells. The light rays then enter the lens which magnifies the image. To calculate the final magnification, just multiply the magnifications of the two lenses together.

The first lens is placed really close to the thing you want to see, while the second lens is what you actually look into at the top of the microscope. The first lens is called the *objective lens* because it's down near the object that you want to see. The second lens is called the *ocular lens* because it's close to your eye (oh yeah, and *ocular* refers to eyes).

The SAT II may ask you about some of these microscope facts and may even ask you about the parts of a light microscope, so Figure 3-1 shows a diagram you can refer to.

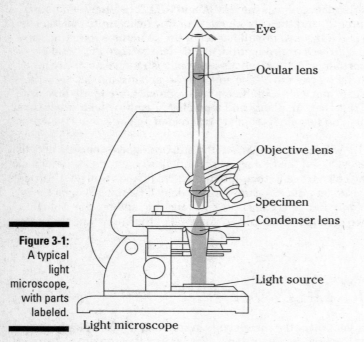

Figure 3-1: A typical light microscope, with parts labeled.

Going hi-tech: Electron microscopes

Another kind of microscope you may be questioned about on the SAT II is the electron microscope. Instead of light rays, the electron microscope uses beams of electrons and special computerized sensors to see really small structures. Electron microscopes produce clearer images and higher magnifications, but they can only see stuff that's been frozen in place. Light microscopes can see cells swimming around and doing their thing, so they are still what most people use for studying living cells. Plus, light microscopes are about a million times cheaper, so you aren't too likely to see an electron microscope in your high school classroom anytime soon.

Now try out these sample SAT II questions on cells.

Which of the following statements concerning light microscopes is true?

   I. They can produce greater magnification than electron microscopes.

   II. They can show active cellular processes while electron microscopes cannot.

   III. They are far cheaper than electron microscopes.

  (A) I and II only

  (B) I and III only

  (C) II and III only

  (D) all are true

  (E) all are false

The electron microscope is a recent high-tech invention that was developed in order to get higher magnifications. That means that any answer with option I can be crossed out, so get rid of answers (A), (B), and (D).

If you look at your remaining choices, you see that you are left with II and III only, which is (C), or neither II or III, which is (E). All you have to do at this point is determine whether one of the statements (II or III) is true. If one is true, the answer is (C); if one is not true, the answer must be (E). You don't need to waste time examining both II and III to get the right answer.

Light microscopes just shine light on what you want to see, so they don't interfere with active cellular processes, while electron microscopes require that what you are magnifying be frozen in place. This means option II is true and you can pick (C). If you read III, you know that light microscopes can be found in every biology class, so they must be pretty cheap, which means that option III is true also. Answer (C) includes these and only these options, so that is the correct answer.

Which of the following is one of the two main tenets of Cell Theory?

  (A) All cells are round

  (B) All cells arise from pre-existing cells

  (C) Cells are too small to see with the naked eye

  (D) Cells arise spontaneously in nutrient-rich water

  (E) All cells have a nucleus

Cells come in lots of different shapes, so (A) is wrong. While it's true that cells are too small to see without a microscope, this fact isn't important enough to be part of the Cell Theory, so (C) can be crossed out also. As discussed later in this chapter, prokaryotic cells do not have a nucleus, so (E) is wrong. That leaves (B) and (D), which are opposites of each other. Cells are way too complex to just arise spontaneously, so they need to be descended from other cells, so (B) is the correct answer. If you are wondering where the first cells came from, check out Chapter 10.

Smaller is better: Cell size

So why are cells so small? It seems weird to have huge animals and trees made up of so many of these teensy little cells that we can't even see. Why aren't there any really big cells? I could just tell you not to worry about it — "Cells are small and that's just the way it is!" — but the SAT II may ask you about the reason, so here's the explanation. Cells need to soak up the oxygen and nutrients like a sponge because they don't have mouths or lungs the way whole animals do. The nutrients move in across the cell's surface, called the cell membrane, and eventually make their way into the center of the cell. The bigger and thicker the cell, the longer it takes to get the nutrients all the way into the center. If you've cooked pasta, you probably know that it takes a lot longer to cook thick linguine all the way through than it does to cook thin angel hair. It's the same idea with cells, and if the nutrients don't get into the middle fast enough, the cell could die. That means that most cells can't be more than 10–20 *thousandths* of a meter thick before they risk facing the size problem, and that's pretty dang small!

Getting Across: Transport Into and Out of Cells

Cells need to take stuff in (like nutrients) and get stuff out (like waste products). There are several ways cells accomplish this. Diffusion moves things around because of different concentration of ions and molecules inside cells and outside cells across the cell membrane (see "Keeping the cell together" later in this chapter). Other means of transportation are a little more complicated.

Diffusion

Ions and molecules have one common theme: They always try to move from high concentration to low concentration, and if nothing stops them, that's exactly what they'll do. Whenever you have a concentration difference from one place to another, it's called a *concentration gradient,* and *diffusion* is the movement of things down their concentration gradient from high to low. To see this happening, get a clear glass of water and drop in a small amount of food coloring. Right where the food coloring went in, the concentration is really high, but then the color molecules immediately start spreading out from that little area of high concentration to the rest of the water, where the concentration of color molecules is really low. Diffusion is a law of nature, and because it doesn't take any energy, diffusion is sometimes called *passive transport.*

There's almost always a concentration gradient across the membrane of a cell, so diffusion happens all the time. The SAT II may include some questions about the technical details of concentration gradients and diffusion, so this section gets those out of the way. Figure 3-2 shows the kinds of diffusion discussed in this section.

Since ocean water is really salty, cells that live in the oceans have a water solution on the outside that is more highly concentrated with salt than the water solution on their insides (called the cytoplasm). The technical term is that the ocean water is *hypertonic* compared to the inside of the cell. *Hyper* means *more,* and *tonic* means . . . well, just pretend it means "salty," and you'll get the idea. Saying that the ocean water is hypertonic means that it is saltier than the inside of the cell, so the minerals in the ocean water will tend to diffuse into the cell if they can find an open channel through the membrane. The hypertonic state also means that water will diffuse out, because the concentration of water is greater on the inside than the outside.

TIP

The direction of water's concentration gradient is always opposite to the direction of the solute's concentration gradient. A solute is anything that is dissolved in water; in this case salt is the solute.

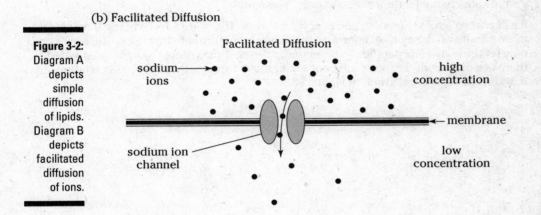

(a) Simple Diffusion

membrane

low concentration
solution

high concentration
solution

diffusion

(b) Facilitated Diffusion

Figure 3-2:
Diagram A
depicts
simple
diffusion
of lipids.
Diagram B
depicts
facilitated
diffusion
of ions.

Facilitated Diffusion

sodium
ions

high
concentration

sodium ion
channel

membrane

low
concentration

The diffusion of water is talked about so much in cell biology that it's been given its own name: *osmosis.* Osmosis is just like regular diffusion, but it only refers to the diffusion of water. The cell membrane is water resistant, but it isn't water proof, so water can still find a way to diffuse down its concentration gradient and go out of the cell. The more hypertonic the environment, the more water will diffuse out (because the salt concentration is greater outside the cell than it is inside), causing the cell to shrink. If too much water flows out, the cell will die. Organisms that live in the ocean have extra-salty insides to slow down the rate of osmosis, but freshwater organisms don't. That means if you put a cell that's used to freshwater into saltwater, it will shrivel up and die, so don't try to raise your freshwater goldfish in a saltwater aquarium. Because of osmosis of water leaving their cells, the poor little fish would actually suffer from dehydration.

Cells in freshwater environments face the opposite problem because their living area is *hypotonic. Hypo* means "less," so fresh water is less salty than the inside of a cell, and this means that water will try to diffuse into the cell. If you put a saltwater cell into fresh water, the fresh water will be way too hypotonic, and osmosis will keep bringing water into the cell until the cell bursts and dies. That means you shouldn't try to raise your tropical angelfish in your freshwater goldfish tank. Because of osmosis of water into their cells, the tropical fish would suffer from extreme water retention.

Oh yeah, one more vocabulary word here. If the concentration on the inside and outside of a cell is exactly the same, then it is called *isotonic* because *iso* means "the same as."

The SAT II may ask questions about the following types of diffusion:

✔ **Simple diffusion:** Lipids (which are molecules that don't dissolve in water) can move right through a cell membrane, so if they have a concentration gradient, lipid molecules will diffuse through right away. The bigger the concentration gradient, the faster the rate of diffusion. This relationship is shown in the first graph in Figure 3-3 and is called *simple diffusion*.

✔ **Facilitated diffusion:** Diffusion will happen all by itself (if there's a concentration gradient) as long as nothing is blocking the path. Cell membranes can block the path of hydrophilic things like ions and charged molecules, so they need to go through channels. Once the channel is open, the ions just flow right through by themselves with no extra help in the form of pumping action. This channel-opening process is called *facilitated diffusion* because the ions and charged molecules need to be helped (facilitated) across the membrane by channels. Just like with lipids, the bigger the concentration gradient, the faster the rate of diffusion, but since ions and charged molecules need to go through channels, their rate can only get so high.

It's like when a movie lets out and everyone leaves. The more people in the theater, the more people will be exiting, but everyone needs to go through the doors. The doors can only let through a few people every second, so even if the theater was really crowded, there is a maximum rate at which people can move through the doors. This relationship is shown in the second graph of Figure 3-3.

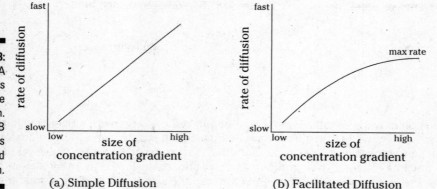

Figure 3-3: Graph A depicts simple diffusion. Graph B depicts facilitated diffusion.

(a) Simple Diffusion

(b) Facilitated Diffusion

Moving molecules in other ways: Active transport, endocytosis, and exocytosis

Diffusion isn't the only way to move molecules in and out of cells. Sometimes ions and molecules need a little more help. For the tougher jobs, there are active transport, endocytosis, and exocytosis.

Sometimes a cell needs to move ions or small molecules across the membrane from low concentration to high concentration, like if it needs to gather up the last few sugar molecules in the area for its internal supply. This means that the ions or small molecules need to go against its concentration gradient, which means going against diffusion. To do this, the cell uses a variety of different little pumps, each of which can use energy to force different ions and molecules to move against their concentration gradients. Since it takes energy, this is called *active transport*. The pumps, which are made out of proteins, get their energy from ATP molecules (see Chapter 7).

Sometimes a cell needs to move really big molecules, like whole proteins or bits of food, into or out of the cell. To do this, the cell uses the following two closely related processes (see Figure 3-4 for a diagram of these two processes.):

✔ **Exocytosis** is the process of moving big molecules out of the cell. During exocytosis, a cell packages the big molecules in a bubble made out of phospholipids, which are the same molecules that make up the cell membrane. The bubble then merges with the cell membrane and dumps the big molecules outside — kind of like a cellular burp.

✔ **Endocytosis** is the process of moving big molecules into the cell. Endocytosis is the same process as exocytosis (see above) but in reverse. The big molecules approach the cell and the cell engulfs them in a bubble and brings them inside.

To keep the two names straight, just remember that *exo* means outside and *endo* means inside.

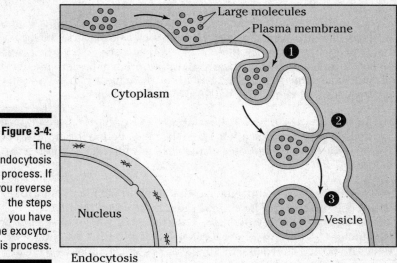

Figure 3-4:
The endocytosis process. If you reverse the steps you have the exocytosis process.

Now for a quick sample question on membrane transport.

A researcher wants to study the rate of sodium uptake by several different samples of the same kind of cell. She adds a different concentration of sodium to each group of cells and finds that at the lower and medium concentrations, the greater the sodium concentration, the faster the uptake. However, at higher concentrations, adding more sodium to the outside has a less and less dramatic effect until the rate of uptake stops increasing altogether. Most likely this uptake of sodium was an example of

(A) active transport

(B) endocytosis

(C) passive diffusion

(D) facilitated diffusion

(E) exocytosis

Endocytosis and exocytosis are used for big molecules like proteins, so (B) and (E) can be crossed out. Active transport can change with concentration, but it tends to stay at a more steady rate than what was depicted in the example, so (A) is wrong also. That leaves the two kinds of diffusion. Remember that facilitated diffusion goes through channels, which is like people all trying to fit through the exit doors at the end of a movie. The more sodium ions there are, the more that will diffuse through, but the channels can only let so many sodium ions through at once, so eventually the rate will stop increasing. That means the answer is (D).

Singing Karyote: Prokaryotes and Eukaryotes

Although all living things are made of cells, bacteria cells are a little different from all others. Bacteria cells are called *prokaryotic cells* or sometimes just *prokaryotes*. They are especially small and also very simple compared to other cells, and they never come together to form a multicellular organism. Sometimes a bunch of prokaryotes form a slimy, stinking blob called a colony, but a colony is just a pile of cells, not a multicellular organism. The cells of everything else — protists, fungi, plants and animals — are called *eukaryotic cells* or *eukaryotes*. These cells are larger and more complex and are capable of forming multicellular organisms like you.

Why the weird names for these two main kinds of cells? Well, the answer may not be very satisfying, but at least it may help you remember. Billions of years ago, the only kind of cells around were all simple bacteria, so bacteria came before all other forms of life. *Pro* means "before," and so bacteria cells have come to be called *pro*karyotes. *Eu* means "new," which is why the larger, more complex cells that came after bacteria are called *eu*karyotes.

All cells, both prokaryotes and eukaryotes, have a cell membrane (outer barrier), a cytoplasm (watery insides), and a cytoskeleton (internal scaffold) (see the next section for more about common cell parts), but prokaryotes and eukaryotes also have a few important differences that just may show up on the SAT II.

Eukaryotes are bigger and they have little compartments that contain the machinery for performing different kinds of cell processes. The compartments are called *organelles* because they are the internal organs of eukaryotic cells. The easiest organelle to see under a microscope is called the nucleus, and that's where a eukaryotic cell's DNA is kept. (See Chapter 7 for more on DNA.) If you see a nucleus, then you know the cell must be a eukaryote. Prokaryotes are much smaller than eukaryotes, and they do not have a nucleus or any other organelles, which means their DNA and cellular machinery is free to float around inside the cytoplasm. Prokaryotes have been around for billions of years, and they still can't get organized like the eukaryotes! See Table 3-1 for a summary of the differences between prokaryotes and eukaryotes, and check out Figure 3-5 for a diagram of typical prokaryotic and eukaryotic cells.

Table 3-1	Basic Differences Between Prokaryotes and Eukaryotes		
	Size	*Organelles?*	*Found In*
Prokaryotes	Smaller	No	Bacteria
Eukaryotes	Bigger	Yes	Protists, fungi, plants, animals

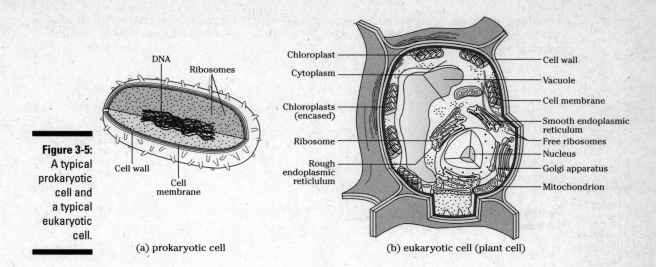

Figure 3-5:
A typical prokaryotic cell and a typical eukaryotic cell.

(a) prokaryotic cell

(b) eukaryotic cell (plant cell)

EXAMPLE

Now for yet another sample question, this time on prokaryotes versus eukaryotes.

Which of the following cell structures do prokaryotes not possess?

(A) cell membrane

(B) nucleus

(C) cytoplasm

(D) cytoskeleton

(E) channels

Only eukaryotic cells have a nucleus, so (B) is the correct answer. Every cell has a cytoplasm, so every cell needs a cell membrane to keep the cytoplasm contained. Also, every cell needs a cytoskeleton to keep it from getting too squashed, and they need channels to let ions and polar molecules get in and out.

Recognizing Common Cell Parts

A few cellular components are found in every kind of cell. Absolutely every cell has a cell membrane with channels and pumps, a cytoplasm, and a cytoskeleton, and this section goes into more detail about these structures.

Keeping the cell together

Here's one of the things that all cells have in common. All cells, both prokaryotes and eukaryotes, have a protective outer barrier called a membrane. Since the membrane is the interface between the living cell and its nonliving environment, the SAT II sometimes includes some important features of cell membranes.

Cell membranes are made of phospholipids, which are big molecules that have an oily section and a charged section (see Chapter 6 for details on phospholipids). The oily *lipid* section is water resistant (hydrophobic) while the charged *phospho* part easily mixes with water (hydrophilic). When they come together to form a cell membrane, phospholipids stack up in a double layer called a phospholipid bilayer. As shown in Figure 3-6, the charged parts stay on the outer and inner surfaces of the membrane while the oily parts form a thick, water-resistant barrier.

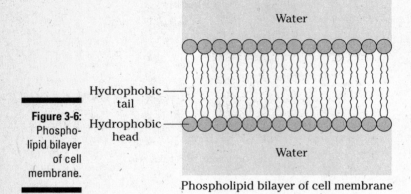

Figure 3-6:
Phospho-
lipid bilayer
of cell
membrane.

Phospholipid bilayer of cell membrane

Almost all cells live in watery environments, plus the inside of a cell (the cytoplasm; see "Getting the inside goop on cytoplasm," below) is also made of water. It's really important for a cell to keep the outside water solution separated from the inside water solution, and the water resistant lipid part of the membrane makes sure this happens. Actually, since the lipid parts of the phospholipids are hydrophobic, which means "water fearing," those parts don't want to touch any water at all. Luckily, the charged parts of the phospholipids don't mind touching water because the phospho parts are hydrophilic, which means "water liking." The charged phospho parts are on both the inside and outside surfaces of the membrane so the hydrophobic lipid parts are kept away from the inside and outside water solutions.

The membrane is water resistant and blocks the movement of any ions or charged mole-cules, but it is not lipid resistant. Fats, oils, and other lipids (see Chapter 6) are not stopped by the membrane and are able to enter or exit the cell pretty easily. Also, as mentioned in the previous section, there are lots of different kinds of channels and pumps that allow different ions or molecules to move into or out of the cell. The channels and pumps are stuck in the membrane, but are free to float around among the phospholipids, which is why this picture of the membrane is called the *fluid mosaic model*. Okay, maybe that's kind of a dumb name, but they may mention it in the SAT II, so be on the lookout.

Getting the inside goop on cytoplasm

The cytoplasm of a cell is the cell's watery interior. *Cyto* is a common prefix in biology that means "cellular," and *plasm* is a variation on "plasma" which means "fluid." The cytoplasm contains lots of different dissolved ions in different concentrations. It also has lots of organic molecules like sugars and amino acids floating around, along with some bigger things like enzymes and RNA strands (see Chapter 6 for more info on important organic molecules). Both prokaryotic cells and eukaryotic cells contain cytoplasm.

Shaping up a cell with the cytoskeleton

The cytoskeleton is made of rigid proteins, and it forms the internal scaffolding of the cell. The cytoskeleton helps the cell keep the right shape, and it keeps each organelle in its proper place inside the cell.

EXAMPLE

Here's some sample questions on common cell parts.

What is the name of the molecule that constitutes all cell membranes?

(A) fatty acid

(B) DNA

(C) cellulose

(D) glucose

(E) phospholipid

The molecules that make up cell membranes need to have an oily hydrophobic part for water resistance, and a charged hydrophilic part to protect the oily part. In a phospholipid, the *lipid* part is hydrophobic, while the *phospho* part is charged and hydrophilic, so (E) is the correct answer. A fatty acid is similar to a phospholipid, but it doesn't have the proper kind of charged portion, so (A) is wrong. The others all have their own separate functions. DNA is the genetic material in the nucleus; cellulose is used to make cell walls; and glucose has many uses, but mainly it's a fuel used in the mitochondria.

EXAMPLE

What kind of molecule is never blocked by the cell membrane?

(A) ions

(B) lipids

(C) charged (polar) molecules

(D) proteins

(E) water

Cell membranes are composed of phospholipids, and the main barrier is the "lipid" part. One kind of lipid cannot block another kind, so (B) is the correct answer. Ions and water both have charges associated with them, so they are blocked. DNA and proteins are way to big, so they are blocked as well.

Dividing the Labor: The Organelles of Eukaryotes

As mentioned before, organelles are only found in eukaryotic cells. Organelles are specialized compartments enclosed in phospholipid membranes and suspended in the cytoplasm of eukaryotic cells.

All eukaryotic cells have the following organelles:

- **The nucleus** is a large compartment bounded by a phospholipid membrane called the *nuclear envelope*. This is the DNA depot because the nucleus is where DNA is packaged and kept safe. See Chapter 8 for how DNA works.

- **The endoplasmic reticulum** is a big, folded membrane that is the construction site for some important molecules. The smooth endoplasmic reticulum (SER) manufactures new lipids, such as the phospholipids that make up all membranes. The rough endoplasmic reticulum (RER) is rough because it has lots and lots of ribosomes stuck all over it. Ribosomes are little protein factories that make all of the different proteins that cells need.

✔ **The Golgi apparatus** is a refinement and distribution center where proteins go after being manufactured in the RER. Inside the Golgi apparatus, raw proteins are modified so that they will be ready to do their job, and then they're packaged up in little membrane bubbles (vesicles) and sent off to where they need to go. Sometimes the proteins are sent all the way out of the cell via exocytosis.

✔ **Lysosomes** are little membrane-bound bubbles that contain digestive enzymes and float around in the cytoplasm. If a cell needs to break down some food particles, some old proteins, or toxic molecules, it sends them into the lysosomes to get chopped up. They're kind of like the cellular garbage disposal.

✔ **The mitochondria** are the power plants because this is where fuel molecules, like sugars and fats, are broken down to release usable energy for the cell. See Chapter 6 for how this works. Mitochondria have a strange structure. They have an outer membrane just like any other organelle, but they also have an inner membrane. The area deep inside the inner membrane is called the *matrix* of the mitochondria (and no, I don't think that's where they got the name for the movie). The space between the inner and outer membranes is called, logically enough, the *intermembrane space*. (See Figure 3-7.)

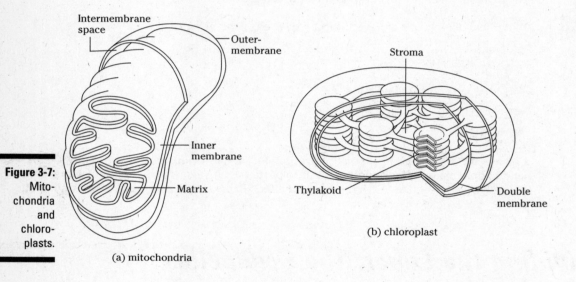

Figure 3-7: Mitochondria and chloroplasts.

(a) mitochondria

(b) chloroplast

The following organelles are found only in plant cells (which are also eukaryotic cells):

✔ **Chloroplasts** are where photosynthesis happens (see Chapter 6), and they are only found in plant cells. Chloroplasts have an outer membrane like other organelles, but they also have stacks of little interior compartments called thylakoids. (See Figure 3-7.)

✔ **Cell walls** can be found in many different kinds of cells, but not in animal cells. A cell wall is an extra-strong barrier around the cell membrane that keeps the cell rigid. Plants and fungi both have cell walls around their cells, as do some protists and some bacteria. Plants cells make their cell walls out of a really strong material called *cellulose*. That's why plants are able to stand up straight even though they don't have any bones. Fungi, like molds and mushrooms, make their cell walls out of a softer material called *chitin*.

✔ **Vacuoles** are found mostly in plant cells and just serve as miscellaneous storage compartments. Some cells use vacuoles to store excess water that has entered the cell through osmosis.

Cilia and flagella are possible cell structures in many plant and animal cells. They are similar to organelles and help cells swim. Many cells use a single, long tail called a *flagellum* to swim (the plural is flagella): other cells use lots of little flippers called *cilia* that look like tiny hairs all over the cells (see Figure 3-8). A cell with a flagellum looks sort of like a microscopic fish, while a cell with cilia looks like it's in bad need of a shave.

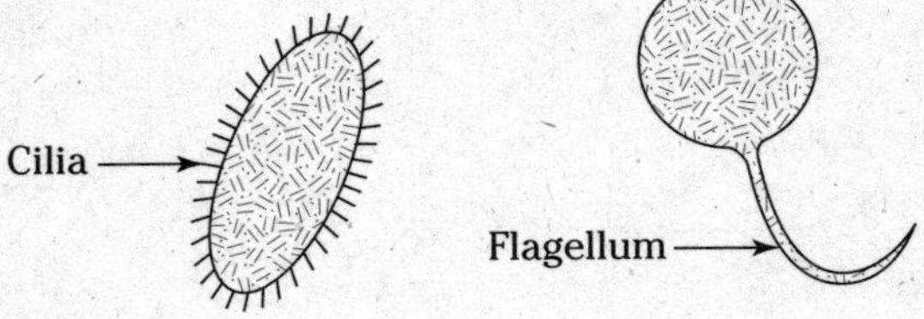

Figure 3-8:
A cell with cilia and a cell with a flagellum.

Cilia ⟶

Flagellum ⟶

Before getting to cell division, try these sample questions on organelles, starting with a set of classification questions, which we haven't seen so far.

Questions 1–3 refer to the following cell parts.

(A) nucleus

(B) cytoplasm

(C) cell membrane

(D) mitochondria

(E) chloroplast

1. Storage area for DNA *A*

2. Found only in plant cells *E*

3. Watery interior of all cells *D B*

For #1, the answer is (A). The only function of the nucleus is to store DNA.

For #2, the answer is (E). Chloroplasts are the organelles in plant cells where photosynthesis happens.

For #3, the answer is (B). The watery interior is called the cytoplasm.

Which cellular components are found in every cell?

I. cytoplasm

II. cell membrane

III. nucleus

IV. membrane channels

(A) I and II only

(B) I, II, III, and IV

(C) II and III only

(D) I, II and IV only

(E) I, II, and III only

The main way to tell the difference between prokaryotes and eukaryotes is that prokaryotes *do not* have a nucleus, so any answer that includes III can be crossed out. That takes care of (B) and (C). Every cell has a cytoplasm and so every cell needs a membrane to keep the cytoplasm contained, and, besides, all of the remaining answer choices, (A), (D) and (E) contain I and II. Therefore, cytoplasm and cell membranes must be components. You don't even have to think about it. Every cell needs channels in its membrane to allow certain ions and molecules to move in and out. So, I, II, and IV are all found in every cell, so (D) is the answer.

The cell walls of plants are made of

(A) DNA

(B) phospholipids

(C) chitin

(D) proteins

(E) cellulose

DNA is the genetic material (see Chapters 6 and 8), so (A) is definitely out of the running. Phospholipids make up cell membranes, so (B) can be crossed out too. Proteins are used for a lot of things, but never cell walls, so (D) is gone. That leaves (C) and (E), which are both good candidates. However, chitin is used in the cell walls of fungi only, while cellulose is used for the cell walls of plants, so (E) is the correct answer.

What structure does a sperm cell use for swimming?

(A) cilia

(B) membrane pump

(C) flagellum

(D) Golgi apparatus

(E) mitochondria

The only candidates here are (A) and (C) because they are the only structures used for swimming. The other options all have distinctly different functions. Sperm cells look sort of like fish, with one long tail flapping to make them swim. A flagellum is a single long tail on a cell, so (C) is the correct answer. Cilia, on the other hand, are tiny little hairlike structures attached all over a cell that all flap in unison to make the cell swim.

Cloning Cells through Mitosis

One of the main characteristics of living things is their ability to reproduce, which means that cells, as the smallest units of life, must be able to do just that. However, cell reproduction is a lot different from the reproduction of an entire multicellular organism: cells don't really mate, don't get pregnant, and don't even produce seeds. Instead, cells just split in half. A cell copies all of its genetic material (DNA), sends one copy to one side of the cell and the other copy to the other side, and then divides itself into two separate cells. The result is that you have two cells with exactly the same genes. In other words, the cells are clones.

Prokaryotic cells, in keeping with their theme of simplicity, just copy all of their DNA and divide — a process called *binary fission.* Eukaryotic cells, as you may predict, are a little more complicated. They reproduce in a process called *mitosis,* which involves chromosomes, chromatids, and a few specific stages covered in this section that may show up on the SAT II.

Fitting mitosis into the cell cycle

Almost all eukaryotic cells go through a cycle of activity that can last anywhere from about 20 minutes to many years, depending on the cell. For most of its cycle, a cell is just going about its regular business doing whatever it is that the cell does. This part of the cycle is called *interphase.* For a small part of interphase, the cell spends some time copying all of its DNA. (See Chapter 7 for more on DNA replication.) After interphase, the cell enters *M phase,* during which the cell divides. You probably already guessed this, but the *M* stands for mitosis. After M phase, the two separated cells go back into interphase and start the whole thing over again.

Splitting eukaryotes: The phases of mitosis

The first stage of mitosis is called *prophase.* This is when the cell's DNA coils up into distinct chromosomes. A chromosome is a big bundle of DNA, as shown in Figure 3-9. Remember that all of the DNA was copied during interphase, so every chromosome has been doubled.

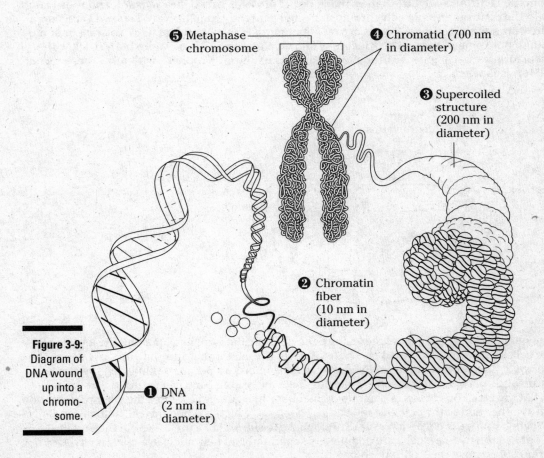

❺ Metaphase chromosome

❹ Chromatid (700 nm in diameter)

❸ Supercoiled structure (200 nm in diameter)

❷ Chromatin fiber (10 nm in diameter)

Figure 3-9: Diagram of DNA wound up into a chromosome.

❶ DNA (2 nm in diameter)

Figure 3-10a shows a chromosome before copying, and 3-10b shows the same chromosome after all of the DNA inside it has been copied. The two copies of the chromosome are called sister chromatids, which are held together by a *centromere*.

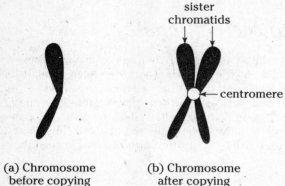

Figure 3-10:
a) a chromosome before DNA copying.
b) a chromosome after DNA copying.

(a) Chromosome before copying

(b) Chromosome after copying

There are a few other important things that happen during prophase. First, the membrane around the nucleus breaks apart, allowing the chromosomes to move around inside the rest of the cell. Also, two little things called *centrioles,* which act as anchors for pulling the sister chromatids to opposite sides of the cell, show up at either end of the cell. Extending out from the centrioles are little cables made out of proteins called *microtubules,* and these latch onto the centromeres of each chromosome and get ready to pull. Okay, I know I've been throwing several technical terms at you about mitosis (it's like a Star Trek episode or something), but some of those terms just may show up on the SAT II, so we're both stuck with them for now. See Figure 3-11 for a diagram of a cell during prophase with all of these technical terms labeled.

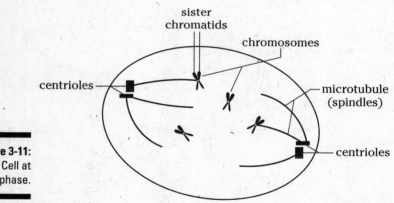

Figure 3-11:
Cell at prophase.

The next phase is called *metaphase.* Here the chromosomes all line up along the middle of the cell, as shown in Figure 3-12a. The area down the center that they line up on is called the *metaphase plate.* Next comes *anaphase* where the microtubules start pulling on the sister chromatids of each chromosome, dragging them away from each other and toward either end of the cell. You can see a diagram of anaphase in Figure 3-12b. After the sister chromatids are at either end of the cell, the cell enters *telophase,* which is when the cell actually splits in half — a process called *cytokinesis.* Telophase is shown in Figure 3-12c. By the end of telophase the two new cells are completely separated and new nuclear membranes have formed to enclose their chromosomes.

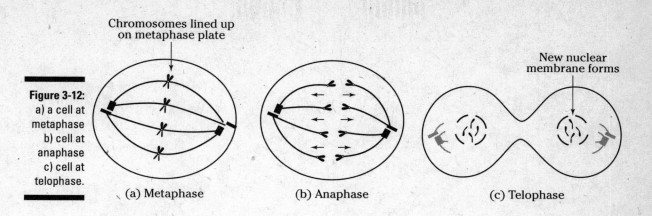

Figure 3-12:
a) a cell at
metaphase
b) cell at
anaphase
c) cell at
telophase.

Chromosomes lined up
on metaphase plate

New nuclear
membrane forms

(a) Metaphase   (b) Anaphase   (c) Telophase

Now for a few more sample questions, starting with another set of classification questions.

Questions 1–3 refer to the following items

(A) interphase

(B) prophase

(C) metaphase

(D) anaphase

(E) telophase

1. Stage in which cytokinesis occurs   E

2. Stage in which chromosomes appear   B

3. Stage in which sister chromatids move apart   D

For #1, the answer is (E). Cytokinesis is the physical act of cell division, which happens at the end of mitosis, and telophase is the last stage.

For #2, the answer is (B). The DNA has been there all along, but it doesn't wind itself up into chromosomes until the first stage of mitosis, which is prophase.

For #3, the answer is (D). The sister chromatids move apart just before the cell splits. The cell splits during telophase, which is the last stage, so separation of the sister chromatids must happen in the stage just before that, which is anaphase.

In which stage of a eukaryotic cell cycle is the cell's DNA copied?

(A) prophase

(B) metaphase

(C) anaphase

(D) telophase

(E) none of the above

When the cell enters the M phase of mitosis, it has already copied all of its DNA. That is, DNA is copied during interphase. All of the choices are stages of mitosis, not interphase, so the answer is (E) none of the above.

"None of the above" doesn't get used all that often, but it does show up once in a while, so I just wanted to keep you on your toes.

Chapter 4

Building A Foundation: Chemical Basics

Wait a minute . . . a whole chapter on just chemistry? You thought this book was about the SAT II *biology* test, not the chemistry test! Did someone screw up? Well, unfortunately, no. It turns out that nailing the biology test means you have to get some chemistry along the way. Organisms are made of molecules, and several different life processes involve chemical reactions, so here's where you can get some of those chemistry basics out of the way.

Getting Down to the Basic Elements

Atoms are really small. Okay, so the cells that Chapter 3 discusses are really small, too, but atoms are really, *really*, small. They're so small that we can't see them through even the most powerful microscopes, but there they are. Everything is made of atoms, and this section covers some of the most important atom information that you may see on the SAT II.

Subatomic particles

As small as atoms are, they are actually made of things that are even smaller. Atoms are made of teeny little subatomic particles called protons, neutrons, and electrons. Protons and neutrons are heavier and denser, and they are packed together in the center of the atom in an area called the nucleus.

Don't get the atom's nucleus confused with the nucleus of a cell! A cell's nucleus is where its DNA is stored, and it's absolutely humongous compared to the nucleus of an atom. Unfortunately, scientists ended up using the same word for both the nucleus of a cell and the nucleus of an atom.

An atom's nucleus is made of protons and neutrons, while the electrons are swirling around outside the nucleus. See Figure 4-1 for a basic picture of an atom.

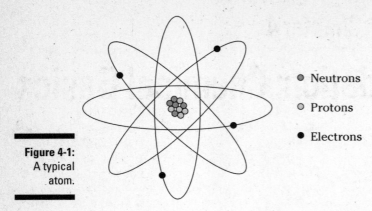

- ○ Neutrons
- ○ Protons
- ● Electrons

Figure 4-1:
A typical
atom.

Elements

There are a lot of different kinds of atoms, though they all have the same basic structure as shown in Figure 4-1. The different kinds of atoms are called *elements,* and the only thing that distinguishes one element from another is its number of protons. Some familiar substances such as carbon, oxygen, and hydrogen are all different elements, so they each have a different number of protons in their nucleus. See Table 4-1 for a list of elements that are important in biology.

Table 4-1		Some Common Elements in Biology	
Element	*Symbol*	*Number of protons*	*Typical ion form*
Hydrogen	H	1	H^+
Carbon	C	6	--
Nitrogen	N	7	--
Oxygen	O	8	--
Sodium	Na	11	Na^+
Phosphorus	P	15	--
Sulfur	S	16	--
Chlorine	Cl	17	Cl^-
Potassium	K	19	K^+

Isotopes

Every atom has protons and neutrons in its nucleus. The number of protons determines which element it is, but the number of neutrons doesn't really matter that much.

In fact, two atoms of the same element, which have the same number of protons, can sometimes have a different number of neutrons. When this happens, the atoms are called different *isotopes* of the same element. For example, carbon is an element that has 6 protons in its nucleus, and there are two isotopes of carbon. One isotope (carbon-12) has 6 neutrons and the other isotope (carbon-14) has 8 neutrons. They're both still carbon because they both have six protons, but they are different isotopes of carbon because they have a different number of neutrons.

Ions

Protons have a positive charge, while the electrons have a negative charge. Neutrons are neutral — they have no charge — and kinda just take up space in the nucleus. Usually, an atom has the same number of protons as electrons, so the positive and negative charges balance each other out. Sometimes, though, an atom has more electrons than protons, so it has an extra negative charge. Other times an atom may have more protons than electrons, leaving it with an extra positive charge. Atoms with an extra positive or extra negative charge are called *ions*. Just to make things a little more complicated, positive ions are called *cations* and negative ions are called *anions*.

Okay, let's get in some sample questions on atoms.

Questions 1–3 refer to the following:

(A) isotopes

(B) ions

(C) protons

(D) electrons

(E) neutrons

   1. An element is characterized by having a certain number of these in its nucleus.

   2. Two atoms with same number of protons, but different number of neutrons.

   3. Atoms with an uneven number of protons and electrons.

For question #1, the answer is (C). The number of protons always determines which element the atom is. The number of electrons or neutrons can matter for other things, but for determining which element the atom is, only the number of protons matters.

For Question #2, the answer is (A). If they are the same element, they must have the same number of protons, but if they are different isotopes then they have a different number of neutrons.

For question #3, the answer is (B). An atom is an ion if the number of electrons does not match the number of protons. More electrons than protons means a negatively-charged ion — an anion. More protons than electrons means a positively charged ion — a cation.

Coming Together: Bonds

Atoms can stick together to form bonded groups of atoms called *molecules*. There are a few different ways that atoms can bond, but whichever way it happens, when you've got two or more atoms stuck together, you've got a molecule. Some common molecules in biology include H_2O (water), O_2 (oxygen gas), NaCl (sodium chloride), CO_2 (carbon dioxide), and $C_6H_{12}O_6$ (glucose). The letters are the symbols for the elements, and the little numbers that sometimes come after the letters tell you how many atoms of that element is in the molecule.

If there isn't a little number, then that means there's only one atom of that element. So, H_2O means that there are two hydrogen atoms and one oxygen in every water molecule. Likewise, in the glucose molecule, there are 6 carbon atoms, 12 hydrogens, and 6 oxygens.

Ionic bonds

Opposite charges always attract, while like charges always repel. That means that if you get two ions that both have a positive charge (cations), they push away from each other, and the same happens if the ions are both negative anions. It also means that if you get two ions that have opposite charges, they stick together. For example, sodium (Na) often has one more proton than electron, making it a cation which is written as Na^+. Chlorine (Cl), on the other hand, often has one extra electron, making it an anion written as Cl^-. If Na^+ and Cl^- get near each other, they stick together in what's called an *ionic bond*. Whenever two or more atoms bond together, the result is called a molecule, and the molecule in this case is NaCl, which also happens to be common table salt.

Covalent bonds

Another way that atoms can stick together to form molecules is by sharing electrons. Two atoms share electrons when a pair of electrons (one electron from each atom) spin around both atoms at the same time. This makes the atoms stick together in what's called a *covalent bond*, which is much stronger than an ionic bond.

Often, two atoms share their electrons equally, but some atoms are a little greedier than others and don't play fair. Greedy atoms share electrons to form a covalent bond, but they don't share evenly because they hog the electrons to themselves most of the time. Since electrons have a negative charge, this uneven sharing makes the greedy atom be a little bit more negative and leaves the other atom a little bit positive. Uneven covalent bonds like this are called *polar covalent bonds,* while covalent bonds with a perfectly even sharing of electrons are called *nonpolar covalent bonds*.

You may find it hard to predict when a covalent bond will be polar or nonpolar, but there are a few things you can count on:

- ✔ Whenever two atoms of the same element are covalently bonded, the bond is nonpolar because they will always be equally greedy for electrons. So for example, carbon-carbon bonds, hydrogen-hydrogen bonds, and oxygen-oxygen bonds are all nonpolar.

- ✔ Whenever carbon and hydrogen bond together, the bond is nonpolar. Carbon and hydrogen are always happy to be together, and they share very evenly.

- ✔ Whenever oxygen bonds with some other element (besides another oxygen) the bond will always be polar. Oxygen is the greediest element out there, so it always pulls electrons to itself when sharing. That means that whenever oxygen bonds with another element, the oxygen side will be a little bit negative.

Figure 4-2 lists some common covalent bonds and whether they are polar or nonpolar.

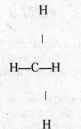

C — C	Nonpolar
C — H	Nonpolar
C — O⁻	Polar
⁻O — H⁺	Polar

Figure 4-2: Some common covalent bonds and their charges (if any).

$$C \overset{O^-}{=\!\!=} OH^+ \quad Polar$$

Forming multiple bonds

Not all elements are able to form covalent bonds, and some elements like to form more bonds than others. The reasons for all this finicky behavior is pretty complicated, but you don't need it for the biology test, so we won't bore you with it here. For now, we'll just get to the specifics about the ways some of the important elements like to bond.

Hydrogen will bond with just about anything, but it can only form one covalent bond at a time. Oxygen, on the other hand, can form two covalent bonds at once, so you can end up with something like this: (The lines represent covalent bonds.)

H—O—H

Notice that the oxygen has two separate covalent bonds and the hydrogens each have one. This molecule is usually written as H_2O and is, of course, water.

Carbon is the most important element in biology, and the rest of this section will explain why. Carbon can form up to four covalent bonds at once, so it could form a molecule with four hydrogens that looks like this:

H
|
H—C—H
|
H

This would be called CH_4, and is natural gas, also known as methane. Not every bond on the carbon has to be taken up by the same element, however, and you could easily get a situation where each of the carbon's four bonds is attached to a different element. For example, take a look at this bond:

H
|
O—C—C
|
N

Notice that the each element bonded to the central carbon is different. Notice also that the element on the right is another carbon. So far, that carbon has only one of its covalent bonds occupied, so it could easily bond to three other elements. If one of those is another carbon, then it could in turn bond to others, creating really large molecules. Since carbon can bond to four other atoms at once and can bond with just about any element, there's a huge variety of carbon-based molecules you could build, all with different shapes, sizes, and chemical properties. Figure 4-3 shows just two examples of big, complicated carbon molecules (and those are tiny compared to the really big ones).

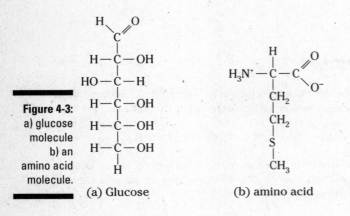

Figure 4-3:
a) glucose
molecule
b) an
amino acid
molecule.

(a) Glucose   (b) amino acid

Because of their great versatility, carbon-based molecules are the most common molecules in biology. All proteins, DNA, fats, and carbohydrates are carbon-based molecules. These are also called *organic molecules* because in chemistry the term *organic* means "carbon-based," unlike in farming where it means something like "all-natural." Chapter 5 goes into a lot more detail about the characteristics of the important organic molecules.

Rearranging Bonds: Chemical Reactions

Some parts of the SAT II will have questions that include chemical reactions. Chapter 5 goes into more detail about reactions, reaction energy, and enzymes, but this is a good spot to cover some basics so that you can recognize chemical reactions and know what they mean.

When different molecules are mixed together, the bonds that hold the atoms together can sometimes get rearranged, and this is known as a chemical reaction. For example, if you mix together H_2 (hydrogen molecules) and O_2 (oxygen molecules), the bonds will rearrange themselves to form H_2O (water molecules).

The famous Hindenberg blimp was filled with hydrogen, and when something lit a spark, all of the hydrogen in the blimp quickly mixed with oxygen in the air to form lots and lots of water molecules. Of course, the people on board were probably more worried about the huge fireball that resulted from this reaction than they were about getting wet from all the water, but hey, a little trivia never hurts.

Anyway, chemists write the reaction out like this:

$$H_2 + O_2 \rightarrow H_2O$$

The molecules before the arrow are called the *reactant*s, and molecules after the arrow are the *products*. Notice that the reactants include two atoms of hydrogen and two atoms of oxygen, and the product has two atoms of hydrogen, but only one atom of oxygen. Where did the other oxygen atom go? That leftover oxygen atom means that this reaction isn't properly balanced. To be balanced, you need to have the same number of each atom on either side of the arrow. You need to add another H_2O after the arrow so that you can have two oxygen atoms on either side. But then that means you'll have four hydrogen atoms after the arrow and only two before, so the hydrogens will then be unbalanced. Luckily, that's easily solved by adding an extra H_2 at the beginning, leaving you with four hydrogen atoms on both sides. Now the balanced reaction looks like this:

$$2 H_2 + O_2 \rightarrow 2 H_2O$$

This says that two hydrogen molecules react with one oxygen molecule to form two water molecules. We haven't changed the reaction because it's still just hydrogen and oxygen molecules getting together to form water, but now the reaction doesn't have any leftover atoms on either side. In other words, the reaction is balanced.

All right, now see if you can bond with these sample questions.

Which of the following covalent bonds is polar?

(A) H—H

(B) O=O

(C) C—H

(D) O—H

(E) C—C

A polar covalent bond occurs when two atoms share electrons unevenly. If the two atoms engaged in a covalent bond are the same element, then they will always share equally, so (A), (B), and (E) can be crossed out. It just so happens that whenever C and H form a covalent bond, the bond is nonpolar, so (C) is out also. That leaves (D) as the correct answer. Oxygen will always be the negative side in a polar covalent bond, unless it is bonding with another oxygen, in which case the bond is nonpolar.

An atom of the element calcium has two more protons than electrons. Based on this information, which of the following best describes the atom?

(A) isotope

(B) negatively-charged ion (anion)

(C) positively-charged ion (cation)

(D) neutral element

(E) none of the above

Protons are positively charged, so if the atom has extra protons, then it will be a positively-charged ion, so the correct answer is (C). It will definitely not be neutral with that uneven number of protons and electrons, and since there are fewer electrons, the overall charge will not be negative, so (D) and (B) are wrong.

I suppose the atom could be called an isotope, but the question didn't say anything about neutrons, so (A) was not the *best* answer based on the given information.

In a common chemical reaction, CO_2 (carbon dioxide) combines with H_2O (water) to form H_2CO_3 (carbonic acid). Which of the following correctly represents this reaction?

(A) $CO_2 + H_2O \rightarrow H_2CO_3$

(B) $2\ CO_2 + 2\ H_2O \rightarrow H_2CO_3$

(C) $CO_2 + 2\ H_2O \rightarrow H_2CO_3$

(D) $2\ CO_2 + H_2O \rightarrow H_2CO_3$

(E) $H_2CO_3 \rightarrow CO_2 + H_2O$

Carbon dioxide and water are the reactants because they are the ones getting mixed together, so they should come before the arrow, which means (E) is wrong. Now we just need to decide which of the other choices shows a balanced reaction. Choice (A) has 1 carbon, 3 oxygens, and 2 hydrogens before the arrow, and the same number of each after the arrow, so (A) is the correct answer. Just one of each molecule was needed to make the whole thing balanced. All of the other choices are unbalanced in one or more ways. For example, (B) and (D) have 2 carbons before the arrow and only one after, while (C) has 4 hydrogens before the arrow and only 2 after.

Throwing Everyone In the Pool: Interacting With Water

Water is one of the most important molecules in biology, and all living things contain a lot of it. Every living cell is full of water and all biological processes happen in the presence of water. As you probably know already, a water molecule is H_2O. That means it has two atoms of hydrogen covalently bonded to one oxygen, and whenever oxygen is involved in a covalent bond, the bond is polar, and water is no exception. The oxygen pulls the shared electrons toward itself, making itself more negative compared to the hydrogens, which end up being a little positive. Figure 4-4 shows the shape of an H_2O molecule and its charges.

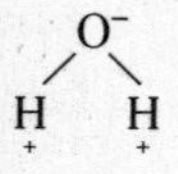

Figure 4-4:
Water molecule showing its polar covalent bonds.

$$O^- $$
$$H \quad\quad H$$
$$+ \quad\quad\quad +$$

The negative oxygen part of H_2O will be attracted to any positively charged ions or molecules in the area, while the positive hydrogen part of H_2O will be attracted to any negatively charged ions or molecules. That means if you throw regular salt (remember that's NaCl) into water, then the Na^+ will stick to the negative oxygen of H_2O, while the Cl^- will stick to the positive hydrogens.

In fact, the water molecules will end up pulling apart the ionic bond holding the Na and Cl together, and the two ions will be surrounded by H_2O molecules, as shown in Figure 4-5. When this happens, the salt is said to have dissolved in the water, and anything with a charge on it — whether it's an ion or a polar molecule — can dissolve in water this way.

Things that can dissolve in water are called *hydrophilic* because *hydro* refers to water, and *philic* means "liking," so it's as if charged ions and molecules enjoy dissolving in water.

Now for a few more quick vocabulary words. Whenever you have some stuff dissolved in water, it's called a *solution*. The water is called the *solvent,* and the stuff that's dissolved is called the *solute*. So, in the example of NaCl dissolving in water, the NaCl is the solute while the water is the solvent, and together they make a saltwater solution. Figure 4-5 shows this saltwater solution.

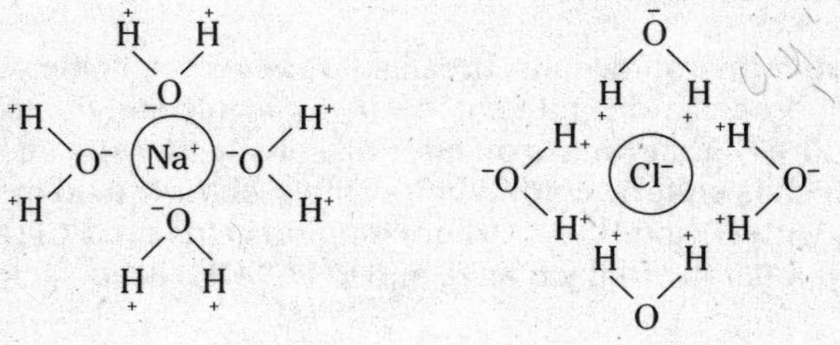

Figure 4-5:
NaCl
dissolved
in water.

Nonpolar molecules do not have any charges for water to stick to, so they cannot dissolve in water. Molecules that can't dissolve in water are called *hydrophobic*, where *phobic* means "fearing." The most common example of a hydrophobic molecule is oil, which is made of just carbon and hydrogen.

When C and H form a covalent bond, they share electrons evenly and are nonpolar. Since there aren't any charges for water to stick to, when you try to mix oil in with water, they move away from each other and stay as far apart as possible. It's like the oil really is afraid of the water.

Now for another sample question.

Which of the following molecules would be most likely to be hydrophilic?

(A) C_2H_6

(B) N_2

(C) $C_6H_{12}O_6$

(D) O_2

(E) Cl_2

Hydrophilic means it can dissolve in water, and in order to dissolve in water, the molecule needs to be polar.

Any molecule with only one kind of element will be nonpolar, which means they would be hydrophobic, which means any answer with only one kind of element is wrong.

(B), (D), and (E) can be crossed out. C_2H_6 has only carbon and hydrogen, and any molecule with only those is hydrophobic, so (A) is wrong also. $C_6H_{12}O_6$, the glucose molecule, contains carbon and hydrogen but it also contains oxygen, and oxygen always forms polar covalent bonds with other atoms. Being polar means having a small charge, which means that glucose is hydrophilic, so (C) is the correct answer.

Behaving Caustically: Acids and Bases

Acids and bases are kinds of polar molecules with interesting properties. They both dissolve in water very easily, in other words, they're hydrophilic, and they have the power to neutralize each other when you mix them. And to test just how acidic or basic a substance is, you can just give the litmus test.

Dissolving acids and bases

When acids or bases get into water, their molecules break apart in very specific ways. When an *acid* is dissolved in water, a hydrogen atom splits off of the molecule and floats around as a hydrogen ion, called H^+. The more H^+ that breaks off after dissolving, the stronger the acid. A common example is H_2SO_4, which is sulfuric acid. When you put sulfuric acid in water, a lot of H^+ breaks off, and you end up with H^+ and HSO_4^-. Other common acids are HCl (hydrochloric acid) which is the main component of stomach acid, and CH_3COOH (acetic acid) which is vinegar.

A *base*, on the other hand, has an oxygen-hydrogen pair break off as OH^- when it is mixed with water. The more OH^- that breaks off, the stronger the base. A common example is NaOH, which breaks into OH^- and Na^+. Other common bases are $NaHCO_3$, which is baking soda, and NH_3, which is ammonia. NH_3 ends up being a base because when you put it in water, it steals a hydrogen from H_2O, leaving lots of leftover OH^-.

Mixing acids and bases

An interesting thing happens when you mix together an acid and a base. The H^+ from the acid gets together with the OH^- from the base, and they form H_2O, which is plain old water. That means strong acids and strong bases, which are pretty caustic chemicals on their own, are able to neutralize each other when they're combined. For example, HCl (hydrochloric acid) is a really strong acid that is used in swimming pools, and NaOH (sodium hydroxide, also called lye) is a really strong base used to unclog drains. When you mix them together, the H^+ from the acid and the OH^- from the base combine to form H_2O, and the Na and Cl combine to form salt, so you just end up with harmless saltwater. I don't suggest you try doing this, however, because if you don't get it just right, then you end up with a highly toxic mess.

Measuring levels of acidity

Chemists use a scale, called pH, to measure acidity. The pH scale runs from 0 to 14, with 7 being neutral (neither acidic nor basic). Anything below 7 is acidic, and anything above 7 is basic. The most common way to test pH is with litmus paper, which is just regular paper with a special pH-sensitive dye. You simply dip some litmus paper into a solution, and the paper changes color depending on the pH. If it is really acidic (near 1 or 2) then the litmus paper will turn bright red, but if it's really basic (near 13 or 14) then the litmus paper will turn a dark blue.

That's right! It's time for another sample question!

Which of the following is false?

(A) acids release H⁺ when mixed with water

(B) when mixed together, an acid and a base will tend to make each other stronger

(C) acids make litmus paper turn red

(D) bases release OH⁻ when mixed with water

(E) bases make litmus paper turn blue

The question asks which of the statement is false, so we can eliminate the ones that are true. For litmus paper, acids make them red and bases make them blue, so (C) and (E) are true. Acids release H⁺ while bases release OH⁻, so (A) and (D) are true also. That means (B) must be false, and here's why.

When you mix together acids and bases, the H⁺ from the acid and the OH⁻ from the base combine to form harmless water. So, the combination of acids and bases actually makes them both weaker rather than stronger.

Chapter 5

Seeing Chemistry in Action: Molecular Biology

Carbon can form a huge variety of different molecules of various shapes and sizes. Carbon can make four bonds at a time with just about any other element, and if you string many carbons together, you can construct all sorts of crazy huge molecules (see Chapter 4 for more on this). Molecules that are based on carbon are called organic molecules. This type of organic is different than the word "organic" as it is used in farming and the food industry, where it means something like "all natural." In chemistry, since *organic* just means "carbon-based," all living things are organic, as well as the products like vegetables and meats that come from living things. Even the things we don't want, like dog poop, are organic. Just about everything inside of a living organism is made of some combination of four kinds of organic molecules that are important in biology: carbohydrates, amino acids, nucleotides, and lipids. We discuss these important organic molecules in this chapter, highlighting areas that the SAT II focuses on.

Sugar-coating Life with Carbohydrates

The word *carbohydrates* (sometimes also called *saccharides*) is really just a fancy name for sugars, but sometimes people think that "sugar" refers to sweet-tasting things, and not all carbohydrates taste sweet. Some diets cut out most or all of the carbohydrates from a person's meals, which includes nonsweet things like potatoes, pasta, rice, vegetables, and bread, in addition to the sweeter things like fruits and desserts. So, if nothing else, maybe this section can show you how to watch your carbs.

Carbohydrates can come in many forms, but they all have one thing in common: They all are made of carbon, hydrogen, and oxygen, and for every carbon in a carbohydrate, there is one oxygen and two hydrogens. Chemists write the generic carbohydrate formula as $C_nH_{2n}O_n$. This means that for any number of carbons, there will be the same number of oxygens and twice as many hydrogens, so you could have $C_4H_8O_4$, $C_5H_{10}O_5$, and so on. The most common carbohydrates in biology have either 5 or 6 carbons. Glucose is by far the most important carbohydrate in biology because it is the primary fuel used by all organisms and it is the main product of photosynthesis, which forms the basis of almost every ecosystem. The chemical formula of this famous carbohydrate is $C_6H_{12}O_6$, and its basic structure is shown in Figure 5-1a. Glucose also comes in a form where it bends around to form a hexagonal ring, which is shown in Figure 5-1b.

Figure 5-1:
a) linear glucose molecule
b) ringed glucose molecule.

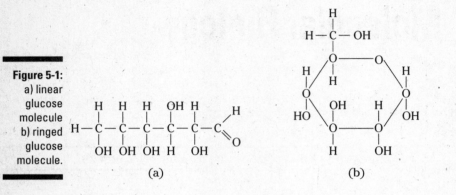

(a)   (b)

When chemists draw ring structures like this, they don't bother showing the carbons at each corner. You can just assume that there's a carbon atom at each corner of the ring unless it shows something else there, like the oxygen atom at the top, right-hand corner of the hexagon.

A single sugar molecule like glucose is called a *monosaccharide,* because *mono* means "one," and saccharide refers to sugars. Monosaccharides can link together to form a bonded pair of sugars called a *disaccharide.* A common example is sucrose, which is the regular sugar you buy from the grocery store and is what makes all fruit taste sweet. Sucrose is a disaccharide made of one glucose and one fructose linked together (see Figure 5-2).

Maybe you noticed that all the sugar names are ending in *-ose.* That's not an accident. All small sugars have a name that ends in *-ose.* Watch out for distinguishing features like that in the names of some of the other kinds of organic molecules.

When two sugars are linked together to form a disaccharide, they go through a standard linking reaction called *dehydration synthesis. Synthesis* means "building," and *dehydration* means "losing water," so in this reaction, a water molecule is lost during the building of the disaccharide. The reaction is shown in Figure 5-2. One sugar loses an OH while the other loses an H, and those get together to form H_2O. The two sugars now each have an open covalent bond, so they bond with each other, and the disaccharide is complete!

Figure 5-2:
Dehydration synthesis reaction joining two monosaccharides into a disaccharide.

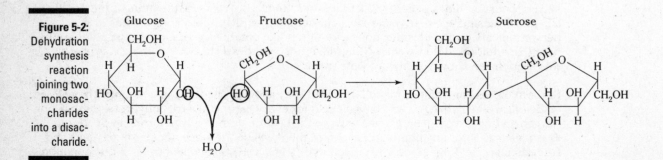

If more than two monosaccharides link together through dehydration synthesis, the result is called a *polysaccharide*. A few important polysaccharides made from glucose may show up on the SAT II. The first one is starch, which is made when plants want to store a bunch of glucose. Starch is the main component of rice and potatoes, which is why low-carb diets want you to reduce or eliminate these foods from your diet. However, meats have some sugar stored in them as well (just not as much). When animals want to store sugar, they link together a bunch of glucose molecules into a different polysaccharide called *glycogen*, which they store in their muscles and liver.

Another important polysaccharide of glucose is cellulose, which is the main component of the cell walls of plants. Even though it is just made of a bunch of glucose molecules all stuck together, cellulose is really strong. In fact, we eat a lot of cellulose whenever we eat plants, but we can't digest any of it because it is too tough. Sometimes cellulose is called *fiber,* and it's the main ingredient in all paper, fabrics, and ropes that are made from plants. Table 5-1 summarizes the main polysaccharides that are made from glucose.

Table 5-1	Common Polysaccharides Made from Glucose	
Name	*Function*	*Found in*
glycogen	sugar storage	animals
starch	sugar storage	plants
cellulose	cell walls	plants

Here are some sweet questions about carbohydrates.

Which of the following molecules is most likely to be a carbohydrate?

(A) $C_5H_{12}O_5$

(B) $C_6H_{14}O_6$

(C) $C_5H_{10}O_5$

(D) $C_5H_{10}O_7$

(E) $C_{12}H_6O_{12}$

The generic chemical formula for a carbohydrate is $C_nH_{2n}O_n$. This means that the number of carbons and the number of oxygens must be the same and that the number of hydrogens is twice the number of the other two. Answer (D) has a different number of carbons and oxygens, so it can be crossed out right away. Answers (A), (B), and (D) all have the same number of carbons and oxygens, but in each of those molecules, the number of hydrogens is not twice the number of carbons and oxygens. The only one that gets it right is (C), so that is the correct answer.

Which of the following is the molecule that plants use to store carbohydrates?

(A) glycogen

(B) glucose

(C) cellulose

(D) starch

(E) fiber

Glycogen is what animals use to store carbohydrates, so (A) is wrong. Cellulose is the polymer that plants use to make cell walls, and fiber is the dietary term for cellulose, so (C) and (E) are wrong. Glucose is the sugar that gets stored, but it is not stored as an individual monosaccharide, so (B) is pretty close to correct, but still wrong. Plants string glucose molecules together into a polysaccharide called starch in order to store carbohydrates, so (D) is the correct answer.

Linking Up: Polymers

Polysaccharides, such as starch and cellulose,, what are called *polymers*. A polymer is a generic name for a big molecule that is made from a long string of smaller molecules. The generic name for the smaller molecules is *monomers*. So, cellulose is a polymer made of many glucose monomers all linked together in a big long chain. Other important organic molecules also form polymers, as you'll see later on in this chapter.

Proteins are polymers made of many amino acids linked together in a chain. DNA is also a polymer, but it is made of many nucleotides linked together in a chain. Table 5-2 lists the important polymers and the monomers from which they are made. Dehydration synthesis is also used to link together the monomers in all polymers (see "Sugar-coating Life with Carbohydrates," above for more on dehydration synthesis).

Table 5-2	Common Polymers and their Monomers	
Polymer	*Monomer*	*Function*
Glycogen	Glucose	sugar storage in animals
Starch	Glucose	sugar storage in plants
Cellulose	Glucose	cell walls of plants
Proteins	amino acids	variable
nucleic acids (DNA and RNA)	nucleotides	genetic material

Here's a quick polymer question before you move on.

What is the name of the reaction that links together the monomers of a polymer?

(A) dehydration synthesis

(B) hydrolysis

(C) photosynthesis

(D) cellular respiration

(E) polymosynthesis

Photosynthesis is the making of glucose molecules from CO_2 and H_2O, so (C) is wrong. Cellular respiration is all about breaking down glucose, so (D) is wrong also. I just made up the word "polymosynthesis," so (E) is definitely wrong. The correct answer is (A) dehydration synthesis, in which the monomers lose a water molecule in order to link together. Hydrolysis is actually the opposite of dehydration synthesis, so (B) was wrong. *Hydro* refers to water, and *lysis* means breaking, so *hydrolysis* means separating monomers by adding water.

Making Everything Work with Amino Acids and Proteins

Proteins are the real workers of every organism. You may have heard somewhere that DNA is the basis for all life. Well, DNA doesn't really do much besides sit around in the nucleus, while proteins do all the real work. Proteins serve as the main structure for hair, skin, muscles, and most internal organs. Some proteins can act as hormones, like insulin. Other proteins act as enzymes that control all of the chemical reactions inside of every cell. In other words, proteins are really what make living organisms function and hold together.

Proteins are polymers, which means they are long molecules made of smaller molecules (monomers) all stuck together in a string. The monomers for proteins are amino acids. Figure 5-3 shows a diagram of a typical amino acid.

Figure 5-3:
A typical
amino acid.

$$ H-N-\underset{\text{variable}}{\overset{H}{C}}-\overset{O}{C}-OH $$

Notice that the middle carbon has the word *variable* attached to one of its bonds. There are 20 different amino acids, and each one has something different attached at that spot. In fact, that's the only thing that makes each amino acid different — everything else is the same as what's shown in Figure 5-3. The other parts all need to be the same in order to make sure that every amino acid can link up properly with every other amino acid. They are sort of like different train cars, where each car has the right hookups to connect to any other car, and you can link them up in any order you want along the chain. The actual sequence of amino acids in a protein chain is called the *primary structure* of the protein. When amino acids are linked together to make a protein polymer, they go through the normal dehydration synthesis reaction, as shown in Figure 5-4. For some reason, biochemists have given the covalent bond that holds two amino acids together the special name *peptide bond*.

Figure 5-4:
Dehydration
synthesis
reaction
linking two
amino acids
to start
a protein
polymer.

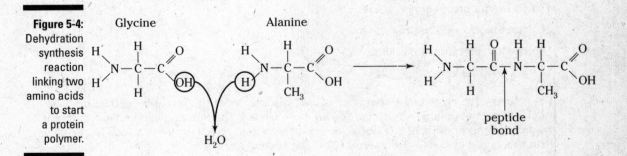

New amino acids can always be tacked onto the end of the chain, creating protein polymers that can be as short as just a few amino acids, or as long as a few thousand amino acids. Once a protein polymer has been built, the string of amino acids bends around to form folds and coils. A fold in a protein is called a *pleated sheet* while a coil is called a *helix*. These pleated sheets and helices are the *secondary structure* of a protein. Once the protein has bent into its secondary structure, then those pleated sheets and helices fold into an even bigger, more complicated 3-D structure called the *tertiary structure* of the protein. Figure 5-5 shows a diagram of a possible tertiary structure of a protein.

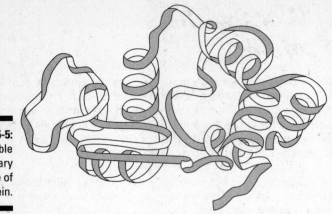

Figure 5-5:
Possible
tertiary
structure of
a protein.

When a protein folds into its secondary and tertiary structures, amino acids at different positions along the chain end up coming very close to each other, and here's where the differences between amino acids finally becomes really important. The only difference between different amino acids is what's connected at the variable position. Some amino acids have atoms at the variable position that form nonpolar bonds (no charges at all), while other amino acids have atoms at that position that form polar bonds (positive or negative charges). See Chapter 4 for more on polar and nonpolar bonds. Suppose one amino acid in the chain has a polar covalent bond with a negative charge, while another amino acid has a polar covalent bond with a positive charge. If these two end up near each other after the protein folds, then they will stick together. The sticking of amino acids like this is what holds together the protein's complicated 3-D shape. As you'll see later, the shape of a protein is really important for its function, so if the shape gets screwed up somehow, then the protein won't work right. Things that can screw up a protein's shape are things like really high or low temperatures or changes in pH.

Now for some protein questions.

The tertiary structure of a protein refers to what feature of the protein?

(A) the overall 3-D shape

(B) the sequence of amino acids

(C) the function of the protein

(D) the local folding and coiling

(E) none of the above

The primary structure is the sequence of amino acids, while the secondary structure is the local folding and coiling, so (B) and (D) are both wrong. The function can be very different from protein to protein, and is not given a generic name, so (C) is wrong also. The tertiary structure is the overall 3-D shape, so (A) is the correct answer.

Which of the following statements about proteins is false?

(A) All proteins are polymers of amino acids.

(B) The shape of a protein is vital to the protein's function.

(C) Proteins make up most of the structure of an animal's body.

(D) The primary structure of a protein helps determine its tertiary structure.

(E) Protein shape is immune to changes in pH.

The question is looking for the false statement, so we can rule out the correct ones. All proteins are made from amino acids, so cross out (A). As explained more fully in the section on enzymes, the shape of a protein is vital to its function, so cross out (B) as well. All hair, skin, muscles, fingernails, connective tissue,and so on are made out of proteins, so (C) is true, which means it should be crossed out also. The primary structure of a protein is the sequence of amino acids, and the exact placement of amino acids along the polymer is important to its overall 3-D shape (tertiary structure) so (D) is also out of the running. That leaves (E) as the false statement. Protein shape can, in fact, be dramatically altered by changes in pH, so (E) is the correct answer to the question.

Building Genes: Nucleotides and Nucleic Acids

Nucleic acids are the polymers that contain the genetic information for every cell. The two main kinds of nucleic acids are deoxyribonucleic acid (DNA) and ribonucleic acid (RNA), and they are both made of monomers called *nucleotides* that are strung together in a long chain. RNA is just a single string of nucleotides, but DNA is actually two chains of nucleotides wound around each other in a spiral structure called a *double-helix*, as shown in Figure 5-7. Table 5-3 lists the main differences between DNA and RNA.

Table 5-3	The Differences between DNA and RNA		
Nucleic acid	*Nucleotides used*	*Number of strands*	*Location in cell*
DNA	A, T, C, G	double-stranded	nucleus only
RNA	A, U, C, G	single-stranded	nucleus, cytoplasm, rough endoplasmic reticulum

The nucleotides are each made of three parts. As shown in Figure 5-6, every nucleotide is made from one sugar (ribose for RNA or deoxyribose for DNA), one phosphate group, and one nitrogenous base. The only thing that makes one nucleotide different from another is the nitrogenous base, so to keep things simple we'll use the terms interchangeably. For DNA, there are four different nitrogenous bases, Adenine, Thymine, Guanine, and Cytosine. RNA uses the same ones, except that RNA uses Uracil instead of Thymine (see Table 5-3).

DNA is double-stranded and twists into a helix. The nucleotides that line up across from each other in the helix need to be arranged very specifically so that Adenine (A) and Thymine (T) always line up across from each other, and Guanine (G) and Cytosine (C) are always across from each other. This matching up of the nucleotides from the two strands helps keep the strands stuck together. The polar covalent bonds of T stick to the polar covalent bonds of A, and the same is true between C and G (see Chapter 4 for more info on polar covalent bonds). The sticking together of nucleotides in opposite strands is what holds the strand together, as shown in Figure 5-7.

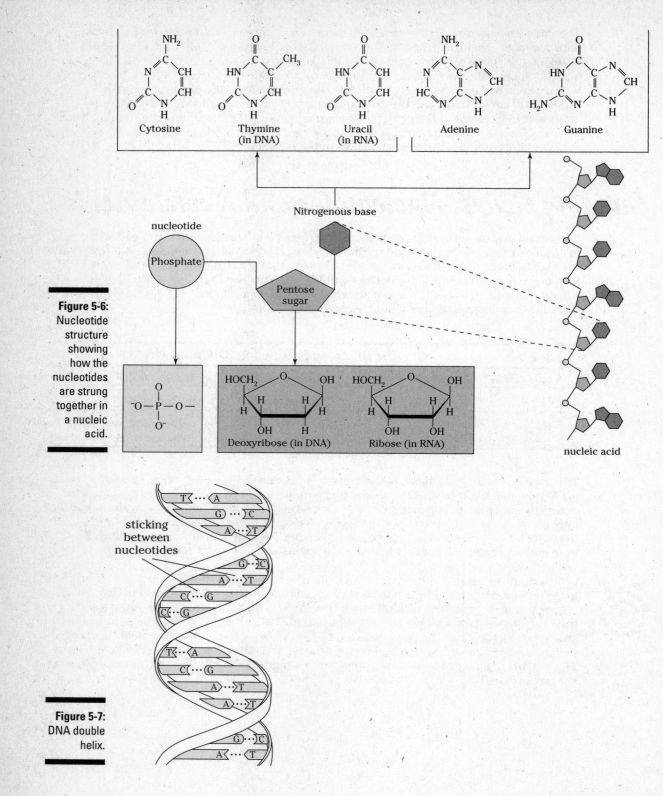

Figure 5-6: Nucleotide structure showing how the nucleotides are strung together in a nucleic acid.

Figure 5-7: DNA double helix.

Try this nucleic acid question.

Which of the following statements about RNA is true?

(A) it is double-stranded

(B) it contains uracil instead of thymine

(C) it is made of amino acids

(D) it is found only in the nucleus

(E) it is found only in the rough endoplasmic reticulum

The question asks which of the statements is true, so we can cross out the false ones. DNA is double-stranded, while RNA is single-stranded, so get rid of (A). Proteins are the polymers made from amino acids, so (C) is wrong also. RNA is found in the nucleus, the rough endoplasmic reticulum, and in the cytoplasm of a cell, so both (D) and (E) are wrong. That leaves (B) as the correct answer. RNA is a single-stranded polymer made from uracil, adenine, guanine, and thymine.

Fearing Water: Lipids

Lipids include fats, oils, and cholesterol, and what all those things have in common is that they're all hydrophobic. Being *hydrophobic* means that the molecule will not mix with water because it has nonpolar covalent bonds. Lipids are made mostly of just carbon and hydrogen, and when these two elements bond, the bond is always nonpolar. Some lipids do have some oxygen or other stuff in there that can make polar covalent bonds, but the vast majority of the bonds in a lipid are just between carbon and hydrogen, making the whole molecule hydrophobic. Lipids used to be avoided by people trying to lose weight, but now it's changed to the carbohydrates.

You don't need to memorize all of the following lipid names for the SAT II, but they may show up in some answer choices here and there, so it would be good to at least be able to recognize them and know that they belong to lipids. Unfortunately, the lipid names don't have little endings that can tell you they are lipids, like the *-ose* that ends the small sugar names, or the *-ine* that ends the names of amino acids and most nucleotides.

Following are some common lipid names you may find on the SAT II:

✔ **Triglyceride:** The most basic lipids are just simple strings of hydrocarbons, as shown in Figure 5-8. The shortest hydrocarbons can be just a few carbons long, while the longest can have up to 20 or so. Simple hydrocarbons, like the one in Figure 5-8, make up oil and natural gas that are used as fuel to run cars or to cook food. More complicated versions, called *fatty acids,* are the ones that are present in food, like in vegetable oil and animal fat. Most fatty acids are found in groups of three that come together in a big molecule called a *triglyceride,* which is three fatty acids stuck to a glyceride molecule, as shown in Figure 5-9.

Figure 5-8: Simple hydrocarbon molecule.

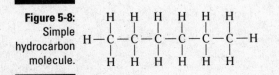

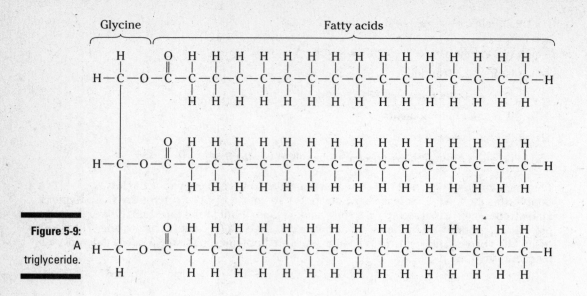

Figure 5-9:
A
triglyceride.

✔ **Phospholipids:** Cell membranes are made of *phospholipids*, which are molecules similar to triglycerides. In a phospholipid, one of the fatty acids is replaced by what's called a *phosphate group*, which is just a phosphorus atom with four oxygens attached to it (see Figure 5-10). The phosphate group makes its end of the phospholipid very polar, which means that phospholipids are actually hydrophobic at one end (the fatty acids) and hydrophilic at the other end (the phosphate group) — this interesting feature of phospholipids is important for cell membranes to be able to do their job properly.

✔ **Cholesterol:** The last kind of lipid is cholesterol, which is used as fuel for cells or for hormones. Cholesterol molecules are big bunches of ring structures all stuck together, as shown in Figure 5-11. All you really need to know about cholesterol for the SAT II is that it is a hydrophobic lipid and it doesn't form polymers.

Okay, it's time for another sample question.

Which of the following lipids is not completely hydrophobic?

(A) basic hydrocarbon

(B) fatty acid

(C) phospholipid

(D) cholesterol

(E) triglyceride

In general, lipids are all hydrophobic, but phospholipids have that phosphate group on them that makes that part of the molecule very hydrophilic. Therefore, phospholipids are not completely hydrophobic, so (C) is the correct answer.

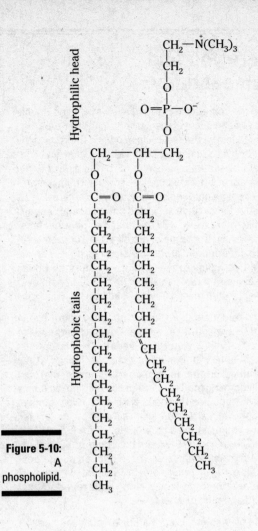

Hydrophilic head

Hydrophobic tails

CH_2—$\overset{+}{N}(CH_3)_3$
CH_2
O
$O{=}P{-}O^-$
O
CH_2—CH—CH_2
O $\quad$ O
$C{=}O$ $\quad$ $C{=}O$
CH_2 $\quad$ CH_2
CH_2 $\quad$ CH_2
CH_2 $\quad$ CH_2
CH_2 $\quad$ CH_2
CH_2 $\quad$ CH_2
CH_2 $\quad$ CH_2
CH_2 $\quad$ CH
CH_2 $\quad$ CH
CH_2 $\quad$ CH_2
CH_2 $\quad$ CH_2
CH_2 $\quad$ CH_2
CH_2 $\quad$ CH_2
CH_2 $\quad$ CH_3
CH_2
CH_3

Figure 5-10:
A
phospholipid.

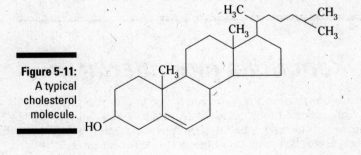

Figure 5-11:
A typical
cholesterol
molecule.

H_3C $\quad$ CH_3
CH_3 $\quad$ CH_3

HO

Chewing the fat: Where you find lipids in the foods you eat daily

Hydrophobic lipids comprise a group of molecules that includes fats and oils, waxes, phospholipids, and steroids (like cholesterol). For decades they have been a major source of dietary controversy. You need fat in your body and in the food you eat. Animals, including humans, use fat for energy storage. Your body also uses fat to protect vital organs like the kidneys and serve as insulation underneath the skin. Nutritionists just can't seem to figure out what fats are good for us and which are bad for us.

Fats and oils consist of glycerol and three fatty acids that are joined together through the process of dehydration synthesis. The have three fatty acids attached to them, which makes them triglycerides. The main difference between fats (like butter) and oils (like olive oil) is that fats are solid at room temperature and oils are liquid. That's because the structures of their fatty acids are different.

You've probably heard about types of fats and how some are better for you than others. But what's the difference? Saturated, mono-unsaturated, and poly-unsaturated labels refer to the number of hydrogens attached to the one end of the fatty acids and the number of double bonds between carbon atoms in the other end. Fats have single bonds between the carbons in their fatty acid tails, which makes the carbons bond to highest possible number of hydrogens. A high concentration of hydrogens gives you saturated fats. Since the hydrocarbon chains in the fatty acids are pretty straight, they can get really close together, so saturated fats, like lard and butter, are solid at room temperature. Saturated fats usually come from animals.

Oils usually come from plants. They have some double bonds between some of the carbons in the hydrocarbon end, which makes the molecule bend and decreases the amount of hydrogens they bond to. So, oils are unsaturated fats. The bends make it hard for the chains to get together, so, unsaturated fats are liquid at room temperature. For a time nutritionists stated that unsaturated fats were better for you than saturated ones. Vegetable shortening, like margarine, was supposed to be a healthier unsaturated oil. But to make the oil a solid at room temperature, laboratories artificially break its double bonds and add hydrogens to make it into a saturated fat, so they're finding that's it really has no health benefit over natural saturated fats, like butter and lard.

Recently scientists have raised concern about transfats. Heating unsaturated oils can cause their bonds to change. Natural unsaturated vegetable oils contain mostly cis bonds (bonds where the two pieces of the carbon chain on the same side of the molecule), but using oil for frying foods can make some of the cis bonds change to trans bonds (bonds where the two pieces of the carbon chain are on opposite sides of the molecule). The more you use the same batch of oil for frying (think fast-food French fries) the more the bonds change. Fatty acids with trans bonds can cause cancer, so the government is going to require that the amount of trans fatty acids appear on food labels along with reports about saturated and unsaturated fats.

So, lipids play an important part in keeping you healthy. It's just hard to figure out which ones are right for the job!

Changing Molecules: Reactions and Energy

In every chemical reaction, molecular bonds are somehow rearranged in order to turn some starting molecules (the reactants) into different molecules (the products). You can classify chemical reactions as endothermic or exothermic depending on how much energy they require to change the reactants into products. Sometimes chemical reactions need a little help to get motivated. They rely on catalysts called enzymes to give them a boost.

Discovering endothermic and exothermic reactions

Some chemical reactions take a lot of energy, especially when you're taking small molecules and putting them together to make a bigger molecule. A good example is photosynthesis, which takes CO_2 and H_2O and builds them into glucose. This reaction needs a lot of sunlight energy to keep it running because the lazy CO_2 and H_2O molecules aren't going to just do it on their own. The other kind of chemical reaction is a lot easier because it just goes on its own, like when H_2 and O_2 gas react together to form H_2O. That reaction will go really fast (explosively fast), as long as you give it a little spark to get it started.

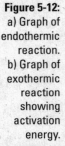

Figure 5-12 shows a graph of these two kinds of chemical reactions. Graph A shows a building-up reaction that takes a lot of energy. Reactions like this are called *endothermic*. *Endo* means inside, and *thermic* refers to energy (especially heat energy) which is supposed to tell you that these reactions absorb energy from their surroundings. Graph B shows the other kind of reaction, where the reactants will naturally turn into the products without any input of energy. Actually, as you can see, these reactions do need a little boost of energy to get them started, called the *activation energy,* but once they get that, they just go on their own. This second kind of reaction is called *exothermic* because they release energy to their surroundings, usually as heat or light.

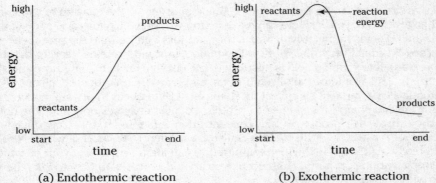

Figure 5-12:
a) Graph of endothermic reaction.
b) Graph of exothermic reaction showing activation energy.

(a) Endothermic reaction   (b) Exothermic reaction

Imagine you are making a big pile of wood. It takes a lot of energy to go around collecting all of those logs and pulling them together into a pile. That is like an endothermic reaction — lots of energy input. Now imagine you set fire to that pile of wood. All you need to do is throw one little match on the pile and pretty soon you'll have a big bonfire that burns the pile down to ashes. That's an exothermic reaction where only a little energy input was needed to get things started, then it all goes on its own and releases a lot of energy into the surroundings.

Helping reactions: Enzymes

A *catalyst* is a thing that makes a chemical reaction work more easily. Enzymes are special catalysts made out of proteins that are set up to help with very specific reactions. For example, there is a specific enzyme called *DNA polymerase* that takes two nucleotides, and makes them bond together in a dehydration synthesis reaction. Names for enzymes always end with "-ase," such as DNA polymerase (which builds DNA), lactase (which breaks down the sugar lactose), and helicase (which unwinds the DNA helix). Almost every important chemical reaction in an organism is helped along by some kind of enzyme.

Every enzyme is an *active site,* where the reactant molecules bind and the reaction happens. Right here is an example of how the shape of a protein is vital to its proper functioning. The shape of the enzyme's active site is very specific, allowing only molecules with the right shape (the shape of the reactants) to fit in. This is sort of like a key fitting into a lock, as shown in Figure 5-13. Once the reactants bind to the active site, the chemical reaction happens, and products are released. The enzyme can then repeat the process with more reactants.

reaction:

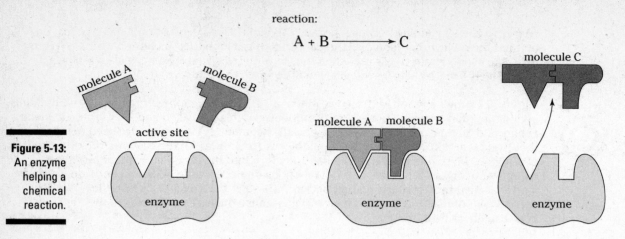

Figure 5-13:
An enzyme helping a chemical reaction.

The active site needs to be a very specific shape in order for the enzyme to work, so anything that changes the enzyme's shape can make it stop working. Enzymes are made of proteins, and the amino acids in the polymer stick together just right to help the protein keep its 3-D shape (see "Making Everything Work with Amino Acids and Proteins," earlier in this chapter for more info). If any amino acid is misplaced, the enzyme may change shape and stop working properly. This would be called a mutation, and for more on those, check out Chapter 7. The protein's environment can affect its shape also. Differences in pH, salt concentration, or temperature can change the shape of a protein, so most enzymes only have the right shape when they are in their proper pH, salt concentration, and temperature. Any deviation away from their ideal range, and the enzyme can stop working. That's part of why it is so dangerous to get a really high fever — the high temperature can mess up some of your enzymes and your brain stops working properly. That means you should probably not try to take the SAT II if you end up with a fever on test day.

EXAMPLE

Okay, now see how you react to these sample SAT II questions.

A chemical reaction is occurring inside of a beaker and the sides of the beaker start to feel hot. Which of the following may you infer about this reaction?

(A) the reaction is endothermic

(B) the reaction is helped by an enzyme

(C) the reaction is very fast

(D) the reaction is exothermic

(E) the reaction is very slow

The question didn't say anything about how fast the beaker heated up, so you can't infer anything about the speed of the reaction, which means (C) and (E) are wrong. The reaction may or may not be helped by an enzyme, but you can't tell just by feeling the temperature, so (B) is wrong also. *Thermic* refers to energy (specifically heat energy). *Endo* means inside, so endothermic reactions absorb energy from their surroundings. If that were happening, then the beaker would feel colder and colder, so the reaction is not endothermic, so (A) is wrong. *Exo* means outside, so exothermic reactions release energy to their surroundings. This would make the beaker feel warmer and warmer, so the correct answer is (D).

The overall 3-D shape of a protein is important for the protein's function. Which of the following factors help determine the shape of a protein?

(A) amino acid sequence of the protein polymer

(B) pH of the protein's environment

(C) temperature of the protein's environment

(D) all of the above

(E) none of the above

The amino acid sequence makes sure each amino acid is in just the right position so that when the protein folds up into its 3-D shape, certain amino acids will stick to each other in just the right way to hold the shape together, so (A) definitely helps determine protein shape. But the pH and the temperature of the protein's environment can also affect the protein's shape, so the correct answer is (D), all of the above.

Chapter 6

Getting Energized: Respiration and Photosynthesis

Life is an extremely active process. Even while you veg out in front of the latest lame reality TV show, the cells of your body are going crazy with activity, and all this action takes a whole lot of energy, whether you feel amped up or not. This chapter may not give you more energy, but it does give you a jump-start on what you need to know about energy on the SAT II for Biology.

Espresso for Cells: ATP and Energy

The energy source for every cell on earth — from your SAT-busting brain cells to the dumbest bacteria — is a tiny molecule that you may have never heard of before: ATP. Every ATP molecule contains a small amount of energy that a cell can use to perform some action, like pumping in tasty nutrients or pumping out nasty waste products.

Getting energy

Since the energy in one ATP (adenosine triphosphate; you can find out more about this in, "Storing and releasing energy," later in this chapter) molecule is so small, a single cell goes through millions and millions of them every day to accomplish the huge variety of tasks involved in staying alive. Luckily, ATPs are recyclable and can be recharged with energy and used again and again. But this recharging process isn't free (nothing is in this harsh world), so cells always need to have a source of energy coming in from outside in order to recharge their ATPs. There are two main outside energy sources that different cells can use: food and light. Cells that use food as their outside energy source are called heterotrophs. Hetero means other and troph refers to eating, so heterotrophs like us eat other organisms in order to steal their energy. These include all animals and fungi, and many varieties of bacteria and protists. Cells that use light are called autotrophs. Since auto means self, these cells feed themselves. They use light energy to make their own food, then use that food to recharge their ATPs! Autotrophs include all plants, and many other varieties of bacteria and protists.

Storing and releasing energy

Unfortunately, we need to deal with a little bit of technical jargon and chemistry here — not because without it you won't understand how cells use energy, but because you just may get asked about it on the SAT II. So, here we go. ATP stands for adenosine triphosphate. As the name suggests, this molecule is made of an adenosine molecule with three phosphates attached. When the molecule is energized and ready to go, the third phosphate is attached. When the molecule gives up its energy, the third phosphate is removed. Recharging of ATP means re-attaching its third phosphate. Figure 6-1 shows an ATP reaction.

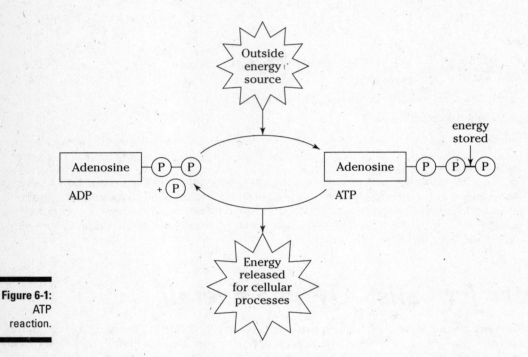

Figure 6-1:
ATP
reaction.

ATP reaction could be tested on the SAT II in the following manner.

Which of the following molecules is the immediate energy source for all cellular processes?

(A) O_2

(B) H_2O

(C) sugar

(D) ATP

(E) DNA

All of the molecules above (except DNA) are involved in aerobic cellular respiration, but only sugar and ATP are used as energy sources, so you can eliminate (A), (B), and (E). The important word to notice in this question is "immediate" because it points you to the correct answer, which is ATP, answer choice (D). Sugars are the original fuel molecules, but they go through the whole long process of aerobic cellular respiration (explained later in this chapter) in which their energy is stored in ATP molecules. Then, when the cell needs to actually use energy to do something, it gets the energy from ATPs.

Questions 1 and 2 refer to the following groups of organisms.

    I Animals

    II Plants

    III Fungi

    IV Bacteria

    V Protists

1. Which of the above groups contain autotrophs?

    (A) I only

    (B) I and II only

    (C) II and III only

    (D) II, III, and IV only

    (E) II, IV, and V only

Autotrophs are organisms that can perform photosynthesis to make their own sugars. Animals obviously don't do this, so you can cross any answer that contains I in it, answer choices (A) and (B). Fungi are always decomposers, so cross answers (C) and (D) because they contain III. This leaves you with the correct answer (E), which contains groups with at least a few species that can perform photosynthesis.

2. Which of the above groups contain heterotrophs?

    (A) I only

    (B) I and III only

    (C) all except II

    (D) I and V only

    (E) II and IV only

The only kingdom that contains only autotrophs is the plant kingdom; all of the other kingdoms contain heterotroph species, so the answer is (C).

Clean-Burning Fuels: Aerobic Cellular Respiration

Now let's focus on heterotrophs and how they use food to recharge their ATPs. The main process has the fancy-sounding name of *aerobic cellular respiration(ACR)*. That's certainly a mouthful, but we can break it down in order to understand its meaning. *Aerobic* means that it uses oxygen — just think of how much oxygen you need when doing aerobics. *Cellular* means, well, you probably get that part. *Respiration* in this context does not refer to actual breathing, though animals do breathe in order to make ACR work right. Instead, it just means that the cell is transferring energy from food molecules (usually the sugar, glucose) to ATP.

Aerobic cellular respiration, or just ACR for short, breaks up glucose ($C_6H_{12}O_6$) molecules in order to release the energy stored inside and then uses that energy to recharge a bunch of ATPs. The overall, balanced chemical reaction is this:

$$C_6H_{12}O_6 + 6\ O_2 \rightarrow 6\ CO_2 + 6\ H_2O + \text{energy for recharging ATPs}$$

In fact, if you burned a pile of sugar in your kitchen table (which I don't recommend because it smells terrible and will probably get you grounded) this chemical reaction would happen, and all of the energy in glucose would be released into the room as heat and light. Cells don't just burn their glucose all at once like that because if they did they would melt and die. Instead, they separate the glucose breakdown process into many small steps to efficiently capture as much energy as possible.

The process of ACR is divided into three main stages in the following order:

1. **Glycolysis:** *Glyco* refers to glucose and *lysis* means breaking, so glucose is broken in half in this first stage.

2. **The Krebs cycle:** Krebs is the name of some famous biochemist — Dr. Krebs — who decided to name this process after himself instead of giving it a name that biology students can understand.

3. **Electron Transport Chain:** This is where most of the ATP gets made and is where water is produced as a by-product.

There's a humongous amount of fascinating details we could talk about in each stage, but to save time and paper, we'll just go through the highlights that you'll need for the SAT II. Try out the following sample questions.

Which of the following molecules contains the energy that is released during aerobic cellular respiration?

(A) ATP

(B) glucose

(C) H_2O

(D) CO_2

(E) O_2

Hopefully this was kind of an easy one. You can for sure eliminate the small molecules in (C), (D), and (E). ATP has some energy in it, but ATP is a product of aerobic cellular respiration, so it can't be the answer either. The correct answer is (B) because glucose is the fuel molecule that is broken down in the aerobic cellular process.

Which of the following states the three main stages of aerobic cellular respiration in their proper order?

(A) electron transport chain, Krebs cycle, glycolysis

(B) Krebs cycle, glycolysis, electron transport chain

(C) electron transport chain, glycolysis, Krebs cycle

(D) glycolysis, electron transport chain, Krebs cycle

(E) glycolysis, Krebs cycle, electron transport chain

Unfortunately, this is just one of those memorization type of questions. The three stages of aerobic cellular respiration are glycolysis, the Krebs cycle, and the electron transport chain, in that order. The correct answer is (E).

Breaking it down with glycolysis

As mentioned before, *glycolysis* splits glucose in half. Each half of glucose that comes out of glycolysis is called pyruvate. Here are the overall inputs and outputs of glycolysis:

$$C_6H_{12}O_6 + 2 \text{ ATP} + 2NAD^+ \rightarrow 2 \text{ pyruvate} + 4 \text{ ATP} + 2NADH.$$

When looking at this, you may have said, "Hey! I thought this was all about *getting* ATPs, so why does this process *use* 2 ATPs?" Well, in the real world, you gotta spend money to make money, and cells are no different. This is a great investment, though, because when ACR is finished, the cell will have recharged up to 38 ATPs — a 1900 percent return! I'd like to see the stock market match that! Notice also that even though glycolysis actually produces four ATPs, you really only get two ATPs overall from this process because the cell had to use two ATPs to get things started.

Those two NAD⁺ things that get turned into two NADHs will become important when we get to stage three: the electron transport chain. What happens is that electrons are pulled off of the glucose molecule and carried by NADH to stage three. For now, though, just remember that glycolysis produces two NADHs. Glycolysis questions may appear in the following ways.

Which of the following are the correct inputs to glycolysis?

(A) 1 glucose and 6 O_2

(B) 1 glucose and 2 NAD⁺

(C) 1 glucose, 2 ATP, and 2 NAD⁺

(D) 2 ATP and 6 O_2

(E) 6 CO_2 and 6 H_2O

Glycolysis is the first step in aerobic cellular respiration, so glucose definitely needs to be included, which means you can cross out (D) and (E). Oxygen doesn't come in until the end of the electron transport chain, so cross out (A) also. That narrows things down to (B) or (C). Remember that the cell needs to add a little energy at the beginning of aerobic cellular respiration in order to get the whole process moving, and whenever the cell needs energy to do something, it uses ATPs. Answer (C) includes the ATPs, so it is the correct answer.

Which of the following are the correct net results of glycolysis?

(A) 6 CO_2 and 6 H_2O

(B) 2 pyruvate and 6 CO_2

(C) 2 pyruvate, 2 NADH, and 6 CO_2

(D) 2 pyruvate, 2 NADH, and 2 ATP

(E) 2 pyruvate, 2 NADH, and 4 ATP

Answer (A) is part of the overall outputs of the whole process of aerobic cellular respiration rather than the outputs of just glycolysis, so cross that one out. Now it gets harder because the answers start to look really similar. CO_2 is a product of the Krebs cycle, so you can safely cross out (B) and (C). That leaves (D) and (E), which differ only in the number of ATPs. Notice that the question asks for the NET. So, the 2 ATPs that are used at the beginning of glycolysis need to be subtracted from the 4 ATPs that are produced, leaving a net total of 2 ATPs. That means (D) is the correct answer.

Joining the dance party in the Krebs cycle

The *Krebs cycle* breaks the two pyruvates from glycolysis all the way down to CO_2, but first they have to get there, and it's a rough trip. Glycolysis happens out in the cytoplasm of the cell — the watery goop in between organelles (see Chapter 3) — while the Krebs cycle and the electron transport chain both happen inside the main ATP recharging center called the mitochondria. On the way there, each pyruvate molecule loses one of its carbon atoms which floats away as CO_2. The leftover 2-carbon molecules are called acetyl molecules, and these are what actually enter the Krebs cycle. Also, this mini-step on the way to the Krebs cycle produces another NADH for each pyruvate (we're up to four total NADHs so far and the fun is just getting started!). Now each acetyl molecule must be ushered into the Krebs cycle by a special escort called coenzyme A, and the combination as they enter the mitochondria is called acetyl-CoA. Like any good usher, though, as soon as the acetyl molecule is inside the mitochondria, the coenzyme A lets go and heads back out to bring in another acetyl.

Luckily, the poor acetyl isn't left all alone in the whirling party of the Krebs cycle. Another escort (whose name doesn't matter) picks up the acetyl from the coenzyme A and helps it move along through the cycle. This new dance partner doesn't treat the acetyl any better, though, because by the time the Krebs cycle is completed, the acetyl has been broken all the way down into two CO_2 molecules, four of its electrons have been stripped away and given to NADHs, and the escort is ready to accept a new victim, er, I mean, acetyl molecule guest.

The outputs of the Krebs cycle are: 2 CO_2, 3 NADHs, 1 $FADH_2$ (which really just acts like another NADH), and 1 ATP. Note that the Krebs cycle can only accept one acetyl at a time, so it must go around twice to handle the two acetyls coming in from glycolysis, which means we need to double all of the outputs listed in order to account for the breakdown of the original glucose molecule. To check out the Krebs Cycle, see Figure 6-2.

Here's our running total so far from glycolysis and two turns of the Krebs cycle:

- 6 CO_2 — that's all the CO_2
- 4 ATP — really six, but remember, we invested 2 ATPs at the very beginning
- 8 NADH — these carry electrons to stage three
- 2 $FADH_2$ — these also carry electrons to stage three

Notice that the original glucose molecule has been completely broken down into CO_2 molecules and we haven't even used any oxygen yet.

Which of the following are the net outputs of one turn of the Krebs cycle?

(A) 6 CO_2, 2 ATP, 6 NADH and 2 $FADH_2$

(B) 6 CO_2, 6 H_2O, and 2 ATP

(C) 3 CO_2, 3 H_2O, 3 NADH, and 1 $FADH_2$

(D) 3 CO_2, 1 ATP, 3 NADH, and 1 $FADH_2$

(E) 2 acetyl, 2 ATP, and 2 NADH

Water is an output of the electron transport chain, which we discuss in the next section, and not a product of the Krebs cycle, so cross out (B) and (C). Acetyl comes in at the beginning of the Krebs cycle, not the end, so cross out (E) also. That leaves (A) and (D). This gets a little tricky because the question specifically asks for the outputs of ONE turn of the Krebs cycle, and the cycle needs to go around twice to handle both of the pyruvates coming from glycolysis. The stuff listed in (A) represents the outputs after two turns of the Krebs cycle, so the correct answer is (D).

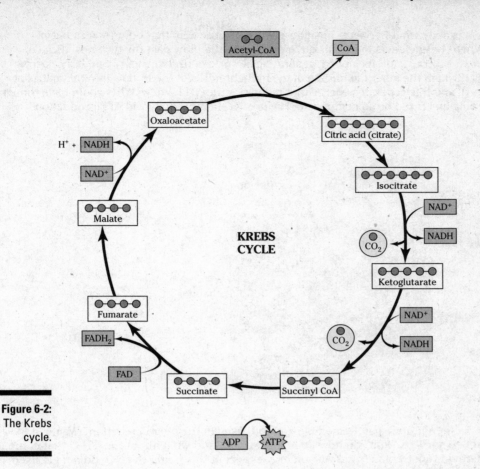

Figure 6-2:
The Krebs
cycle.

Charging toward the finish line: The electron transport chain

Okay, you've made it this far, so now comes the stage where the investment really pays off. The first two stages of ACR are really just geared toward getting electrons from the glucose molecule over to the electron transport chain, and now it's time to use those electrons. The *electron transport chain (ETC)* is a series of molecules that sit along the inner membrane of the mitochondria. These molecules do two things:

1. As the name suggests, the molecules of the ETC accept electrons from NADH and $FADH_2$ and send the electrons down the chain. This process releases a little energy.

2. The molecules of the ETC do use that energy to pump H^+ (hydrogen ions) across the inner membrane of the mitochondria, from the inner space (called the matrix) to the space between the inner and outer membranes (called the intermembrane space). At first this seems like an odd thing for them to do. Why not just use the energy for recharging the ATP instead of messing around pumping these hydrogen ions? Well, just wait, because the ATP-recharging is coming up! It turns out that the pumping action of the ETC is building up a whole bunch of H^+'s in the intermembrane space, and as soon as a channel opens in the inner membrane, they're all going to come flooding back into the inner matrix.

And that's exactly what happens. Imagine a hydro-electric dam that holds back a big lake of water. When the engineers open the narrow channels that flow past the turbines, the lake pushes water through at high speed, generating all sorts of usable energy. Similarly, narrow channels through the inner membrane of the mitochondria let the H⁺ flow into the matrix at high speed, and this generates energy that recharges the ATP! Whew! Who would have thought that burning fuel could be so complicated! Figure 6-3 shows H⁺ flow and ATP production.

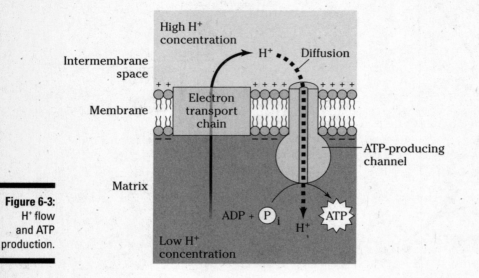

Figure 6-3:
H⁺ flow
and ATP
production.

But wait, we're not done yet. Remember the 6 O_2 used in the overall reaction? We need to breathe O_2 to survive, right? So how does it get used? And what about the 6 H_2O that come out? Where do those come from? As you may expect at this point, the 6 O_2 do *not* get used to make the 6 CO_2, because all the CO_2 has already been made directly from the breakdown of glucose in the first two stages of ACR. Instead, O_2 gets used in the production of H_2O.

All those H⁺ flowing back into the matrix could cause the matrix to get really acidic (see Chapter 4 for info on acids and bases), so the mitochondria needs some way to painlessly get rid of them, and a painless way to get rid of anything is to turn it into water. But to do that, you need oxygen, so here's where the O_2 gets used. A special enzyme at the end of the ETC called cytochrome oxidase catalyzes this reaction: $4 H+ + O_2 \rightarrow 2 H_2O$ and it does this six times for every glucose that enters aerobic cellular respiration. Figure 6-4 provides a picture of O_2 use and H_2O production.

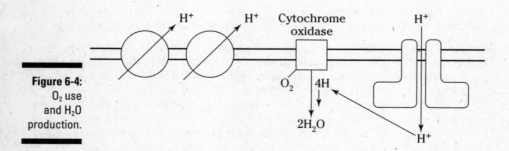

Figure 6-4:
O_2 use
and H_2O
production.

To test your knowledge of the electron transport chain, the SAT II may present you with questions like these.

Passing electrons down the electron transport chain releases energy. What is that energy used for?

(A) to make more ATP

(B) to make H_2O

(C) to pump H_2O into the intermembrane space

(D) to pump CO_2 out of the mitochondria

(E) to pump H^+ into the intermembrane space

Ultimately, the electron transport chain will produce lots of ATPs, but the energy from the redox reactions is actually used to pump H+ ions into the intermembrane space, so the correct answer is (E).

What is the role of O_2 in stage 3 of aerobic cellular respiration?

(A) It is attached to carbon and turned into CO_2

(B) It is used to make glucose

(C) It is attached to 4 H^+ and turned into 2 H_2O

(D) It is released unchanged

(E) It is attached to NAD^+ to make NADH

Aerobic cellular respiration breaks down glucose instead of making it, so (B) can't possibly be the right. Also, O_2 is definitely consumed in the process, so (D) is wrong also. Sometimes people think that the O_2 gets used to make CO_2, but that actually isn't correct. CO_2 comes from the breakdown of pyruvates, so (A) must also be wrong. Plus that happens in the Krebs cycle, which is stage 2 of aerobic cellular respiration and the question asks about stage 3, which is the electron transport chain. At the end of the electron transport chain, hydrogens are added to the O_2 to produce H_2O, so the correct answer is (C).

Which of the following is a result of H^+ flowing back into the matrix from the intermembrane space during stage 3 of aerobic cellular respiration?

(A) recharged ATP is produced

(B) NADH turns back into NAD^+

(C) NAD^+ turns back into HADH

(D) O_2 is produced

(E) glucose is broken down

The ultimate purpose of stage 3 of aerobic cellular respiration is to produce lots of ATP. The energy for producing these ATPs comes from the flowing of H^+ through that special channel into the matrix, so the correct answer is (A). NADH doesn't come into play after the very beginning of the electron transport chain, so (B) and (C) are both wrong. O_2 is consumed in this process, and glucose has already been broken down in steps 1 and 2, so (D) and (E) are both wrong also.

Which steps of aerobic cellular respiration produce CO_2?

(A) glycolysis only

(B) Krebs cycle only

(C) glycolysis and Krebs cycle only

(D) glycolysis and electron transport chain only

(E) glycolysis, Krebs cycle, and electron transport chain

This is pretty much just a memorization type question. Only the Krebs cycle produces CO_2, so the correct answer is (B).

Understanding Anaerobic Respiration

Anaerobic means without oxygen, so this kind of cellular respiration does not use O_2. As a result, anaerobic respiration is much less efficient at recharging ATPs, but the upside is that it is much faster. There are two varieties of anaerobic respiration that could show up on the SAT II. The basic process of both is just like glycolysis, but since they don't include the Krebs cycle or the electron transport chain, they need an extra step at the end of glycolysis to keep the process moving.

Fermentation is one variety of anaerobic respiration that is used by single-cell organisms like yeast, which ends up making ethanol, which is the drinkable kind of alcohol. The basic process is just like glycolysis, but a new step is added on at the end. Remember that the net outputs of glycolysis are 2 pyruvate, 2 NADH, and 2 ATP. The recharged ATPs are ready to be used by the yeast cells, but in order to keep glycolysis moving, the cells need to get rid of the pyruvate molecules and recycle the NADH back into NAD^+. So here's the extra step that has been turned into a multibillion dollar worldwide industry:

$$2 \text{ pyruvate} + 2 \text{ NADH} \rightarrow 2 \text{ ethanol} + 2 \text{ } CO_2 + 2 \text{ } NAD^+$$

So in addition to keeping glycolysis moving, this extra little step turns sugar into alcohol, carbonates your beverage with those little CO_2 molecules and — tada! — everybody's happy! In fact, these products sometimes make people get a little bit too happy, especially on New Year's Eve.

The other kind of anaerobic respiration happens in the cells of animals like us when we just can't get enough O_2 to our muscles fast enough to keep ACR working. Of course, when our muscle cells do anaerobic respiration they don't end up producing alcohol. If they did, then hard exercise would get us drunk! Here is the extra step that we do:

$$2 \text{ pyruvate} + 2 \text{ NADH} \rightarrow 2 \text{ lactic acid} + 2 \text{ } NAD^+$$

Instead of making us feel tipsy, lactic acid makes our muscles start to burn, so we can't keep doing this for very long. This is just an emergency process that helps us recharge some ATPs really fast for quick bursts of energy for things like sprinting and jumping when O_2 supplies aren't coming in fast enough. The more O_2 you can get to your muscles the less you'll have to use anaerobic respiration, and this is what people mean by "getting into shape." Through rigorous exercise, you increase your ability to deliver O_2 to your muscles and decrease the need to produce lactic acid. In the long run, this keeps your muscles from burning, but in the meantime you have to put up with a lot of sore arms and legs, but hey, no pain, no gain, right? It's the same thing with studying for the SAT II. Exercise your brain with the following SAT II type questions involving anaerobic respiration.

What step do aerobic cellular respiration and anaerobic respiration have in common?

(A) Krebs cycle

(B) alcohol production

(C) glycolysis

(D) electron transport chain

(E) lactic acid production

The Krebs cycle and the electron transport chain can only happen in aerobic cellular respiration, so cross out (B) and (D). On the other hand, alcohol and lactic acid are only produced in anaerobic respiration, so you can cross out (B) and (E) also. That leaves (C) as the correct answer.

Which of the following processes produces alcohol?

(A) Krebs cycle

(B) electron transport chain

(C) glycolysis

(D) photosynthesis

(E) fermentation

Only fermentation, which is a kind of anaerobic respiration, can produce alcohol, so the answer is (E).

Under which conditions would an animal's muscles be expected to produce lactic acid?

(A) muscle cells do not have enough O_2

(B) muscle cells have too much O_2

(C) muscle cells have too much NAD^+

(D) muscle cells do not have enough NADH

(E) muscles are relaxed

Lactic acid is produced during anaerobic respiration, and "anaerobic" means without oxygen. This means that the answer is (A), where not enough O_2 is available to allow for aerobic cellular respiration.

Which of the following processes takes place exclusively in the mitochondria?

(A) fermentation

(B) lactic acid production

(C) photosynthesis

(D) Krebs cycle

(E) protein synthesis

Photosynthesis happens in plants, so cross out (C) right away. Fermentation and lactic acid production are variations of glycolysis, which happens in the cytoplasm of a cell, not in the mitochondria, so cross out (A) and (B) also. Protein synthesis actually does sometimes happen in the mitochondria, but it happens other places as well, and the question asks which one happens EXCLUSIVELY in the mitochondria, so (E) is also wrong. That leaves the Krebs cycle, which happens in the mitochondria and nowhere else, so (D) is the correct answer.

Going Green: Photosynthesis

The autotrophs (remember that means self-feeders) that you will be asked about on the SAT II all do photosynthesis, so that's what we'll focus on now. The *photo* part refers to the fact that this process uses light as its energy source, and *synthesis* refers to how the process synthesizes glucose. The glucose that is synthesized in photosynthesis can then be used in aerobic cellular respiration just as described above. That's why things that can do photosynthesis, like plants and algae, get the name autotrophs.

Here is the overall reaction in photosynthesis:

$$6\ CO_2 + 6\ H_2O + \text{light energy} \rightarrow C_6H_{12}O_6 + 6\ O_2$$

Notice that this is almost the exact reverse of the overall reaction for aerobic cellular respiration. (This is important in Chapter 12, which discusses nutrient recycling.) In fact, a lot of the things that happen in photosynthesis just look like the reverse of ACR, but there are big enough differences that we need to go through it all separately. Also like ACR, the overall reaction in photosynthesis is actually done in many small steps, though here the whole thing is separated into only two stages: the light-dependent reactions and the light-independent reactions. The light-dependent reactions in the first stage of photosynthesis trap light energy and use it to temporarily recharge some ATPs. Those ATPs are then used in the light-independent reactions of the second stage to power the production of glucose.

The SAT II may test photosynthesis with questions like this one.

Which of the following best represents the correct overall inputs and outputs of photosynthesis?

(A) $C_6H_{12}O_6 + 6\ O_2 \rightarrow 6\ CO_2 + 6\ H_2O$

(B) $6\ CO_2 + 6\ H_2O \rightarrow C_6H_{12}O_6 + 6\ O_2$

(C) $C_6H_{12}O_6 + 2\ ATP + 2NAD^+ \rightarrow 2\ \text{pyruvate} + 4\ ATP + 2NADH$

(D) $3\ CO_2 + 3\ H_2O \rightarrow C_6H_{12}O_6 + 3\ O_2$

(E) $2\ \text{pyruvate} + 2\ NADH \rightarrow 2\ \text{ethanol} + 2\ CO_2 + 2\ NAD^+$

The question asks about photosynthesis, and (C) and (E) contain molecules used in cellular respiration, so cross them out right away. Answer (D) is an unbalanced reaction because fewer atoms go in than come out, so cross that one out as well. That leaves (A) and (B), which are exact opposites of each other. Photosynthesis produces glucose, so glucose must be one of the outputs instead of one of the inputs, which means the correct answer is (B).

Catching some rays: The light-dependent reactions

The leaves of plants act like big solar panels soaking up as much light energy as they can. Leaves contain something called chlorophyll that is the molecule that actually absorbs the incoming energy. Have you ever asked yourself why grass is green? While the Hulk is green because he got an overdose of gamma rays, plants are green because of chlorophyll. Perhaps you remember from physics class that the white light from the sun is actually a blend of many different colors of light, as we can see in a rainbow. Chlorophyll absorbs all colors of light except green. Since it isn't absorbed, the green light bounces off of the leaves and enters our eyes, making us see green. Okay, so maybe that seems like a pretty useless bit of trivia, but it just may show up on the SAT II.

The light energy that is absorbed by chlorophyll is used to break apart H_2O molecules, and some electrons from the H_2O are fed into an electron transport chain. The electrons get passed down the chain and this ends up recharging a bunch of ATPs the same way as it did in aerobic cellular respiration. The breakup of H_2O results in the production of O_2, which is released into the atmosphere so that things like us can breathe it in and use it for ourselves. At the end of the electron transport chain, the electrons are given to $NADP^+$ to make NADPH. NADPH then carries the electrons over to the light-independent reactions. See what light-dependent reactions look like in Figure 6-5.

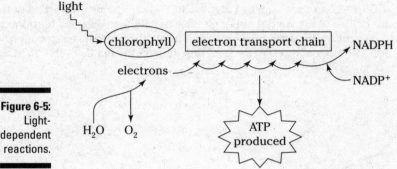

Figure 6-5: Light-dependent reactions.

Here are some typical SAT II questions on light-dependent reactions.

Which colors of light would be least likely to help a plant perform photosynthesis?

(A) blue

(B) red

(C) white

(D) green

(E) yellow

This may seem like a weird question at first, but remember why the leaves of plants appear green. All of the colors in white light are being absorbed by the plant except green, which bounces off the leaves and makes it to our eyes. That means plants can't really use green light as an energy source for photosynthesis, so plants would grow really poorly under green light. That means the correct answer is (D).

The O_2 produced in photosynthesis results from the breakup of which molecule?

(A) glucose

(B) CO_2

(C) NADPH

(D) $NADP^+$

(E) H_2O

Glucose is produced in photosynthesis, not broken up, so cross out (A). NADPH and $NADP^+$ are not directly involved with O_2, so cross out (C) and (D) also. H_2O is split apart at the beginning of photosynthesis to liberate H atoms, leaving O_2 as a byproduct, so (E) is the correct answer.

Heading for the shade: The light-independent reactions

The light-independent reactions, also called the Calvin cycle, are sort of like the Krebs cycle in reverse. CO_2 comes in, ATPs and NADPHs get used, and half of a glucose comes out. It even uses escort molecules like the Krebs cycle, though the Calvin cycle uses ribulose bisphosphate, which is called RuBisCo for short, to accompany the molecules around the cycle. Since each turn of the Calvin cycle produces half of a glucose, the cycle must go around twice to synthesize one whole glucose (see, those math skills are really working).

The glucose coming out of the Calvin cycle can be used for all sorts of things. Almost all of the structures found in a plant cell are constructed out of glucose molecules. Also, as mentioned above, the glucose could be sent to the mitochondria inside of plant cells and sent through aerobic cellular respiration to recharge more ATPs. It all depends on the needs of the plant. Figure 6-6 demonstrates the Calvin cycle.

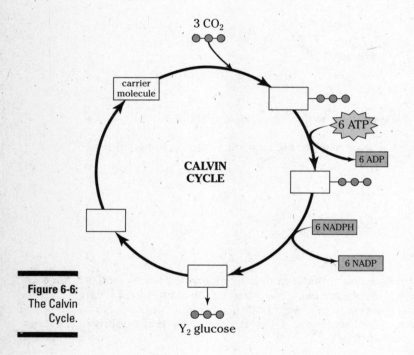

Figure 6-6:
The Calvin Cycle.

Here are a couple of ways the SAT II may test you on the Calvin cycle.

Which of the following is not an input into the Calvin cycle?

(A) CO_2

(B) glucose

(C) ATP

(D) NADPH

(E) products from the light-dependent reactions

First notice that the question asks which is NOT an input into the Calvin cycle, so you can cross out all the things that are inputs. The products from the light-dependent reactions are what enter the Calvin cycle, and that includes ATP and NADPH, so cross out (C), (D), and (E). The Calvin cycle produces glucose, so glucose can't be an input, so cross out (B) also. That glucose is made (in part) from CO_2 molecules, so CO_2 is definitely an input, which means that the correct answer is (A).

Which of the following processes consumes O_2?

(A) Calvin cycle

(B) fermentation

(C) electron transport chain

(D) Krebs cycle

(E) light-dependent reactions of photosynthesis

Photosynthesis produces O_2 instead of consuming it, so cross out (A) and (E) because they are part of photosynthesis. Fermentation is a kind of anaerobic respiration, which means it does not use O_2, so cross that one out as well. The Krebs cycle is part of aerobic cellular respiration, but not the part that actually uses the O_2. The electron transport chain is the part that uses oxygen, so the correct answer is (C).

Chapter 7

Working from the Blueprints: DNA and Proteins

You may have heard somewhere that DNA is the basis for life. Well, sort of. Actually it's more like the blueprint for life because DNA contains the assembly instructions for all of the proteins that an organism will ever need, and proteins are what really make organisms work. So that you know what's coming, here's the basic idea: A section of DNA that contains information for how to make one protein is called a gene. (See Chapter 8 for more on genetics.) When a cell needs to make a certain protein, it first copies the gene that contains information for that protein. The copy is called mRNA (for reasons you'll see later). The mRNA is then used to direct the construction of the protein. Normally this process works flawlessly, but occasionally the information on genes or mRNA gets messed up, which is called a mutation (more on that later). A mutation usually has bad consequences, but sometimes it doesn't make any difference at all, and every once in a while it even turns out to be a good thing.

This chapter tells you what you need to about how cells copy their DNA in order to pass it on to their offspring. It then explains how cells read the information in DNA and how they use that info to make their proteins. Like so much else in molecular biology, cells use a pretty weird, round-about way to get these projects done, but this chapter shows you how it all works without any more jargon or technical mumbo jumbo than you actually need for beating the SAT II.

Makin' Copies: DNA Replication

Since the *DNA* (deoxyribonucleic acid) tells a cell how to make its proteins, every cell needs a full set of DNA in order to function. Therefore, whenever a cell divides, it must make a complete copy of all of its DNA for the new cell because if any DNA is missing, the cell would be in big trouble because it would have incomplete instructions for how to build its proteins. Imagine trying to bake a cake with only half the recipe — it would end up as a useless pile of goop. But to understand how DNA works and how it gets copied, you must first understand what DNA looks like. (See Chapter 5 for more details on the structure of important molecules like DNA.)

DNA is a long molecule made up of smaller molecules linked in two strings lined up together, forming what's called a double-stranded DNA. The smaller molecules that are linked together to make the strands of DNA are called nucleotides. There are four different nucleotides in DNA: Adenine, Thymine, Guanine, and Cytosine, or just: A, T, G, and C. Nucleotides can be strung together in any sequence, sort of like different kinds of train cars. Each kind has the right hookups to connect to any of the others, so you can shuffle and reconnect them however you like. The exact sequence of nucleotides in an organism's DNA is vitally important, but unfortunately you need some really fancy equipment to figure out the sequence for yourself, so it will always be given to you in some way when you come across this stuff on the SAT II. DNA is just sneaky that way.

The good news is that all you really need to know is the nucleotide sequence for one of the strands in a double-stranded DNA. This is because when the two strands line up together, there are strict rules for which nucleotides can be across from each other. Check out this example of a small section of double-stranded DNA. Don't worry too much about the 5' and 3' stuff because the story behind it is just too darn complicated. Just remember that if one strand goes from 3' to 5', then the other goes from 5' to 3'.

5'—ATGCAACTCGAC—3'   3'—TACGTTGAGCTG—5'

As this example shows, A and T must always be across from each other, while G and C must always be across from each other. It's like when you always want to sit next to your best friend on the bus. A and T are best friends, and so are G and C. This is called the *complimentarity rule,* so you would say that A and T are complimentary nucleotides, and so are C and G. Because of this complimentarity between nucleotides, if you are given the sequence of one strand, you can automatically figure out the sequence on the other strand — just match up each nucleotide on the first strand with complimentary nucleotides on the other strand.

Here's a helpful hint for some questions you might see on the SAT II: Because of these complimentary matching rules, every cell's DNA has an equal amount of A and T, and also an equal amount of G and C. So if I tell you that a certain cell's DNA is 20% A and 30% G, then you know right away that the DNA must also contain 20% T to match up with the As, and 30% C to match up with the Gs.

Cells take advantage of this rule when copying DNA — a process called *replication,* which is just a scientist's fancy name for copying. During DNA replication, the two strands come apart and new nucleotides are matched up with each old strand according to the matching rules (see Figure 7-1). Here's the result of replicating the DNA shown above (the newly added strands are in bold):

5'—ATGCAACTCGAC—3'   **3'—TACGTTGAGCTG—5'**

5'—ATGCAACTCGAC—3   3'—TACGTTGAGCTG—5'

You may be tested on DNA replication with questions like these:

Consider the following nucleotide sequence for a section of one strand in a double-stranded DNA: 5'— TACAGTACCAGTT—3'. Which of the following correctly represents the other strand?

(A) 5'—ATGTCATGGTCAA—3'

(B) 3'—AUGUCAUGGUCAA—5'

(C) 3'—ATGTCATGGTCAA—5'

(D) 5'—TACAGTACCAGTT—3'

(E) 3'—TACAGTACCAGTT—5'

The correct answer is (C) because it gets the nucleotide matching correct and it goes from 3' to 5'. The matching rules say that A and T go across from each other, and so do G and C. That means (D) and (E) can be crossed out because they mistakenly try to match T with T, A with A, and so on. The "U" nucleotide only belongs in RNA, so (B) is wrong also. That leaves (A) and (C), which have the same nucleotide sequence. Notice that the strand given in the question goes from 5' to 3'. Remember that the second strand needs to be the opposite of whatever the first strand is, so the correct answer must have its strand going from 3' to 5', which means that (C) is the correct strand. See how many annoying little details they can pack into just one question?

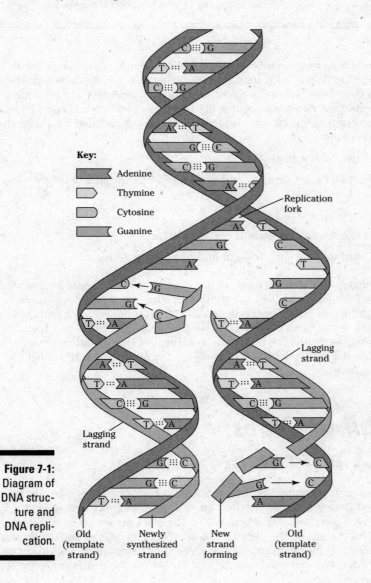

Figure 7-1:
Diagram of DNA structure and DNA replication.

One big happy family

As different as life on seems, living organisms actually have a lot in common. All store genetic information with the same molecules, DNA and RNA. Even though higher life forms have to develop new genes to survive, they still have many of the same genes that control basic functions in primitive life forms.

In another more direct means of sharing, organisms can rip off genes from other organisms. Viruses can inject their genes into the cells of a host organism, and some viruses have been known to take genetic material from a host and then give that gene to another host. We guess you could say the viruses are great levelers of society.

A researcher grows bacteria in a nutrient medium that contains special, heavy-isotope versions of the four DNA nucleotides. When he tests a sample of the bacteria, he finds that their DNA is all composed of two strands of "heavy" nucleotides. He then removes any remaining heavy nucleotides from the medium and adds regular, light-isotope nucleotides. Then he lets the bacteria go through one round of replication and tests the DNA again. What would be the most likely result of this second test?

(A) All of the DNA contains two heavy strands.

(B) 50% of the DNA contains two heavy strands and the other 50% contains two light strands.

(C) All of the DNA contains two light strands.

(D) All of the DNA contains one heavy strand and one light strand.

(E) All of the DNA strands contain a mixture of light and heavy nucleotides.

The original strands in the experiment were all made of heavy nucleotides. After the researcher removed the spare heavy nucleotides and added in light nucleotides, any new DNA strands would be built out of only light nucleotides. Remember that in DNA replication, the two DNA strands are separated and new nucleotides are added to the old strands according to the matching rules. This results in DNA molecules that each have one old strand and one new strand. In this experiment, that would mean they each have one heavy strand and one light strand, so (D) is the correct answer.

Following the Building Codes: Working From DNA to Protein

As you already know, DNA contains the super-important information for how to make all of the cell's proteins. If the DNA gets damaged somehow, then the cell may not know how to make certain vital proteins. To prevent this, the DNA is kept safe in the cell's nucleus. Unfortunately, though, proteins are actually made *outside* the nucleus in the cytoplasm or the rough endoplasmic reticulum (RER). (See Chapter 3 for more info on cell parts.) So the cell must find a way to transmit its protein-building information from the nucleus out to where the proteins are made.

Actually, you've probably faced problems like this yourself. Imagine you need to write a research report on World War I, and you need information from an encyclopedia. The library won't let you take the "W" volume back to your house where you do your writing because the encyclopedia needs to be kept safe in the library. So what do you do? If you have enough nickels, you copy the pages you need and leave the whole big encyclopedia volume in the library. Well, that's exactly what happens with DNA. If the cell needs to make a certain protein, it copies just the section of its DNA that contains the information for how to make that protein (in other words, it copies just that one gene) and leaves the whole huge volume of DNA safe in the nucleus. The copy is then taken out to the RER or the cytoplasm (see Chapter 3 for more on cell parts) to direct the construction of the protein.

Sending a memo: transcription of RNA

The copy of a gene that is taken out of the nucleus is called RNA. RNA is a lot like DNA because it is a long string of nucleotides, but RNA is single-stranded instead of double-stranded. Also, RNA contains U (uracil) instead of T. (See Chapter 5 for the main differences between DNA and RNA.) When the RNA copy of a gene carries a message about how to build a protein, it is called *messenger RNA* or just *mRNA* for short.

DNA is double-stranded, but only one strand gets copied, and this is called the *template strand.* Here's a possible DNA template strand:

3'—TACGTTGAGCTG—5'

The mRNA copy would look like this:

5'—AUGCAACUCGAC—3'

Notice that the same matching rule for complimentary nucleotides applies here, except that whenever you see an A on the DNA, you match it with a U on RNA (instead of T). Since the copying of DNA to RNA only involves nucleotides, and since the matching rules are basically the same, it is sort of like DNA and RNA are written in the same language. When you copy something without changing the language, you are performing "transcription", which is exactly what this process is called.

Here's how the SAT II may test this information:

Here is a nucleotide sequence for a section of a template DNA strand:

3'—TACGCATTCGAT—5'

Which of the following shows the correct mRNA that would be copied from this template?

(A) 5'—AUGCGUAAGCUA—3'

(B) 3'—ATGCGTAAGCTA—5'

(C) 3'—AUGCGUAAGCUA—5'

(D) 3'—TACGCATTCGAT—5'

(E) 3'—UACGCAUUCGAU—5'

Remember that the matching rules for going from DNA to mRNA are the same as DNA to DNA, except that you never put a T in mRNA. Instead of T, RNA contains U. Answers (B) and (D) both contain "T," so they are both wrong. Answer (C) gets the matching wrong, so it can be crossed out, too. That leaves (A) and (C) which have the same nucleotide sequence. The template strand given in the question goes from 3' to 5', which means a matching strand must go from 5' to 3', so (A) is the correct answer.

Which of the following statements is false?

(A) mRNA can be found either inside or outside the nucleus.

(B) RNA contains uracil instead of thymine.

(C) Only one strand of DNA is copied during transcription.

(D) RNA is single-stranded.

(E) DNA must exit the nucleus in order to direct protein production.

First, be sure to notice that the question asks which statement is *false*, which means that four of them will be true. (A) is true because mRNA is made inside the nucleus during transcription and then exits the nucleus and goes out to where proteins are constructed. Two of the main differences between DNA and RNA is that RNA is single stranded and it contains uracil instead of thymine, so (B) and (D) are true. (C) is also true because only the template strand is copied during transcription, and so that leaves (E). As we know, DNA must be kept safe in the nucleus, which means that (E) is false, so that's the correct answer to the question.

Getting lost in translation: from mRNA to protein

A protein is a long string of small molecules called amino acids. (See Chapter 5 for more info on proteins.) Amino acids are also like little train cars because they can be hooked up in any sequence whatsoever. The sequence of nucleotides on the mRNA contains the information for what the exact sequence of amino acids should be for a given protein. Going from mRNA to a protein is a little bit more complicated than transcription, because now you're going from the nucleotide language to the amino acid language. When you go from one language to a different one, you are performing *translation*, and that's exactly what this process is called. Translating is hard enough when going from something like English to Spanish, but as an added complication for cells, there are 20 different amino acids that can go into making a protein, while there are only four different nucleotides in RNA. So we have to translate a language with just 4 characters into a language with 20.

The cell solves this problem by arranging its nucleotides into short 3-letter words called *codons,* and each codon can be translated into a unique amino acid. Here's an example mRNA

　　　5'—AUGCAACUCGAC—3'

AUG is the first codon, and it just so happens that AUG is translated into the amino acid methionine. The next codon, CAA, is translated into glycine. Luckily, you don't need to know the whole translation dictionary from codons to amino acids for the SAT II, but you do need to know a couple bits of trivia that may show up on the test. Here's a sample:

- ✔ There are 64 possible codons, but only 20 different amino acids. So some amino acids are associated with more than one codon.

- ✔ Also, just like words in a regular English sentence, codons never overlap. So in our example, if AUG is a codon, then you can't use that G to start the next codon and have it be GCA.

In order to translate from nucleotide language to amino acid language, cells need a translator. This is done by another kind of RNA called *transfer RNA* or just *tRNA.* The tRNA needs to be able to read the codon on the mRNA and match the correct amino acid with that codon. To do so, tRNA makes use of the complimentarity between nucleotides. As shown in Figure 7-2, every tRNA has a set of three nucleotides that can match up with the three nucleotides of a codon. The set of three nucleotides on the tRNA is called an anticodon, and the cell has a tRNA with an anticodon to match any possible codon on mRNA. So, if the codon on mRNA is AUG, then there is a tRNA with UAC as its anticodon. The tRNA with UAC as its anticodon always carries the amino acid methionine because the AUG codon means methionine. When the UAC anticodon on the tRNA sticks to the AUG codon on mRNA, the methionine is placed in the proper spot over that codon and — bingo! — the AUG codon has been successfully translated into methionine!

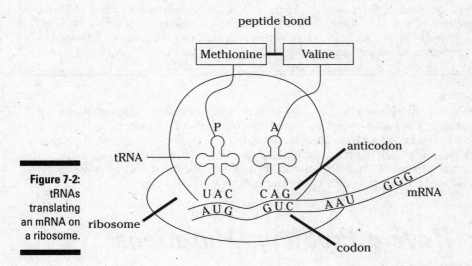

Figure 7-2:
tRNAs
translating
an mRNA on
a ribosome.

Once the first codon has been translated, then another tRNA can come in and translate the next codon. The next tRNA should have an anticodon of GUU to match up with the CAA codon on the mRNA, which brings in glycine to that spot because CAA means glycine. Once the first two amino acids are next to each other, a peptide bond (see Chapter 5) links them together and the processes of protein-building (also known as protein synthesis) officially begins. New tRNAs keep coming in to translate each codon, connecting the amino acids as they go, until they come to the end of the mRNA. Then the newly completed protein is released and the mRNA can be used again to build another one of those proteins. After being used a few times, the mRNA is broken down by an enzyme that specializes in breaking down nucleic acids, and its nucleotides are used to make a different mRNA.

Do bacteria and viruses have sex lives?

Until the 1940's scientists debated whether or not single-celled bacteria had genes or whether they shared common characteristics with more complex life forms. The question was answered when scientists discovered that bacteria mate through a process called conjugation, which means that two bacteria get together just long enough to exchange genetic material before they go their separate ways.

Then electron microscopes show that bacterial viruses also hook up. The virus attached itself to a host bacterium and uses its tail to inject its DNA into the host. The DNA then reproduces new viruses in the contaminated cell. Scientists now use viruses and bacteria to study the principles of genetics.

We wonder what a bacterium gets another bacterium for Valentine's Day.

DNA finally gets some respect

Biochemists knew that DNA and protein made up the chromosomes as early as the late 1800s, but for the next four decades they thought that protein was the substance that carried the genetic code and DNA just sort of held the whole thing together.

Then in the 1940s and 1950s along came Avery and Hershey, whose studies showed that DNA was the carrier of the genetic code. Later work proved that each chromosome provides the package for a long unbroken strand of DNA, and in more complex organisms it's actually the protein that provides support for the DNA. DNA finally got the recognition it deserved.

Protein is no slouch, though. DNA gives out the genetic information, but proteins encoded with DNA actually do the dirty work of accomplishing the cellular reactions that produce what we know as life. Scientists still aren't sure exactly how proteins achieve this goal, however.

Protein synthesis usually happens in the rough endoplasmic reticulum, although it can occur in the cytoplasm also. The RER is rough because it is dotted with hundreds of little protein factories called *ribosomes,* where translation actually happens. Each little ribosome is made of yet another kind of RNA called *ribosomal RNA,* or just *rRNA.* I promise that this is the last kind of RNA you need to know. The rRNA provides a platform for the mRNA to stay steady and allows the tRNAs to come in and translate the codons into amino acids.

Houston, We Have a Problem: Mutations and Their Consequences

A mutation is when the genetic information gets messed during replication, transcription, or translation. If the sequence of nucleotides on DNA or mRNA is changed, then the protein-building information also changes, and since proteins help keep cells alive, mutations are usually really bad. For example, a mistake could be made during replication of DNA, which would screw up that cell's genetic code forever. It's like if your encyclopedia volume has mistakes in it, then your research report is going to have mistakes also, although I've tried that excuse with my teachers before and it didn't work. A less severe mutation would be a mistake during transcription, because the cell can just try again and make new a mRNA if an old one isn't working right. Similarly, if the toner smudged the memo describing the exact requirements for software you needed while you were printing it, you could just throw that one away and try again. It seems like a waste of paper, but getting the information correct and clear is very important. For you, getting accurate copies is necessary for getting an A on your report, but for a cell, accurate mRNA copies are a matter of life or death!

Kinds of mutations

The two most common kinds of mutations questioned on the SAT II are point mutations and frameshift mutations.

A *point mutation* is when a single nucleotide gets changed. For example, suppose the first A on our mRNA gets changed to C. This means the first codon has to be CUG, which the anticodon GUC translates into the amino acid leucine (instead of methionine). That can be a problem, but it's really just one amino acid out of perhaps hundreds or thousands of amino acids that make up the protein, so it sometimes isn't that big of a deal. Following, I've listed three results of a point mutation:

"Good" breeding

Advancements in genetics didn't always bring out the best in folks. In the early 20th century when genetic research uncovered the secrets of heredity, a eugenics movement emerged that revealed the undesirable human trait of discrimination. Eugenics was an effort to breed more perfect human beings by promoting reproduction between people who were considered to have good genes (in the eyes of those who were selectively breeding). Members of the movement lobbied the American government to segregate racial and ethnic groups to keep gene pools separate, to keep out immigrants from backgrounds that they thought were ethnically inferior to keep the American gene pool pure, and to sterilize people they thought should not be allowed to reproduce. The Nazis jumped on the eugenics movement in their attempt to create a "super race," and the ultimate result was the Holocaust.

- **Missense mutation:** When the mutation results in the wrong amino acid, then it's called a *missense mutation* because the codon can still be translated — although it's a mistake, it still makes sense to the tRNAs.

- **Silent mutation:** When a point mutation doesn't make any difference at all, it's called a *silent mutation*. Suppose the second codon had a point mutation and it changed from CAA to CAG. This is technically a mutation, but it turns out that CAG also gets translated into glycine, just like CAA does, so the protein is totally unaffected.

- **Nonsense mutation:** When a point mutation just completely scrambles a nucleotide so that the codon can't be translated at all, it's called a *nonsense mutation*. If AUG were changed to XUG, because the tRNAs don't know how to translate that, protein construction would just fail at that point in translation.

The other general kind of mutation is a *frameshift mutation,* which is when a single nucleotide is removed or one is added. Adding or subtracting a single nucleotide throws off the whole sequence after the mutation. For example, here's that original sample sequence we keep using:

5'—AUGCAACUCGAC—3'

The codons here are AUG, CAA, CUC, GAC. Now suppose a nucleotide were added (in bold):

5'—AUGUCAACUCGAC—3'

The first codon is unaffected, but the rest are shifted by one, making everything after the mutations different. Now the sequence of codons is: AUG, UCA, ACU, CGA, C. Now when the codons are translated into amino acids, all the amino acids after the frameshift mutation will be different, leading to the construction of a protein with a completely different amino acid sequence. (See Chapter 5 for info on why the amino acid sequence is so important for the function of a protein.)

Consequences of mutations

Mutations are random, unpredictable events that are caused by things like high-energy radiation and toxic chemicals. A mutation on DNA is usually permanent and can have the following possible consequences:

- **The cell no longer works correctly.** If a mutation ends up causing a different protein to be made (as in missense and nonsense mutations), then something about the cell usually doesn't work right anymore. Sort of like when a doorway is sized incorrectly, the doors don't close properly.

✔ **The cell dies.** If the protein that was supposed to be made was really important (but a missense or nonsense mutation caused a different one to be made in its place), the cell could die. Imagine you're building a skyscraper and someone messed up your original blueprints so that they showed one supporting column to be 5 feet too short. We're not engineers, but we're pretty sure that would be really bad for the building. The same thing is true if the original DNA of a cell gets messed up.

✔ **The cell is unaffected.** On the other hand, sometimes a mutation affects a part of the protein that was never all that important, and the cell never notices. That would be like having the change in your blueprints only affect the size of the drinking fountains. Okay, so it's different from the original plan, but the building isn't going to fall down or anything.

✔ **The cell works better than before.** Every once in a while, a cell gets lucky and a mutation happens in just the right way to make a protein that actually works better than before. Suppose those blueprints of yours were accidentally changed so that all the doors were six inches wider than you had planned. Now suppose this change turned out to make the pedestrian traffic through the building work way better than you had imagined. You would probably be really surprised when you found out what happened, but also pretty happy because it was actually a good mistake for you. Well, the same sort of thing can happen for an accidental mutation in a cell. Sometimes mutations make a protein stronger or faster or in some other way better than it used to be, and that's good for the cell. As you might suspect, these lucky mutations are pretty rare, but it turns out that they help drive evolution. (See Chapter 10 for more on evolution.)

Mutation questions on the SAT II may look like this:

A point mutation occurs in a cell's DNA, but it turns out that the amino acid sequence of the resulting protein is unaffected. This is an example of a

(A) silent mutation.

(B) corrected mutation.

(C) nonsense mutation.

(D) missense mutation.

(E) frameshift mutation.

If a mutation in a gene does not affect the amino acid sequence of the protein, then it is a silent mutation, so (A) is the correct answer. There's no such thing as a corrected mutation, so (B) can be crossed out. A missense mutation changes one amino acid, and a frameshift mutation changes many amino acids, so (D) and (E) are also out of the running. A nonsense mutation will cause translation to just stop, so (C) can't be the answer either, leaving us with only (A).

Questions 1–3 refer to the following items:

(A) mRNA

(B) tRNA

(C) rRNA

(D) rough endoplasmic reticulum

(E) gene

1. This translates codons into amino acids.

2. This is the main component of ribosomes.

3. This stays in the nucleus and contains the information for how to construct one protein.

The "t" in tRNA stands for "transfer," but I like to think of it as "translator RNA" because that's what it does. That means that (B) is the correct answer to question 1.

This one's easier because the "r" in RNA stands for "ribosomal," which means that (C) is the answer to question 2.

Both a gene and mRNA are things that contain information for how to construct a single protein, but only genes stay in the nucleus, so (E) is the correct answer for question 3.

Which of the following statements is true?

(A) Mutations are always detrimental to the organism.

(B) Sometimes mutations are beneficial to the organism.

(C) An organism can decide what kinds of mutations it needs.

(D) All mutations cause permanent changes in a cell.

(E) Mutations always tend to bring evolution to a halt.

If you aren't sure which of these is true, you can try using the trusty process of elimination. Mutations on DNA are permanent, but mutations on RNA are temporary because a messed up RNA can be tossed out and the cell can just transcribe a new one, so (D) can be crossed out. Mutations are random, unpredictable events, so an organism could never decide what mutations to make, which means (C) is eliminated. Also, mutations are necessary for evolution to move forward, so (E) is wrong, which leaves (A) and (B) which are directly opposing answers. Even though it is rare, lucky mutations do sometimes happen and can be good for an organism, so (B) is the correct answer.

Chapter 8

Inheriting the Wind: Genetics

*I*n this chapter we discuss genes and how they get passed on from one generation to the next. A *gene* is a small section of DNA that contains the information for how to build one protein. Chapter 7 explains how the information coding and protein building works. A protein that gets made from a gene then goes on to produce some sort of effect in an organism. For example, a protein could help an organism break down a certain kind of food, or it could help an organism move around, or it could cause an organism to grow hair of a particular color or have a certain blood type. These kinds of effects in an organism are called *traits,* which are also known as characteristics. In genetics, we don't really have to bother mentioning all that stuff about the proteins, so we just say that a certain gene can produce a certain trait in an organism. For example, Mike's gene for eye color produces brown eyes in him.

Passing On Genes: Sexual and Asexual Reproduction

In asexual reproduction, a single parent produces an offspring with exactly the same genes as the parent. Single-cell organisms are asexual because they just copy all of their genes and then split in two, producing two cells that have identical DNA. Since there is no mixing of genes, there is no such thing as males or females in species that only reproduce asexually. So there's no little boy or little girl bacteria, they're all just bacteria. Also, since the offspring from asexual reproduction are just clones of their parents, there isn't too much variety in their family line. Differences can only come from occasional mutations in their DNA.

Sexual reproduction, by contrast, produces a lot of variation because the offspring are a combination of genes from two different parents. Males and females mix their genes together so that their offspring ends up with some traits from their mothers and some from their fathers. Biologists have figured out how most of this works, and it is all based on the fact that every individual in a sexual species actually has two genes for every trait. When it's time to reproduce, each parent passes on only one of its two genes for each trait, so that the offspring ends up with two genes for every trait — one from the mother and one from the father (see Figure 8-1). This gene-combining happens in every generation, so the members of a sexual species are shuffling their genes together in different ways every time they reproduce. That's why children so often resemble their parents, but usually don't look exactly like either of them.

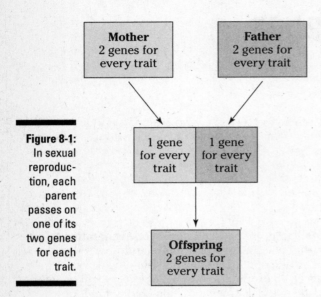

Figure 8-1:
In sexual reproduction, each parent passes on one of its two genes for each trait.

Going From Genes to Traits

The offspring's traits result from the genes they receive from their parents. The chromosomes they get from their mothers contain genes for specific traits, and those they get from their fathers usually have genes for those same traits. How the genes actually show up as a specific characteristic depends on whether the offspring get dominant or recessive genes for that trait.

Discovering the difference between genotypes and phenotypes

For sexual species, the two genes that an individual has for a certain trait is called his *genotype*. On the other hand, the trait that he actually ends up with is called the *phenotype*. For example, Mike has two genes for eye color, one from his mom and one from his dad. The eye color gene from his dad codes for brown eyes while the eye color gene from his mom codes for blue eyes, so his genotype for this trait is "brown-blue." Different versions of a gene are called different *alleles*, so another way of stating his genotype is to say that Mike has one brown-eye allele and one blue-eye allele. Now, even though Mike has these two different alleles, he has only one actual eye color, which is brown, so his phenotype for this trait is brown eyes.

Examining how dominant and recessive alleles function

TIP

So, if Mike has one brown-eye allele and one blue-eye allele (see more about alleles above, in the section, "Discovering the difference between genotypes and phenotypes") why does Mike have brown eyes instead of blue eyes? Why not some combination of brown and blue? Well, sometimes one allele is *dominant* over the other, while the other allele is *recessive.* Whenever the dominant allele is part of the genotype, then the dominant allele becomes the trait (or phenotype). It just so happens that the brown-eye allele is always dominant over the blue-eye allele, so even though Mike has both alleles, he ends up with pure brown eyes. His mom, on the other hand, has two recessive blue-eye alleles. Since the brown-eye allele isn't there to dominate the blue, she ended up with beautiful blue eyes.

Mike's mom's genotype is blue-blue, and his dad's genotype is brown-brown (if all this talk of genotypes and phenotypes has your head swimming, check out "Discovering the difference between genotypes and phenotypes"). Because both of his parents have the same allele for both of their eye-color genes, his parents are called *homozygous* for eye color — his mom is homozygous blue and his dad is homozygous brown. *Homo* means "same" and *zygous* refers to genes. Unlike his parents (Mike's always been a rebellious kid), Mike has two different alleles for his eye color genes, so his genotype is brown-blue. That means Mike is *heterozygous* for eye color, where *hetero* means "different." See Table 8-1 for a summary of Mike's family's genotypes and phenotypes for eye color. The brown allele is dominant over the blue allele.

Table 8-1	Eye Color Genotypes and Phenotypes in Mike's Family	
Person	*Genotype*	*Phenotype*
Mom	Blue-blue	Blue eyes
Dad	Brown-brown	Brown eyes
Mike	Brown-blue	Brown eyes

Compromising on traits: Incomplete dominance and co-dominance

For some traits, the alleles aren't strictly dominant or recessive like they are for eye color. Sometimes the phenotype ends up being a blend of the two alleles, a situation called *incomplete dominance.* An example of this is when a red rose and a white rose produce a pink rose. The red allele and the white allele are incompletely dominant, so an offspring whose genotype is red-white will end up with a pink phenotype.

For other traits, both genes are *co-dominant,* which means they both end up fully expressed in the phenotype. For example, in human blood type, both the A blood type gene and the B blood type gene are co-dominant, so if your genotype is A-B, then your phenotype will be AB blood type. There isn't a blending of the A and B genes because both are expressed fully and independently. When you say it like that it sort of sounds like a legal arrangement.

Actually, the SAT II often includes a question or two about the genetics of human blood typing, so we should tell the whole story. There are three different alleles for human blood type: A, B, and O. The type-O allele is recessive, while the A and B alleles are co-dominant. There are four different phenotypes for blood type that a person could have: type A, type B, type AB, and type O. The O allele is recessive, so in order to get type O blood, you cannot have either of the dominant alleles. In other words, your genotype must be O-O (homozygous recessive). As already mentioned, in order to end up with type AB blood, you must have the A-B genotype. The A-A and A-O genotypes both result in type A blood because A dominates over O, while the B-B and B-O genotypes both result in type B blood because there B dominates over O.

Now try to dominate these sample questions.

Questions 1–3 refer to the following:

(A) homozygous

(B) heterozygous

(C) genotype

(D) asexual reproduction

(E) sexual reproduction

1. The two genes that an individual possesses for a certain trait.

2. The situation in which an individual's alleles for a certain trait are the same.

3. The offspring has the exact same genetic makeup as its parent.

This is one of those classification questions where the answer choices appear before the questions. Questions 1–3 all have the same possible answer choices (but not necessarily the same correct answer). You need to quickly glance through the answer choices and then more carefully read the questions to determine which answer choice complements which questions. It is possible to use the same answer choice more than once.

For #1, the answer is (C). The genotype refers to the two genes that an individual has for a certain trait. Phenotype, remember, is the actual characteristic or trait that the individual ends up with.

For #2, the answer is (A). *Zygous* refers to the genotype. Homozygous means that the two genes are the same allele, while heterozygous means that the two genes are different alleles.

For #3, the answer is (D). In asexual reproduction, there is only one parent, and the offspring is genetically identical to that parent.

An orange tree with large fruit breeds with an orange tree that has small fruit. The offspring of this breeding are orange trees with some small fruit and some large fruit. Which of the following best explains these results?

(A) Fruit size is not influenced by genes.

(B) The genes for fruit size are co-dominant.

(C) The large-fruit allele is dominant over the small-fruit allele.

(D) The small-fruit allele is dominant over the large-fruit allele.

(E) The genes for fruit size are incompletely dominant.

Before you check out the answer choices for this question, ask yourself what is going on here. Two trees with different size fruits produce a tree that contains both sizes of fruit. Hmmm . . . one size doesn't seem to dominate the other because both fruit sizes are produced by the offspring. The offspring doesn't have fruit sized differently than either of its parents. Sounds like co-dominance; now take a look at the answer choices.

There's nothing in the question that would make us think that a basic trait like fruit size is not influenced by genes, so (A) can be crossed out. Now, the offspring trees have big fruit and small fruit, which means that both the large-fruit allele and the small-fruit allele are fully expressed in the phenotypes of the trees. This situation is called co-dominance, so (B) is correct. Incomplete dominance results in a blending of the two characteristics, which would have resulted in the offspring trees all having medium-sized fruit. This is not the case, so (E) isn't right. If one allele was dominant and the other recessive, then the offspring would have had either all large fruit or all small fruit; so that knocks out (C) and (D).

Predicting Genes

Phenotypes are usually pretty easy to see because you can just observe the color or test the blood type or whatever. Genotypes are a lot trickier. Suppose you meet someone with brown eyes. You know what their phenotype is, but what's their genotype? This is tough to say because their genotype could be brown-brown, or it could be brown-blue. Both of those genotypes will result in the brown eyes phenotype. If you feel like finding out (and who wouldn't, right?), the way you do it is by looking at the phenotypes of the person's parents and the person's children (if they have any). This section explores the different ways you can predict traits that may be examined on the SAT II.

Using Punnet squares

To see why Mike has brown eyes, look at Mike and his parents (see Table 8-1). Mike has brown eyes, so at least one of his genes must be the dominant brown-eye allele (brown eyes can result from having either brown-blue or brown-brown alleles). His mom has blue eyes, so, as listed in Table 8-1, her genotype is be blue-blue because the recessive blue-eye trait is only expressed if she has both blue alleles. That means that the eye color gene Mike got from his mom must be the blue-eye allele. Therefore, we know that his genotype must be brown-blue. Figure 8-2 shows the possible eye color gene combinations from Mike's parents. This kind of diagram is called a *Punnet square,* and it shows that Mike's parents' children all were bound to end up with the brown-blue genotype.

Figure 8-2:
Punnet square showing the possible gene combinations from Mike's parents' genotype.

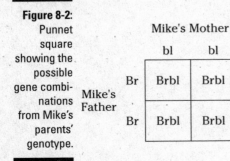

Genotypes — 100% Brbl   Phenotypes — 100% Brown

Now suppose Mike gets married and has kids with a woman who also happens to have the brown-blue genotype. Figure 8-3 shows the possible gene combination that their kids could have. Notice that even though Mike's wife and he both have brown eyes, there is a 25% chance that one of their kids will end up with blue eyes.

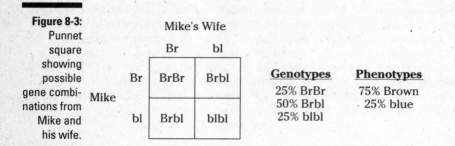

Figure 8-3:
Punnet square showing possible gene combinations from Mike and his wife.

Mike's Wife

	Br	bl
Br	BrBr	Brbl
bl	Brbl	blbl

Mike

Genotypes
25% BrBr
50% Brbl
25% blbl

Phenotypes
75% Brown
25% blue

Predicting traits through a test cross

A Franciscan monk back in the 1860s named Gregor Mendel was the first person to analyze genetics by analyzing the parents. That's why this stuff is sometimes called *Mendelian Genetics*. Mendel was studying the traits of pea plants and was able to determine the genotypes of his plants by breeding them together and observing the phenotypes of the offspring. He called this procedure a *test cross*. For example, he started with two parent plants, called the *P generation,* one of which was tall and one of which was short. He knew that their genotypes for height must be different, but he couldn't be sure exactly what they were or how they interacted, so he did a test cross. Mendel allowed the plants to breed, and he called the offspring of these P generation plants the *F1 generation.* It turned out that all the plants in the F_1 generation ended up tall, which told Mendel that the tall allele must be dominant over the short allele.

Figure 8-4 shows the possible ways that the height alleles from the P generation could have been combined in the F_1 plants. Notice that the tall parent was homozygous for the tall allele, while the short parent was homozygous for the short allele. That resulted in all of the plants in the F_1 generation being heterozygous for the height gene, and since the tall allele is dominant, the plants all became tall.

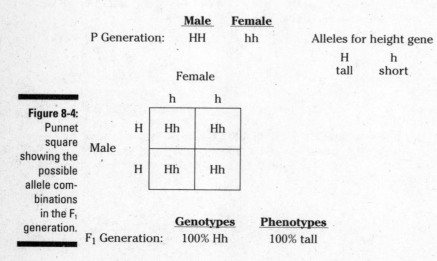

	Male	**Female**
P Generation:	HH	hh

Alleles for height gene

H   h
tall   short

Female

	h	h
H	Hh	Hh
H	Hh	Hh

Male

Figure 8-4:
Punnet square showing the possible allele combinations in the F_1 generation.

	Genotypes	**Phenotypes**
F_1 Generation:	100% Hh	100% tall

Just to be sure he had it right, Mendel took two plants from the F_1 generation and allowed them to breed. Their offspring were called the F_2 generation. The Punnet square in Figure 8-5 shows the possible combinations of alleles that could result from the breeding of two heterozygous F_1 plants. It predicts that about 25% of the F_2 offspring will be short because they end up with two recessive short alleles, while the other 75% will all end up tall because they would all receive at least one dominant tall allele. Of course, that's exactly what happened: About 75% were tall and about 25% were short. Mendel was a meticulous and single-minded studier of pea plants, and while that probably made him really boring at cocktail parties, he did manage to get a whole field of biology named after him, so that's pretty good.

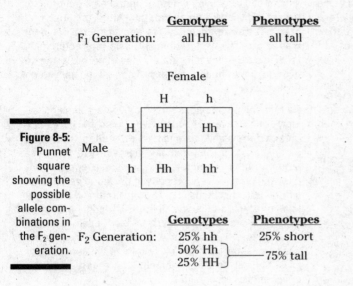

Figure 8-5:
Punnet square showing the possible allele combinations in the F_2 generation.

Okay, now here's some more sample questions.

The gene for brown hair color (Br) is dominant over the gene for red hair color (rd). A man with brown hair and a woman with red hair have four children. Two of their children have brown hair and two of them have red hair. What were the genotypes of the parents?

(A) Father: Br Br; mother: Br rd

(B) Father: Br Br; mother: rd rd

(C) Father: Br rd; mother: Br rd

(D) Father: Br rd; mother: rd rd

(E) Father: rd rd; mother: Br Br

Knowing what you do about dominant and recessive genes, look for easy ways to eliminate answer choices. The gene for brown hair (Br) is dominant over the gene for red hair (rd), so the mother, who has red hair, must not have the dominant Br gene at all. That means her genotype is rd-rd, so any answer that doesn't include rd-rd must be wrong. Cross out (A) and (C). Now, if the father were Br-Br, he wouldn't be able to pass on a red gene to produce the red-haired child, so any answer that includes Br-Br must also be wrong. That eliminates (A), (B) and (E). That leaves (D) as the correct answer, and if you make a Punnet square using those genotypes, you'll see that it works out.

The amazingly anonymous Mendel

Though Monk Mendel didn't necessarily take a vow of silence, his revolutionary theories of heredity were virtually unheard of for almost forty years — several years after his death. His anonymity may be attributed to that whole "those who can't — teach" attitude. You see Mendel wasn't a well-known scientist. He was just a lowly high school natural sciences teacher who came up with some pretty incredible discoveries about how plants and other organisms pass on their traits to their offspring. So, when he put short and tall together and came up with tall, nobody really noticed.

Not the majority of 19th century scientists. They held to a "blended theory" that maintained that traits from the parents got blended in the offspring. So, they didn't put much stock in Mendel's idea that the genes from each parent don't change in the children.

And not Charles Darwin. He thought that that organisms had "particles" in their systems that got affected by the stuff they did while they were alive. These environmentally changed particles would then cruise around in the blood stream and enter the reproductive cells where they would get passed down to the next generation. This theory was called "pangenesis," and it was, of course, wrong!

Mendel started out his experimentation testing the environmental impact idea that Darwin adopted. He was walking around the monastery one day when he came across a strange looking version of one of the garden plants. He decided to plant it next to a normal looking plant of the same variety to see if a similar environment would cause the offspring to be normal looking instead of strange looking. Then he grew the offspring side by side to see what would happen in the next generation. What he discovered was that the plants' offspring had the basic traits of their parents, and so the environment wasn't a factor in determining basic characteristics. From this experiment he got the idea of heredity, and he got hooked on finding out how living things passed on their traits.

He focused on pea pods for seven years and painstakingly proved several theories. He showed that hereditary factors don't blend, instead they pass intact, that each parent passes on only half of its hereditary factors to its progeny and some factors are dominant over other factors, and that different progeny of the same parents get different combinations of hereditary factors. Notions we take for granted today. Then in 1866, Mendel published his ground-breaking findings, but nobody seemed to take note. So, for the rest of his life he happily carried out his position as abbott of the monestary in obscurity, never knowing that he would someday be regarded as the father of modern genetics.

Two parents have a child with type O blood. The mother has blood type A, and the father has blood type B. What is a possible set of genotypes for the parents?

(A) Mother: A-A; father: B-B

(B) Mother: A-O; father: B-B

(C) Mother: A-O; father: O-O

(D) Mother: O-O; father: B-O

(E) Mother: A-O; father: B-O

Mother is blood type A and the father is type B, so the mother must have at least one A allele, and the father must have at least one B allele. That eliminates answers (C) and (D). The child is type O, and the only way you can have that phenotype is if your genotype is O-O. Therefore, each parent must have one O allele to pass on to the child, which means (A) and (B) are wrong also. Answer (E) is correct because it is the only one that matches the situation in the question.

You can probably figure out this question without setting up a Punnet square. But if it takes you too long to figure out the answers in your head (say, more than 20 seconds), by all means whip up a quick Punnet square to help yourself out.

Checking out sex-linked traits

You may have heard somewhere that humans have 46 chromosomes. *Chromosomes* are large bundles of DNA, and each chromosome contains many genes. So while we humans have only 46 chromosomes, we have somewhere around 30,000 genes. 44 of a person's chromosomes contain genes for all of his or her basic traits, while the other two chromosomes contain the genes that help determine the person's sex. Logically enough, these are called the *sex chromosomes*. There are two versions of the sex chromosome: X and Y. If a person has two X chromosomes, she will be female, and if a person has one X and one Y, then he will be male. This means that in sexual reproduction, the mother can only pass on an X chromosome, while the father can pass on either an X or a Y. If he passes on an X, the child will be a girl, and if he passes on a Y, the child will be a boy.

The X and Y chromosomes also have some other genes that have nothing to do with gender, but since those genes are carried on the sex chromosomes, the resulting traits are sometimes called *sex-linked traits*. An example is color blindness. The X chromosome carries a gene that contributes to color vision, but the Y chromosome does not have that gene. There are two alleles for this gene: one that produces color vision (which is dominant) and one that produces color blindness (which is recessive). The only way the recessive gene for color blindness will result in a phenotype for color blindness (meaning that a person will actually be color blind) is if a person does not have another chromosome with the color vision gene to dominate the recessive color blindness gene. Most people's X chromosomes have the dominant color vision allele, but some people have an X chromosome with the recessive color blindness allele. A female with that recessive allele has a backup X chromosome that is likely to have the dominant color vision allele, so it is really rare to find a girl with color blindness. However, if a male ends up with an X chromosome that has the recessive allele, he does not have a backup X chromosome with the dominant allele, so he will end up with color blindness. Boys with color blindness aren't very common, but they are way more common than color blind girls.

A female who has only one recessive allele on one of her X chromosomes will not end up with the recessive phenotype, but she is a *carrier* of the recessive allele. That means that if she passes the gene on to her child, and the father passes on a Y chromosome, then the child will end up being a boy with color blindness. The Punnet square in Figure 8-6 shows this situation. It looks like boys are just unlucky when it comes to chromosomes.

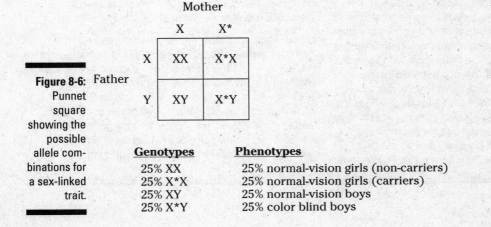

X = X with color vision allele
X* = X with color blindness allele

Figure 8-6:
Punnet square showing the possible allele combinations for a sex-linked trait.

	Mother	
	X	X*
Father X	XX	X*X
Y	XY	X*Y

Genotypes
25% XX
25% X*X
25% XY
25% X*Y

Phenotypes
25% normal-vision girls (non-carriers)
25% normal-vision girls (carriers)
25% normal-vision boys
25% color blind boys

Okay, one last set of sample questions . . .

A man and a woman have 10 children, 5 boys and 5 girls. The mother is a carrier for a sex-linked trait called hemophilia, while the father does not carry the hemophilia gene. The gene that carries hemophilia is recessive. Which of the following scenarios is most likely given this information?

(A) Three of the boys and two of the girls have hemophilia. One other girl is a carrier.

(B) None of the children have hemophilia. Three of the girls are carriers.

(C) Two of the boys and none of the girls have hemophilia. Three other boys are carriers.

(D) Two of the boys and none of the girls have hemophilia. Three other girls are carriers.

(E) All of the girls and none of the boys have hemophilia.

Since actually having hemophilia is sex-linked, it is only expressed if a person has a recessive gene on the X chromosome and a Y chromosome (without any gene for the trait) or two X chromosomes, each with the recessive gene for hemophilia. The mother is a carrier, so her genotype is X^*-X (the * stands for the hemophilia gene on the X chromosome), while the father does not have the gene, so his genotype is X-Y. You probably need to take the time to draw a Punnet square for this problem.

If you draw out the Punnet square for these parents, you will see that there is no way for a girl (X-X) to end up without at least one normal X chromosome, so no girls in this family can have hemophilia. That means (A) and (E) can be crossed out. A boy in this family has a 50-50 chance of getting the X chromosome with the hemophilia gene, and because the boys don't get a backup X from their dad, some will end up with hemophilia. So you can expect that about two or three boys out of five will have hemophilia. You need to find an answer that is most likely; so, (B) can be crossed out, too. A boy can't be a carrier of hemophilia without actually having hemophilia, so (C) can't be right. That leaves (D) as the correct answer, which is the one that best matches the result of the Punnet square.

This question gives you two answer choices that are possible, but it asks you which is more likely. This is why it is so important for you to read ALL of the answer choices before making your selection. B is possible, but it is much less likely than D. If you choose B before you read D, you'll get this question wrong.

Does DNA have fingerprints?

Remember that genes are sections of DNA. Chapters 5 and 7 both talk about how DNA is made of strings of nucleotides and that the information on genes is coded into the nucleotide sequence. Modern technology has made it possible to find out the exact nucleotide sequence of a section of DNA, and this has been big news in the world of genetics. We already knew that the more closely related individuals are, the more genes they will have in common, but we've always had to guess at exactly how many genes they share based on their phenotype and (if possible) on test crosses. Now we can find out the exact nucleotide sequences of their genes and find out how much they match. If they are 50% the same, then the two individuals are very closely related, perhaps siblings.

This is also important in crime investigation because modern forensics experts can test the nucleotide sequence of a DNA sample from a crime scene and compare it to the nucleotide sequences of the suspects. The one who is guilty will match the sample DNA 100%, while nobody else will come anywhere near that close (unless one of the other suspects was the guilty person's identical twin). They call this *DNA fingerprinting* and it is much more reliable than regular fingerprinting.

Which of the following is false about human chromosomes?

(A) Humans have 46 chromosomes.

(B) Each chromosome contains one gene.

(C) All chromosomes contain genes for non-sexual characteristics.

(D) If the sex chromosomes are X-X, the person will be female.

(E) If the sex chromosomes are X-Y, the person will be male.

The questions asks you to identify the false statement, so you can cross out all the answers that are true.

Humans have 46 chromosomes, so cross out (A). Answers (D) and (E) get the sex chromosome stuff right, so they can be crossed out, too. Even though the two sex chromosomes contain the genes for sexual traits, they also do carry some non-sexual genes as well, so (C) is true. That leaves (B) as the false one. Every chromosome has a huge number of genes — up to several thousand.

Chapter 9

Mixing It Up: Meiosis and Sexual Reproduction

This chapter builds off of the concepts you study in genetics. If you need more information about genetics, you can find it in Chapter 8. That chapter discusses how genes mix from two parents to produce an offspring. Each parent passes on one gene for every trait to the offspring, so that the offspring will end up with two genes for every trait, one from mom and one from dad. This chapter explains how the process actually happens. (And, no, we're not going to give you the birds and the bees talk.)

Preparing Gametes: Meiosis

In meiosis cells divide to produce gametes, which are commonly known as eggs and sperm. Before you get into the actual steps of division, you should know a little bit about chromosomes.

Packaging DNA in chromosomes

If you look at Figure 3-9 in Chapter 3, you can see a diagram of how DNA is packed into a chromosome. A chromosome is just a large bundle of DNA, and each chromosome contains many genes. Human cells have over 30,000 genes, all contained in just 46 total chromosomes! Other organisms have different numbers of chromosomes, but everything we say about meiosis in this chapter holds true for any species that reproduces sexually.

Every chromosome in a eukaryotic cell has a partner, and the two partner chromosomes carry genes for the same traits. For example, consider the hair color trait. There's a certain pair of chromosomes, one of which carries (among other things) one of the genes for hair color, while the other chromosome carries the other gene for hair color. A chromosome pair like this is called a *homologous pair*. Figure 9-1 shows a diagram of a homologous pair of chromosomes that contain the hair color and eye color genes. This person's genotype for hair color is Brown-red, and the genotype for eye color is Brown-blue. Hhhmmm . . . do you wonder what this person's phenotype would be? If you do, check out Chapter 8.

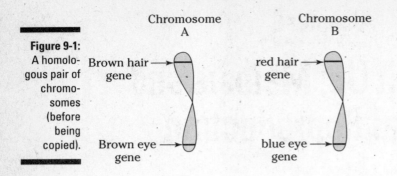

Figure 9-1:
A homologous pair of chromosomes (before being copied).

Getting an overview of meiosis

Most of the cells in a multicellular organism are called *somatic* cells. These are just the regular cells that make up things like skin or muscles (in animals), or stems or leaves (in plants). There are a few cells, though, that are specialized for sexual reproduction. These sexual cells have been given the very un-sexy name of *germ cells*. In order to get ready for sexual reproduction, each parent takes some of its germ cells and sends them through a special cell division process called *meiosis*. Meiosis results in special cells that have only one chromosome from each homologous pair, which means that they have only one gene for every trait. Those special cells are called *gametes*, and when a gamete from one parent is combined with a gamete from the other parent, they form a single cell called a *zygote*, and the zygote will develop into the offspring.

The process of producing gametes is called meiosis. In some ways, meiosis is a lot like mitosis (see Chapter 3); but mitosis is the *asexual* splitting of a single eukaryotic cell into two cells, and the result is two identical cells each of which has two genes for every trait. Meiosis, on the other hand, goes through two rounds of division, resulting in four cells, each of which has just one gene for every trait. A regular cell with two genes for every trait is called *diploid*, while a cell with only one gene for every trait is called *haploid*.

When the SAT II asks you about meiosis, it'll almost certainly use those two vocabulary words. A diploid human cell has all 46 chromosomes, while a human gamete (a haploid) has only 23 chromosomes (one chromosome from each homologous pair).

Before the cell even starts meiosis, it copies all of its DNA so that the chromosomes are doubled up, as shown in Figure 9-2. The two copies of each chromosome are called *sister chromatids*, and they stay stuck together until the second round in meiosis. We've labeled some of the genes on these chromosomes so you can track where each chromosome goes as the cells start dividing.

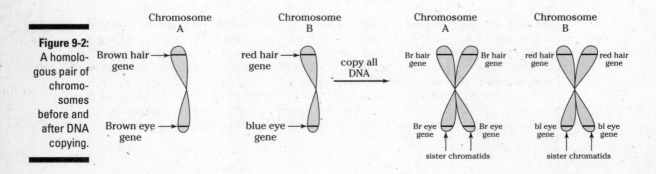

Figure 9-2:
A homologous pair of chromosomes before and after DNA copying.

Do chromosomal disorders pass from generation to generation?

Some types of chromosomal abnormalities pass to the next generation, but most chromosomal disorders aren't inherited. Knowing whether an abnormality is inherited or not is important to parents who have a disorder or who have already had a child with a chromosomal disorder.

Chromosomal conditions that are caused by changes in the number of chromosomes (like Down syndrome or Turner syndrome) aren't inherited. They occur randomly during meiosis while the reproductive cells are forming. If an error in cell division occurs, the result can be reproductive cells with an abnormal number of chromosomes. If one of these reproductive cells is part of the genetic makeup of a person, each of the person's cells will contain an extra or missing chromosome. But a child with Down syndrome has not inherited that trait from the existing chromosomal makeup of his or her parents.

Disorders that result from changes in chromosome structure may or may not be passed down to future generations. There are several types of chromosomal changes that result in disorders.

Deletions happen when a portion of the chromosome is missing.

When a portion of the chromosome is duplicated, called (not surprisingly) **duplication**, the result is that the person has extra genetic material.

When a portion of the chromosome breaks off, turns upside down and reattaches, the genetic material is inverted. This is called an **inversion**.

A piece of a chromosome can break off and form a circle or **ring**, which can cause a loss or no loss of genetic material.

Translocation occurs when a part of one chromosome transfers to another chromosome. There are two main types of translocations. Reciprocal translocation happens when segments from two different chromosomes exchange. With the other type, Robertsonian translocation, an entire chromosome attaches to another at the centromere, which can cause serious problems or no problems at all. Translocations can be inherited, however, so an apparently normal parent with translocated chromosomes could pass down the abnormality to his or her children. The children could then have problems that the parent didn't.

So, the bottom line is that chromosomal disorders are so complex, it's difficult to determine whether they are inheritable or not, which is why many parents with histories of disorder seek genetic counseling before they have children.

Getting from diploid to haploid: The first division

The first stage of meiosis is prophase I, where the cell is still diploid. The cell's nuclear membrane disappears, and the homologous pairs join up. Figure 9-3a shows a human cell in prophase I, with two homologous pairs that have some of their genes labeled. This person's genotype for blood type is A-O. Hhhmmm . . . know what their phenotype would be? If not, you can always consult Chapter 8.

A real human cell would have 23 homologous pairs, for a total of 46 chromosomes, but we cut that down to two in the diagrams in order to keep things simple. After prophase I comes *metaphase I*, where the homologous pairs all line up along the middle of the cell, called the *metaphase plate*, as shown in Figure 9-3b.

After metaphase I, the cell moves into *anaphase I*, where the homologous pairs separate and one pair is sent to either side (see Figure 9-4a). The cell then splits apart in *telophase I*, and the result is two cells (see Figure 9-4b).

After this first round of division, the two cells are left with only one chromosome from every homologous pair. That means they are now haploid cells.

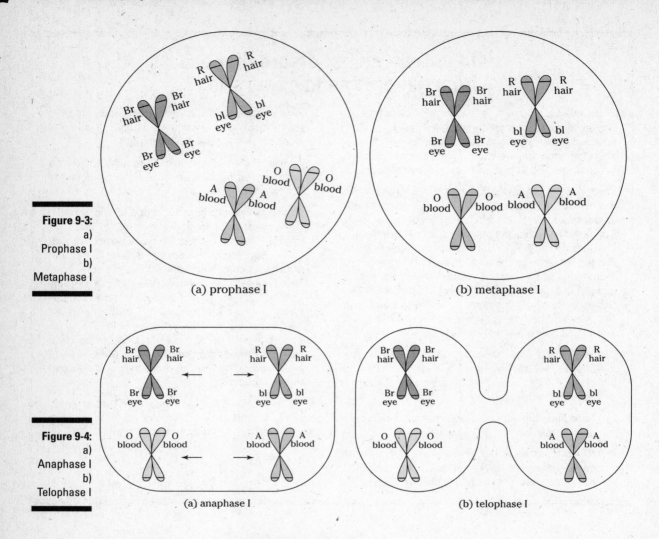

Figure 9-3:
a)
Prophase I
b)
Metaphase I

(a) prophase I

(b) metaphase I

Figure 9-4:
a)
Anaphase I
b)
Telophase I

(a) anaphase I

(b) telophase I

Generating gametes: The second division

The two haploid cells still need to go through another round of division in order to become gametes. *Prophase II* is exactly the same as the very end of telophase I, so just look at Figure 9-4b for prophase II. Next comes *metaphase II*, when the chromosomes line up along the center of each cell again, as shown in Figure 9-5a. *Anaphase II* is when the two copies of each chromosome are pulled apart and one copy is sent to either side of the cell, as shown in Figure 9-5b.

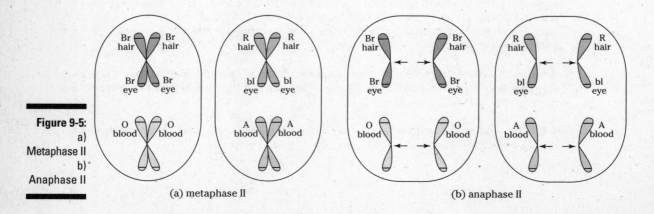

Figure 9-5:
a)
Metaphase II
b)
Anaphase II

(a) metaphase II

(b) anaphase II

The cells then split in half during telophase II, and you end up with four cells, each of which has just one copy of one chromosome from each homologous pair, as shown in Figure 9-6. These are the gametes, and in animals, these develop into either sperm or eggs, depending on the sex of the animal. If one of these gametes combines with a gamete from someone else of the opposite sex, then the resulting zygote would once again be diploid. That is, the zygot would have homologous pairs again, providing it with two genes for every trait. That zygote would then develop into a full-blown offspring baby.

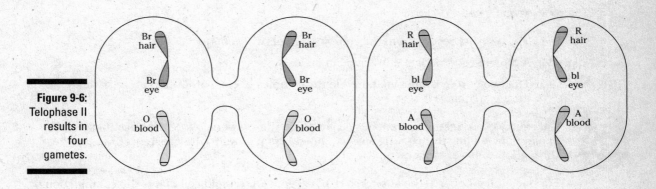

Figure 9-6: Telophase II results in four gametes.

Now that you've completed the second division, try these sample questions.

During which phase of meiosis are homologous pairs separated?

(A) prophase I

(B) telophase II

(C) anaphase II

(D) anaphase I

(E) metaphase I

The first division in meiosis is designed to separate homologous pairs, so anything from the second division can be crossed out.

So, (B) and (C) are gone. Anaphase is always the phase where chromosomes move to opposite ends of the cell, so the answer is (D), anaphase I.

Which phase of meiosis results in haploid cells?

(A) anaphase I

(B) telophase I

(C) metaphase I

(D) prophase I

(E) none of the above

A haploid cell has only one chromosome from each homologous pair, and all the homologous pairs are separated during anaphase I of meiosis, but it is still just one cell at that point, so (A) is wrong. The cell doesn't actually split until telophase I, so at the end of that stage you've got two separate haploid cells, so (B) is the correct answer.

Questions 1–3 refer to the following:

(A) homologous pair

(B) gamete

(C) zygote

(D) sister chromatids

(E) somatic cell

1. The cell that results from the combination of two gametes.

2. A diploid cell that is not involved in meiosis.

3. The two chromosomes that are identical copies of each other that are separated during anaphase II.

This funky classification question type gives you the answers before the questions. Don't spend time reading through the answer choices. Skip down to the questions first; then read through the answer choices.

For question number 1, the answer is (C). A zygote is a diploid cell that is the combination of two haploid gametes. The zygote develops into the offspring.

For question number 2, the answer is (E). Somatic cells are just normal body tissue cells, like skin or muscle cells, that are not used to make gametes.

For question number 3, the answer is (D). Sister chromatids are identical copies of a chromosome that are stuck together all the way until anaphase II.

Jumbling the Genes: Diversity and Crossing Over

Gametes turn into either sperm cells (called *pollen* in plants) or egg cells, depending on the sex of the organism. The sperm from a male is combined with the egg of a female to produce a zygote, which grows into an offspring. The whole point of going through meiosis and sexual reproduction is to make offspring that are a mixture of the genes from two parents.

This mixing of genes increases diversity within the species, and diversity is what helps species adapt through evolution by natural selection (see Chapter 10). As long as all the off-spring end up as normal diploid organisms with two genes for every trait, then the more mixed up the genes are in the next generation, the better. It seems like the older generation always thinks that kids these days are pretty mixed up, and when it comes to the genes that the kids inherited from their parents, those folks are absolutely right!

It's hit and miss: Random chances

One way for different chromosomes to mix is through the random chances that occur during meiosis. Notice in Figure 9-6 there are four cells, and in two cells the chromosome with the brown hair and brown eye genes ended up with the chromosome with the type O blood gene. This is purely an accident of how the homologous pairs lined up during metaphase I. It could just as easily have turned out that the homologous pairs lined up slightly differently during metaphase I, resulting in the chromosome with the type A gene being in the same gamete as the chromosome with the brown hair and brown eye genes (see figure 9-7).

The chromosomes in the gametes can be combined in any old way, as long as the gametes each end up with one gene for every trait. If any genes are missing, then that gamete may not be able to produce an offspring.

Figure 9-7:
Alternate chromosome combinations from figure 9-6.

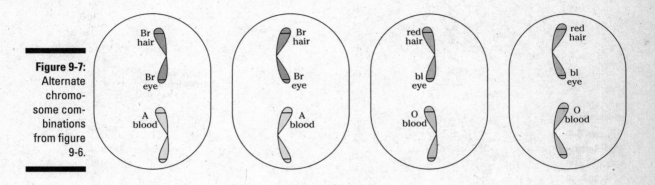

Safe passage: Crossing over

Another way the cells can mix up the genes even more is through a process called ***crossing over***, which happens during metaphase I. As shown in Figure 9-8a, the homologous pair gets really close together until each has one of its sister chromatids overlap the sister chromatid from the other chromosome. The chromosomes then swap the overlapping part. So, for example, the eye color gene on one chromosome will be exchanged for the eye color gene on the other chromosome, resulting in even more mixing of genes than already took place.

What did your parents give you?

We'll bet you're pretty familiar with the standard genetic traits, like hair color and eye color, but did you know that the following traits are also inherited?

✔ **Dimples:** You can thank your parents for hose cute little indents on your face that make your Great Aunt Harriet pinch your cheeks everytime she sees you. You can take comfort in knowing that she probably pinched your parent's cheeks, too.

✔ **Curled tongue:** You can't learn to roll your tongue up on both sides; you can either do it or not based on heredity.

✔ **"Hitchhiker's thumb":** If your thumb curls back when you make the "thumbs up" sign, that's a gift from your parents.

✔ **Long second toe:** Some people get toes that decrease in size from the big toe on down to the little one; others get a second toe that is longer than all of the other toes, including the big toe.

✔ **Earlobes:** You inherit your earlobes from your parents. Some have lobes that attach to the face at their lowest point. Others have unattached earlobes that don't attach to their faces at the bottom.

✔ **Left or right thumbed:** Whether you're right or left thumbed depends on heredity. The way to tell is by interlocking your hands together without thinking about it. If when you look at your hands, your left thumb's on top, you're left thumbed. If the right one's on top, you're right thumbed.

✔ **Vulcan hands:** Can you spread out your hands leaving a space between your two middle fingers and no spaces between the first and last two fingers? If so you've inherited the ability to make the Vulcan "V" just like Mr. Spock on *Star Trek*. We don't think this makes you an alien, however.

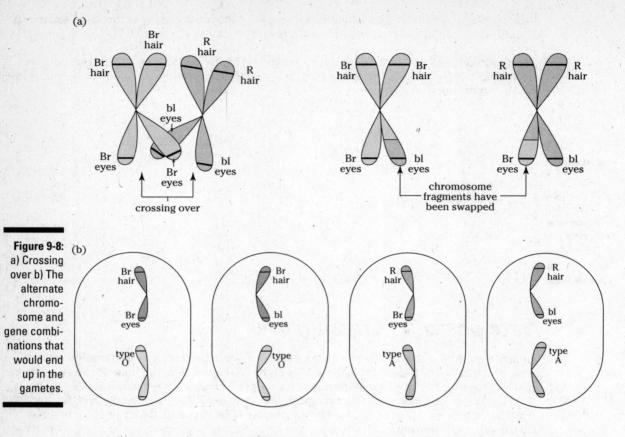

Figure 9-8:
a) Crossing over b) The alternate chromosome and gene combinations that would end up in the gametes.

Figure 9-8b shows the possible gametes that could result after crossing over has happened. Now an offspring can inherit brown hair and blue eyes together, which wasn't possible before crossing over. That's why siblings don't always look exactly the same. They each receive a different set of genes from each parent, and as long as they end up with two genes for every trait, everything should work out okay.

EXAMPLE

Try a few more sample questions.

Crossing over occurs between which of the following?

(A) sister chromatids

(B) two gametes from the same parent

(C) two gametes, one from each parent

(D) random chromosomes

(E) homologous pairs of chromosomes

Crossing over is the exchange of chromosome sections in order to increase the possible gene combinations that end up in gametes. Sister chromatids are exact copies of each other, so there would be no point in them exchanging chromosome sections, so (A) is wrong. Crossing over happens way before we get to gametes, so (B) and (C) are wrong. If it happens between random chromosomes, you can't be sure that you'll end up with exactly one gene for every trait in the gametes, so (D) can't be right either. Homologous pairs have genes for the same traits, so when they exchange chromosome sections, they mix up gene combinations while still ensuring that the gametes end up with all the genes they need, so (E) is the correct answer.

Crossing over helps to increase the diversity in the next generation. Why is this considered beneficial for a species?

(A) increased diversity aids adaptation through evolution by natural selection

(B) increased diversity helps the individuals in a species tell each other apart

(C) increased diversity prevents inbreeding

(D) all of the above

(E) none of the above

If you are confronted with a question with an "all of the above" answer choice, you have some help in the answer elimination process. If you know one of the answer choices is wrong, you know that all of the above cannot be right, which means that (D) must be wrong as well. You can eliminate two answer choices in one fell swoop! The same treat is true for "none of the above" answer choices. If you find an answer choice to be true, you know that your "none of the above" answer is wrong and you can eliminate it, raising your possibilities of answering the question correctly even if you can't decide whether another answer works or not.

Choice C is meant to throw you off. Inbreeding may cause a lack of diversity, but diversity has nothing directly to do with prevention of inbreeding, so (C) is wrong. The SAT II makers are hoping you are reading too quickly to catch the inverse cause and effect relationship.

Diversity in some species could help the individuals tell each other apart, but that is not a general advantage of diversity, so (B) is wrong. Evolution by natural selection can only work if there is diversity in the species. The more diversity there is, the more nature has to select from, which increases the rate of adaptation by evolution, so (A) is the correct answer.

Part III

Environmentally Aware: Evolution, Ecology, and Other Stuff on the Biology-E Section

The 5th Wave   By Rich Tennant

"I'm really pumped for this test. I can feel the whatcha ma call it flowing through those little round tube things in my body."

In this part . . .

Part III focuses on the Biology-E section material, which includes ecology, taxonomy, and evolution. Unfortunately for you cellular and molecular biology fans who plan on doing the Biology-M section instead of the Biology-E section, you still need to know a lot of this ecology and evolution stuff because it makes up about 30 percent of the Biology E/M core section that everybody has to do. At least this part covers stuff that you can see happening out in nature, or at least in nature documentaries that you watch on TV.

Chapter 10

Understanding Origins and Evolution of Life

The theory of evolution explains how organisms change over the generations and what guides that change. Using the theory of evolution, biologists can understand why living things have the characteristics they have and how different characteristics may change in future generations. The explanatory power of evolution is so important to biology that it ends up being an underlying theme of much of the SAT II. In this chapter I discuss the fundamentals of the theory of evolution as well as the leading theory of how life got going on earth in the first place.

Starting Up: Origins of Life

Cell theory, discussed in more detail in Chapter 3, says that all cells arise from previous cells. Why is that? Why can't cells just form on their own if you mix the right molecules together? The problem is that even the simplest prokaryotic cells are amazingly complicated and finely structured organisms, and organization like that doesn't just pop up on its own. That means every new cell needs to be built by a previous cell. But, wait a minute . . . this can't be completely right because we know that life on earth had to start sometime in the past, and whatever the first cells were, they didn't come from previous cells. So how did the first cells arise? The answer is that nobody really knows, because nobody was around to see it happen 4 billion years ago, and nobody's seen it happen again since then. Nevertheless, biologists have some interesting guesses (as they always do), and the SAT II just may ask you about the most famous theory (as it always does).

Early atmosphere

I wish somebody would finally manage to build a time machine with a decent safety rating so we could just go back 4 billion years and see how life first formed. I should admit, however, that even if we could go back that far, I wouldn't want to step outside because the atmosphere of the very ancient earth was a lot different than it is now. Instead of the nice, fresh mixture of oxygen (O_2) and nitrogen (N_2) that we have today, the early earth atmosphere had a toxic mixture of methane, hydrogen gas, and ammonia. So how could life arise in that? Well, a scientist tried to answer that question by re-creating the conditions of the early earth in a big beaker in his lab. Amazingly, he found that organic molecules like sugars and amino acids formed automatically, and these molecules are part of what go into making cells. The results from this experiment form the basis of the current theory for the origins of life.

First cells

We now know that the building blocks of life were present in the oceans of the early earth, forming an organic mixture called the *primordial soup*. As time went on, the molecules of the primordial soup got more and more complex and they engaged in complex chemical reactions. In some of these reactions, big molecules like proteins and nucleic acids could actually copy themselves. Then, when the right kinds of self-copying molecules were trapped inside of the right kind of oil droplets, the first prokaryotic cells were formed!

These first cells could reproduce themselves and were therefore subject to evolution by natural selection. They were also able to use the organic molecules floating around in the primordial soup as fuel and nutrients. To break down their fuel, they used anaerobic respiration.

A change of atmosphere

Anaerobic respiration tends to produce carbon dioxide (CO_2), which is a molecule that was not present in the atmosphere before then. Once CO_2 was around (after a few hundred million years), other cells could use it to perform photosynthesis. Photosynthesis produces free oxygen (O_2), another molecule that had never been around before. Once photosynthesis had produced enough O_2, the atmosphere started to become a lot more like it is today. The O_2 allowed complex eukaryotic cells to emerge using aerobic respiration, which is a very efficient way to break down fuel. (See Chapter 6 for more information on cellular respiration and photosynthesis.) These eukaryotes gradually became more complex and eventually began forming multicellular organisms, until we finally end up with all of the varieties of life we see on earth today! Okay, that's the whole story of four billion years of evolution in a few paragraphs. Whew.

To test your understanding of the workings of billions of years of evolution, the SAT II may present questions like the following.

Which of the following was not a component of the early earth atmosphere?

(A) ammonia (NH_3)

(B) oxygen (O_2)

(C) water (H_2O)

(D) methane (CH_3)

(E) hydrogen (H_2)

This is a tough one if you aren't good at straight memorization. One thing you may remember is that O_2 is a big part of our atmosphere today, and the atmosphere of the early earth was completely different than it is now. Also, the first O_2 molecules weren't produced until photosynthesis finally got going, and that didn't happen until life had been around for a long time. So, the correct answer is (B). Water is always around on the earth, and the other gasses were all toxic components of the early atmosphere that are found only in very small amounts in the atmosphere today.

Which is the correct sequence for evolution of life on earth?

   I. eukaryotic cells emerge

   II. anaerobic respiration develops

   III. prokaryotic cells emerge

   IV. pre-biotic primordial soup

   V. photosynthesis develops

(A) I, III, V, II, IV

(B) IV, II, III, V, I

(C) IV, III, II, V, I

(D) II, III, V, I, IV

(E) IV, II, III, I, V

The pre-biotic soup (IV) has to be first, because *pre-biotic* means "before life," so (A) and (D) can be crossed out right away. The first cells were simple prokaryotes, so III must come next, which eliminates (B). Anaerobic respiration paved the way for photosynthesis, and then that allowed complex eukaryotic cells to emerged. That means (C) must be the correct answer.

Providing Evidence for Evolution

How do we know that the overall theory of evolution is at all plausible? It seems weird to think that all life on earth evolved from the same basic, simple cells so long ago. Darwin made an amazing claim when he said that all life on earth is fundamentally related, so scientists have needed some strong evidence to be convinced.

Molecular similarity

One really strong line of evidence has been uncovered only in the last several decades when molecular biology got better technology for studying cell processes. It turns out that all cells are based on the exact same set of molecules and the same basic sets of metabolic reactions. Even the genetic code is exactly the same for all cells on earth, which is just too big of a coincidence to ignore. The only scientific explanation is that the first living things had these molecules, metabolic reactions, and genetic code, and that all modern organisms have inherited these things together. See Chapter 5 for more info about the common biological molecules, Chapter 6 for common metabolic pathways, and Chapter 7 for DNA and the genetic code.

Comparative anatomy

You can use the following two types of anatomical evidence to support the theory of evolution:

✔ **Homologous structures:** When looking at a certain branch of animals, you may notice some really similar structures in different lineages. For example, mammals such as whales, dogs, horses, and humans all use limbs for moving around, and their limbs all have the same basic bone structure. This is an example of what's called *homologous structures,* and it suggests that modern mammals all inherited their limbs from the same distant ancestors. If the mammals weren't evolutionarily related, it seems weird that they would all end up with such similar bones.

✔ **Vestigial structures:** Another bit of anatomical evidence for evolution comes from what are called *vestigial structures*. These are things that no longer serve any purpose in an organism. For example, the appendix in humans serves no purpose, but a similar structure in other mammals helps them digest tough plants. That suggests humans had a distant ancestor that needed to digest tough plants, and for some reason we eventually didn't have that need anymore. Having an appendix usually doesn't harm us, so it still hangs around as a vestigial structure.

You have to be careful when using anatomy as evidence for evolutionary relatedness, though. Sometimes two different lineages develop similar characteristics completely independently, a process called *convergent evolution*. For example, insects and birds both have wings, but insect wings and bird wings have totally different structures even though they are both used for flying. Another example is sharks and dolphins. They have similar streamlined bodies and fins specialized for swimming, but again, they evolved totally separately and are genetically unrelated. The underlying genes are very different in sharks and dolphins, but the different genes produce body structures that look and perform a lot alike. Characteristics that are produced by convergent evolution are called *analogous traits*.

The fossil record

If an organism is covered by sediment soon after it dies, then after a few million years of more sediment piling on and turning into rock, the organism's tougher structures can turn into fossils. Newer fossils form in each subsequent layer of sediment that gets laid down, so the deeper the fossil, the older the organism. By examining the fossils in each layer of rock, we can see how anatomical structures have changed throughout the history of life, giving us pretty direct evidence for some kind of evolution. Plus, if it weren't for fossils, we wouldn't have all the great dinosaur museums and movies!

Unfortunately, the fossil record is far from perfect. In order to get fossilized, an organism has to be covered up pretty quickly and the process of rock formation has to happen just right. That means most organisms just die and decompose without fossilizing. Plus, only the really tough parts like shells, bones, and leaves tend to fossilize, so we can't tell what the soft tissues of these organisms were like at all. Even when some parts of an organism do fossilize, they can still be ruined by geological forces like earthquakes, volcanoes, and plain old erosion. Nevertheless, paleontologists (fossil scientists) have found enough intact fossils to have a pretty good idea of how things like the limbs of mammals changed over millions of years.

Try your hand at a few SAT II type evolution questions.

All mammals have very similar four-chambered hearts. Based on this information, which of the following is not true?

(A) This is an example of analogous structures.

(B) An animal with a two-chambered heart probably is not a mammal.

(C) This is an example of homologous structures.

(D) This is evidence that all mammals shared a common ancestor with a four-chambered heart.

(E) If a new mammal were discovered, it would be likely to have a four-chambered heart.

The question is asking which of the answers is false, so we can cross out the ones we know are true. Since the question states that *all* mammals have a four-chambered heart, then any new mammal we find would definitely have a four-chambered heart. Also, anything with a two-chambered heart is definitely not a mammal, so (B) and (E) are true. When a group of animals all have a very similar anatomical structure, this indicates a close evolutionary relationship, so (D) is true also. That leaves (A) and (C), the two vocabulary words. Analogous structures are ones that do the same sort of thing but have a very *different* internal structure, like bird wings and insect wings. That is not going on here because mammalian hearts have very *similar* structure, making them homologous structures, so (C) is true while (A) is false, which means (A) is the correct answer to the question.

Which of the following is not evidence for the evolutionary relatedness of all organisms on earth?

(A) all organisms use DNA as their genes

(B) all organisms use the same genetic code

(C) all organisms have cells with a nucleus

(D) all organisms use similar metabolic pathways

(E) all organisms have cells with phospholipid membranes

Evidence of relatedness from molecular biology includes things that are common to every single organism on the planet, so this question asks which of the answers is not common to all organisms. All organisms use DNA and a similar genetic code, so (A) and (B) can be crossed out. All organisms use similar metabolic pathways, so (D) is out also. Options (C) and (E) ask you to draw on information from Chapter 3, which covers the characteristics of cells. It turns out that all cells use the same kind of phospholipid membrane, so (E) is not the answer. Chapter 3 also explains that prokaryotic cells never have a nucleus, so (C) is the correct answer because it's the false one.

Paleontologists have little fossil evidence for the evolution of the brain. Which of the following is the most likely explanation for this fact?

(A) erosion has worn away most of the fossilized brains

(B) animals with brains tend to die in areas with little or no sedimentary rock

(C) paleontologists haven't searched for fossilized brains

(D) brain tissue is too soft to fossilize easily

(E) the development of brains is too recent to have been found in ancient fossils

You may be able to jump right to the answer on this one, but I'll go through the process of elimination anyway. We all know that fossilized dinosaurs have been found all over the world, and that dinosaurs were animals with brains. That means (B) and (E) are both wrong. Paleontologists make a living out of searching for all kinds of fossils, so (C) is wrong as well. Answer (A) could be true, but it's a very unlikely explanation for the complete lack of fossilized brains. Answer (D) is definitely true and seems a much simpler explanation than (A), so (D) is the correct answer.

Making Change: Two Theories of Evolution

Once people started to realize in the 1800s that the species around today evolved and changed over many generations, people wanted to know how this worked. Two main theories of evolution were proposed, but only one was right. You may not remember a guy named Jean-Baptiste Lamarck, but he came up with a theory that turned out to be wrong, though it still may show up on the SAT II as a sort of "history of biology" question. The other theory, Charles Darwin's, turned out to be right, so he went on to become one of the most famous scientists of all time, and the SAT II focuses a lot of questions on his theory of evolution.

Lamarck and acquired characteristics

Lamarck thought that an organism could, over the course of its life, acquire characteristics that help it to survive better in its environment. For example, if a squirrel lived in a cold environment, Lamarck thought the squirrel could manage to grow thicker fur over its lifetime. Lamarck also thought that the squirrel could then pass that trait on to its offspring so the babies could start off with thicker fur than their parents had when they were born. That sounds like a good theory — the only problem is that it's completely wrong. Lamarck didn't know that the characteristics of an organism are determined by its genes and that you can't change your genes during your lifetime in order to make yourself somehow better. Also, even when you do manage to acquire a new characteristic during your lifetime, like if you learn to speak French or something, you can't automatically pass that characteristic on to your offspring. The only thing you can automatically pass down are your genes. If Lamarck's theory were true, then basketball players could get taller just by playing basketball, and they could then pass that tallness on to their children. Sorry Lamarck, but it just doesn't work that way.

Darwin and natural selection

Darwin's theory turned out to be correct, so he's the scientist we remember. Darwin didn't know anything about DNA or genes, but he did know that you could not develop an in-born characteristic just by trying really hard. He realized that evolution works on a population — a group of organisms of the same species — and not on individuals. The source of evolution is the diversity of characteristics that are always present in any population. Think of cold-weather squirrels. Among that population, some squirrels are born by chance with thicker fur while some are born with thinner fur. Since their environment is cold, the squirrels that were lucky enough to be born with thicker fur are more likely to survive long enough to produce offspring, and since fur thickness is a genetic trait, their offspring will also have thick fur like their lucky parents. There's always some small differences between siblings, so among those thick-fur offspring, some will inevitably have fur that's a little thicker than the others. Then, just as before, the squirrels with slightly thicker fur will be able to survive and reproduce better in the cold environment. After many generations of this, very few thin-furred squirrels are around, and the only squirrels left in the population are ones with thicker fur. In other words, thicker fur evolved in the population! Remember, they can't *try* to get thicker fur. Some squirrels were just lucky and some weren't. Since the naturally cold environment only allows thick-furred squirrels to survive, it is sort of like nature is *selecting* squirrels with thick fur. Hence, Darwin's theory is called *evolution by natural selection*.

Here are the main points in Darwin's theory:

- The individuals in a population are not all identical — there is variation within the population.

- Populations tend to produce more offspring than the environment can support, leading to competition.

- The individuals with characteristics that help them better survive in the environment are the ones who win the competition.

- The individuals that win the competition are able to produce more offspring, and the offspring will have winning characteristics similar to their parents. In this way, the winning characteristics become more and more common in the population.

- The individuals who do not have the best characteristics do not produce as many offspring, so their characteristics tend to be less and less common in the population.

Notice that it is not good enough just to *survive* in the environment. What's important is that you produce as many offspring as possible. This is called *reproductive fitness,* so Darwin's theory is sometimes called *survival of the fittest.* This is the true reality show, where those that are voted off by Mother Nature are actually eliminated from the gene pool!

A great place to see this selection in action is dog breeding. Since humans are controlling it, dog breeding is called *artificial selection,* but it works just the same as the natural kind. Suppose some dog breeders really like small, fluffy dogs. What they'll do is find two dogs that are sort of small and sort of fluffy, and have them breed together. Among their puppies, some will inherit just the right combination of genes that determine body size and fluffiness of fur. The breeders will then take those smallest, fluffiest offspring and, after they grow up, breed them with small, fluffy dogs from other breeders, leading to even smaller and fluffier puppies. After a few generations of doing this, the breeders can end up with *really* small and *really* fluffy dogs. Different breeders can select for different traits like speed, friendliness, alertness, sense of smell, and so on, leading to the crazy diversity of dogs we have today. That's reproductive selection in action, only in the real world, the natural environmental conditions do the selecting instead of humans.

To test your knowledge of Darwin you may see some questions like these on the SAT II.

Which of the following individuals has achieved the most reproductive fitness?

(A) An Olympic athlete with no children

(B) A 35-year-old widow with four children

(C) An 85-year-old woman with four children and three grandchildren

(D) A newly married couple in their mid-20s

(E) A 40-year-old man with two children

Reproductive fitness is all about having the greatest number of offspring — especially offspring that can have children of their own. It doesn't matter how many children you could have or may have. It only matters how many you *do* have, so any information about age, gender, and athleticism is only there to distract you from the important facts. The 85-year-old woman in (C) may not be as physically vigorous as some of the others, but she's got the most offspring, so she has achieved the most reproductive fitness.

Why is it impossible for a population of genetic clones to evolve?

(A) there would be no selection pressure on the population

(B) there would be no diversity within the population

(C) there would be perfect cooperation within the population

(D) there would be too much competition within the population

(E) a population of genetic clones actually can evolve

A population of clones cannot evolve, so (E) is wrong. The amount of cooperation or competition can affect evolution in different ways, but they would not cause evolution to cease, so (C) and (D) can be crossed out also. The environment would never stop applying selection pressure, so (A) is wrong. If there's zero diversity, as there would be in a population of clones, then it doesn't matter who ends up reproducing or how much because the exact same genes will be passed on no matter what. That means (B) is correct.

Traveling the Road of Life: Patterns of Evolution

Even though the basic mechanism in evolution is the same everywhere, the actual results of evolution depend on a whole bunch of different factors like environmental conditions, what kind of food is available, what kinds of predators are around, and so on. This section covers the main patterns of evolution that you may see on the SAT II.

Moving right along: Directional selection

Think about squirrels in a cold-weather environment. Over the generations, more and more squirrels are born with thicker fur. Another way of saying this is that the average fur thickness in the population is increasing. Since the squirrel population is moving in the direction of thicker fur, this is an example of *directional selection* (see Figure 10-1).

Figure 10-1: Graph showing directional selection in a population.

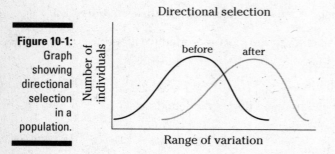

Taking the middle way: Stabilizing selection

A different type of selection is where extreme versions of a characteristic are being eliminated in favor of the average. Think of the tusk size of modern-day rhinos. If a rhino is born with a small tusk, he won't be able to defend himself or fight for mates as well as the other rhinos, so he won't be able to pass on his small-tusk genes. On the other hand, if a rhino grows a tusk that is too big, he won't be able to lift his head up anymore, so he won't be able to pass on its big-tusk genes either. Only rhinos with medium-sized tusks survive and mate, so only the average-tusk genes get passed on to the next generation. This is called *stabilizing selection* because it is keeping the tusk size in the population stable: not too big, not too small (see Figure 10-2).

Figure 10-2: Graph showing stabilizing selection in a population.

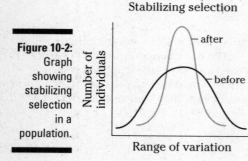

Causing a split: Disruptive selection

A third type of selection is when a characteristic is going in two directions at once. Consider a forest where a population of birds feeds on two different kinds of nuts. One kind of nut is bigger and harder, so birds with a bigger, stronger beak are better at eating these nuts. The other kind is smaller and softer, so birds with a smaller beak are better at eating these. Birds with medium-sized beaks can't eat either nut all that well. Since big beaks and small beaks both provide a better fitness advantage than medium beaks, medium-sized beaks will tend to disappear in favor of the two extremes. This is called *disruptive selection* because it is the opposite of stabilizing selection (see Figure 10-3).

Figure 10-3:
Graph
showing
disruptive
selection
in a
population.

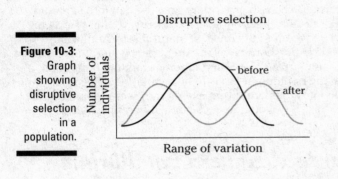

Disruptive selection may be tested on the SAT II in this way.

A species of bird uses large, colorful tails to attract mates. Since the females prefer males with larger tails, the large-tailed males in the population tend to mate more often. This an example of _____.

(A) stabilizing selection

(B) artificial selection

(C) disruptive selection

(D) Lamarckian evolution

(E) directional selection

Since the females always mate with the males who have the biggest tails, the big-tail genes will be passed on more often than small or medium-tail genes, leading to bigger and bigger tails in the population with each generation. That is, evolution in this population is going in the direction of bigger tails, so this is directional selection which means that (E) is correct. Stabilizing selection would have the average tail size becoming more common with each generation, while disruptive would have two different sizes being selected, so (A) and (C) are both wrong. Artificial selection is done only by humans, and Lamarckian evolution never happens.

Parting ways: Speciation

If destabilizing selection continues, it could result in a splitting of the species, called *speciation*. A species is defined as a group of individuals capable of breeding to produce fertile offspring, and the individuals of a certain species are closely genetically related. As long as their DNA is similar enough, two individuals can still produce offspring and are considered members of the same species. For example, humans are a pretty diverse bunch, but our DNA is all very similar; so any human man and woman of the right age are capable of having children together. If the DNA is too different, like between humans and monkeys, then they are not able to produce offspring (even if they tried) and are definitely considered different species.

A group of individuals of the same species that are living in the same area is called a population. Individuals in a population can all interbreed with each other, mixing together their genes in different ways all the time. Because of this, the collection of genes present in a population is sometimes called a *gene pool*. Evolution happens when some genes in the gene pool become more common than others as a result of natural selection. New genes can be added to the gene pool by random mutations (see Chapter 7 for more on DNA and mutations).

Think of cold-weather squirrels. Suppose that a group of those squirrels migrated a little further south where the weather is warmer. The two groups are now divided into separate populations — separate gene pools. For the southern squirrels, thick fur wouldn't be as big of an advantage. In fact, it may even cause them to overheat, so natural selection would cause them to evolve thinner fur than their northern cousins. After many generations, the two populations would evolve further and further apart, and different random mutations would show up in each gene pool, leading to different kinds of new variations. Eventually, the DNA of the two populations would become so different that even if they were reunited, they would not be able to interbreed anymore. They would have become different species!

Coming to a halt: Hardy-Weinberg Equilibrium

Scientists sometimes like talking about hypothetical situations that never exist in reality, but it isn't because they've lost touch with the real world. Rather, it's because they like to have a very simple, basic situation to compare with the complex world of organisms and populations. Imagine a population that is just like a regular population except that there's no evolution. In other words, the frequency of the different genes in the gene pool stay the same generation after generation. Biology textbooks call this *Hardy-Weinberg equilibrium* after the guys who thought it up. In order for a population to be at Hardy-Weinberg equilibrium (no evolution), the following five basic conditions need to be met:

- ✔ **There must be random mating within the population.** If males or females choose their mates based on some specific characteristic, then that characteristic will become more common, and that would be evolution, so mating has to be random.

- ✔ **There is random reproductive success.** As in the first condition, if individuals with a certain characteristic are able to reproduce more than anyone else, then that characteristic will become more common, and that would be evolution, so reproductive success has to be random — that is, not based on anything special about the parents.

- ✔ **There must be no immigration or emigration.** Immigration of newcomers brings in new genes, which would alter the makeup of the gene pool, so that can't happen. Same thing goes for emigration. If individuals leave the population, they take their genes with them, thereby changing the gene pool.

- ✔ **There must be a large population.** This is a statistical point, because when a population is small, weird chance events can change the makeup of the gene pool in just one generation. In large populations, chance events here and there tend to even each other out. Suppose you flip a coin only 10 times. There's a small (but very reasonable) chance that it will come up 8 heads and 2 tails, even though the coin has a 50-50 chance of falling either way. If you flip another 990 times, then any more weird, uneven results like that would tend to average out, and you can be sure it will come up right around 500 heads and 500 tails. So, having a big population size ensures that no statistical flukes change the makeup of the gene pool.

- ✔ **There must be no mutations.** Mutations change genes, which would obviously change the makeup of the gene pool. See Chapter 7 for more on DNA and mutations.

When all five of these conditions are met, no evolution would happen in the population. Of course, no actual population meets all of these conditions, so all real populations are evolving at least a little bit. The job for biologists studying one of these populations is to find out which conditions aren't being met and why.

A Hardy-Weinberg question may appear like this.

Which of the following is not a requirement for a population to be in Hardy-Weinberg equilibrium?

(A) no mutations

(B) all individuals must be genetically identical

(C) no immigration or emigration

(D) random mating

(E) large population size

A population is in Hardy-Weinberg equilibrium when the overall makeup of the population's gene pool does not change over time. This doesn't say anything about the genes that any individuals possess or how similar they all are to each other. That means (B) is correct because it is not a requirement for Hardy-Weinberg equilibrium. Having a large population size prevents the chance of weird statistical fluctuations in the gene pool from one generation to the next, so the answer can't be (E). Mutations and immigration introduce new genes, and emigration takes genes out, so those would all change the makeup of the gene pool, so (A) and (C) can be crossed out. There needs to be random mating to ensure that individuals with certain characteristics aren't getting a reproductive advantage, so (D) is out also.

Chapter 11

Following the Hierarchy: Taxonomy

There are tons and tons of different species on earth. In fact, some biologists estimate that there's over 60 *million* different species alive today, and that over *a billion* different species have been around at one time or another during the history of life on earth. That's way too much for anybody to keep track of, so biologists have developed a method of sorting all of the species into groups based on their evolutionary relatedness. This classification method is called *taxonomy*. In this chapter, we not only introduce you to the classification system, but we also give you an overview of the five kingdoms that divide all the species as well as give you some pointers on viruses.

Filling Out the Family Tree: The Levels of Classification

Chapter 10 talks about how all organisms on earth are ultimately related to one another. All organisms have evolved from the first organisms, with groups branching off from one another and forming their own genetic lineage. First off, all of the species on earth are separated into five big groups, called *kingdoms*. The official names of the five kingdoms are Monera (bacteria), Protista, Fungi, Plantae, and Animalia. Figure 11-1 shows a diagram of the family tree for all life on earth, and you can see from that diagram how the kingdoms are related to each other.

Each of the five kingdoms is broken down into different *phyla*, which are separated in to different classes (which is called *classification*), then orders, then families, then genera, and finally species. Table 11-1 lists all of the levels of classification along with the names of all the groups for humans and for wolves. This process of breaking the groups down into smaller and smaller groups only stops when you reach the species level. A **species** is a group of closely related individuals that are able to reproduce, and this is the most basic level of classification.

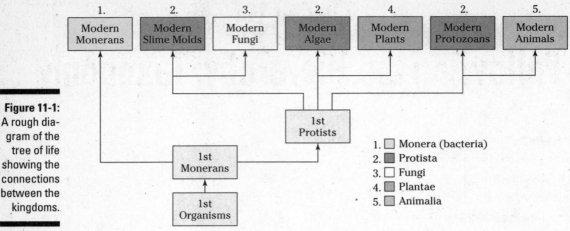

Figure 11-1:
A rough diagram of the tree of life showing the connections between the kingdoms.

The SAT II may ask you a question or two about how to determine relatedness. For those questions, follow these steps:

1. Look at general, obvious characteristics like anatomy and feeding style. At the higher levels this is really easy. Plants and animals have some really huge structural differences that are tough to miss, and not many people would think something with leaves and flowers was an animal. On the other hand, horses and donkeys have a lot in common, and sometimes it may even be hard to tell them apart, so you know that they are closely related.

   Sometimes things can get a little tricky. You may come across two groups that look and act a lot alike, but actually aren't related very closely at all. Think of sharks and dolphins. In a lot of ways, they look and act in very similar ways — they both have fins and streamlined bodies to swim in the ocean, and they're both fish-hunting carnivores — but sharks are fish while dolphins are mammals, so you have to be careful when relying on superficial appearances. This is the problem of homologous structures versus analogous structures, which Chapter 10 discusses in more detail, so I won't clog up space in this chapter by explaining it all again.

2. When the obvious characteristics don't give you a clear answer, then you can go on to features that are harder to test, such as biochemical similarities or something complicated like that.

3. The final test of relatedness is the DNA. The more similar the DNA, the more close the relationship. It can be pretty expensive and time consuming to do DNA tests, so biologists try to look for more obvious stuff first.

It's hard to remember all of the levels of classification in order, so sometimes people make up weird sentences using the first letter of each level: K, P, C, O, F, G, and S. We've heard lots of sentences that do this (some of them too dirty to print here). My favorite G-rated version is, "**K**ings **p**lay **c**hess **o**n **f**ine-**g**rain **s**and." We don't know why, but that one has really stuck in our head.

Table 11-1	The Seven Levels of Classification with Two Examples	
Levels of Classification	**for Humans**	**for Wolves**
Kingdom	Animalia	Animalia
Phylum	Chordata	Chordata
Class	Mammalia	Mammalia

Levels of Classification	for Humans	for Wolves
Order	Primates	Carnivora
Family	Hominidae	Canidae
Genus	Homo	Canis
Species	Homo sapiens	Canis lupus

Before moving on to the descriptions of the different categories, try this sample question.

Taxonomists try to classify organisms according to features that are easily detectable, but which of the following is the ultimate basis for classification?

(A) genetic relatedness

(B) anatomical similarity

(C) biochemical similarity

(D) habitat similarity

(E) none of the above

Habitat similarity has nothing directly to do with taxonomy because all sorts of different organisms can live in the same habitat, so (D) is definitely wrong.

Make sure you read the question carefully. Anatomy and biochemical makeup are fairly easy to determine, so they are what taxonomists tend to look at first, but they are not the ultimate basis for classification, which is what the question is looking for; so (B) and (C) are also wrong.

Ultimately, the basis for taxonomic classification is genetic relatedness, so (A) is the correct answer.

Starting Small: Monera

This kingdom contains all of the prokaryotic cells. See Chapter 3 for the details on what makes a cell prokaryotic. Bacteria are microscopic, single-celled organisms that are usually associated with food poisoning and other diseases, though really only a small percentage of all bacteria cause disease. This kingdom is by far the most abundant and is very diverse, so you can find bacteria living in all sorts of different habitats and eating every conceivable kind of food (including toxic molecules from volcanic vents). Since they're so small, we don't notice the major ways that bacteria help to sustain all ecosystems (see Chapter 12), but without them, many of our nutrient cycles would soon grind to a halt.

Since there are so many different kinds of bacteria, it's kind of hard to fit them into any neat and tidy classification, so we'll just give you the four groups of bacteria that may show up on the SAT II. Microbiologists divide bacteria into the following four different groups according to the kind of cell wall they have:

✔ **Gram positive bacteria:** Microbiologists have a special dye called a *Gram stain* that they use to make bacteria easier to see under a microscope, and Gram positive bacteria have the kind of cell walls that the Gram stain sticks to. This phylum includes bacteria that cause diseases, such as salmonella and E. coli.

- **Gram negative bacteria:** Bacteria that have cell walls that the Gram stain has no effect on are called *Gram negative* bacteria. While this phylum also contains bacteria that cause diseases, such as salmonella and E. coli, like the Gram positive bacteria, the Gram negative phylum also includes some of the most ecologically important bacteria, the cyanobacteria. Cyanobacteria includes most of the bacteria species that do photosynthesis, which produces most of the world's oxygen. Also, the nitrogen-fixing bacteria are in the cyanobacteria group. See Chapter 12 to find out about the importance of photosynthesis and nitrogen fixation in nutrient cycles.

- **Bacteria with no cell walls:** The third phylum in the kingdom Monera contains bacteria that have no cell walls at all. You aren't likely to see any questions on these, so we won't bother saying any more about them.

- **Archaebacteria:** The fourth phylum contains bacteria with cell walls that are totally different from all the others. The Archaebacteria phylum contains some of the toughest organisms on the planet, which are called "extremophiles." This name may sound like something out of the X-Games, but these bacteria can manage tricks that Tony Hawk and Dave Mirra could never dream of doing. Thermoacidophiles, for example, live their whole lives in highly acidic water that is at or above the boiling point, 220° F (100° C). These bacteria are the only things that can live in the sulfurous, boiling pools of Yellowstone Park and are what give those pools their green, red, and blue colors. Another example is the halophiles that live in extremely salty lakes and ponds, where nothing else can survive, such as the Dead Sea (they don't call it that for nothing). This last phylum is sort of a miscellaneous category and shows how difficult it is to come up with a clear system of classification for bacteria. Table 11-2 provides a summary of the four phyla of bacteria.

Table 11-2	The Four Groups of Bacteria within the Kingdom Monera
Phylum	**Example**
Gram positive	Streptococcus (strep throat)
Gram negative	Cyanobacteria
No cell walls	Mycoplasm
Archaebacteria	Thermoacidophiles, halophiles

Here are some sample questions on the kingdom Monera.

Which of the following processes are accomplished by bacteria species in the cyanobacteria group?

(A) photosynthesis

(B) O_2 production

(C) nitrogen fixation

(D) all of the above

(E) none of the above

Cyanobacteria are the most ecologically important group of bacteria because without them many of the world's nutrient cycles would come to a halt. Some bacteria in the cyanobacteria group do nitrogen fixation while others do photosynthesis. Photosynthesis naturally produces O_2, so those two answers go together. The correct answer, then, is (D) all of the above.

As you may have noticed, "all of the above" and "none of the above" answer choices are rarely correct answers, but sometimes they are correct, so don't immediately dismiss them from contention.

Which of the following bacteria is most likely to belong in the Archaebacteria group?

(A) a species that causes food poisoning in meats

(B) a species that causes diseases in tainted drinking water

(C) a species that lives in the mud in a deciduous forest

(D) a species that lives near volcanic vents at the bottom of the ocean

(E) a species that lives in the stomachs of cows

Archaebacteria are famous for containing species that live in really extreme environments, such as high temperatures, high acidity, or high salt concentration.

Food and water that we would consume are not normally extremely hot, acidic, or salty, so (A) and (B) can be crossed out. Deciduous forests are pretty mild, so (C) can be crossed out, too. A cow's stomach may seem like a pretty inhospitable place to us, but for most bacteria it's warm and cozy, so (E) is also wrong. The correct answer is (D) because that is the most extreme environment on the list. The water coming out of those vents is very, very hot and may contain some highly acidic molecules.

Which of the following kingdoms includes only prokaryotes?

(A) Animalia

(B) Plantae

(C) Monera

(D) Protista

(E) Fungi

For this question, you also need to know what a prokaryote is. Most prokaryotes are bacteria. The kingdom Monera includes all of the bacteria, and that accounts for all prokaryotes, so the correct answer is (C). All of the other kingdoms contain only eukaryotes. (See Chapter 3 for more about prokaryotes and eukaryotes.)

Getting More Complex: Protists

The protist kingdom, like bacteria, is sort of hard to classify because it's so diverse. First of all, before we even get to the phyla, protists are broken down into three main groups: protozoans, algae, and slime molds. These three groups are thought to be distantly related to three other kingdoms: Animals, Plants, and Fungi (see Figure 11-1).

Acting like animals: Protozoans

Protozoans are unicellular protists that feed on bacteria cells and on other protists. They swim around and survive as heterotrophic hunters, sort of like regular animals. In fact, *Protozoan* means "early animal."

The following bullets list the three most important phyla of protozoans that may show up on the SAT II:

- **Apicomplexa:** This phylum of protozoans contains some famous unicellular parasites, including the one that causes malaria. Protozoans in this phylum live part of their lives inside animal cells — in red blood cells in the case of malaria. Then they produce spores that are picked up by another host, like a mosquito, and transferred to another animal. Humans have been battling this phylum for thousands of years, and modern medicine is finally starting to give us a real advantage.

- **Ciliophora:** This phylum contains protozoans that are fast swimmers, such as paramecium. They use little hairlike structures called cilia to swim around in fresh water ponds and rivers. See Chapter 3 for more detail on cilia.

- **Rhizopoda:** The Rhizopoda phylum contains amoeba, which are protozoans that stretch out part of their cell membranes in order to grab onto stuff (see Figure 11-2). The stretched out part is called a *pseudopod,* which means "fake foot." If the pseudopod grabs onto another cell, the amoeba will consume it using phagocytosis (see Chapter 3 for a description of endocytosis, which is just like phagocytosis). If the pseudopod grabs onto something big and solid, the amoeba can use the pseudopod to pull itself along.

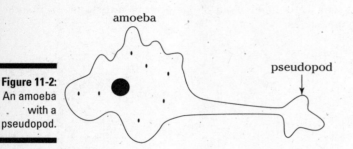

Figure 11-2:
An amoeba with a pseudopod.

Acting like plants: Algae

All algae are protists that perform photosynthesis. Some of them are big, multicellular organisms that seem a lot like regular plants, while others are unicellular swimmers in oceans, lakes, and rivers. Table 11-3 provides a summary of all of the protists in this section.

Following we list the phyla that may show up on the test:

- **Chlorophyta:** This phylum includes algae that have chloroplasts that are very similar to those of plants. In fact, the whole plant kingdom just may be a descendant of very ancient chlorophyta. These algae are found just about everywhere there's water (and warm enough temperatures). The green, slimy stuff in stagnant ponds, and the long, stringy stuff in lakes and rivers are all part of the chlorophyta phylum.

- **Dinoflagellates:** These algae are unicellular and only live in the oceans. Dinoflagellates produce a large amount of the world's oxygen, and are the basis for most ocean food chains. *Plankton* is a general term for the large groups of unicellular organisms that live near the surface of the ocean, and this plankton consists mostly of dinoflagellates. Small animals like shrimp feed on plankton, as do the largest animals ever, the baleen whales.

- **Euglenophyta:** This phylum is made of unicellular algae that typically live in freshwater ponds and rivers. Most of them have little flagella that they use to swim around (see Chapter 3 for more details on flagella).

✔ **Phaeophyta:** This phylum includes the algae that look the most like plants. All the big seaweed and kelp in the oceans are all brown algae (even though a lot of them are green). This phylum makes up the forests of the oceans and supports some very dense ecosystems with lots of variety of organisms.

Acting like fungi: slime molds

Protists in this category are all decomposers, similar to fungus, and it's thought that the whole fungus kingdom evolved from ancient slime molds. You aren't too likely to find questions about the specific phyla of slime molds, so here are some general facts. Slime molds live in freshwater biomes and mostly just decompose plant material. When their food starts to run out, they produce spores that float away. If any of these spores fall on dead plant material, they grow into regular slime molds again and start decomposing the dead plants.

Table 11-3	The Main Phyla within the Protista Kingdom	
Category	*Characteristics*	*Examples*
Protozoans		
Apicomplexa	Live as parasites	Malaria
Ciliophora	Swim with cilia	Paramecium
Rhizopoda	Move with pseudopods	Amoeba
Algae		
Chlorophyta	Plant-like chloroplasts	Pond scum
Dinoflagellates	Unicellular marine algae	Phyto-plankton
Euglenophyta	Unicellular fresh water algae	Euglena
Phaeophyta	Long marine algae	Seaweed, kelp
Slime Molds	Decomposers	Yuck

Now for some more sample questions.

Questions 1–3 refer to the following:

(A) Protozoans

(B) Algae

(C) Slime molds

(D) all of the above

(E) none of the above

1. The group of protists that all perform photosynthesis.

2. The group of protists that are all decomposers.

3. The group of protists that are all eukaryotes.

TIP

This is that classification question type appearing again. It gives you the answers before the questions. Remember to read the questions first; then read through the answer choices.

For # 1, the correct answer is (B). Algae are the protists that perform photosynthesis. They are the most like plants.

For #2, the correct answer is (C). Slime molds are the slimy, moldy protists that act as decomposers. Some protozoans may act as decomposers as well, but *all* of the species in the slime molds group are decomposers.

For #3, the answer is (D). The only kingdom that does not contain exclusively eukaryotes is Monera. That kingdom includes *all* of the prokaryotes, while the other four kingdoms are all eukaryotes.

Decomposing Full Time With Fungi

All fungi are decomposers. They grow on the surface of the organic material they are going to eat, and they secrete digestive enzymes onto their food. The enzymes break up the organic material so that the fungus can absorb the bits and pieces of nutrients. Most fungi are multi-cellular organisms, such as molds and mushrooms, though some are unicellular, like yeast. The cells in a fungus have cell walls made of *chitin*, which is a little softer than the cellulose in the cell walls of plants. The cells of a multicellular fungus are lined up in chains called *hyphae*, as shown in Figure 11-3. Sometimes the fungus has its hyphae packed really closely together, like in mushrooms; but then sometimes the hyphae are really loose, as in the thin, hairy mold that grows on bread and cheese.

When fungi are going to reproduce, they grow a large structure called a *fruiting body*. Fungi that live out in nature (as opposed to your refrigerator) have most of their hyphae under the soil, and only the fruiting body sticks up into the air. When you see a mushroom, that is the fruiting body of a much larger fungus that runs all through the soil in the area around the mushroom. The fruiting body needs to be up in the air so that when the wind blows, the wind can carry spores away to grow somewhere else.

Figure 11-3:
The hyphae of a multi-cellular fungus such as bread mold.

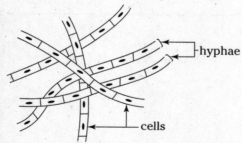

hyphae

cells

EXAMPLE

Here's a quick question on Fungi before you move on to Plants and Animals.

Which of the following is the term for the part of a fungus that contains spores?

(A) spore body

(B) mushroom

(C) hyphae

(D) spore fruit

(E) fruiting body

All of these may sound plausible, but the correct answer is (E), fruiting body.

A mushroom is an example of a fruiting body, but not all fungi produce mushrooms, so (B) was close, but still wrong.

Peeking In On Plants

Now we are finally getting to the more familiar kingdoms. Plants are all organisms that perform photosynthesis and have cell walls made of cellulose. Chapter 13 goes into a lot more detail on the different kinds of plants, but we'll summarize the different kinds of plants for you here.

The two main categories of plants are nonvascular and vascular. Nonvascular plants don't have elaborate transport systems for nutrients, so their structures have to be close to the ground where the food and water are. Examples of nonvascular plants are mosses and hornworts. Vascular plants have nutrient transport systems that allow them to grow away from the ground. You can break vascular plant into two groups, seedless and seed plants. Seedless plants, like ferns and horsetails, shed spores to reproduce because they don't have seeds. Seed plants come in two types, gymnosperms and angiosperms. Gymnosperms have cones, like pine trees; angiosperms are all of the flowering trees and plants with seeds that don't produce cones.

Getting Big and Active: Animals

This, of course, is your kingdom. All animals are multicellular and are heterotrophs (that is, none of them do photosynthesis), and they do not have cell walls. Most animals have more distinct organ systems, such as digestive and circulatory systems, than do those in the other kingdoms, and most animals have some kind of muscles for quick movements or locomotion.

There are a few themes in the descriptions of animals below. First of all, almost all animals have bodies with either radial symmetry or bilateral symmetry. *Bilateral symmetry* is when the right and left sides of the animal are mirror images of each other, as with all mammals, including humans. Along with bilateral symmetry usually comes a distinct head and tail. *Radial symmetry* is when the animal is constructed in a circular pattern, such as a starfish or sea urchin. Animals with radial symmetry may have a top and bottom, but they won't have a distinct front and back or left and right.

Another theme is the complexity of the organ systems. Animals that have more advanced digestive and circulatory systems can support faster metabolisms, so those animals are more active. They usually have a more advanced nervous system as well, so the animals with faster metabolisms are usually smarter than the slow animals. You should also watch out for what kind of skeleton (if any) the animals have. Table 11-4 provides a summary of most of the animal groups covered in this section.

Table 11-4	The Main Groups within the Kingdom Animalia		
Phylum	*Symmetry*	*Distinguishing Characteristics*	*Examples*
Porifera	None	No differentiated tissues	Sponges
Cnidaria	Radial	Stinging cells	Jellyfish, Hydra

(continued)

Table 11-4 *(continued)*

Phylum	Symmetry	Distinguishing Characteristics	Examples
Echinodermata	Radial	Endoskeleton, spines	Starfish, Sea Urchin
Platyhelminthes	Bilateral	Act as parasites	Flatworms
Nematoda	Bilateral	Act as decomposers, parasites	Roundworms
Annelida	Bilateral	Act as decomposers, parasites	Segmented Worms
Mollusca	Bilateral	Most have exoskeleton	Snails, Clams, Octopus
Arthropoda	Bilateral	Exoskeleton, jointed appendages	Insects, Spiders, Crustaceans
Chordata	Bilateral	Spinal chord, endoskeleton, advanced central nervous system	Fish, Reptiles, Birds, Mammals

The simplest animals: Porifera and cnidaria

Porifera is the animal phylum that contains sponges, which are the simplest possible kinds of animals. They are just masses of cells with neither radial nor bilateral symmetry. They don't move at all, and they feed by filtering organic material out of whatever seawater happens to flow through it. These guys just barely qualify as animals, and only because their cell structure and feeding pattern is more similar to animals than it is to any other kingdom.

The cnidaria phylum includes jellyfish, sea anemone, hydras, and coral. These animals have radial symmetry and often have a simple neuromuscular system that can manipulate tentacles. Some cnidarians feed just by filtering food out of the seawater like sponges, but the more famous ones, like the jellyfish, can provide a powerful sting to immobilize unfortunate passing fish. After the fish is paralyzed, the cnidarian pulls the fish into its stomach where the food in digested and absorbed. Cnidarians are pretty slow because they don't have a heart or circulatory system or anything like that.

Spiny sea creatures: Echinodermata

This phylum includes the starfish, sea urchin, and sea cucumber, which all have radial symmetry. They have muscles, but they tend to move very slowly. Starfish, also called sea stars, have many little suction cups on the undersides, and they use those to pull open clamshells so that they can digest the soft clam inside. Sea urchins are very spiny, spherical animals that look a lot like a pincushion. Their spines are usually very sharp and contain some nasty, stinging chemicals.

The worms: Platyhelminthes, nematoda, and annelida

In this phyla, the animals are bilaterally symmetric. The three worm phyla have increasingly complex digestive systems, and they breathe by absorbing oxygen through their skin. They are typically found in aquatic habitats or very moist soil or mud. In the following list, we describe the three worm phyla:

- **Platyhelminthes** are the flatworms. They have a slightly more advanced digestive system than cnidarians, but not by much. Some flatworms are parasites that either feed off of the blood or in the digestive tract of a larger animal. Either way, they're pretty disgusting.

- **Nematoda**, the roundworms, aren't much better. Some types of nematodes live in soil and act as harmless decomposers, but others also act as blood parasites.

- The **annelid** (segmented) worms are ones that you may have actually seen before, because they include earthworms and leeches. The annelids have a more advanced central nervous system with sort of a brain in the front, with smaller nerve bundles called *ganglia* in each segment. Annelids have one-chambered hearts, allowing them to have a somewhat higher metabolism than the others.

Walkers, swimmers, and fliers: Arthropoda

Arthropoda is one of the biggest phyla because it contains all of the insects, spiders, and crustaceans such as shrimp and crab. The animals in this phylum are bilaterally symmetric. The body plan of arthropoda is extremely successful, and they inhabit almost every area on earth. Arthropods generally have an exoskeleton made out of chitin, along with hinged appendages, and their bodies are divided into segments. They have more advanced nervous systems than the annelids, especially when it comes to sensory systems and movement. Lots of insects have advanced eyes, ears, antennae (for detecting chemicals) and sense of touch. The flying abilities of some insects, such as dragonflies, houseflies, and bees are unmatched in the animal kingdom.

Arthropods have two-chambered hearts. Some of the aquatic groups breathe through gills, while the terrestrial types breathe through little air holes along the sides of their bodies. Most arthropods live solitary lives, but some of the insect species, such as bees and ants, live in very tight-knit social groups.

The other shellfish: Mollusca

This phylum includes clams, oysters, snails, squid, and octopus. The clams, oysters, scallops, and other such creatures are called *bivalves,* and they are enclosed by a strong shell made of calcium carbonate. They can open and close the shell using strong muscles. The squid and octopi, on the other hand, have no rigid skeleton at all. Most mollusks have simple nervous systems and sensory apparatus. The squid and octopi, though, have fairly advanced central nervous systems and are capable of some very intelligent tasks such as visual communication and problem solving. Also, they have very advanced vision.

The fastest and smartest of all: Chordata

This phylum includes animals that have a distinct spinal chord as part of their central nervous system. Of course, it contains humans along with most of the other animal species that humans are interested in. That means that we'll break this phylum down into different classes, and even mention some orders. Before that, though, let us mention the three subphyla under Chordata.

The subphyla urochordata and cephalochordata have only a few species in them and are generally ignored by test makers. The vertebrata subphylum, however, is given a whole lot of attention.

All members of the vertebrata subphylum show bilateral symmetry, and have a central nervous system with a spinal cord encased in a spinal column. Vertebrata includes all of the really big animals because this group has a rigid endoskeleton that provides good internal support. In addition, most of the smartest species on the planet are part of the Vertebrata subphylum. The rest of this section will list the characteristics of the important classes of vertebrates, which are summarized in Table 11-5.

Table 11-5	The Classes within the Order Vertebrata	
Class	Distinguishing Characteristics	Examples
Agnatha	Jawless fish	Lampry
Chondrichthyes	Cartilaginous fish	Sharks, rays
Osteichthyes	Bony Fish	Trout, goldfish
Amphibia	Change from aquatic to semi-aquatic	Frogs, salamanders
Reptilia	Scaly skin, leathery eggs	Lizards, snakes, turtles
Aves	Feathers, flight, endotherms	All birds
Mammalia	Hair, mammary glands, live birth, endotherms	Cows, whales, dogs, apes

Fish

All fish live full-time underwater, they breathe using gills, and most have skin with scales. They also have a full digestive system and two-chambered hearts. Some of them are pretty fast, such as the tuna, salmon, and marlin. When fish reproduce, the female releases eggs into the water, and the male fertilizes them by releasing sperm. This is called *external fertilization*, and is also common among many of the invertebrates.

There are three different classes of fish. First is the agnatha class, which is the jawless fishes such as the lamprey. Next is chondrichthyes, which are the fish with skeletons made out of cartilage, though their jaws are made of bone. These include sharks and rays. Third is the osteichthyes class, which are all the regular fish you know of such as goldfish, tuna, and trout. Fish in this last class all have skeletons made of bone.

Amphibia

This class contains frogs, toads, and salamanders. The most distinctive thing about amphibians is their dramatic metamorphosis into adults. Amphibians start off more like fish. They are full-time swimmers with fins, gills, and skeletons made of cartilage. These fully aquatic young amphibians, such as tadpoles, are called *larvae*. As they age, the larvae slowly change into adults with lungs, legs, and skeletons made of bone, and they spend part of their time on land.

Other distinguishing features of amphibians are their three-chambered heart and their thin, bare skin. Amphibian skin is so thin that they can actually breathe by letting oxygen just diffuse across into their bodies. That's how frogs can live so easily underwater even though they don't have gills. Like fish, amphibians use external fertilization to reproduce.

Reptilia

The reptile class includes dinosaurs (an order that's now extinct), along with lizards, snakes, and turtles. Reptiles engage in *internal fertilization*, and lay eggs with a leathery shell. They have skin with tough scales for protection, very advanced digestive systems, and rudimentary four-chambered hearts, which allow them to have pretty fast metabolism compared to most of the animals that have come so far.

All of the animals up until this point, including reptiles, are considered to be *ectotherms*, which is a fancy name for cold-blooded. This means that the temperature of their environment determines their body temperature. If it is cold outside, then they are cold on the inside as well because their metabolism isn't fast enough to generate enough body heat to keep them warm. Reptiles, if they want to warm up, will often go sit in a patch of sun and soak up some rays.

Aves

This is the class of birds. They have advanced digestive systems, lungs, and four-chambered hearts. They have skin with feathers, and most of them can fly. They engage in internal fertilization and lay eggs with hard shells made of calcium carbonate. Birds and mammals are the two classes that contain *endothermic* (or "warm-blooded") animals. This means that their metabolism is high enough to produce lots of body heat so that when it is cold outside, their bodies stay warm.

Mammalia

Mammals have skin with hair or fur, four-chambered hearts, and advanced digestive systems and lungs. They engage in internal fertilization and bear live young. The young are fed using milk from the mammary glands of the mother. There are three sub-classes of mammals.

- ✔ **Monotremes** lay eggs sort of like birds, but they still qualify as mammals because they have mammary glands and hair. The best-known example of a Monotreme is the platypus.

- ✔ The **marsupial** subclass includes koala bears and kangaroos. I don't know why marsupials tend to have names starting with *k*, but for some reason it worked out that way. Marsupials bear live young, but the young are very underdeveloped and they spend the rest of their development in their mother's pouch.

- ✔ The third subclass is the **placental** mammals, which have a more complex uterus (the females do, anyway) that allows the mother to provide nutrients to the offspring internally until they are ready to be born as regular babies. The placental mammal subclass includes most of the animals you are most familiar with, so we'll break it down into a few orders.

  - • The **artiodactyla** order includes the hoofed mammals such as sheep, cows, pigs, deer and giraffe. Most of these are grazing herbivores.

  - • Order **carnivora** includes dogs, cats, bears, and seals. As the name suggests, members of this class tend to be carnivores, though some of them are omnivores that will eat just about anything (like my dog will eat carrots).

  - • **Cetacea** is the order that includes the fully aquatic marine mammals such as whales and dolphin. These animals are usually very social and intelligent, and many of them are able to navigate and communicate using sonar.

  - • **Primates** is the order that includes monkeys, apes, and humans. These are the species with the most complex social behavior and most advanced intelligence. Chimps, gorillas, and orangutans (and even dolphins) have shown themselves to be a lot smarter than people once realized, but humans are still the smartest animals on the planet. Of course, we do some really dumb things, but at least we're smart enough to realize just how dumb we can be. Other animals have no idea.

Okay, now that you've read all about animals, try these sample questions.

Which of the following animal groups possess skeletons?

   I. Porifera

   II. Mollusca

   III. Annelida

   IV Arthropoda

   V. Vertebrata

(A) I only

(B) II and IV only

(C) II, III, and IV only

(D) II, IV, and V only

(E) V only

You can benefit from the process of elimination with questions that contain Roman numeral lists. Once you have determined one of the elements of the list to be incorrect, you can eliminate any answer choice that contains it. When you determine one of the elements to be correct, you can eliminate any answer choices that don't contain it. Sometimes by eliminating answer choices, you won't even have to read through all of the elements in the numbered list.

Remember that a skeleton can be either an endoskeleton (on the inside) or an exoskeleton (on the outside). Porifera are the sponges and annelids are segmented worms, and neither of those has a skeleton at all. They are just soft-bodied animals, so any answer that contains I or III is wrong, which means (A) and (C) can be crossed out.

If you look at your remaining answer choices (B, D, and E), you see that (E) presents V only. A quick glance at the list tells you that this cannot be right. Arthropoda have obvious skeletons, so the answer must include at least IV and V. You can eliminate (E).

You don't even have to consider whether mollusca have skeletons. Both remaining answer choices, (B) and (D), contain II. (B) doesn't include arthropods, so (D) is the correct answer. Mollusks and arthropods have exoskeletons, while vertebrates have endoskeletons.

Which of the following is a distinguishing characteristic of most mammals?

(A) hair

(B) birth of live young

(C) mammary glands

(D) endothermy

(E) all of the above

Once you notice that at least two of the answers are true, then you can jump to the correct answer, which is (E), all of the above.

Which of the following groups of animals shows radial symmetry?

   I. Porifera

   II. Cnidaria

   III. Annelida

   IV. Echinodermata

   V. Vertebrata

(A) I, II, and IV only

(B) II and IV only

(C) I, II, and III only

(D) V only

(E) II and III only

This is a tough one because it involves some straight-up memorization.

Remember that porifera is the sponges, and they don't have any specific symmetry at all, so (A) is definitely wrong. Now you can eliminate both (A) and (C). Take a look at what's left: (B), (D), and (E). Vertebrates (as in humans) definitely have bilateral symmetry, not radial, so V is wrong. You can eliminate (D) from contention.

Since (B) and (E) remain and both of them contain II, you know you don't have to consider cnidaria. It must show radial symmetry. You know you need to choose whether annelida or echinodermata show radial symmetry.

The really tough one is annelida, which consists of the segmented worms. They have a sort of head and tail to them, so they count as having bilateral symmetry, so (E) is wrong. The echinoderms (starfish) have radial symmetry, so (B) is the correct answer.

A certain species of animal is able to keep its body temperature fairly high despite its cold environment. Which of the following groups does this animal most likely belong to?

(A) Aves

(B) Mollusca

(C) Arthropoda

(D) Reptilia

(E) Nematoda

This question requires you to know what characteristic an organism must possess to keep its body temperature warm despite cold weather. Then it requires you to know which organisms possess this characteristic.

If an animal can stay warm despite a cold environment, then it must be endothermic. The only endothermic groups of animals are the birds and mammals. Aves is the class of birds, so (A) is the correct answer.

Living on the Edge: Viruses

Viruses cause lots of diseases such as colds, flu, hepatitis, and AIDS, but viruses don't fit into the normal taxonomy anywhere because biologists aren't sure they even count as being alive. Viruses have DNA and they spread, proliferate, and evolve, so some people consider them to be living. On the other hand, viruses don't actually *do* anything. They don't have a metabolism or any cellular activity of any kind. In fact, they aren't even made of cells! They can't reproduce themselves on their own, and they rely on regular cells to do all the work for them. For these reasons, some biologists consider viruses to be, at most, "life forms" rather than technically living.

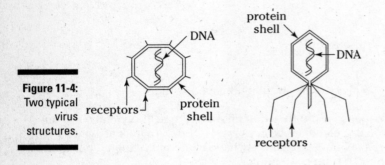

Figure 11-4:
Two typical virus structures.

As shown in Figure 11-4, viruses are just little protein shells with receptors on the outside, and DNA on the inside. When the receptors on the virus attach to just the right kind of receptors on just the right kind of cell, the virus is pulled inside through endocytosis (see Chapter 3 for more on that process). The protein shell opens up and the viral DNA is let loose inside the cell. Another possibility is that the protein shell stays on the outside and the virus injects its DNA into the cell through the cell membrane.

Now cells are amazing little things, but they're also kind of stupid in a lot of ways. Cells don't know the difference between their own DNA and the viral DNA, so they end up using the viral DNA as if it were their own, which ends up being a big mistake. The viral DNA contains instructions on how to build more viruses, so that's exactly what the cell starts doing. The cell uses its own amino acids and nucleotides to build hundreds (or even millions) of new viruses that are all exactly the same as the virus that originally came in. Once the cell is full of new viruses it breaks open and dies, letting loose all those new viruses to go infect other cells. Sometimes during the manufacturing of new viruses, the cell can make little mistakes, leading to slight changes in the new viruses that get made. These slight changes are the source of diversity in the virus population that can lead to the evolution of viruses. This is why there's no flu vaccine doctors can give you that lasts a lifetime. A flu vaccine may work on a particular flu strain one year but not on the strain that comes around the next year. See Chapter 12 on evolution for more on the importance of diversity.

Okay, before finishing this chapter, try this sample question on viruses.

Which of the following is not a characteristic of viruses?

(A) They possess a protein shell.

(B) They cause many diseases.

(C) They possess receptors.

(D) They use glucose as fuel.

(E) They possess genetic material.

Remember that viruses aren't cells, and they don't have any internal activity at all. The only one of the choices that would count as cellular activity is the use of glucose as fuel. To use glucose as fuel, an organism would need to perform some kind of cellular respiration Viruses can't do that. So the correct answer is (D).

Chapter 12

Bringing It All Together: Ecology

his is one of the most important chapters in this whole book. If you plan on taking the E version of the SAT II, then about 23 percent of the test will include something directly from this chapter! Even if you plan on taking just the M version, around 13 percent of your test will be from here, so beating the SAT II means spending time getting familiar with ecology.

The reason this chapter is so important is because this is where we see all of the stuff from the other chapters come together in real-world situations. Other chapters discuss molecules and cells and other things we can't really see, or they run through the basic characteristics of living things separate from the rest of the world. In this chapter, we show you how ecology covers the real lifestyles and interactions of all the different species on earth as well as how ecology may be covered on the SAT II.

This chapter links up a lot with the theory of evolution from Chapter 10 because ecology provides the selection pressures that drive the evolution of populations.

Finding Your Favorite Climate: Biomes

Biomes are the major biological divisions of the earth. Biomes, such as oceans, deserts, and savannas, are characterized by the area's climate, plus the particular organisms that live there. The living organisms make up the *biotic* components of the biome while everything else makes up the *abiotic* components. The most important abiotic aspects of a biome are its amount of rainfall and its amount of temperature variation. More rain and more stable temperatures means more organisms can survive. It turns out that these two abiotic components are usually linked because the wetter a biome is, the less its temperature changes from day to night or from summer to winter. That's why so many people want to move to southern California and Florida — the weather is never too hot and never too cold. The number of organisms that can survive in a biome is called that biome's "carrying capacity" (see "Carrying capacity: Ecosystems at maximum occupancy" later in this chapter). This section contains some quick facts about the different biomes, including the size of their carrying capacities.

Drying out in the desert

Deserts are areas that get less than about ten inches of rain per year. Although most of the deserts we know of are hot (like the Sahara), some are actually cold (like parts of Antarctica), so the real distinguishing characteristic of deserts is their extreme dryness.

Temperatures in deserts change a lot from day to night and from summer to winter. The organisms that live in a desert need to be able to survive these drastic temperature swings along with dry conditions, so the density and diversity of species are very low. In other words, the desert has a low *carrying capacity*. One of the few plants that can survive the hot deserts are cacti, which can store water after a rainstorm in order to have a nice supply during the frequent droughts. Animals in the desert include reptiles like lizards and snakes, along with some arachnids like spiders and scorpions. That makes the desert seem pretty nasty, but I grew up in a desert, and it's really a lot nicer than it sounds, I swear! Well . . . as long as you have air-conditioning and a lot of water, anyway.

Getting drenched in the tropical rainforest

A *tropical rainforest* is the exact opposite of a desert. Tropical rainforests get lots of rain and the temperatures are very steady and mild all year round. These are perfect conditions for most terrestrial organisms, so the tropical rainforest has by far the greatest density and diversity of life. This means that the tropical rain forest has the greatest carrying capacity of all terrestrial biomes. The best known tropical rain forests are in South America and southeast Asia, and they contain densely packed trees, plants and vines that are home to millions of insect species, along with lots of rodents, reptiles, monkeys, birds, and just about every other kind of terrestrial animal there is. Personally, I like the desert more than the rain forest because the desert's got fewer bugs.

Enjoying the fall colors of the temperate deciduous forest

The *temperate deciduous forest* is sort of average, with an average carrying capacity. It gets more rain than the desert, but less than the tropical rain forest. Its temperature changes quite a bit from season to season, but not as dramatically as the desert. Temperate biomes have a medium density and diversity of species, with big trees that lose their leaves in the winter (that's what *deciduous* means), and lots of mammals like rodents, deer, and many types of song birds. You find this biome in the eastern U.S. and Europe. The changing of the leaves in autumn can really be a wonderful sight, but the winters can be pretty harsh.

Seeing the taiga for the trees

A *taiga* is another forest biome, but it has mostly evergreen trees like pine and spruce, along with animals like squirrels, deer, moose, wolves, bears, and birds. The taiga's carrying capacity is a little lower than the temperate deciduous forest because the taiga is a little colder and it usually gets less rain. Good examples are the forests of northwestern North America and northern Europe and Asia.

Outrunning lions in the savanna

The *savanna* biome is mostly grasslands with a few trees here and there. It has one good rainy season with long periods of drought every year, so its carrying capacity is below average. Because of all the grass, this biome supports lots of grazing mammals such as antelope, zebra, and bison, along with the famous feline predators such as lions and cheetahs. The best known savanna is in central Africa, but the central prairies of the U.S. count as well.

Freezing fields of the tundra

The main characteristic of the *tundra* is that the ground stays permanently frozen. The extreme tundras like those near the north and south poles are too cold for almost anything to live there, so the carrying capacity is really low. The less extreme tundras can support lots of mosses and grasses, along with mammals such as caribou and bears. The tundra can actually be pretty nice in the summer, but winter turns the place into a deep freeze.

Splashing around in freshwater

The *freshwater* biome includes things like rivers, lakes, and ponds. These areas can be affected by temperature swings, the amount of available O_2, and the speed of water flowing through. All of these are affected by the larger climate area the freshwater biome is in, which also affects the biotic components. For example, lakes and rivers near the tropics can have really high carrying capacities, while those in the tundra will have very low carrying capacities. Algae, fish, amphibians, and insects are found in freshwater biomes. Lakes and rivers are a nice place to visit, but I don't think I'd live there. I just wouldn't fit in with the locals.

Bearing the biomes: Biosphere 2

In the late 1980s, Texas oil tycoon Edward Bass provided the funding for building Biosphere 2, an airtight imitation of the earth's environment, just outside of Tucson, Arizona. The huge structure consisted of a lot of steel and glass and contained five biomes. It housed its own ocean, rain forest, and desert, and had a living environment for humans, including areas where they could grow crops to sustain themselves and apartments to provide them with shelter. The next step was to populate the space to see just what would happen if you put human beings in a closed system.

In September of 1991, four men and four women from seven countries and various background committed to spending the next two years of their lives living and working in this mini-Earth environment. Despite troubles raising food in the agricultural environment, the crew stuck out their two-year commitment to self-sufficiency and emerged without killing each other.

The second installment didn't fare so well. In 1994, seven others entered the oversize terrarium to live off the land.

They didn't even make it a year, though. Because of some physical maladies and some social issues, the second crew called it quits. The carrying capacity of the Biosphere 2 biome must have been less than seven! The failed experiment drew a lot of negative attention, and the public generally scorned the scientific value of the experiment. Since 1994 nobody has actually lived in Biosphere 2, and there are no plans to allow crews to inhabit Biosphere 2 again in the future.

So, you won't be able to live in this habitat, but you can visit it. You can check out an ocean, a rain forest, a desert, a marsh, and a savannah all in one day. And you can see where scientists continue to collect data about climate changes and the effects of global warning from the ecological systems that still exist within the giant glass greenhouse. Heck! Maybe after studying for the ecology questions on the SAT II Biology E/M exam, they'll let you work as a tour guide and you can introduce the public to the wonderful world of biomes.

Exploring the open oceans

The *oceans* cover about 70 percent of the earth's surface, so this is by far the biggest biome. The temperature swings aren't nearly as big in the oceans as they are on land, and there's plenty of water to go around (duh, it's the ocean) so the carrying capacity of the oceans is really huge. The density and diversity of organisms isn't quite as high as in the tropical rain forest, but the total number of organisms in the oceans is way bigger than all the terrestrial biomes put together.

The ocean biome is divided into the following different regions, as shown in Figure 12-1:

✔ *Intertidal zone:* The intertidal zone is the beach. This area is covered by water during high tide and is exposed during low tide. Lots of seaweed, crabs, sea urchins, and starfish tend to live here.

✔ *Neritic zone:* Notice in Figure 12-1 how the continental shelf extends out pretty far before dropping off to the really deep ocean — that part after the beach but before the drop-off is called the neritic zone. The diversity and density of species here is pretty high, with lots of fish, seaweed, and crustaceans.

✔ *Pelagic zone:* The pelagic zone is out in the really deep water and is divided into two layers:

• *Photic zone:* The photic layer is where sunlight penetrates to promote photosynthesis. Lots of phytoplankton live here, so that's also where plankton-feeders like blue whales hang out.

• *Aphotic zone:* The aphotic zone is completely dark because sunlight does not penetrate, so there's no photosynthesis. Down there live a lot of decomposers that eat the bits and pieces of dead stuff that sink down to the bottom, and there's also some freakish looking predators that feed on the decomposers. I definitely don't want to hang out there.

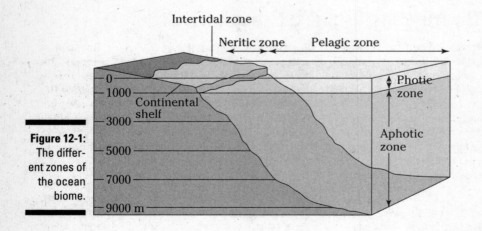

Figure 12-1: The different zones of the ocean biome.

Now for some sample biome questions.

Which of the following biomes has the lowest carrying capacity?

(A) temperate deciduous forest

(B) tropical rain forest

(C) savanna

(D) taiga

(E) desert

The desert is the driest biome among the choices, plus it has the largest temperature swings, so it definitely has the lowest carrying capacity, so (E) is the correct answer. Some deserts have a decent number of cacti and reptiles, but some, like the Sahara, are almost nothing but sand dunes.

Which part of the ocean biome is likely to have the most decomposers?

(A) intertidal zone

(B) aphotic zone

(C) photic zone

(D) neritic zone

(E) continental shelf

When something dies in the ocean, it usually sinks to the bottom. Decomposers feed on dead things, so they probably hang out near the bottom. *Aphotic* means "no light," so the aphotic zone is where light does not penetrate, which is in the deepest part of the ocean. That means (B), the aphotic zone, is the correct answer.

Spinning the Web of Life: Trophic Levels and Nutrient Cycles

No species can live completely on its own, because eventually it will run out of nutrients or energy. Imagine if suddenly humans were the only species on earth — no other plants or animals or anything. We've got a lot of food stored up right now, but it wouldn't take long for that to run out, and if there's no more plants or animals to harvest, then we'd soon die of starvation. Another problem is that there's a limited supply of oxygen in the atmosphere, and if there are no plants or bacteria to replenish it through photosynthesis, then not only would we starve, but we'd also suffocate. The same goes for every other species too, because all the different life forms on earth cooperate to recycle all of the nutrients, and if somebody stops doing their job, we all suffer. An ecosystem is the name given to all of the organisms in an area that are supporting each other by helping to keep the nutrient cycles going. Sometimes this cooperative relationship is called "the great web of life." This section explains how all the organisms in an ecosystem are connected in that great web.

Finding food and energy: Trophic levels

All organisms on earth are made mostly from carbon, hydrogen, nitrogen, and oxygen (for more details read Chapter 6), so these are the nutrient cycles that are most important. To get a sense of how these nutrients are cycled through an ecosystem, you first need to understand the food chain. The food chain starts with little nutrient molecules like carbon dioxide (CO_2), water (H_2O), nitrogen (N_2), and oxygen (O_2) all floating around in the environment. These nutrient molecules get picked up and used to make the organic molecules that make up organisms. This section follows those organic molecules as they get passed along the food chain. Each stage in the food chain is called a *trophic level* because *trophic* refers to eating. See Figure 12-2 for a picture of the trophic levels.

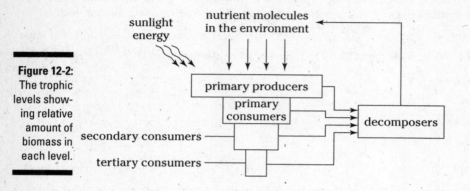

Figure 12-2:
The trophic levels showing relative amount of biomass in each level.

Primary producers

The first organisms to use those small nutrient molecules are the ones that do photosynthesis, such as plants, algae, and some bacteria. They absorb CO_2 and H_2O from the environment and use them to produce organic molecules, especially glucose. Therefore, these organisms are called *primary producers*. Building organic molecules takes a lot of energy, and primary producers get theirs from sunlight (see Chapter 6 for more on photosynthesis). The sunlight energy is trapped inside the organic molecules, and the primary producers use those molecules to build their cells and to run their life processes (called *metabolism*). Since there are a lot of basic nutrient molecules in the environment and a lot of sunlight shining down to provide energy, there are a lot of primary producers. They are by far the largest trophic level in the food chain.

Primary consumers

As you know, if there's plants around, then there's probably going to be some herbivores eating the plants. Herbivores are called *primary consumers* because they consume the organic molecules that the primary producers have already produced. Instead of making their own molecules, the primary consumers just steal them from the producers and use those molecules to construct their own tissues and run their own metabolism. Unfortunately for the primary consumers, though, a lot of the energy that was originally trapped in the organic molecules has already been used to run the metabolism of the primary producers. Plus, the primary consumers can't eat *all* of the producers, so a lot of the nutrients are lost back into the environment before the consumers can get at them. Because of all this energy and nutrient loss, there aren't as many consumers around as producers. In fact, if you gathered up all the primary consumers and weighed them, they would weigh only about 10 percent of the total weight of all the primary producers.

Secondary consumers

Now things get a little more exciting (I'll bet you thought that wasn't possible) because the next step in the food chain is the carnivores who eat the herbivores. Carnivores are called *secondary consumers* because they eat the primary consumers in order to steal the organic molecules that the primary consumers stole from the primary producers. Thanks to the secondary consumers, we have all those gory nature documentaries showing predators with big teeth and claws ripping through their poor, defenseless prey. Just like before, though, a lot of energy and nutrients get lost before the secondary consumers can get a hold of primary consumers, so an ecosystem only supports about one tenth the number of secondary consumers as primary consumers. If you think about it, this makes sense, because we can think of a huge number of herbivores — insects, fish, rodents, hoofed mammals, birds, and so on — but not quite as many carnivores. There are always a lot more prey species than predator species.

Tertiary consumers

This gets even more dramatic when we go to the next level — the tertiary consumers. These are carnivores that eat other carnivores, like sharks that feed on seals that feed on fish that feed on seaweed. Can you think of any other examples? It's not so easy, is it? So much of the energy and nutrients has been lost by the time we get to this level that not many species can be supported anymore. Maybe you can think of a few tertiary consumers, and if you think really hard, you may even be able to come up with an example of a carnivore that eats tertiary consumers. These *quaternary consumers* are really, really rare and usually extremely vicious. If a bigger, meaner shark could eat our seal-eating tertiary consumer, then it would be a quaternary consumer.

Omnivores

Most consumers eat more than one thing, and sometimes they eat things from more than one level. For example, certain birds will eat both seeds and insects, making them an herbivore (primary consumer) and a carnivore (secondary consumer) at the same time. Animals like this are called *omnivores* because *omni* means "all," and omnivores will eat just about anything.

Decomposers

Standing outside of the normal trophic levels are the decomposers like fungus and some kinds of bacteria. The decomposers get their organic molecules from dead organisms and organic wastes (poop). It doesn't matter what it is or how it died, the decomposers will break it down. The organisms in this group may be pretty disgusting, but they're also super important. Their job is to take dead organic material and return the nutrients back into the environment. If it weren't for the decomposers, we'd all be neck deep in dead animals.

Okay, ready for some sample questions about the trophic levels? Well, let's do it anyway.

Giraffes have long necks because they eat leaves out of tall trees. They also eat grasses. What trophic level does the giraffe occupy?

(A) primary producer

(B) primary consumer

(C) secondary consumer

(D) decomposer

(E) omnivore

The giraffe is eating, which means it must be some kind of consumer, so (A) can be crossed out. Decomposers feed on dead things, and the leaves in the question are right off the trees, so (D) is wrong also. Secondary consumers are carnivores that eat primary consumers, while omnivores eat both plants and animals, and the question doesn't say anything about the giraffe hunting down prey, so both (C) and (E) are gone. That means the correct answer is (B). The tree with its leaves is a primary producer, so the giraffe feeding on it must be a primary consumer.

How are energy and nutrients lost before they move from one trophic level to the next?

- (A) cellular respiration
- (B) photosynthesis
- (C) decomposition
- (D) parasitism
- (E) none of the above

Photosynthesis brings energy and nutrients *into* the trophic levels, so (B) can't be right. Decomposers and parasites are consumers that feed on all the trophic levels, so they can't be solely responsible. Cellular respiration is the use of organic molecules as fuel, which uses energy and returns nutrients to the environment, causing them to be lost before the next trophic level can get ahold of them. That means (A) is the correct answer.

A little pollution goes a long way: Biological magnification

One thing they may ask you about on the SAT II is *biological magnification,* which has to do with the way toxic molecules can become more concentrated (and more dangerous) the higher up the food chain you go.

Suppose a forest area is contaminated with a small amount of some toxic pollutant like arsenic. A little bit of arsenic will soak into each plant, but not really enough to hurt the plants. This harmless amount is magnified when the herbivores spend years eating as many plants as they can, not realizing that there's a little bit of arsenic in each mouthful. Eventually, the herbivores can build up a truly dangerous amount of arsenic in their bodies. Then, if a carnivore eats just one of those arsenic-laden herbivores every day, the carnivore could die from arsenic poisoning — all from just a little bit of arsenic getting into each plant. Because of biological magnification, the Atlantic swordfish, which often acts as tertiary consumers, now contain so much mercury that they've been banned from fish markets in the United States. Another example is the damage done to bald eagles by the pesticide DDT.

Reusing and recycling: Nutrient cycles

Here's the basic pattern for all of the nutrient cycles: Small nutrient molecules like CO_2, H_2O, and N_2 are taken in from the environment by primary producers and are used to make organic molecules. Those organic molecules are then passed along through the trophic levels. At each level, a lot of the organic molecules are broken down in cellular respiration, releasing the nutrient molecules back into the environment. Only about 10 percent of the energy and organic molecules get passed on along to each trophic level. When a plant or animal dies, whatever organic molecules are left in its tissues are broken down by decomposers and returned to the environment so that the whole process can start over again. The cycle for each nutrient follows this same basic pattern (see Figure 12-2), but there are also some variations that you may need to know for the SAT II.

Carbon cycle

This is the simplest of the nutrient cycles. Carbon starts off as CO_2 in the environment. It is absorbed by primary producers and used in photosynthesis to make organic molecules. (See Chapter 6 for more on photosynthesis.) Consumers eat the organic molecules and break some of them down in a process called cellular respiration. (See Chapter 6 again for more on cellular respiration.) During cellular respiration, the consumers release the carbon back into the environment as CO_2, and the process repeats. Any carbon left over in dead organisms or wastes are broken down to CO_2 by decomposers. See Figure 12-3 for a picture of the carbon cycle. Human activity is speeding up part of the carbon cycle by returning too much CO_2 into the environment through the burning of fossil fuels. The other parts of the cycle are staying the same, which is causing the buildup of CO_2 in the atmosphere which contributes to global warming. Now, we're not the only species that can throw off the nutrient cycles, but we sure are good at it.

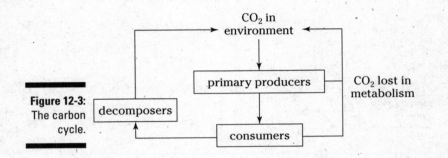

Figure 12-3: The carbon cycle.

Water and oxygen cycles

Water is also absorbed by primary producers during photosynthesis, and they split the H_2O into hydrogen and oxygen. The hydrogen atoms are used to make organic molecules while the oxygen is released as O_2. Consumers eat the organic molecules and breathe in the O_2 for cellular respiration, and then they release the hydrogen and oxygen back into the environment as H_2O. You can see this water in your own breath when you fog up a mirror by breathing on it up close. See Figure 12-4 for a picture of the water and oxygen cycles.

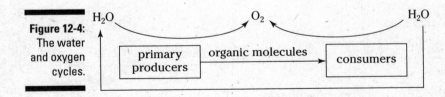

Figure 12-4: The water and oxygen cycles.

Another part of the water cycle involves the weather. Water evaporates out of the oceans, lakes and rivers, and it evaporates out of plants (called *transpiration*). Evaporated water in the atmosphere forms clouds which then rain the water back down onto the earth.

Nitrogen cycle

The nitrogen cycle is definitely the most complicated of the nutrient cycles. In fact, it's sort of a tangled mess. That must be why the SAT II so often includes questions about it. Most of the nitrogen in the environment is trapped as N_2 gas in the atmosphere. In fact, about 80% of the air we breathe is N_2 gas. The problem is that very few organisms are able to use N_2 as a source of nitrogen for building organic molecules like amino acids and nucleotides (see Chapter 5). Only a certain kind of bacteria is able to absorb N_2 and convert it into something usable. This special bacteria converts the N_2 into NO_3, a process called *nitrogen fixation,* and NO_3 can be used by primary producers to make organic molecules. Without those nitrogen-fixing bacteria, nobody else would ever be able to get any nitrogen and we'd all die. Luckily, those bacteria can be found in the soil of most ecosystems, as well as in the roots of some kinds of plants. Some species of bean plants called "legumes" have little nodules on their roots where the nitrogen-fixing bacteria can live. The bacteria receive food and protection from the plants, while the plants receive usable nitrogen from the bacteria (a situation called "mutualistic symbiosis").

Once the nitrogen has been incorporated into the organic molecules of the plants, it travels through the trophic levels like normal. Dead organisms are broken down by the decomposers who release the nitrogen as ammonia, NH_3. The NH_3 can then go one of two ways. It can either be re-absorbed by primary producers to make more organic molecules, or it can be converted back into N_2 by a different kind of bacteria and returned to the atmosphere to start the whole process over again. See Figure 12-5 for a picture of the complicated nitrogen cycle.

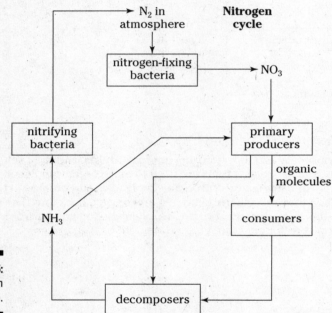

Figure 12-5:
The nitrogen
cycle.

Here's some examples of nutrient cycle questions.

Which of the following nutrients does not pass through photosynthesis as part of its cycle through an ecosystem?

(A) water (H_2O)

(B) carbon

(C) oxygen

(D) nitrogen

(E) none of the above

Photosynthesis is the process of making glucose, which is $C_6H_{12}O_6$. The only element not in the glucose molecule is nitrogen, so the answer is (D). Nitrogen is converted from N_2 to NO_3 in nitrogen fixation, and then plants take the NO_3 to help build amino acids and nucleotides. Amino acids and nucleotides are not constructed during photosynthesis.

Which of the following best characterizes the main role of primary producers in the nutrient cycles?

(A) Take dead organic material and break it down into basic nutrients

(B) provide energy and nutrients to secondary consumers

(C) convert N_2 into NO_3

(D) take basic nutrients out of the environment and use them to make organic molecules

(E) take in organic molecules made by other organisms

Primary producers use basic nutrients to produce organic molecules, so the correct answer is (D). Dead organic material is broken down (decomposed) by decomposers, so (A) is wrong. Secondary consumers are carnivores, so they don't get their nutrients from plants. If (B) had said that primary producers provide energy and nutrients to *primary* consumers (herbivores), then it would have been worthy of consideration. The nitrogen fixation in (C) is done by specialized bacteria, not by primary producers, and only consumers take in (eat) whole organic molecules from other organisms.

Surviving as a Team: Populations

A population is a group of individuals from the same species that are living in the same general area and are able to interbreed. Notice that a population is a subgroup within a species. You can have a single species that is separated into two groups, and if the two groups don't have contact with each other, then they can't mate, and so they are different populations. A big part of ecology is tracking populations, especially population size and population growth. As you may expect, the growth rate of a population is determined by the total number born each year minus the total number that die each year. Birth rates are based on how many individuals are able to find mates and how many offspring each pairing produces. Some species, like most insects and fish, produce a lot of offspring from each mating, while other species, like elephants and humans, produce only one or two. Death rates, on the other hand, are affected by old age, lack of nutrients, diseases, predators, and other such dangers.

Pushing the boundaries: Carrying capacity of populations

Every ecosystem has a limited amount of resources such as water, food, and territory — enough to supply a population of a certain size. The maximum sustainable size of a population is called the "carrying capacity" (that term gets used a lot in ecology). The carrying capacity is the number of individuals in that population that the ecosystem can support. If the population is below the carrying capacity, then they have room to reproduce more and increase their numbers. If the population is above the carrying capacity, then there are not enough resources to go around, and some of the individuals will die off, bringing the population size back down.

Getting out of control: Exponential growth

When a species is really far below its carrying capacity, then there are plenty of resources to go around and just about all of the offspring of every generation can survive to produce yet more offspring. Suppose we introduce a mating pair of mice into an area with plenty of food and water and almost no predators or competitors. This would be a great situation for the mice because the carrying capacity of that ecosystem would be really high. The first generation would produce, say, ten offspring, all of which would survive just fine. In the next generation, those 10 offspring could produce 50 more offspring of their own. In the generation after that, those 50 could produce 250 more, then those 250 could produce 1,250, and then those 1,250 could produce 6,250. You can see that if all of the offspring of every generation survive, the population can start to grow really, really fast. If this keeps up, then after just ten generations, the population size would be over 19.5 million! This unchecked population growth is called *exponential growth,* and you can see a graph showing exponential growth in Figure 12-6. The only thing that can stop exponential population growth is when the population finally hits its carrying capacity.

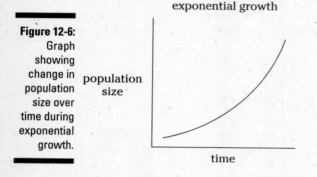

Figure 12-6:
Graph showing change in population size over time during exponential growth.

Caring for just a few: K-selected species

Some species tend to stay as near their carrying capacity as they can. They produce only a few offspring each year — just enough to replace those that have died. These kinds of species are called *K-selected species* because K is the symbol used by ecologists to represent carrying capacity. Yes, the ecologists know that it isn't spelled "karrying kapacity," but they use K anyway. See Figure 12-7 for a graph showing the population size of a K-selected species over time. Since K-selected species produce so few offspring, they tend to spend a lot of time caring for their young to make sure they survive. Most of the big mammals follow this pattern, such as whales, elephants, bears, and humans.

Maximizing offspring: R-selected species

Other species try to maximize their rates of reproduction in order to go way over their carrying capacity. They then let their offspring fend for themselves in the furious competition for resources. These species are called *r-selected species* because r is the symbol used for population growth rate. Just remember that the population sizes of r-selected species rise really rapidly (and they also fall really rapidly). See Figure 12-7 for a graph showing the population size of an r-selected species over time. Notice that each generation has a huge population boom and then a huge population crash after most of the resources are gone. Even so, if you average it all out over the years, the population size over time still stays right around the carrying capacity. The parents are no help to the offspring of an r-selected species, so only the toughest (and luckiest) individuals survive long enough to reproduce and start the whole boom and bust cycle over again. Most insects are r-selected species, as are many kinds of fish and amphibians, with some of them laying thousands of eggs at a time. Also, most bacteria are r-selected even though they use asexual reproduction. Bacteria will just grow and grow until they run out of resources, then most of them will die. Bacteria are pretty short-sighted little buggers.

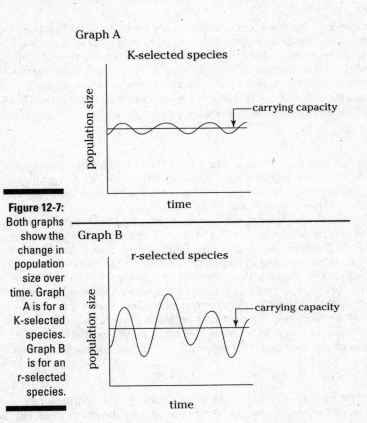

Figure 12-7: Both graphs show the change in population size over time. Graph A is for a K-selected species. Graph B is for an r-selected species.

Dealing With the Neighbors: Population Interactions

Whenever two populations of different species are living near each other in the same ecosystem, there's a good chance they will interact in some way. There are a bunch of different ways that populations can interact, and in this section you will learn the main ones that they may ask about on the SAT II.

Finding a place to call home: Competition for niches

Since there's usually a limited amount of resources in an ecosystem, organisms are always competing with each other for things like nutrients, energy, and territory. As stated in Darwin's theory of evolution (see Chapter 10), competition for resources is what drives evolution, so most of an organism's characteristics and behaviors have evolved in order to improve its ability to compete and survive in the ecosystem. This means that over the generations, each species in the ecosystem will settle into its own way of carving out a living. Another way of saying this is that each species establishes its own *niche* in the ecosystem. A niche includes the species' diet, territory, behaviors, roles in the nutrient cycles, and anything else that helps define the species' lifestyle.

Niche components

There are two components to every niche: the abiotic components and the biotic components. *Abiotic* means nonliving, so this includes things like the physical terrain of the area, the yearly amount of rainfall, and the average daily temperature. *Biotic* means living, so this part of the niche includes all of the other species in the community with which it interacts — all the predators, prey, parasites, competitors, and so on that the species is likely to face during its life. While studying for the SAT II, your niche may be little more than your own bedroom, your test-prep book, and the PB&J your mom made for you.

Interspecific competition

Whenever the niche of two or more species overlaps, like if they try to live in the same space or eat the same food, then the species are automatically in competition. It's like if your little brother tries to take part of your PB&J. The two of you will then engage in some kind of competition for that yummy sandwich. Competition in the wild can take many forms and only occasionally involves direct combat. A species can win a competition by being faster, more efficient, smarter, more colorful, or any of a huge number of other ways. In the end, there are only three possible results of a competition: winning, losing, and compromising. A species may win the competition and take over that part of the niche, or it may lose and be forced to retreat from that part, or the two species could find a way to divide that part of the niche so that they can coexist peacefully. For example, you can snatch back your sandwich, or you can decide to just give it up rather than bother, or maybe you could split it with him. Any of these would resolve the competition (for now). The conflict between you and your brother is called sibling rivalry, but competition in the wild between two or more different species is called *interspecific competition* because *inter* means "between," and *specific* refers to species.

Intraspecific competition

In addition to interspecific competition, there can be competition between individuals of the same species, which is called intraspecific competition because *intra* means "within." In addition to food, water, and territory, members of the same species fight over mates. This is a whole different kind of competition because it can lead to the development of unusual qualities like vibrant color, alluring scents, or a beautiful singing voice. Sometimes only the prettiest, the smelliest, or the loudest are able to win the competition for mates and only they are able to pass on their pretty, smelly, or loud genes.

Hunting and escaping: Predator-prey interactions

Predators are hunting animals, and the prey are what the predators eat. When two species are involved in a predator-prey relationship, the sizes of their populations are linked together. If the size of the prey population goes up, then the predators have more food to eat, so their population will increase also. But then all those extra predators end up eating a lot more prey, which brings the prey population back down. When that happens, the predators start to run out of food, and their population goes back down, too, which then allows the prey population to increase again. The graph in Figure 12-8 shows how the populations of a predator and its prey track each other over time.

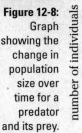

Figure 12-8:
Graph
showing the
change in
population
size over
time for a
predator
and its prey.

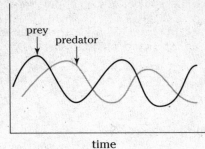

Moving in together: Symbiosis

Sometimes two species can form an even more intimate relationship than any described so far. If two species live together in close contact for extended periods of time, then their relationship is called *symbiosis.*

We've listed the the three kinds of symbiosis below:

- *Parasitism:* With parasitism, one species is helped, and the other is harmed. An example of this is when a smaller species, such as a tick, leech, or a tapeworm, lives on the skin or in the digestive system of a bigger species in order to steal the bigger species' nutrients. This sucks for the bigger species, but it's great for the parasite.

- *Commensalism:* With commensalisms, one species is helped, and the other is unaffected. An example of this are the little mites that live in your eyelashes. You may think that's totally gross, but the mites are just looking for a nice, cozy place to live and they don't really harm you at all.

- *Mutualism:* With mutualism, both species are helped. A famous example of this is the bacteria that live in the stomach of cows. The bacteria break down grass for the cow and the cow supplies the bacteria with food and a safe living space, so it's a win-win situation. Another example is the bacteria that lives in the root nodules of legumes, as described in the section, "Nitrogen cycle," earlier in this chapter.

Making each other better: Co-evolution

Another thing that happens when two populations interact with each other is what's called *co-evolution,* which is when the two species drive each other to evolve increasingly dramatic characteristics. For example, in the predator-prey relationship, the prey will tend to evolve better defenses like armor and camouflage, which in turn forces the predator to evolve better methods for finding and killing the prey. The result is a sort of ecological arms race in which the predators become expert hunters and the prey become tough-skinned escape artists. Co-evolution can also happen between two species that are trying to help each other, like flowers and pollinators. The flowers evolve more and more dramatic ways to attract pollinators, such as brighter colors and stronger smells, while the pollinators evolve better ways to get at the nectar, such as color vision and long noses. Hummingbirds would never have evolved their amazing hovering ability if flowers didn't provide nectar, and flowers would never have evolved their bright colors if that didn't attract hummingbirds; so the two species evolved together in the process of co-evolution.

We haven't had any sample questions for a while, so try a few on populations.

A species fish called remoras attaches to the skin of some sharks. The remoras eat the bugs and debris that is stuck on the shark's skin, and the sharks tend to scare away the remoras' natural predators. This is an example of

(A) parasitic symbiosis

(B) mutualistic symbiosis

(C) interspecific competition

(D) commensalistic symbiosis

(E) ecological succession

Both species are helped in this example. The sharks get clean skin and the remoras get safety from predators, so the correct answer is (B) mutualistic symbiosis. If the remoras were sucking the shark's blood instead of cleaning its skin, then it would be parasitic symbiosis, and if the shark was unaffected then it would be commensalistic symbiosis. As it is, (A) and (D) are both wrong. The shark and the remora aren't competing for any resources, so (C) is also wrong. Answer (E) ecological succession, has nothing to do with the situation in the question.

In which of the following situations is exponential growth least likely to happen?

(A) Food is plentiful

(B) The species has no competition

(C) The population size is low

(D) The spring season brings warmer weather to a cold biome

(E) The species has no predators

Notice first that the question asks which is the least likely situation to see exponential growth. Exponential growth happens when there are lots of excess resources, little or no competition, and no significant predators. This eliminates (A), (B), and (E). When population size is low, then there is likely to be excess resources and little competition, so (C) is out also. The coming of spring may make growth conditions better, but it is not as clear of a case as the others, so (D) is the least likely to result in exponential growth.

The population of a certain species X goes up and down over the years. The population of another species Y, in the same ecosystem, goes up and down along with, but lagging slightly behind species X. Based on this information, which of the following could be the relationship between species X and species Y?

(A) Species Y is a parasite of species X

(B) Species Y is a predator of species X

(C) Species Y is in mutualistic symbiosis with species X

(D) all of the above

(E) none of the above

If the population size of species Y track the population size of species X, then Y must be dependent on X somehow. Parasites are dependent on their hosts, predators are dependent on their prey, and mutualistic symbionts are dependent on each other. So, based on the information provided in the question, all of the first three are a possible relationship between species X and Y. That means (D) all of the above is the correct answer.

Working Together: Ecosystems

An ecosystem is a large area with many different species of organisms in different trophic levels all doing their parts to keep the nutrient cycles moving. Notice the levels of organization here because they just may show up on the SAT II. A group of individuals of the same species is called a *population*. All of the populations within an ecosystem put together are collectively called a *community* of populations. The community plus the physical territory in which it resides is called an *ecosystem*. A group of ecosystems in a general climate zone is called a *biome*. Since there are all these different levels involved, ecologists need to pay attention to a lot of things at once in order to study an ecosystem. Things like the climate, the terrain, and, of course, the variety of organisms and their interactions, all go into determining the characteristics of an ecosystem.

Keeping your balance: Healthy ecosystems

Every ecosystem needs to be balanced. The nutrient cycles are crucial to the long-term survival of the ecosystem, so all of the organisms need to work together to keep things running smoothly. Of course they're all just trying to survive as individuals, but the various species still end up working together, because if one of the nutrient cycles speeds up or slows down, then the whole ecosystem will be out of balance, which means big trouble. Sometimes a renegade species will throw the ecosystem out of balance by releasing or taking up too much of one nutrient too quickly, leaving almost none for everyone else. For example, the bacteria in a stagnant or polluted body of water can use up all the O_2, leaving none for any of the other organisms. This stops the oxygen cycle, causing the death of all the various animal and plant species that were living in the water, which creates what is sometimes called a *dead zone,* which is definitely not a name given to a healthy ecosystem. Another example is when humans release CO_2 into the atmosphere too quickly, as described in the section, "Carbon cycle," earlier in this chapter.

Carrying capacity: Ecosystems at maximum occupancy

Every ecosystem has a limited amount of resources. There are only so many nutrients to go around, and only so many places to live, so there is a limit on the number of organisms that can survive in a single ecosystem. This is called the *carrying capacity* of the ecosystem, and it determines how many individuals of each species can be sustained over the long term. For example, the desert has a very low carrying capacity because there is not enough water to sustain very many organisms. The tropical rain forest, on the other hand, has a huge carrying capacity because it gets drenched with rain all year long.

The following two sorts of factors determine the carrying capacity of an ecosystem:

- *Density-independent* factors are ones that are always there no matter what, such as when an area gets hit by a hurricane every summer. The hurricane will come ripping through every year no matter how many or how few organisms are around, and either way it will probably manage to kill off a lot of the plants and animals in the area. That kind of thing lowers the carrying capacity of an ecosystem.

- *Density-dependent* factors, on the other hand, are ones that get more severe as the density of organisms increases. In the desert example, the more plants that are living there, the less water each individual plant can soak up for itself, making the dryness problem even harder to deal with. As a result, the density of plants in the desert is usually really low. Another density-dependent factor is disease. If the area is densely packed, then the chances of spreading diseases increases a lot, which can limit the number of organisms that can survive in the area. Just think of the guy spraying juicy sneezes on the bus. If he's the only passenger, then maybe only the bus driver will get sick, but if it's really crowded, there's a good chance of him infecting ten or more other people with his nasty germs.

Making a comeback: Ecological succession

When every niche in an ecosystem is filled and all of the nutrient cycles are moving along smoothly, then there isn't really any room for new species to move in. A full, healthy ecosystem like this is called a *climax community*. A climax community can be disrupted when something dramatic happens, like when a hurricane comes through and kills off half the plants and animals in the area. When something like this happens, the ecosystem will gradually work its way back to being a climax community, but it may take many decades. Sometimes a climax community can get completely wiped out, like when a volcano erupts and covers the whole place with hot lava, or a glacier slides through and scrapes the ground clean.

Ecosystems work their way back to being a climax community through what's called *ecological succession*. More and more species move back in as the conditions improve, until all the niches are filled and the nutrient cycles are running smoothly again. Consider an old forest that gets covered by a volcanic eruption. Once the lava cools, ecological succession can begin. The problem, though, is that the area is covered by packed lava and plants need soil to put down their roots. Luckily, there are a few species that can live in a completely lifeless rocky place like this. They are called *pioneer species* because they are the first to move in.

Lichen is a tough organism that can act as a pioneer. Lichen can perform photosynthesis, so it doesn't need to eat other organisms, and it also has the ability to break the rock down to dirt in order to get some extra energy and minerals. This is important for ecological succession because after a long time of lichen breaking down the rock, enough dirt can build up to support some grasses. Once you have grass, then you can start to get larger plants and some animals coming in. Then, after a few hundred years, the area can be back to a full-blown forest — a climax community!

Now for some ecosystem questions!

Questions 1–3 refer to the following:

(A) Climax Community

(B) Ecological Succession

(C) Carrying Capacity

(D) Density Dependent Factor

(E) Density Independent Factor

1. Competition for space limiting a population size

2. The maximum number of individuals that an ecosystem can support

3. The spread of diseases limiting a population size

For #1, the correct answer is (D). The more crowded the ecosystem is, the more competition there will be, so this is a density dependent factor limiting population size.

For #2, the correct answer is (C). The carrying capacity of an ecosystem refers to how many individuals the ecosystem can support. Answer (A) is wrong because a community may still be a climax community even when it is not quite at the ecosystem's carrying capacity.

For #3, the correct answer is (D) again. Diseases spread faster in crowded conditions, so the denser the population, the more diseases will be spread, causing the population to go down.

Remember that in these classification type questions, some choices may be used more than once and others not at all.

Which of the following is a biotic component of an ecosystem?

(A) temperature range

(B) amount of O_2

(C) yearly rainfall

(D) altitude

(E) presence of lichen

Biotic components are the living parts. Answers (A) through (D) are all about nonliving, abiotic components of the ecosystem. Only lichen is alive, so the answer is (E).

Part IV
Constructing Creatures: Organismal Biology

The 5th Wave ©RICHTENNANT By Rich Tennant

"If it's okay for them to ask experimental questions, I figure it should be okay for me to give some experimental answers."

In this part . . .

Part IV is all about organismal biology, which focuses on the structures and processes of plants and animals. Chapter 13 is all about plants and their various adventures. Chapter 14 is about how animals function, and Chapter 15 is about how animals behave. The three chapters of organismal stuff will make up about 35 to 40 percent of the Biology E/M core section of the SAT II, so everybody needs to know this material whether they're planning to focus on the Biology-M section or the Biology-E section.

Chapter 13

Going Vegetarian: Plant Structures and Functions

••

In This Chapter
▶ Categorizing plant types
▶ Exploring plant circulation
▶ Investigating plant structures
▶ Getting a grip on plant growth
▶ Following plant reproduction

••

Chapters 13, 14, and 15 cover the organismal information on the SAT II, which will make up about 20 percent of the test. Most of the organismal questions will be on animals, but the E and M versions will both contain at least a few plant questions, so this chapter gets you ready for the most likely topics.

Plants perform photosynthesis and are the most important primary producers in terrestrial biomes. All animals (including you!) rely on plants in a big way — both for food and for breathable oxygen. In this chapter you'll find out about plant types, plant structures, plant functions, and plant reproduction. Sound like fun? Well, then plant yourself down in a comfortable spot and plow through this chapter.

Sorting Things Out: Plant Types

Table 13-1 lists the main categories of plants that may show up on the SAT II. The two main categories of plants are the *tracheophytes* and the *nontracheophytes* (sometimes they're called *vascular* and *nonvascular*). The difference between these two main categories is that one kind has a circulatory system that moves fluids through the plant and the other kind does not. Nontracheophytes are the ones that don't have a circulatory system while tracheophytes do have a circulatory system. Most of the trees, bushes, and flowers you're familiar with are tracheophytes.

Table 13-1	Categories of Plants
Category	**Example**
Nontracheophytes	mosses, hornworts
Tracheophytes	
- Seedless plants	ferns, horsetails
- Seed plants	
- Gymnosperms	pine and fir trees
- Angiosperms	
- monocots	grasses and grains
- dicots	all other flowering plants

As you can see in Table 13-1, there are a few more divisions that you should be aware of, but since they're all explained in more detail later on in this chapter, we'll just briefly mention them here. The tracheophytes are broken down into seedless plants and plants that produce seeds. Then, the seed-bearing plants come in two varieties: the gymnosperms and the angiosperms. *Gymnosperms* are the trees that produce cones, while the *angiosperms* (by far the biggest category of plants) include all of the plants with flowers. The angiosperms can then be broken down even further into the monocots and the dicots. That's a lot of plant divisions to remember, but you can take comfort in the fact that any plant-related questions on the SAT II are most likely to be about angiosperms. Okay, we're not sure that's particularly comforting, but hey, it's not as bad as it looks. If you can answer the plant questions in this chapter and the practice tests, you will be just fine. The next two sections take a closer look at the two main categories of plants.

Laying low: Nontracheophytes

Nontracheophytes are the simplest kinds of plants. They don't have the fancy leaves or seeds or flowers or anything. You've seen the mosses that grow all over the place like a bright green carpet in really wet forests? Those mosses are nontracheophytes. Some other examples you may know about are liverworts and hornworts. Actually, we'd be surprised if you knew about those because we don't think we've ever recognized one in the wild.

Since they don't have a circulatory system, nontracheophytes have a hard time getting enough water to every part of the plant. That's why they only live in wet areas and why they're so small. In order to saturate the whole plant, the water just has to soak in from every direction. If the plant gets too thick, the interior won't be able to get enough water and it will die from dehydration.

Living large: Tracheophytes

Tracheophytes are more diverse and complex than nontracheophytes. They include all the trees, grasses, grains, bushes and flowers. Some tracheophytes are small like the mosses, but some of them are really huge, like giant sequoia trees. There's no way a humongous tree trunk like that could just soak up enough water if it acted like a nontracheophyte. So, in

Pumping fluids

Plants don't have a heart or anything else to pump water through the xylem, so how does the fluid move? To get an idea of how this works, dip the corner of a paper napkin into a glass of water and watch what happens. Go ahead and get the napkin and the water, we'll wait . . . Okay, see how the water soaks right up and keeps moving until it's saturated the whole napkin? Well, the xylem works exactly like that. In fact, the paper in the napkin is made out of shredded wood pulp, and wood mostly consists of old xylem tubes, so it only makes sense that the napkin would soak up water so efficiently. Without the xylem tubes, a plant could still absorb some water, but it would go much, much more slowly. In fact, it would be too slow for a large plant to survive.

order to supply the whole plant with nutrients, all tracheophytes have a kind of circulatory system that moves things around pretty fast. Well, pretty fast for a plant that is, which isn't really all that fast compared to animals, but it's fast enough. The circulatory systems of tracheophytes are more like two circulatory systems in one: the xylem and the phloem.

Soaking it up: Xylem

The *xylem* (pronounced "ZIE-lum") is the network of tubes that brings water and other simple nutrients (such as minerals and ammonia) up from the roots and delivers them to the rest of the plant. One special fact is that the tubes of the xylem are the nonliving remains of old cells. As the plant first sprouts and starts to grow, some of the tube-shaped cells in the stalk of the plant die and leave behind tubes made of cellulose (in most trees, the xylem tubes are made of wood). The xylem, then, is like thousands of microscopic drinking straws inside the stalk of the plant.

The next important point about the xylem is that once the plant is saturated with water, it can't absorb any more. That leads to a problem because a plant can't just stop absorbing water once all its tissues are saturated. That's because the plant needs to keep soaking up water from the soil in order to keep absorbing all the other nutrients down there, like minerals, ammonia, and sulfides. The plant is growing and developing, so it always needs new nutrients. So, in order to keep drawing nutrients out of the soil, the plant needs a way to get rid of some old water to make room for the new water coming in through the roots. The leaves take on this job by letting water evaporate out of little pores on their surface. This water loss through the leaves is called *transpiration*, which helps keep fluid flowing through the xylem from the roots up to the leaves. You'll see transpiration pop up again in this chapter's section on leaves.

Spreading the wealth: Phloem

The *phloem* (pronounced "FLOW-um") is the network of tubes that brings fluid from the leaves to the rest of the plant. The phloem tubes are made of living cells, unlike the nonliving tubes of the xylem, and they can deliver the fluid all around the plant, not just in one direction. The leaves are where photosynthesis happens, and photosynthesis produces glucose. The rest of the plant needs glucose for fuel and to make cell walls, and so the phloem delivers a steady supply. The fluid traveling through the phloem is very thick and sticky with lots of sugars and amino acids. Sometimes it's called sap, and the sap of maple trees is where maple syrup comes from, so next time you're eating waffles, ask the person next to you to "Please pass the phloem."

Before heading to the next section, try out these sample questions on plant types.

Which of the following is false about xylem?

(A) it is only found in tracheophyte plants

(B) it can flow either up or down the stem of the plant

(C) it carries water and minerals from the soil

(D) it is able to continue because of transpiration

(E) the cells that constitute the xylem tubes are nonliving

First, notice that this is one of those questions that ask you to look for the only false answer. That means you can cross off any that you know to be true.

Tracheophytes have their name because they are the ones that have a circulatory system. Xylem is part of the circulatory system, so A is true. Xylem is the one that is made of dead tube cells, and it brings soil nutrients up from the roots to the leaves, so (C) and (E) are also true. Transpiration is the evaporation through leaves that keeps the xylem moving, so (D) is true as well. Phloem is the one that can travel in any direction. Xylem can only flow from the roots where it is soaked up from the soil, to the leaves where the water evaporates in transpiration. So, the answer is (B).

Which of the following best explains why nontracheophytes tend to be smaller than tracheophytes?

(A) nontracheophytes need to be less conspicuous because they are more susceptible to being eaten by herbivores

(B) tracheophytes grow taller in order to get beyond the reach of most herbivores

(C) nontracheophytes need to stay closer to the ground to regulate their temperature

(D) a large nontracheophyte could not absorb enough water to supply its inner tissues

(E) tracheophytes simply grow faster than nontracheophytes

The question asks which is the *best* explanation, which means that all of them could be possible explanations. You have to determine which is best.

Both (A) and (B) would apply equally to tracheophytes and nontracheophytes, so it couldn't account for a major difference between the two groups. You can cross them out. Answer (C) may seem reasonable, but plants aren't too worried about temperature changes, as long as it doesn't get really, really cold or hot, so that one is pretty unlikely. Even if tracheophytes grew faster, that doesn't automatically mean that they would grow taller, so (E) is also pretty unlikely. Nontracheophytes don't have a circulatory system, so they can't move fluids around inside their tissues very fast, at least not fast enough to adequately supply the interior of a big stalk, so the correct answer is (D).

Plant Structures

Chapters 3 and 5 both contain a lot of information about plant cells so we won't go into any more detail about that here, but let us briefly remind you about some of the highlights. Plant cells are eukaryotes, so they have a nucleus and a variety of other organelles. For example, they have mitochondria for aerobic cellular respiration, and they also have chloroplasts for photosynthesis. That means plants can make their own glucose in the chloroplasts and then use that glucose as fuel in the mitochondria. Plant cells also use glucose to make cellulose, which is the rigid polymer that makes up their cell walls.

This whole section applies to all tracheophyte plants, but it focuses on the monocots and dicots because they are more likely to show up on the SAT II.

There are a few major differences between these monocots and dicots, but the one that gives them their name is based on how they sprout. The little sprout that comes out of a seed is called a cotyledon, and *monocots*, such as the grasses and grains, sprout with one leaf coming out of the seed. *Dicots*, on the other hand, sprout with two leaves emerging from the seed. The following sections of this chapter talk a little more about some of the differences between monocots and dicots, and those differences are summarized in Table 13-2.

Table 13-2	Main Differences between Monocots and Dicots				
	# of cotyledons at sprouting	leaf veins	vascular structures	root systems	examples
Monocots	One	parallel	xylem and phloem in bundles	fibrous	grasses grains
Dicots	Two	branching	xylem on inside phloem on outside	tap root	most fruit and vegetable plants

Letting it all hang out: Leaves

Leaves are where most of the real action takes place in a plant. It may not look like it from the outside, but at the microscopic level, leaves are a real whirlwind of activity. Seriously . . . they are. Leaves do most of the photosynthesis and use most of the water, so they get the most access to xylem and phloem, as shown by their obvious leaf veins. As you can see in Figure 13-1, the veins run parallel to each other in the leaves of monocots, while they follow a branching pattern in the leaves of dicots.

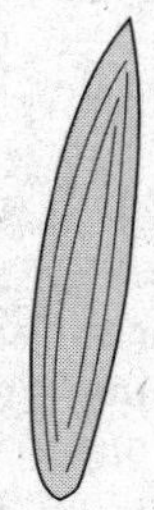

Figure 13-1: Leaf veins in a) a leaf from a monocot and b) a leaf from a dicot.

(a) monocot leaf with parallel veins

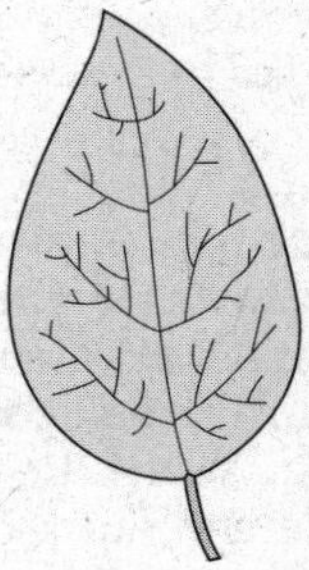

(b) dicot leaf with branching veins

Most leaves have the same basic structure. The inner cells of a leaf are called *mesophyll cells,* and these are the ones that are tapped into the vascular system and are where photosynthesis happens. The outermost layer of cells is tougher than the interior cells, and they form a kind of skin that is called an *epidermis.* That's the same word as they use for animal skin, but animal skin has a completely different structure to it (see Chapter 14). The epidermis of the leaf is covered by a waxy layer called the *cuticle* to keep it waterproof. See Figure 13-2 for a cross-section of a typical leaf.

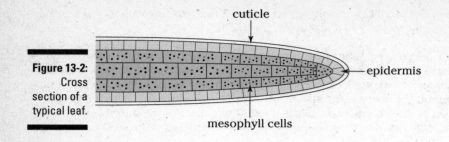

Figure 13-2:
Cross section of a typical leaf.

There are also little pores in the epidermis of a leaf called *stomata*. The stomata are used to absorb CO_2 and get rid of O_2. Take a look at Chapter 6 to see how these molecules are used in photosynthesis. The stomata also release a lot of H_2O. Remember from earlier in this chapter that this is called transpiration, and it's how the plant gets rid of excess water in order to keep soaking up more xylem.

The size of leaves varies depending on the biome the plant is in. In the tropical rain forest, for example, most of the leaves are really wide because other plants block a lot of the light and the leaves are trying to soak up as much energy as they can. In the desert, on the other hand, the leaves are really small because getting enough light is not a problem. The real danger is losing too much water, so the leaves are both small and especially thick and waxy. The most extreme example are the cactus whose leaves have turned into spines, so they do all their photosynthesis in their stems.

Stems

Stems serve two main purposes. First, they hold the plant upright so the leaves can soak up as much sunlight as possible. The more shade they get from other plants, the higher the plant tends to grow. Just like the leaves evolve to suit their habitat, some plants have evolved stalks that allow them to be really tall in order to get above everyone else and soak up all the sunlight. Some of the trees in the tropical rain forest can be over 100ft high, and the tallest redwoods can be over 300 feet tall! That crazy height pretty much maxes out the ability of the xylem to deliver water, and also maxes out the structural capacities of wood to support that much weight.

The second function of stems is to house the circulatory system. There is a difference between monocots and dicots to mention here that has to do with how the xylem and phloem are contained within the stem. In dicots, the phloem usually runs near the surface of the stem, while the inside is reserved for the xylem. In monocots, the tubes of the xylem and phloem run in little bunches throughout the stem. Each little bunch contains one xylem tube and one phloem tube. Figure 13-3 shows this difference in stem design between monocots and dicots.

Figure 13-3:
Xylem and phloem within the stem of a) a monocot, and b) a dicot.

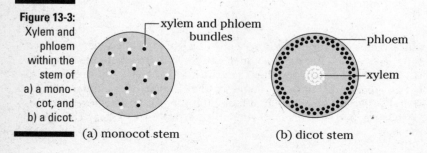

(a) monocot stem   (b) dicot stem

Roots

Roots soak up water and other small nutrients from the soil, plus they serve as anchors for the plant to stay upright. For both these reasons they need to maximize their contact with the soil, so they grow in a complicated branching pattern, as shown in Figure 13-4. Monocot roots branch the most, forming what's called fibrous roots, while dicots tend to have one main root called the taproot, with lots of smaller branches coming off that taproot. If you look closely at roots, you'll notice that they have really tiny branches called root hairs that provide even more surface area for soaking up nutrients.

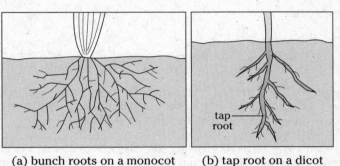

(a) bunch roots on a monocot   (b) tap root on a dicot

Figure 13-4:
a) fibrous roots of a monocot; b) tap root of a dicot; c) a close-up of roots hairs.

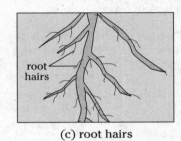

(c) root hairs

Now try some questions on plant structures.

Which of the following is a structure not possessed by monocots?

(A) taproot

(B) leaves

(C) root hairs

(D) xylem

(E) flowers

Monocots have fibrous roots instead of a taproot. Both monocots and dicots are members of the angiosperm category of plants, and all of those have leaves, xylem, and flowers, and they all have little hairs on the roots. The right answer is (A).

Which of the following is a role of the stomata on leaves?

    I. absorb CO_2

    II. absorb O_2

    III. allow for transpiration

    IV. get rid of H_2O

  (A) I and II only

  (B) I and IV only

  (C) I, III, and IV only

  (D) III and IV only

  (E) I, II, III, and IV

Stomata are the little pores on the surface of leaves that allow for things to go in and out. One thing that moves out is O_2, which is a waste product of photosynthesis that we need to breathe, so II is definitely wrong. Therefore, you can cross out (A) and (E).

Eliminating (A) and (E) leaves you with (B), (C), and (D). All three of the answer choices contain IV, so you don't even have to take time to consider IV. You know getting rid of H_2O must be a role of stomata without even thinking about it.

CO_2 is needed for photosynthesis (see Chapter 6), so I needs to be included. You can eliminate (D). The stomata also allow water to evaporate in order to keep the xylem moving up from the roots, and "transpiration" is the name given to this process, so III is a role and (C) is the right answer.

Stretching Skyward: Plant Growth

Unlike animals which grow for a while and then stop once they're adults, plants tend to grow continuously throughout their lives. This section deals with how plants grow longer and how their growth can be modified by factors in their environment.

Like before, this section will focus on monocots and dicots because they're covered the most on the SAT II.

Getting longer every day: Primary growth

Most plants tend to grow longer from their tips. The middle parts of a stem or root do not grow longer; instead they do grow wider as the plant ages. The tip of a stem or root is called the *apical meristem*, and it's where cells go through a lot of mitosis in order to make the plant grow longer. In the roots, the apical meristem has a tough little cap, called the root cap, to help it burrow through the soil. On the stem, the apical meristem prevents the growth of new stem just beneath it. However, once the apical meristem has grown past a certain point, new branches can start to grow further down.

This helps gardeners, because if you cut the apical meristem off of a plant, it will stop growing longer at that spot and can start new branches right where you cut. So, if you clip your plants at just the right place, you can make them grow fuller and bushier rather than taller.

Monocots do things a little differently because they don't have an apical meristem. Instead, they have areas of growth all through the stem, so they can grow longer even if you cut off the tip. This works out great because monocots include the grasses, which usually have their tips cut off by grazing herbivores. Since they don't use apical meristems, grasses can just continue to grow taller after every nibble from a passing deer or antelope.

Finding some direction: Tropisms

Tropism refers to the direction that plants grow. The roots, for example, tend to grow toward where there's more water, and the stems and leaves can also grow in specific directions. The most obvious example is when plants grow toward a source of light. This is called *phototropism*, and it helps plants grow up toward the sun. It also causes them to grow sideways if something is blocking direct light. Indoor plants grow toward artificial light sources and you can make them grow in crazy twists and turns if you keep changing the placement of your lamps.

The other kind of tropism is called *gravitropism*, and it happens when the plant grows away from the source of gravity. Normally, of course, this just means growing straight up from the ground, but if the plant happens to be growing on a steep slope, it needs to figure out which way is up. If the plant just grew straight out from the sloping ground, it would eventually topple over. By instead growing directly away from the pull of gravity, the plant can stay balanced.

Going through cycles: Photoperiodism

Photoperiodism is when plants change their activity based on the amount of light they're getting. The simplest case is when certain species of flowers fold up when they stop receiving light at sunset. Beside the basic day-night difference, many plants are also sensitive to much longer cycles in sunlight. Believe it or not, they are able to keep track of the changing *amount* of light and dark they receive each 24-hour period and change their activity as the seasons change from summer to winter and back again. For example, when the amount of darkness starts to become greater than the amount of light, then the plants know winter is coming on. For deciduous trees, this means losing their leaves and going dormant. On the other hand, when the amount of light starts to be longer than the amount of darkness, then the plant knows that it must be springtime, and it will start to grow again and produce flowers.

Before you go onto plant reproduction, see if these questions grow on you.

Questions 1–3 refer to the following:

(A) apical meristem

(B) phototropism

(C) photoperiodism

(D) gravitropism

(E) branching

1. inhibited by hormones from the growing tip of a plant

2. growth toward a source of light

3. results in seasonal changes in plant activity

Number 1 is (E). The apical meristem is where the plant grows longer, and it prevents the branching of the plant right below the meristem. When the meristem has grown past a certain point or has been clipped off, then the plant can start branching at that point.

Number 2 is (B). This question mentions light, and there are two answers with "photo" in their names, which refers to light. "Periodism" refers to changing activity over a certain period of time, while, "tropism" refers to growth, and so phototropism is the correct answer.

Plants keep track of the seasons by keeping track of how long the days and nights are. They can also keep track of the temperature, but day length is a much more reliable indicator of the seasons. Photoperiodism is when a plant changes its activity based on difference in the amount of light during the seasons. So 3 is (C).

Making More: Plant Reproduction

In Chapter 9 you discover that there are two basic kinds of reproduction: sexual and asexual. Asexual reproduction results in the production of offspring that are genetically identical to the parent, and sexual reproduction involves the mixing of genes from two parents to produce an offspring with a unique combination. Most plants reproduce sexually, but most of them can also reproduce asexually in certain situations.

Taking a clipping: Asexual reproduction

Lots of plants can accidentally reproduce asexually when a significant piece breaks off and lands in such a way that it's able to form roots and start growing. The simple plants, like the nontracheophytes, can do this really easily. For the more complicated tracheophyte plants to do this, however, the piece that breaks off needs to have a significant amount of xylem and phloem and a way to get fuel fast — either with some functioning leaves or some stored fuel. Anyway, the piece that has broken off (gardeners call it a clipping) will re-grow the rest of the plant when it is placed in good soil.

Maintaining a long-distance relationship: Sexual reproduction

If the SAT II asks you about plant reproduction at all, it will most likely ask something about gymnosperms (cone producing plants) or angiosperms (flowering plants), which are both seed-bearing tracheophyte plants. They aren't too likely to ask about sexual reproduction in nontracheophyte plants, but in the unlikely chance of a question on this, or if you are just interested, it turns out that nontracheophytes reproduce in a weird, complicated way called alternation of generations. Male and female gametes, called spores, do not combine to form a zygote. Instead, they develop into full-grown haploid plants. Then the haploid plants of both sexes produce new gametes that combine to produce diploid offspring.

Tracheophyte plants can be divided according to whether they reproduce using seeds. The seedless plants, like ferns and horsetails, reproduce pretty much like the nontracheophytes with that weird alternation of generations. The plants that produce seeds are the ones most likely to show up on the SAT II, so we'll focus on them for the rest of this section.

The seeds in plants come from the normal combination of a male gamete and a female gamete to produce a zygote. The male gamete is called *pollen* and the female gamete is called an *ovum* (plural = ova). Using methods described below, the pollen from the male parts manages to get over to the female parts and fertilize the ovum. The ovum then develops into a seed. Some plants produce just a few seeds while others produce hundreds or even thousands of seeds at a time. The seed-producing plants can be separated into two big categories: the kind that produces cones and the kind that produces flowers.

Living in the taiga: Gymnosperms

Gymnosperms are the kind of seed-bearing plants that produce cones, which includes trees like pine, fir, and juniper. Gymnosperms dominate the temperate taiga biomes, and are sometimes called evergreens because they stay green all year round. Most of the species of gymnosperms have leaves in the shape of needles in order to protect them from the cold winters.

The male trees produce cones that contain pollen. When the wind blows, the pollen is blown out of the male cones and some of it lands on female cones, which contain the ova. The pollen only land on the right cones by pure chance, so the male cones crank out huge amounts of pollen to make sure at least some of it finds its proper destination. During the summer in the taiga biome you can sometimes see big clouds of yellowish green pollen all over the place. If you live in an area with lots of pine trees, the summer pollen season can be pretty messy.

After the ova inside the female cones are fertilized by pollen, they develop into seeds. The cones eventually drop onto the ground and, if the conditions are just right, they sprout into new plants. Good conditions include fertile soil, a reliable source of water, a nice clear area where the new seedling can have access to light, and a small-scale forest fire.

Wait . . . forest fire? While forest fires are usually thought to be really terrible events for a forest, it turns out that they actually play a big role in helping the new gymnosperms to sprout. Of course, if the fire is really intense and sustained, then everything will be turned to ash, and that doesn't help at all. Gymnosperms are hoping instead for a quick brush fire so that the high heat will cause the cones to pop open and release the seeds like popcorn. If the temperature never gets high enough, then the cones never pop open and the seeds never sprout, so fires are actually required for gymnosperm reproduction.

But that's not all. Not only do quick forest fires open up the cones, they also clear away any dead brush covering the ground so that the new seedling can have ready access to light as it sprouts. Plus, the ashes left behind can make good fertilizer. Pretty smart, huh? But even that's not all. One more benefit is that natural forest fires are almost always caused by lightening, and lightening usually happens during thunderstorm season, which is a good time to sprout because of the likelihood of plenty of rain. Nature is pretty smart!

Considering the most common: Angiosperms and flowers

Angiosperms are the kind of plants that produce flowers, which includes all of the grasses and grains (the monocots) and all of the plants that produce regular fruits and vegetables (dicots). Just like with the gymnosperms, the male parts of a flower produce pollen and the female parts produce ova; but instead of relying on the wind to carry their pollen, angiosperms rely on animal helpers called *pollinators*. These animals, such a bees, butterflies, and hummingbirds, pick up pollen from male plants and deliver them to the female plants, but more on that later. First, take a look at the flower structure in Figure 13-5.

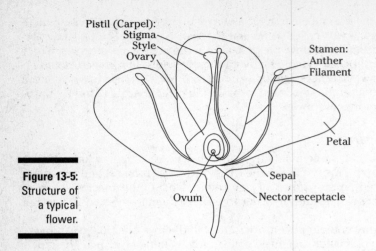

Figure 13-5:
Structure of
a typical
flower.

Okay, here comes a big flurry of technical terms. The *stamen* is the male part of the flower, and the *carpel* is the female part. The important part of the stamen is the *anther*, which is where the pollen is located. The *filament* just holds the anther up in the air. The top of the carpel is called the *stigma*, and that's where the female parts accept the pollen. The opening in the stigma leads to a tube called the *style* that leads down to where the ovum is located, inside the ovary. When the pollen gets in there, it fertilizes the ovum, forming a zygote, which then turns into a seed. Whew.

Every flower has petals and sepals. *Sepals* cover and protect the flower before it is ready to open, but after that, they don't serve much of a purpose. The *petals*, though, are the main advertisement for pollinators, so they need to make themselves as noticeable as possible. Red and yellow flowers stand out really well against the green background of leaves, so these are the most common flower colors. Some pollinators, though, can actually see better in the violet range (even the ultraviolet range), so you can also find lots of blue and purple flowers. Not only do flowers look pretty, they usually smell really good, too, so not only do they attract pollinators, they attract us as well.

The relationship between flowers and pollinators includes plants, animals, and special ecological and evolutionary relationships, which means it's just the kind of bug question the SAT II likes to ask about. Luckily, the relationship is a pretty straightforward exchange.

Inside the flower, the plant produces a thick sugar water called nectar. The pollinators use the nectar as food; and when they come for the nectar, they brush past the anthers, picking up some pollen. Then they go to another flower of the same species to find more nectar. When they get there, they brush some of the pollen off on the stigma of the other flower, thereby delivering right where it needs to go. So, the pollinators and the angiosperms have a pretty good deal worked out. The animal gets tasty sweet nectar, and the plant gets help with reproduction. This deal has worked out great for both of them. Angiosperms are the dominant kind of plants on earth, and pollinators (especially the insects) spread like crazy.

Okay, so what happens after fertilization? Like so many times before, it's a little different in monocots than it is in dicots. In monocots, the ovary develops into a seedpod that eventually opens up and lets the seeds be carried away by the wind. In dicots, the ovary instead develops into a fruit with the seeds embedded inside. The fruit is rich in carbohydrates (mostly sucrose) and can provide good fuel for the seeds when they start to sprout.

On the other hand, some fruits are designed to be eaten by herbivores. That sounds weird at first because the seeds have been consumed, but the seeds are pretty tough, so they usually don't get broken down in the animal's digestive system. Instead, they pass right through, and the animal deposits them somewhere far away, along with a nice little supply of fertilizer (also called "poop"). Just like with flowers, the fruits are supposed to attract animals, so they're usually brightly colored red, yellow, or orange.

See how you fare on these sample questions about plant reproduction.

Which of the following is the best explanation for the red, yellow, or orange coloration of fruit?

(A) herbivores see green better than any other color, so non-green fruit keeps herbivores from eating them

(B) bright colors attract bees and other insects that pollinate the plant

(C) fruits contain vitamins, and the vitamins are brightly colored

(D) bright coloration makes it more likely that animals will find and eat the fruit

(E) it is the result of random mutations and has no cost or benefit to the plant

This is one of those "best explanation" question, so all of the answers could be possible explanations. You need to eliminate the less likely ones.

In general, fruit is supposed to be eaten by fruit-eating herbivores so that the animals carry the seeds far away. The plants want to attract the animals to their food, so (A) doesn't make a lot of sense. It also means that (D) is a good explanation, and it is the correct answer.

You know that (E) is not correct. The bright colors attract animals, and this is beneficial to plant reproduction. The presence of vitamins does not necessarily contribute to fruit's color, so you can eliminate (C).

(B) seems to be true, but you are looking for the best answer. Pollinators work in the flowers of the plant rather than the fruit, so (D) is a better answer than (B).

Which of the following is true of gymnosperms?

(A) they often need wind in order to reproduce

(B) they are most commonly found in tropical biomes

(C) they require the help of pollinators to reproduce

(D) they usually lose their leaves during the winters

(E) they occasionally produce flowers

The question asks you to find the true answer, so you can either find one that you know is true or you can eliminate the ones you know are false.

Some gymnosperms live in the tropics, but they are most common in the temperate taiga, so (B) is false. Angiosperms are the ones that produce flowers, and they make use of pollinators, so both (C) and (E) are false also. Most gymnosperms, like pines and firs, are evergreens, which means they do not lose their leaves in the winter, so cross out (D) as well. The plants that lose their leaves during the winter are called deciduous trees. The true answer is (A). Without wind, male gymnosperms could not spread their pollen to female plants to produce seeds and new plants.

Chapter 14

Making A Body Work: Animal Organ Systems

All animals are eukaryotes and are multicellular. All animals are also heterotrophs, which means they need to find food. In fact, most of what animals do centers around finding food and avoiding being food for someone else. They use their digestive and respiratory systems to take in whatever nutrients they need, and their circulatory systems deliver all those nutrients to every individual cell. Animals move around using their muscular and skeletal systems, and they find food using their senses, all of which are controlled by the nervous system. Animals also use skin for protection, and their endocrine system regulates their growth and development. All in all, animals are amazing, complex organisms, and we'll break down the structures and functions of each individual organ system in order to give you just the information you need to tackle the questions on the SAT II.

In this chapter we focus exclusively on animals and explore their inner workings a little more closely. The first thing to know about animals is that they're the most active of the five kingdoms. They get up, move around, and sometimes even fight each other, so they need organ systems that will support all that activity. Because the SAT II is a lot more likely to ask questions about the digestive system of a human than the digestive system of a clam, this chapter goes through all of the typical animal organ systems, with special emphasis on mammals and, in particular, on humans. (Although we do mention some non-mammalian animals and their special features, but we won't go into much detail.)

Keeping Track of Everything: The Nervous System

The nervous system is the main control system for the body. It monitors what's happening everywhere inside the body and outside in the environment, and it makes quick changes to respond to anything important. Okay, that was a big mouthful of a sentence, so here's an example. Suppose you accidentally touch a hot stove. Your nervous system (which has been keeping track of the location of your hand) will register the pain and quickly cause your arm to pull back to protect your hand. That's the kind of quick, precise action that only an animal could manage, and the nervous system makes it all happen. So, when you save your hand from the hot stove, you're showing yourself to be much swifter than a tree or a fungus. Congratulations. This section explains how that communication works within your nervous system.

Exciting cells: The neurons

The main cells of the nervous system are called *neurons*, which are the cells that can send information back and forth really fast (for more on this process see, "Sending signals: Neuron action potentials," below. Figure 14-1 shows a diagram of a neuron. The *cell body* is the part that's just like any generic cell because it's got the nucleus and other organelles. The *dendrites* receive signals from other neurons or from sensory receptors, and the *axon* is the part that sends signals to other neurons or to muscle cells. The *synapse* is the connection between the axon of this neuron and whatever cell it's sending a signal to.

Usually a single neuron will send signals to many other cells at once, so the axon will branch off in lots of different directions and have synapse connections to many other cells. For some neurons, the axons are very short and just connect to other cells in the immediate area, but other neurons have axons that stretch a few feet and connect all the way over on another part of the body. For example, whenever you accidentally hurt your foot, information needs to get to your brain really fast in order to be figure out how to get your foot out of harm's way. To make sure it happens as fast as possible, the route for pain signals contains only a few neurons, even in people that are seven feet tall, so some neurons need to be really long.

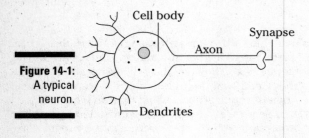

Figure 14-1:
A typical
neuron.

Cell body

Synapse

Axon

Dendrites

Sending signals: Neuron action potentials

The way a neuron sends a signal — also called an "action potential" — is a complicated process that involves concentration gradients, channels, diffusion, and active transport, which are all covered back in Chapter 3. If you need to refresh your memory about this stuff, you should take a peek there before moving on.

To lay a groundwork for understanding the signal-sending process, first look at a section of a neuron that is not sending a signal, as shown in Figure 14-2. Notice that the sodium ion (Na^+) concentration is much higher on the outside than on the inside, so the Na^+ would like to diffuse into the axon. However, the Na^+ is blocked from coming in because the sodium channels are all closed. Also notice that there's an active transport pump moving even more Na^+ out of the cell, while also pumping potassium ions (K^+) into the cell. The potassium doesn't really get a chance to build up inside, though, because there are some small K^+ channels open so they can diffuse back out. Anyway, there's a huge concentration gradient across the membrane, and sodium is just waiting to flow in.

Since there's so much positively charged Na^+ on the outside compared to the inside, the outside of the cell starts to become more positively charged overall, leaving the inside a little more negative. A difference in charges like this is called a *voltage,* which is sometimes called an *electrical potential,* and the inside of the neuron ends up having a voltage of −70 millivolts (mV) — that's 70 thousandths of a volt. Since the neuron is like this when it's not sending a signal, −70 mV is called the *resting potential* of the neuron.

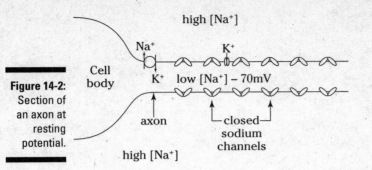

When the neuron is prompted to send a signal (for reasons you'll read about later), some of the sodium channels open at the beginning of the axon, as shown in Figure 14-3a. This allows Na^+ to flow in and change the potential of that little area inside the axon by the open channel. The sodium channels next door are called *voltage gated* channels because they open and close depending on the voltage in the immediate area. When the incoming Na^+ raises the inside voltage to –50 mV, then the next-door sodium channels open up and allow even more sodium to flow in, as shown in Figure 14-3b. Since the channels are set to open at –50 mV, that voltage is called the *threshold potential*. Once the Na^+ starts flowing through the first few sodium channels, this causes the area further along the axon to raise to –50 mV which then triggers even more sodium channels to open, as shown in Figure 14-3c. This continues along the axon, opening more and more sodium channels down the line, and that's the *signal* that a neuron sends down its axon.

It's not over yet, though, because a single sodium channel doesn't have to be open for long before the area inside the cell gets all the way up to about +30 mV. This is called the *action potential* and is the point at which the sodium channels snap back shut, as shown in Figure 14-3c. The active transport pump then pushes all the Na^+ back out of the cell until it gets back to the resting potential of –30 mV again. This may seem like a lot of complicated work for a signal that's supposed to be sent really fast, but it turns out that the whole process of going from resting potential to action potential and back to resting potential only takes about two milliseconds!

Once an area of the axon reaches threshold, there's no going back. The sodium channels are already opening and they won't close again until they've hit the action potential. This all-or-nothing aspect of the action potential means that the axon either hits threshold and goes all the way to action potential, or it doesn't hit threshold and just stays at resting potential. There's no halfway action potential, and there's also no extra-big action potential. Sometimes, however, a neuron needs to send a more intense signal, like when there's a serious pain coming in. To make a signal more intense, a neuron can't make a bigger action potential, so instead it produces lots of action potentials right in a row really fast. The faster the action potentials come in, the more intense the signal. A really intense signal can generate over 100 action potentials per second.

Although the action potential signal can travel down the axon pretty fast (about 3 feet per second) some signals need to go really, really fast, like the ones carrying serious pain signals that were mentioned earlier. These neurons have axons that are wrapped up by specialized cells called *Schwann cells*. Schwann cells contain a kind of lipid called *myelin* that forms a good insulation around the axon, called a *myelin sheath*. Because of the insulation, the action potential can only happen at the spaces between the myelin sheaths, called the *nodes of Ranvier* after the guy who first discovered them. All the channels and diffusion and stuff happens only at the nodes, so the signal jumps from node to node and skips the 1 mm spaces in between where the myelin is located. This strategy can increase the signal speed up to around 350 feet per second!

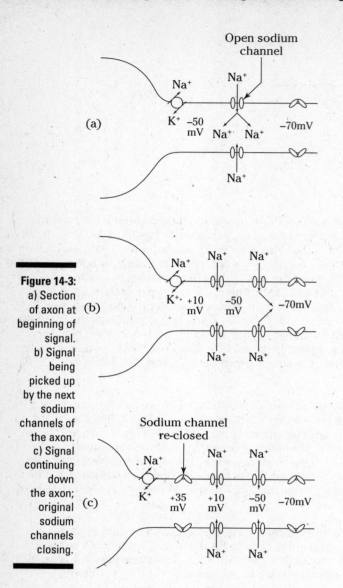

Figure 14-3:
a) Section of axon at beginning of signal.
b) Signal being picked up by the next sodium channels of the axon.
c) Signal continuing down the axon; original sodium channels closing.

Communicating: Neurotransmitters and the synapse

When the action potential finally gets to the end of the axon (after less than 5 milliseconds), it hits the synapse. When the area around the synapse gets to the threshold potential of −50 mV, calcium channels open instead of sodium channels. When the calcium comes rushing in, it causes the release of a specific kind of molecule called a *neurotransmitter* that relays the signal to the next neuron. The neurotransmitter molecules (different neurons use different neurotransmitters) were waiting inside vesicles at the end of the axon, and when the signal arrived, the neurotransmitter molecules were dumped outside the neuron through exocytosis, as shown in Figure 14-4.

When they're released, the neurotransmitters move over to the next neuron and attach to its receptors. Very soon after that, the neurotransmitter molecules are reabsorbed by the first neuron so that it can use them again when the next action potential comes in. Some examples of neurotransmitters are acetylcholine, serotonin, dopamine, and norepinephrine.

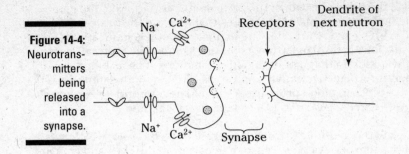

Figure 14-4: Neurotransmitters being released into a synapse.

When a neurotransmitter binds to the receptors of the next cell, there are two possible effects, depending on which particular neuron we happen to be examining. One possibility is that the neurotransmitter will cause sodium channels in the next neuron to open, starting a whole new action potential signal in the next neuron. This would be an *excitatory* signal because it would cause the next neuron to become active. The other possibility is that binding the neurotransmitter will cause sodium channels to stay shut, which would be an *inhibitory* signal because it would *prevent* the next neuron from becoming active. By the way, most drugs that affect the brain do their work by attaching to receptors that are normally reserved for neurotransmitters. Sometimes they do the same thing as the normal neurotransmitter, and sometimes they do the opposite.

Finding the parts: General anatomy of the nervous system

The main division in the nervous system is between the central nervous system (CNS) and the peripheral nervous system (PNS). The CNS is the brain and spinal cord and is where most of the actual control and regulation functions are located. The PNS includes all of the nerves running through your whole body, and they all have myelin sheaths. These nerves will either carry information from the sensory systems inward to the CNS, or control signals out from the CNS to the muscles or other tissues. The incoming sensory signals are called *afferent signals,* and the outgoing control signals are called *efferent signals.*

The Central Nervous System

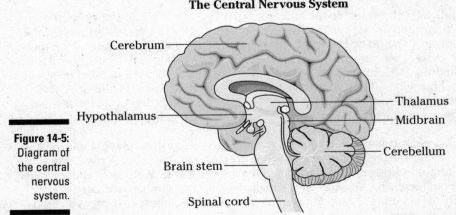

Figure 14-5: Diagram of the central nervous system.

As you can see in Figure 14-5, the brain consists of the brain stem, the midbrain, the cerebellum, and the cerebrum. The brain stem contains structures that activate the basic automatic functions of the body like breathing and heart rate. The midbrain contains more advanced structures that exert subconscious control over the body. For example, the *hypothalamus* is an important structure in the midbrain that monitors bodily functions such as blood pressure, blood pH, body temperature, digestive activity, and so on. If the hypothalamus detects something out of balance, like a rise in blood pressure, it will initiate appropriate responses. Keep an eye out for the hypothalamus in various places later in the chapter.

Just above the hypothalamus in the midbrain is a structure called the *thalamus*, which acts as a gatekeeper for most of the sensory systems. Sensory signals from the eyes and ears are sent through the thalamus, and it decides if they are important enough to be sent through to the cerebrum. If so, the thalamus directs the sensory signals to the part of the cerebrum that handles that sense, such as the vision area or hearing area. The thalamus is kind of like the front desk receptionist for the rest of the brain.

The cerebrum is the biggest part of the human brain, and it's the part with all of the big folds. This is where perception, thinking, and memory happen, especially in the outermost layer, called the *cerebral cortex*. The cerebellum is the wrinkly part underneath and behind the cerebrum. This is where the brain controls the muscles in order to maintain balance and avoid obstacles. Almost all sports rely heavily on the cerebellum because they involve catching and avoiding stuff, which requires lots of quick movements and good balance.

Speeding up and calming down: The sympathetic and parasympathetic systems

In addition to the parts of the nervous system described so far, the whole thing can be divided in another way. For example, there are the somatic and autonomic systems within the overall nervous system. The *somatic* system is the part that is associated with the higher brain centers, so it includes incoming sensory signals and outgoing commands to the muscles, such as intentional movements and speaking. The *autonomic* system, on the other hand, is responsible for controlling all of the internal organ systems, and this part is usually not under conscious control. In fact, the autonomic nervous system is largely under the control of the hypothalamus, and there are two basic things that it can do to each organ system: It can either speed them up or it can slow them down.

With that in mind, you can subdivide the autonomic nervous system into the sympathetic system and the parasympathetic system. The *sympathetic* system is active when the animal needs to be more alert and ready for action, like when it is faced with a predator. That means the sympathetic system will speed up heart rate and breathing rate, and it will open blood vessels (vasodilation) in the muscles and lungs, and the animal will feel a burst of energy. At the same time, the sympathetic nervous system will also slow down the digestive and reproductive systems and will close down blood vessels (vasoconstriction) in those areas because they are not necessary for immediate survival in emergency situations.

The most common neurotransmitters used by the sympathetic system are epinephrine and norepinephrine. You know the feeling you get when you have an "adrenaline rush" like when you realize you forgot to bring number 2 pencils to your SAT II test? Well, "adrenaline" is just another name for epinephrine, so what you're really feeling is a "sympathetic nervous system rush." This is sometimes called the *fight-or-flight response* because it gets you ready for serious action, whether it's fighting or running away.

The *parasympathetic* system does the exact opposite of the sympathetic system, and it is active when the animal is calm and resting. The digestive and reproductive systems start working normally, and the heart and lungs are working at their resting rate. The most common neurotransmitter used in the parasympathetic system is acetylcholine, and it is most active during sleep. It is also active right after a meal, which is why you're not supposed to go swimming for at least a half hour after eating. The parasympathetic nervous system diverts blood to the digestive system and away from everything else, so your muscles aren't ready for serious swimming action.

Before moving on to the sensory systems, try these questions about the nervous system.

Which of the following is most likely to be caused by the sympathetic nervous system?

(A) decreased digestive system activity

(B) increased immune system activity

(C) decreased heart rate

(D) vasodilation in digestive system

(E) decreased breathing rate

This is one of those "most likely to" questions, so read them all carefully because more than one may be a possible effect.

The sympathetic system initiates the fight or flight response, so it will increase activity in organs associated with immediate action and will decrease activity in the long term growth and maintenance organs. The heart and breathing rates will definitely go up during the fight or flight response, so (C) and (E) can be crossed out. The immune system is not part of immediate response to emergencies, so it will be suppressed, so cross out (B) as well. The digestive system is not immediately needed for fighting or running away, so it will be suppressed. Vasodilation opens up blood vessels to organs that are more active, so (D) is out, and (A) is the correct answer.

Which of the following is least likely to be caused by the parasympathetic nervous system?

(A) increased digestive system activity

(B) increased reproductive system activity

(C) increased sense of alertness

(D) decreased heart rate

(E) decreased breathing rate

This one is a "least likely to happen" question, so four of the choices will be clear results of parasympathetic system action, and you need to find the one that doesn't belong.

The parasympathetic system works against the sympathetic system in order to calm the animal down and promote the long-term growth and maintenance organs. The digestive and reproductive systems are definitely part of that program, so (A) and (B) can be crossed out. Breathing and heart rates will both decrease, so (D) and (E) can be crossed out as well. That leaves (C), because increased alertness is associated with the high energy sympathetic system, not the low key parasympathetic system.

Which of the following is true about a section of axon of a neuron during action potential?

(A) neurotransmitter is reabsorbed

(B) sodium channels are closed

(C) potential is at approximately –70 mV

(D) sodium channels are open

(E) potential is at approximately –50 mV

The question is looking for the true answer, so you can cross out ones you know are false.

Neurotransmitters are involved in the synapse, not in the axon, so (A) is out because it is irrelevant. Answers (C) and (E) are also wrong because –70 is the resting potential and –50 is the threshold potential. The action potential is +30 mV, and that's not one of the choices. The potential gets up to +30 because of all the Na+ rushing in, and for that to happen the sodium channels must be open, so the correct answer is (D).

Which of the following brain structures is most responsible for regulating autonomic functions?

(A) hypothalamus

(B) thalamus

(C) cerebellum

(D) cerebral cortex

(E) brain stem

This is just a basic memorization question, but some of those are on the SAT II.

The correct answer is (A), the hypothalamus, because it is the structure in control of the autonomic functions. The thalamus is the gate keeper for incoming sensory information, so (B) is wrong. The cerebellum is for balance, so cross out (C). Answer (D) can't be right because, the cerebral cortex is for conscious thinking, and (E) is wrong because the brain stem is for initiating autonomic functions rather than regulating them.

Taking It All In: The Sensory Systems

The senses are how animals get information about the outside world and about how things are going inside the body. All sensory organs, such as eyes, ears, nose, and so on send their sensory information to the brain via the peripheral nervous system. This section will cover the basic five senses that you're familiar with — sight, sound, taste, smell, and touch — plus the sense of balance.

Seeing is believing: Vision

This is, of course, the detection of light coming at you from the environment. The eyes are the sensory organs, and as you can see in Figure 14-6, they allow light to come in through holes called *pupils,* which are the dark spots in the middle of your eyes. The size of each pupil is controlled by the *iris,* which is the colored muscle around the pupil. If there's not much light around, then the pupils get bigger to allow in more light so you can see better.

As the light comes in, it passes through the *lens,* which focuses the light on the *retina,* which is where the actual photoreceptors are located. When the photoreceptors are triggered, they activate neurons that send the information to the brain through the optic nerve.

There are two types of photoreceptors, rods and cones. **Rods** are good at picking up different intensities of light and dark and are located at the edges of the retina, which is your peripheral vision. You may not notice it all the time, but your peripheral vision is not very sharp. Try looking about an inch off of this page and then read these words without looking back. You may not even be able to tell exactly where the words are, let alone be able to read them. You can really only read what's right in the middle of your vision, which is where the cones are located. The **cones** detect color and are packed in really tight in the center of the retina so that you can pick out a lot more details.

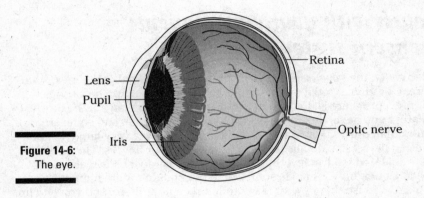

Figure 14-6:
The eye.

Lens —
Pupil —
Iris —
Retina
Optic nerve

Sounding it out: Hearing

The outer ears are just the external parts of our hearing system, sometimes called the *auditory system,* and all that those flappy, wrinkled things do is focus incoming sound down to the ear canal like a funnel. Sound waves are vibrations in the air, and when they come into the ear canal, they hit the ear drum, also called the *tympanic membrane,* and they cause it to vibrate. The inside of the ear drum is attached to the smallest bones in the body, the inner ear bones, and the vibration is transferred through them to the *cochlea.* Inside the cochlea are little receptor cells called hair cells. The different hair cells are sensitive to vibrations of different frequencies, also called different pitches of sound, such as high squeaky sounds and low rumbling sounds. When a sound of a certain frequency comes in, the corresponding hair cells pick up the vibrations and activate specific neurons that tell the brain that a sound of that frequency has been detected.

Keeping your balance: The vestibular system

The sense of balance is mostly handled by a set of structures in the inner ear called the *vestibular system.* The vestibular system consists of hollow structures called the *semicircular canals,* the *utricle,* and the *saccule.* The names aren't as important as remembering how they work. Each structure contains a kind of specialized fluid, and when the position of the head changes, the fluid in these chambers sloshes around. This sloshing is detected by receptors that activate neurons that send the information to the brain about which direction the fluid sloshed. Although these are the main sensory organs for balance, you also use your eyes and feet. Your eyes tell you if your leaning a little bit one way or the other, and your feet can detect whether the pressure you're putting on them is even or not.

Sampling the cuisine: Taste and smell

These two go together because they're both set up to detect the presence of certain chemicals. The taste buds on the tongue detect chemicals inside things you eat or drink, and the scent receptors inside the nose are detecting chemicals in the air. The sense of taste is sometimes called *gustatory system*, while the sense of smell is sometimes called the *olfactory system*. There are different receptors for different kinds of chemicals, and when a receptor detects the presence of its chemical, it activates a neuron which send that information to the brain. The four basic kinds of taste receptors are sweet, sour, bitter, and salty. Our sense of smell is way more fine-tuned than our sense of taste, so there aren't just a few neat and tidy categories of olfactory receptors.

Getting in touch with your environment: The somatosensory system

The sense of touch, also called the *somatosensory system*, includes a lot of subcategories, such as detection of pressure, vibration, stretch, temperature, texture, and so on. The various kinds of somatosensory receptors are all located in the skin, and also in many of the internal organs. The more receptors you have, the more sensitive you are to touch, and some areas of skin have more receptors than others. For example, the fingertips have a very large number of receptors so that we can detect fine details how things feel with our fingers. This is different from an area like the ankle, which can feel things okay, but it just doesn't feel as much detail. Have you ever had an itch on your ankle somewhere but couldn't quite pinpoint where to scratch it? That's because there's a lot fewer touch receptors there, and you end up just scratching the whole area in order to make sure you get at the source of the problem. Just like always, when one of the touch receptors is activated, it activates a neuron that carries the information to the brain.

Okay, now check your knowledge with these sensory systems questions.

Questions 1–4 refer to the following:

(A) auditory system

(B) olfactory system

(C) vestibular system

(D) visual system

(E) somatosensory system

1. The sensory system that detects chemicals in the environment.

   The two sensory systems that detect chemicals are taste and smell. Taste is not one of the options, so you should choose smell, which is also called the olfactory system.

2. The sensory system primarily responsible for helping to maintain balance.

   Balance is maintained by the vestibular system. "Vestibules" are little enclosed spaces, and the vestibular system is made of hollow chambers.

3. The sensory system that detects temperature differences.

   The somatosensory system covers all forms of touch, that is, all things you can feel with your skin, and temperature definitely falls into this category.

4. The sensory system that detects stretching of tissues.

   Detection of stretching also falls into the group somatosensory receptors.

Which of the following is the part of the eye that contains the photoreceptors?

(A) lens

(B) optic nerve

(C) semicircular canal

(D) retina

(E) pupil

The lens focus the light that comes through the pupil and lands on the retina. The retina is where the actual photoreceptors are, so the correct answer is (D). The optic nerve carries information from the receptors on the retina to the brain. The semicircular canals are part of a different sensory system entirely.

Getting All Hormonal: The Endocrine System

For most of you life, you don't really think too much about your hormones, but from around middle school up through high school they make themselves known in a big way. It's kind of hard to miss the changes that happen during puberty, what with all the hair, the zits, and the daily emotional dramas. All of those changes are triggered by just a few hormones that can affect every organ in the body. The endocrine system is all about those hormones and a whole bunch more.

The SAT II isn't likely to have more than a few questions that cover the endocrine system, and this section will cover the most likely topics.

The nervous system exerts really fast and precise control over the various organ systems. Hormones also control organ system activity, but unlike the nervous system, the effects of the endocrine system are slow and steady. This feature makes them bad candidates for things like muscle coordination during complex movements, but it makes them great for long-term things like the crazy growth and development that happen during the teen years.

Hormones are produced inside of **endocrine glands** that send the hormones out into the blood stream at just the right time. Before continuing, we should mention the difference between an endocrine gland and an exocrine gland. Both types of glands produce and release certain substances, but *endocrine* glands release their substances (usually hormones) into the blood stream, while *exocrine* glands, such as sweat and oil glands, release their substances out onto the surface of the skin. This section focuses on the endocrine glands, while exocrine glands are covered in more detail in "Protecting the Insides: The Skin" later in this chapter.

Figure 14-7 shows the locations of the main endocrine glands in the human body. Different hormones have different functions, but the basic mode of action is the same for all of them. First, a gland is prompted by the nervous system to release a hormone into the blood stream, where it travels to every tissue in the body. Some cells will have receptors that the hormone can attach to, and when that happens, the hormone will change the activity of the cell in some specific way, either speeding it up or slowing it down.

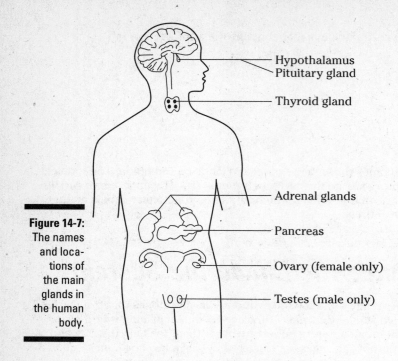

Figure 14-7:
The names and locations of the main glands in the human body.

Hypothalamus
Pituitary gland

Thyroid gland

Adrenal glands

Pancreas

Ovary (female only)

Testes (male only)

Exerting wide influence: The pituitary gland

The gland that produces the greatest variety of hormones is the pituitary gland, which is stuck just underneath the brain. The pituitary gland is controlled by the hypothalamus, which is the part of the brain that controls most of the autonomic functions. The pituitary gland is divided into two sections, called the *anterior* (front) pituitary, and the *posterior* (rear) pituitary. The posterior pituitary releases two main hormones. The first is called *oxytocin*, and it is released when a woman needs to deliver breast milk to her baby. The other hormone from the posterior pituitary is called *antidiuretic hormone*, and it slows down urine production in the kidneys.

The anterior pituitary releases a whole bunch of different hormones, and while it's active for a person's entire life, it is *especially* active during puberty. Here are the main hormones from the anterior pituitary:

- **Adrenocorticotropic hormone.** This causes the adrenal glands to release hormones associated with the fight-or-flight response.

- **Thyroid stimulating hormone.** As the name suggests, this hormone stimulates the thyroid gland to produce and release thyroid hormone.

- **Growth hormone.** This name is also pretty self explanatory. This hormone promotes growth of all tissues, especially bones and muscles, and it also promotes healing. Growth hormone is released every night during deep sleep.

- **Luteinizing hormone.** This one promotes puberty by causing the gonads (testes or ovaries) to grow and become active. The gonads are what produce sperm or eggs (see Chapters 9 and 15) and they also produce sex hormones. Luteinizing hormone specifically promotes the *release* of the sex hormones, and also helps prepare the uterus for pregnancy.

✔ **Follicle stimulating hormone.** This one also starts being released during puberty. It promotes the production of gametes in the gonads.

✔ **Prolactin.** This is yet another hormone associated with reproduction, though it is only produced in females. Prolactin promotes the production of breast milk by the mammary glands.

Keeping you going: The thyroid gland

The thyroid gland is in front of the throat, and it produces thyroid hormone, which helps maintain basic metabolic rate. When someone says that they don't gain weight because they have a high metabolism, it's because they produce a lot of thyroid hormone. This is also the only place in the body that needs the element iodine in order to function. For some strange reason, iodine is needed for the thyroid gland to release thyroid hormone. If you don't have iodine in your diet, the gland will make the hormone but it won't release it, and you'll end up feeling less energetic. That's why most table salt has been "iodized."

Getting an energy burst: The adrenal glands

The adrenal glands are located just above the kidneys, and they are each separated into two parts. The cortex is the outer surface of the adrenal glands, while the medulla is the interior part. The hormones coming from this gland are all associated with the fight-or-flight response, which is triggered during emergency situations by the sympathetic nervous system and by adrenocorticotropic hormone from the pituitary gland. The adrenal cortex produces a hormone called *cortisol,* which helps the fight or flight response by suppressing the activity of the immune system, the digestive system, and the reproductive system. These need to be suppressed because they aren't needed for the moment to moment survival during an emergency and you don't want them taking resources away from the muscles, lungs, and heart.

The adrenal medulla produces epinephrine, which is also called adrenaline. When this is released it causes the activity of most cells to increase, especially the muscle cells. If something scares you, your adrenal gland will give you an adrenaline rush in order to deal with the possible emergency.

This is a good example of how the endocrine system is different from the nervous system, because once the adrenaline has been released, there's no recalling it. If the thing that startled you turns out to be no big deal, you'll still feel a little bit jumpy until the adrenaline effect wears off.

Regulating fuel supply: The pancreas

The pancreas is an organ that serves double duty. It's involved in digestion by producing enzymes needed for breaking down food, but it also works as an endocrine gland. The pancreas releases the hormone *insulin* which helps store away excess glucose after a meal. The digestive system absorbs the sugar into the blood, and then insulin helps get the sugar into storage in the liver. The other hormone that the pancreas releases is called *glucagon*, and this one does the exact opposite of insulin. Glucagon is released when you haven't eaten for a while and need some extra fuel, and it causes any stored sugars and fats to be released into the blood stream so that they can be used by the muscles and other tissues.

Driving for reproduction: The gonads

The gonads are the final glands discussed in this section. Male gonads are testes, while females have ovaries. The testes, in addition to producing sperm, also produce and release testosterone. This hormone is most directly responsible for the changes that happen during male puberty such as bigger muscles, broader shoulders, and more body hair. It's also responsible for male pattern baldness later on in life. The ovaries, on the other hand, produce eggs (also called *ova*) and release the female sex hormone estrogen. Estrogen does the same as testosterone, but for girls, so it causes wider hips, and only a little extra body hair (usually not nearly as much as boys).

Okay, now you can check your knowledge of the endocrine system with these sample questions.

Which of the following hormones is most directly responsible for sexual development in humans?

(A) growth hormone

(B) thyroid hormone

(C) adrenocorticotropic hormone

(D) luteinizing hormone

(E) cortisol

Notice that the question asks for the hormone *most* responsible, which can sometimes be a little tricky. The best possible answer may not even be on the list at all, and in this case it is not. Testosterone and estrogen are *most* directly responsible for puberty from among *all* the hormones, but they are not included in the choices. Even so, you can still determine a winner from this list by judging the effects of the different hormones.

Cortisol and adrenocorticotropic hormone are both involved in the fight or flight response, so they would actually slow down sexual development, so cross out (C) and (E). Thyroid hormone sets basic metabolic rate, and growth hormone helps with general growth and development, so they both indirectly help with sexual development, but there may be an even better answer. Luteinizing hormone directly promotes greater activity in the gonads, which leads to more testosterone and estrogen release, so (D) is the one that's most directly responsible for sexual development from among the choices.

Which of the following glands produces hormones involved in the fight or flight response?

I. pituitary

II. thyroid

III. adrenal

IV. pineal

(A) I only

(B) I and III only

(C) III only

(D) I and IV only

(E) II only

The fight or flight response has to do with an energy burst from an adrenaline rush. The adrenal gland produces adrenaline (also known as epinephrine), so III must be included, which narrows things down to either (B) or (C). The pituitary gland produces a lot of hormones that have nothing to do with the fight or flight response, but it can also release adrenocorticotropic hormone, which activates the adrenal gland, so I needs to be included also. That means the correct answer is (B).

Breaking It Down and Soaking It Up: The Digestive System

The obvious purpose of the digestive system is to break down food into nutrients and then absorb the nutrients. In animals, this all starts with the mouth. Some just suck in their food whole and send it right to the stomach. Others, especially the herbivores and carnivores, use teeth to slice, grind, or crush their food before swallowing it. In fact, you can tell a lot about an animal just by looking at its teeth. The teeth are specialized for the typical diet of the animal, so if they're wide and flat, then the animal is probably an herbivore that needs to grind up leaves and other plant material. On the other hand, if the teeth are sharp and pointy, then the animal is probably a carnivore that needs to kill its food and slice it up into manageable chunks.

As you can see in Figure 14-8, after coming in through the mouth, the food goes down a tube called the esophagus and ends up in the stomach. There are smooth muscles lining the esophagus that help push the food down to the stomach, which is part of the basic swallowing reflex. In fact, there are smooth muscles lining the whole digestive tract, and they continually push food through the different digestive organs in a process called *peristalsis*.

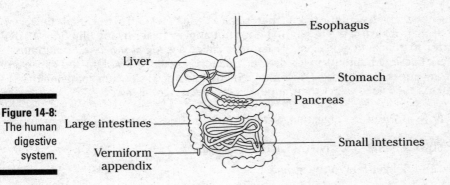

Figure 14-8:
The human digestive system.

Scorching with acid: The stomach

Most animals have a very acidic stomach to start the breakdown process and for killing off some of the bacteria and fungus that may be in the food. Stomach acid is at about pH 1, which makes it very good at breaking down proteins and for dissolving minerals and sugars. The stomach lining can also absorb a lot of water and some nutrients, but most of the absorption happens in the small intestine. Some herbivores, like cows, have extra stomachs that contain a special kind of bacteria that helps the animal break down the cellulose in all that plant material they consume. Without the bacteria, the animal wouldn't get enough nutrients, and without the animal, the bacteria wouldn't get any food at all, so this is a great example of mutualistic symbiosis (see Chapter 12).

Doing most of the work: The small intestine

After the stomach, the food goes to the main digestive organ, the small intestine, which is where most of the breakdown occurs. In a typical human, the small intestine is around 6 feet long because the longer the food stays in there, the more time it has for digestion. Digestive enzymes are produced in the pancreas and then sent to the small intestine where they systematically break down all the proteins, carbohydrates, lipids, and nucleic acids. The liver also helps out by producing a nasty green substance called bile which is sent to the small intestine. Once there, the bile helps to break up fats and oils. As the digestive enzymes break down the food into basic monosaccharides, amino acids, and things like that, the lining of the small intestine absorbs the nutrients and sends them into the blood stream where they are delivered to the rest of the body.

In order to pick up all these nutrients, the small intestine receives a huge blood supply. Right after a meal the blood vessels in the small intestine will undergo vasodilation, which allows more blood to flow through. Since more blood is going to the digestive system after a meal, less of it is available to the rest of the body, especially the muscles. As discussed right at the end of the section of the nervous system, this is why you shouldn't go swimming right after eating a big meal.

Holding it in: The large intestine

After the small intestine comes the large intestine, which is mostly just a storage area, though some water is absorbed so that it isn't wasted. The stuff that's left over after digestion in the small intestine is kept in the large intestine until the animal can find a convenient time and place to poop it out. For some animals this is just wherever they happen to be standing, but the more civilized creatures need to learn to hold it in.

One weird thing about the large intestine is that it has a little dead end area called the vermiform appendix. This is a part of the organ that does not appear to serve any function. As discussed in Chapter 10, this kind of useless structure is called a *vestigial structure*. Sometimes people get excess bacteria building up inside the appendix, making it swell up and cause an appendicitis. If the appendix ruptures, it would be really bad news, so when someone develops an appendicitis they need to get their appendix removed right away.

Now that you know all about the digestive system, you can chew on these sample questions.

Which of the following is the digestive role of the pancreas?

(A) to produce and deliver bile to the stomach

(B) to produce and deliver bile to the small intestine

(C) to produce and deliver digestive enzymes to the stomach

(D) to produce and deliver digestive enzymes to the small intestine

(E) none of the above

First of all, the pancreas produces digestive enzymes, while the liver is the organ that produces bile, so cross out (A) and (B). The digestive enzymes that are produced by the pancreas are sent to the small intestine, where the majority of the actual breakdown of food happens, so the correct answer is (D).

Which of the following is not a function of the small intestine?

(A) use digestive enzymes to break down food

(B) absorb nutrients from broken-down food

(C) use acids to kill bacteria and fungus

(D) move food along the tube via peristalsis

(E) receive bile from the liver

The small intestine receives bile from the liver and digestive enzymes from the pancreas. It then breaks down the food and absorbs the nutrient molecules into the blood stream. The only thing on the list that the small intestine doesn't do is C. The stomach uses strong acids, not the small intestine.

Exchanging Gasses: The Respiratory System

The basic purpose of the respiratory system is to get O_2 and to get rid of CO_2, a process called *gas exchange*. Some animals, like jellyfish, anemone, and worms, don't really have a specific respiratory system because they just let the gasses diffuse across their skin. For most animals, however, this diffusion process isn't fast enough, so they use gills or lungs to get the job done. Animals with gills are things like mollusks and crustaceans and, of course, fish, which are all things that live full time in the water. The gills are made of many thin layers of tissue with lots of blood vessels. Water flows over the gills and gas exchange happens between the water and the blood.

Taking a deep breath: The lungs

Lungs are for air breathers, which includes all mammals, birds, reptiles, and adult amphibians. Mammals and birds have the fastest metabolisms, so they need really rapid gas exchange, so their lungs are the most complex. Air is drawn in through the mouth or nose, and travels through the trachea to the bronchi, and then down into the lungs (see Figure 14-9). If it goes through the nose, the air will also go through an area called the *pharynx* which includes the sinuses back inside the head. Eventually, the air reaches little air sacs called *alveoli* deep inside the lungs. The alveoli have very thin walls and have blood vessels running right up against them, which allows O_2 to diffuse in and CO_2 to diffuse out. In mammals, the muscle that pulls air into the lungs is called the *diaphragm*. The diaphragm is unusual because it's normally under autonomic control, but we can easily bring it under conscious control like when you speak or hold your breath to go underwater.

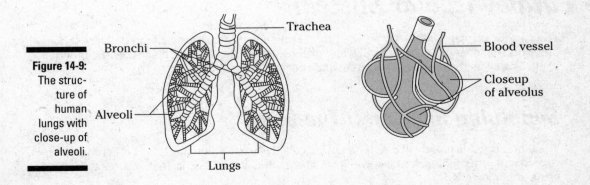

Figure 14-9: The structure of human lungs with close-up of alveoli.

Trachea

Bronchi

Blood vessel

Closeup of alveolus

Alveoli

Lungs

Controlling acidity: pH regulation of the blood

Although the main purpose of the respiratory system is for basic gas exchange to keep the mitochondria working (see Chapter 6), the respiratory system also works to regulate the pH of the blood. Chapter 4 tells you that pH is a measure of acidity, and when pH goes down, that means things are more acidic. The pH of blood is supposed to be kept at around 7.3 to 7.4, which is just above neutral. If it goes too much above or below that value, the red blood cells stop working correctly and they can't carry O_2 anymore, so obviously it's really important to keep the pH of the blood closely regulated. As always, it's the job of the hypothalamus in the brain to keep track of all of this.

It just so happens that when CO_2 is dissolved in water (blood plasma is mostly water) it forms carbonic acid, and this lowers the pH. That means too much CO_2 in the blood can lower the pH out of the safe range. To bring the pH back up, you need to get rid of some excess CO_2, which you can do by breathing a little faster and deeper. The normal time for doing this is when you are exercising because when you're exercising, you're producing extra CO_2. Surprisingly, the main trigger for making you breathe faster is not the need for more O_2. Instead, the main trigger for the brain to increase breathing rate is a decrease in the pH of the blood caused by excess CO_2.

Okay, just one quick sample question on the respiratory system before moving on to the cardiovascular system.

Which of the following is the part of the lungs in which gas exchange occurs?

(A) pharynx

(B) diaphragm

(C) trachea

(D) bronchi

(E) alveoli

The air comes in through the mouth or the nose and then into the trachea. If air comes in through the nose, it will go through the pharynx (sinuses) before entering the trachea. The trachea then branches off into the two bronchi that go to the two lungs. So far, this is all just tubing that leads down to where the real action happens, and no gas exchange happens in the tubing. Only when you get to the alveoli do you finally see gas exchange. So (E) is the correct choice.

Pumping and Delivering: The Cardiovascular System

The cardiovascular system moves the blood around inside the body. Blood delivers O_2 and other nutrients, and it clears out CO_2 and other wastes. This section discusses the blood itself, as well as the circulatory system and the heart.

Supplying nutrients: The blood

The blood is made mostly of a water solution called *plasma*, which has lots of different minerals, sugars, and other molecules dissolved in it. Suspended in the plasma are the three different kinds of blood cells.

The most important kinds for the SAT II are the red cells, also called *erythrocytes*, because these are the ones that carry O_2 and CO_2.

The second kind are the white blood cells, also called *leukocytes*, which are part of the immune system. Leukocytes attack invading viruses and bacteria with antibodies and break them down into basic nutrient molecules. The third type of blood cells are the *platelets* which are involved in blood clotting. When the wall of a blood vessel is damaged, platelets stick to the damaged area to reduce leakage and give the vessel a chance to heal.

Red blood cells contain a special protein called *hemoglobin* that is important for carrying O_2. Stuck right in the middle of the hemoglobin protein is a iron atom (chemical symbol = Fe), and when O_2 comes by, it sticks to the iron. This forms FeO_2, also known as iron oxide, which is known as rust when it builds up on metal objects. Rust, as you know, is a kind of reddish-orange color, so this rusting of your blood is the main reason the blood looks red. The hemoglobin is very sensitive to changes in pH, so the pH of the blood needs to be very closely regulated, as discussed in earlier in this chapter in "Exchanging Gasses: The Respiratory System."

Sometimes the SAT II asks a question about *anemia*, which is a general term for an inability to deliver enough O_2 to the various tissues of the body. In *iron deficiency anemia,* the reason is that the person does not have enough iron in their red blood cells to pick up enough O_2. Another type of anemia, called *pernicious anemia,* is caused by a lack of vitamin B12, which is required for making functional red blood cells in the bone marrow.

Delivering the blood: The circulatory system

Some animals have a really simple circulatory system where the blood isn't even really contained inside blood vessels except around the heart. This is called an *open circulatory system* and is used by things like insects. Vertebrates, which are more likely to show up on the SAT II, use a closed circulatory system where the blood stays inside the vessels at all times, and is pumped around by a bigger heart.

The vertebrate circulatory system is actually two systems in one. The *pulmonary circulation* is the part that carries blood through the lungs (or gills) to pick up O_2 and get rid of CO_2. The *systemic circulation*, on the other hand, carries blood through the rest of the body to deliver O_2 and pick up CO_2. See Figure 14-10 for a diagram of these two systems as they go through the heart. Blood vessels carrying blood away from the heart are called *arteries,* and the ones carrying blood back to the heart are called "veins." The smallest blood vessels that run through all of the tissues of the body are called "capillaries."

Since most of the bigger blood vessels, especially the arteries, are lined with smooth muscle, they can change their size to allow more or less blood to flow through. For example, if you start swimming, you need to send more blood to your muscles, so the blood vessels in your swimming muscles open up in a process called *vasodilation.* On the other hand, you don't need to send as much blood to your digestive system while you're swimming, so the smooth muscles around the blood vessels in your small intestines contract, which restricts the blood flow. This squeezing off of the blood supply is called *vasoconstriction.* So, your mother was right. Don't go swimming right after a meal! Your digestive system and your muscles will be fighting each other for blood, and you won't do a good job of either digesting or swimming.

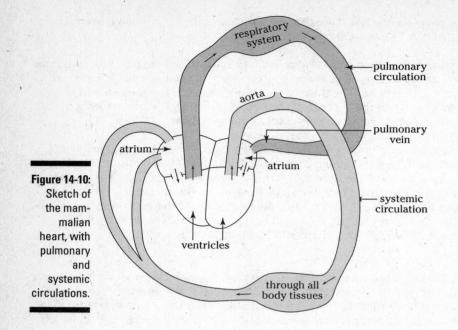

Figure 14-10:
Sketch of the mammalian heart, with pulmonary and systemic circulations.

Keeping it moving: The heart

The heart is a strong, high-endurance muscle for pumping blood through the circulatory system. This section will focus on the mammalian heart, but we should mention other kinds of animals, just in case. Small, simple animals such as worms have one-chambered hearts. Fish have hearts with two chambers, one atrium and one ventricle. The *ventricle* is the really strong chamber that pushes blood through the circulatory system, while the *atrium* just squeezes blood into the ventricle. Amphibians and reptiles are a little fancier because they have three-chambered hearts with two atriums and one ventricle. One atrium receives blood from the pulmonary circulation while the other atrium receives blood from the systemic circulation, though they both squeeze blood into a single ventricle.

The most efficient kind of heart is the four-chambered heart of mammals and birds. A four-chambered heart keeps the systemic and pulmonary sides completely separate so that oxygenated blood from the lungs doesn't mix with de-oxygenated blood from the rest of the body. See Figure 14-10 for a diagram of a standard mammalian heart.

Hopefully some vasodilation in your brain will help you answer these sample questions about the circulatory system.

EXAMPLE

Questions 1–4 refer to the following:

(A) erythrocytes

(B) leukocytes

(C) platelets

(D) pulmonary circulation

(E) systemic circulation

1. blood cells that contain hemoglobin

   The erythrocytes are responsible for carrying oxygen, and they do it with hemoglobin, so (A) is correct.

2. carries blood through the respiratory system

   The pulmonary circulation carries blood through the respiratory system (sometimes called the pulmonary system) to pick up O_2 and drop off CO_2. Then the systemic circulation sends the blood through all the other tissues of the body to drop off O_2 and pick up CO_2. So (D) is the correct answer here.

3. blood cells that carry O_2

   Just like in #1, the erythrocytes use their hemoglobin to carry oxygen; again (A) is the correct choice.

4. blood cells directly involved in immune responses

   The leukocytes are the white blood cells, which are the cells of the immune system, so (B) is the correct answer.

Taking Out the Trash: the Excretory System

The excretory system, also called the *renal system*, includes the kidneys, the urinary bladder, and the tubes that are used to get rid of urine. The overall purpose of the excretory system is to control the contents of the blood. For example, if there are any waste products or foreign molecules in the blood, the kidneys filter them and they are eventually released through urine. Also, if there's too much salt or sugar or something in the blood, the kidneys filter them out, too.

The kidneys are made of many thousands of microscopic little filtration systems called *nephrons,* one of which is shown in Figure 14-11. Each nephron receives blood from a single vessel and filters out most small molecules and lots of water. Most of the water and the good stuff, such as minerals, sugars, amino acids, and things like that are reabsorbed back into the blood. Whatever's left is called urine, which gets stored in the bladder until the animal can find a convenient time and place to urinate. Of course, some animals just go wherever, but the classy ones consider that impolite.

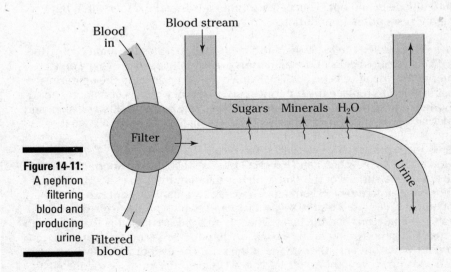

Figure 14-11: A nephron filtering blood and producing urine.

If the animal's blood contains too much of any of the good molecules, such as excess minerals or amino acids, then the nephron will reabsorb less of those good things and let them pass out in the urine. The nephron can also adjust how much water it reabsorbs in order to help regulate blood pressure. If the blood pressure is too high, the hypothalamus in the brain will detect it and will tell the nephrons to let more water be released in the urine. This brings the total volume of the blood down, which in turn brings overall blood pressure down. By the way, the most common medication for high blood pressure is a *diuretic,* which is a pill that makes you urinate more.

If you think you can hold it in a little longer, try this sample question on the excretory system.

Which of the following is most likely to be a response of the excretory system to high blood pressure?

(A) retain more minerals

(B) release more minerals into the urine

(C) release more water in the urine

(D) retain more water

(E) retain more sugars

If your blood pressure is too high, you can bring it back down by releasing some extra water. Just like if you let some of the water out of a water balloon, the pressure in the balloon will go down. The nephrons in the kidneys filter a lot of water out of the blood and then reabsorb much of it back into the blood. If blood pressure is high, the nephrons will reabsorb less water and allow it to be released in the urine, bringing the overall pressure inside the circulatory system down. The answer is (C).

Protecting the Insides: The Skin

This is the only organ that you typically see of an animal. The main purpose of the skin is to provide protection for the soft juicy parts underneath, so most skin is covered by scales, feathers, or fur. Amphibians are the biggest exception because their skin is really thin and allows a lot of stuff to diffuse in and out. This helps amphibians breathe underwater, but it also makes them highly susceptible to pollution.

The outer part of the skin is called the *epidermis*, and that's what provides the main protection and waterproofing. The outermost cells of the epidermis are actually dead, leaving a dense layer of protein covering the living cells below. The living cells lower down in the epidermis reproduce really fast in order to replace the outermost layer of skin which is constantly being rubbed off. Actually, most of the dust in your house is made of tiny bits of rubbed off skin, and while you may think that's gross, the tiny dust mites that feed on it think it's really great.

Below the epidermis is the layer of living cells called the *dermis* (see Figure 14-12) This is where the hair follicles (which produce new hair) and exocrine glands are located. Exocrine glands secrete a substance out on the surface of the skin, which is different from an endocrine gland which secretes its hormones into the blood stream. There are two main kinds of exocrine glands in the skin of humans. First, there's the *sebaceous* glands which produce the oil that protects and waterproofs the epidermis and the hairs. Then there's the *sweat* glands that help with cooling the body down. When body temperature rises, the hypothalamus in the brain triggers the sweat glands to send water out onto the surface of the skin. The evaporation of water cools the skin down, which ends up cooling the whole body down. One other kind of exocrine gland is the *mammary gland,* which produces milk for newborn offspring (in female mammals only, of course).

Underneath the dermis is the *hypodermis*, which is where the bigger blood vessels run and where you can find subcutaneous fat, which is sometimes called *adipose tissue*. We all store at least a little subcutaneous fat, though serious marathon runners and Tour de France cyclists have almost none. Below the hypodermis is connective tissue that connects the skin to the underlying muscles and bones.

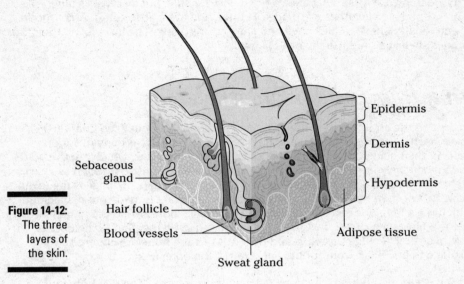

Figure 14-12: The three layers of the skin.

Epidermis

Dermis

Hypodermis

Sebaceous gland

Hair follicle

Blood vessels

Sweat gland

Adipose tissue

Your skin can't protect you from SAT II questions, so you may as well practice on this one.

EXAMPLE

Which of the following is not an example of an exocrine gland?

(A) mammary gland

(B) adrenal gland

(C) sebaceous gland

(D) sweat gland

(E) all of the above are exocrine glands

Exocrine glands secrete their stuff onto the surface of the skin. All of the choices do that except the adrenal gland, which secretes hormones like epinephrine and cortisol into the blood stream. That makes the adrenal an endocrine gland. The answer is (B).

Standing Tall: The Skeletal System

All animals have some kind of skeleton, even if it's really soft like a jellyfish, amoeba, or worm. Even those mushy animals have what's called a "*hydrostatic skeleton,* which is just a tough skin holding everything in. Even though they're mushy, animals with a hydrostatic skeleton can still hold their shape fairly well. All other animals have a hard skeleton, which come in two basic types, exoskeletons and endoskeletons. *Exoskeletons,* sometimes just called "shells," are on the outside of the animal because *exo* means "outside." *Endoskeletons,* on the other hand, are on the inside of the animal and are usually made of bones.

Living in a shell: Exoskeletons

Animals with exoskeletons include all the insects (arthropods) and shellfish (mollusks). The exoskeletons of most mollusks, such as clams and oysters, are made of calcium carbonate, which is hard as rock. The only mollusks that don't have shells are the squid and octopus, which have a hydrostatic skeleton. This makes them very flexible, but also very vulnerable to predators. Arthropod exoskeletons are made of chitin, and are a little softer. Arthropods such as crabs and lobsters have a thick shell and can get pretty big. The insects, on the other hand, have thinner shells and are usually pretty small.

Supporting from inside: Endoskeletons

The echinoderms and the chordates are the animals with endoskeletons (see Chapter 11). Echinoderms are starfish and sea urchins, and the SAT II isn't likely to ask any questions about the details of their skeletons, so we'll just focus on the chordates, which are the vertebrate animals. Most endoskeletons are made of bone, but some types of fish, such as sharks and rays (the chondrychthyes) have endoskeletons made of cartilage. Cartilage is made out of tough proteins rather than bone, so it's a lot softer. Regular bone is made out of calcium phosphate, which is Ca_2PO_4. The calcium part makes the bones hard, while the phosphate part helps keep the bones a little bit flexible. Bones are connected together by ligaments, which are made of strong, flexible proteins, and the ends of each bone are covered by a padding of cartilage to protect it from rubbing up against the bone next to it.

Endoskeletons have a lot of different functions in vertebrate animals. The most obvious functions include supporting the animal's shape, protection of the vital organs, and working with the muscles to produce movement. A less obvious function is the storage of minerals. Calcium and phosphorus are important minerals for many different bodily functions, so if there's ever a shortage somewhere, more calcium or phosphorus can be taken out of the bones. Normally this is just a temporary situation because when you eat these minerals in your food, any extras get stored in the bones to replace whatever was taken out before. Another less obvious function of bones is to enclose the bone marrow, which is where new blood cells are made.

To help you bone up on your knowledge of the skeletal system, try this sample question.

EXAMPLE

Which of the following is not a function of the skeletal system?

(A) protection of internal organs

(B) storage of excess phosphorus

(C) storage of excess calcium

(D) storage of excess water

(E) support for overall body shape

This question is asking which is *not* a function, so that means you should try to eliminate the ones you know *are* functions of the skeletal system. Obviously, support and protection are functions of the skeletal system, so (A) and (E) can be crossed out. Bones are made of calcium phosphate, so they can act as a storage depot for both calcium and phosphorus, which means you should cross out (B) and (C) as well. That leaves (D). The bones contain some water, but they definitely don't function as water storage.

Beefing Up: The Muscular System

Muscles are made of a special group of proteins that are able to pull or squeeze, and the two most important proteins in muscles are *actin* and *myosin*. As shown in Figure 14-13, muscles are arranged in little subunits called *sarcomeres,"* and when a muscle contracts, all the sarcomeres get shorter.

Figure 14-13: Arrangement of sarcomeres in a skeletal muscle.

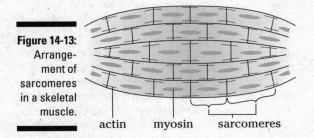

actin   myosin   sarcomeres

In order for a sarcomere to contract, the myosin binds to the actin (see Figure 14-14a) and pulls it toward the center of the sarcomere. Next the myosin lets go and grabs onto the actin one spot back and pulls again, causing the sarcomere to shorten (see Figure 14-14b and c). When it's time to relax, the myosin just lets go and the actin slides back to where it was. Now, you only have to do a little bit of exercise to know that muscle contractions take a lot of energy. To keep themselves running, muscles contain a lot of mitochondria that use a lot of fuel to make ATP. They also produce a lot of CO_2 as a result of all that fuel use.

Figure 14-14: a) attachment of myosin to actin, with pulling action. b) actin and myosin in a sarcomere. c) sarcomere shortening as a result of myosin pulling the actin in toward the center.

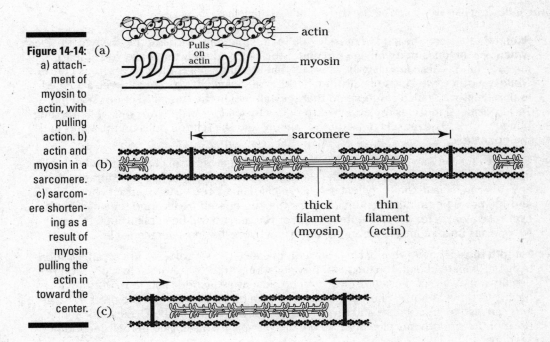

System breakdown: When things go wrong with the endocrine system

Since the endocrine system affects so many of the workings of the human body, when it breaks down the results can be pretty devastating. Here are just a few of the things that can happen when there's a system failure:

Type 1 diabetes. This complicated disease occurs when the pancreas fails to produce enough insulin. It usually appears in children and teens and can cause kidney problems, nerve damage, blindness, and early coronary heart disease and stroke. Those who have this disease have to control their blood sugar levels with regular injections of insulin.

Growth hormone problems. A tumor on the pituitary gland can cause it to produce too much growth hormone and make the bones and other body parts grow abnormally. If the pituitary gland doesn't produce enough growth hormone, a person can just stop growing. Growth hormone problems are often responsible for the world record holders for height that you see in the Guinness books.

Precocious puberty. Puberty isn't a particularly fun time for anyone, and for some the pituitary hormones stimulate the sex hormones to create a situation where the onset of puberty occurs too early. These children experience the body changes associated with puberty at a very young age.

Thyroid problems. Too much or too little of the thyroide hormones can also create difficulties. People with high levels of hormones can lose weight and experience nervousness, tremors, excessive sweating, and increased heart rate and blood pressure. Those with too little have the opposite result: weight gain, fatigue, dry skin, and a slow heart rate.

With increased understanding of how the endocrine system does its thing, medical research has come up with ways to control an endocrine system gone mad or at least the resulting symptoms. Hormone therapies and medications have made a huge difference for those who are at the mercy of their endocrine glands.

In the following list, we describe the three kinds of muscles:

✔ **Skeletal muscles:** The kind of muscle you're most familiar with are the skeletal muscles which are the ones that you can see under the skin and are what make you able to move around. These are also the muscles that are under your direct conscious control, while the other two kinds usually aren't. Skeletal muscle has its sarcomeres arranged in parallel fibers called *striations* so that they all pull in the same direction (see Figure 14-14). Skeletal muscles are attached to bones by *tendons,* which are sort of like strong bungee cords. The muscle pulls on the tendon, and the tendon pulls on the bone, and the bone moves.

✔ **Cardiac muscle:** As you may have guessed, the heart is made of cardiac muscle. Cardiac muscle isn't as strong as some of the skeletal muscles, but it has more endurance than any other muscle in the body by far. In a typical human, the heart contracts between 65 and 120 times per minute continuously for the person's entire life, and the heart can't ever take a break for a few minutes to rest or the person will be in big trouble. Cardiac muscle has its sarcomeres arranged in parallel fibers like in skeletal muscle.

✔ **Smooth muscle:** Smooth muscle is smooth because the sarcomeres are arranged more irregularly instead of in the neat and tidy striations in the other muscle types. You're usually not aware of these muscles at all because they just do their jobs without you having to think about it. Smooth muscle lines the blood vessels and the digestive tract, and can also be found here and there throughout the whole body. The specific functions of the smooth muscles in these organ systems are discussed in their individual sections.

Now try to flex your brain muscles on this sample question before moving on to Chapter 15.

Which of the following is false about smooth muscle?

(A) the main contractile proteins are actin and myosin

(B) it is arranged in contractile units called sarcomeres

(C) it uses a lot of ATP when contracting

(D) it is found in the lining of most large blood vessels

(E) most of it is under conscious control

The question asks for the *false* statement, so you can eliminate the ones that you know are true.

All muscles are arranged in sarcomere subunits that are made primarily of actin and myosin, and all muscles use a decent amount of ATP when they're contracting, so (A), (B), and (C) can be all crossed out for sure. Now notice that the question asks about smooth muscle rather than skeletal or cardiac muscle. Smooth muscle is located in the lining of large blood vessels in order to control how much blood they allow through, and that activity is definitely not under conscious control, so the correct answer is (E).

Chapter 15

Dating and Behaving: Animal Behavior and Reproduction

*T*he most distinctive thing about animals is that they *do* stuff. Other things like bacteria, plants, and fungi just sit around all the time, or if they really are doing something interesting, the action is too small to see without a microscope. Animals, on the other hand, get up and run around and attack each other and sometimes they fall in love . . . well, they mate anyway. This chapter covers all that exciting stuff, starting with all the different categories of animal behavior, and then moving on to mating and reproduction.

Acting Up: Animal Behavior

Animal behavior is all about how an animal moves or reacts to a stimulus, and a stimulus is some kind of sensory signal that the animal picks up from the environment. Sometimes the stimulus is really simple like a specific shape, color, or sound, and sometimes it can be really complicated like a sophisticated bird song or some kind of social interaction.

The behavior an animal performs in reaction to a stimulus can be either instinctual or learned. *Instinctual behavior* is something that is automatic, while a *learned behavior* takes the animal some time to figure out. This chapter is pretty fun because it involves lots of interesting examples of weird animal behavior. We use examples from as many different kinds of animals as we can, but we should warn you that we're big fans of dogs and birds, so they'll show up more often than anything else.

Running on automatic: Instinctual behavior

Instinctual behaviors are hard-wired responses, which means they are genetic traits that an animal is born with. In fact, most of the time, animals tend to act exclusively on instinct. Dogs wag their tails when they're happy, frogs snatch flies out of the air, and moths fly toward lights for some stupid reason that only the moths understand. Most animals can't really think things through and decide what course of action to take, so instead they just react however they've been designed to react — they can't help it.

In the following sections, we explain the two main kinds of instinctual behavior: fixed action patterns, like the moth flying toward the light, and simple reflexes.

Quick and simple: Reflexes

Reflexes are fast, simple motions in response to very specific stimuli, and they usually only involve a few neurons and one muscle, as shown in Figure 15-1. For example, if something touches your eyelashes, you will respond by blinking. That's a reflex. You don't need to think about it or learn how to do it, it just happens automatically. In fact, even newborn babies will do it the very first time it happens because the behavior has been hard-wired into their neuro-muscular system by their genes.

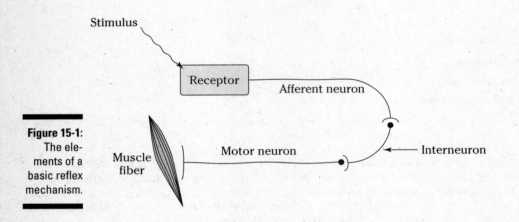

Figure 15-1:
The elements of a basic reflex mechanism.

A basic reflex system contains the following four (sometimes five) simple parts:

1. First, there is the *sensory receptor* that is tuned to the proper kind of stimulus. In the eye blink example, the receptor is a touch receptor. Other receptors involved in reflex systems could be sound receptors or visual receptors.

2. When the sensory receptor receives the right kind of stimulus, it activates a neuron called an *afferent neuron*. As described in Chapter 14, *afferent* means "incoming," so this neuron carries incoming information.

3. The afferent neuron then activates a specific motor (*efferent* or "outgoing") neuron that activates a specific muscle fiber.

4. When the muscle fiber contracts, the reflex action occurs.

5. Sometimes there is an "interneuron" between the afferent neuron and the motor (efferent) neuron to help regulate the reflex. Interneuron becomes important when you don't want the reflex to happen, like when you're sleeping. During such times, the interneuron can shut off the reflex response.

Reflexes are important for survival because sometimes there isn't enough time to react to important stimuli. That is, if you take too much time to figure out what's really going on and what you should do about it, something bad could happen before you have a chance to react. In the eye blink example, if something is close enough to your eye to touch your eyelashes, then you are better off just closing your eyes right away and figuring out later what actually touched you. Your eyes are too fragile and important to take any chances. Another example is a snail that will quickly withdraw into its shell if it gets poked. I don't know why you would want to poke a snail, but if you did, that's what would happen. This helps the snail survive because whatever poked may want to try to eat it. Again, I don't know why you would want to eat a snail, but some kinds of birds (and some weird gourmet chefs) think they're pretty tasty.

Sometimes, though, reflexes can cause problems. For example, most vertebrate animals will turn their head whenever they hear a loud, sharp sound. That makes sense because the sound may be coming from something dangerous, so you should turn your attention to it right away. However, since the whole point of reflexes is to react without taking time to think about what you're doing, you may end up doing the wrong thing. For example, if you are trying to balance a full cup of hot coffee, then reacting to a loud, sharp sound with a startled turn of your head could make you spill the coffee. Okay, so maybe that's not a life or death example, but when you spill your coffee it could make you pretty irritable.

Getting fancier: Fixed action patterns

Fixed action patterns are similar to reflexes because they are triggered by some basic stimulus. However, the resulting behavior is a lot more complex than a simple one-muscle reflex. Fixed action patterns involve many muscles that must contract and relax in a complicated sequence to produce some sort of bodily motion. For example, if a male stickleback fish sees the red underbelly of a rival male, he will charge the rival and try to drive him away. As you probably know from splashing around in a pool, efficient swimming is not easy. For sticklebacks, swimming uses every major muscle in the fish's body in precise coordination in order to propel it in a particular direction. It's certainly more complicated than just triggering the eye blink muscle.

Here's a more complicated example that has become famous among biologists that study animal behavior. Female gray geese build their nests on the ground, and like any other birds, they need to keep their eggs inside the nests where they'll be safe and warm. If a female gray goose sees one of her eggs out of the nest, she will walk over to it and roll the egg back into the nest using her beak. Even though this looks like something we may do if we needed to keep our eggs in a nest, this is actually a fixed action pattern that's hard-wired by the goose's genes.

The stimulus that triggers the behavior (generally called the **key stimulus**) is the shape and color pattern of the egg outside the nest. Whenever the goose sees that key stimulus, it runs through the exact same egg-rolling fixed action pattern no matter what. Even if you remove the egg after the goose sees it, the goose will still go through the motions as if it were actually rolling an egg. Also, the goose will go through the motions for any object that looks roughly the same as the key stimulus, even if it's just an old can that someone threw away. This brings up some important points about fixed action patterns. As long as the key stimulus is present, the behavior is triggered, even if the stimulus is coming from something that the animal isn't really interested in. Also, once a fixed action pattern is triggered, it just starts running until it's finished, whether it's actually accomplishing the right task or not.

Another crazy example is a species of beetle in Australia. The females are brown and bumpy, and whenever a male sees that stimulus, it tries to mate. Unfortunately, an Australian beer company produced bottles that were brown and bumpy just like the female beetles, and when people chucked the bottles on the ground, the male beetles all tried to mate with it. It got so bad that the males were totally ignoring the real females and the beer company had to change their bottles.

Recognizing mom: Imprinting

Usually the exact stimulus that triggers a fixed action pattern is pre-set by the animal's genes. Sometimes, though, a key stimulus needs to be learned very early in the animal's life, and this is called *imprinting*. To use geese as an example again, when the babies hatch, they look at the first living creature that they find (presumably the mother goose), and they pick out some obvious feature such as a big yellow beak. That feature becomes the key stimulus that triggers the "following" behavior. In other words, whatever has a beak like that will cause the little goslings to follow no matter what. Normally, of course, the thing they imprint on is their mother, but if the goslings accidentally see you when they first hatch, they will imprint on you and follow you wherever you go as if you were their mom. That sounds like a lot of responsibility, but we think you're up to it, at least once you've finished taking the SAT II.

Finding food or becoming food: Hunting and escaping

A special class of fixed action patterns involves obtaining food. Every animal is hard-wired to pick up on certain stimuli, such as smells and tastes, that automatically mean "this is food" or "I may be lunch!"

The "this-is-food" stimuli trigger fixed action patterns that make an animal go get the food and eat it. For herbivores this is easy because their food doesn't run. If they see green leafy stuff, then they wander over and munch on it, and that's pretty much it. For carnivores this is a lot more complicated. Hunters usually have more than one fixed action pattern associated with catching prey. For example, some stimuli will make a cat crouch and stay perfectly still, others will cause it to creep forward quietly, and still others will cause it to pounce and grab.

However, if prey has its "I-may-be-lunch" stimulus triggered because it's discovered by a predator, a pretty straightforward behavior results. The animal needs to get as far away as fast as it can, and it will have some sort of in-born fixed action pattern that does nothing but that. When this behavior gets triggered, all others are immediately stopped in favor of the escape motion.

Prey species sometimes take advantage of the instinctual behaviors, like the eating fixed action pattern, of their predators. For example, a predatory fixed action pattern for insect-eating birds is triggered by the sight of a juicy, defenseless, little bug. Sensibly enough, the birds' predatory action is not activated by the sight of leaves because if it were, then the birds would be frantically pecking at every leaf on every tree. Some insects take advantage of this by having bodies that look almost exactly like leaves, so as not to trigger the birds' fixed action pattern for hunting behavior. Pretty clever, huh?

Changing instincts: Daily and seasonal behavior cycles

Some fixed action patterns can only be activated at certain times. Following are some examples of such patterns that may be tested on the SAT II:

- **Circadian rhythm:** The most obvious example of a fixed action pattern that can only be activated at certain times is the daily cycle that most animals go through, called the *circadian rhythm.* When an animal is asleep, its fixed action patterns are suppressed so that even if the key stimulus is present, it won't trigger the associated behavior. Most animals, such as birds, insects and reptiles, are active during the day and sleep at night, and these are called *diurnal* animals. Animals that are active at night, on the other hand, are called *nocturnal*, such as bats and most rodents.

- **Migration:** Migration follows a long-term seasonal cycle. Not very many animals migrate, but a lot of birds do it, as do several kinds of mammals, and even some insects. In fact, one of the most dramatic examples of migration is the monarch butterfly, which travels from the rainforest of South America to the southern parts of Canada every year. In all of these cases of seasonal changes in behavior, different hormones are present inside these animals' bodies at different times of the year, and this causes them to change their sensitivity to key stimuli. For example, during the spring, lots of species of birds suddenly become sensitive to the direction of the sun, which causes them to get up and head north for the summer. In the fall, the opposite happens, and they fly back south to where it's warmer.

- **Hibernation:** Hibernation also follows a long-term seasonal cycle and usually only happens in the winter, and during that time the animal is almost completely unresponsive to key stimuli. If a mouse comes across a hibernating snake, the mouse could do a little jig right in front of the snake's nose without fear of triggering a fixed action pattern, which, of course, would normally involve the capture and consumption of the talented little mouse.

✔ **Courtship rituals:** Another important kind of fixed action pattern in animals that is seasonally affected is courtship rituals. We explain a lot about courtship rituals later in this chapter (see "Finding a date: Courtship"), so we won't go into much more detail here. The important issue in this section is that the key stimuli that trigger the courtship action patterns are the sight, sound, or smell of a potential mating partner. Sometimes the key stimuli are always around, but the animals are only sensitive to it during mating season, such as when a bird is only attracted to the color of members of the opposite sex during spring time. In other species, the animals are always sensitive to the key stimulus, but the stimulus is only present during mating season, such as when females only produce pheromones during spring.

Now see if your biological instincts can help you answer these questions on instinctual behavior.

Which of the following is not a reflex behavior?

(A) a clam snapping shut its shell when it is touched

(B) a frog hopping away immediately upon seeing a predator

(C) a person giving a small kick when their patellar tendon is tapped

(D) a turtle pulling its head inside its shell upon hearing a loud sound

(E) a dog gagging on a piece of food

Reflex behaviors are very simple motions, so they usually don't involve anything complicated like locomotion.

The only choice that involves something complicated is the hopping of the frog. It isn't as complicated as something like a courtship ritual in a mammal, but hopping involves a lot of different muscles and is a form of locomotion. All of the other choices only involve one or a few muscles and they each last around a second or even less, so (B) is the correct answer.

Which of the following instinctual behaviors is least likely to be affected by changes in the seasons?

(A) migration

(B) predation

(C) courtship

(D) escaping from predators

(E) mating

This one may be a little harder than it first seems. First of all, it asks which behavior is *least* likely, which means it could be that *all* of the behaviors are affected by the seasons, so make sure you read every answer carefully before deciding.

Migration, courtship, and mating are all behaviors that are pretty obviously affected by the seasons in most animals, so those can all be crossed out. Predation, on the other hand, is not normally affected by the seasons because the animal needs to eat all year round. However, if the prey species changes from season to season, then a predator's hunting style would probably change as well. For example, some wolves hunt elk in the summer and then switch to hunting mice in the winter. Also, in the hibernation example above predation behavior is shut off entirely. That means this answer is a good candidate if we can't find something else that is even less likely to be affected by the seasons.

So how about escaping from predators? Most animals have one basic escape strategy: Get away as fast as you can! I suppose it is possible that a prey species somewhere could encounter different predators from summer to winter and it is also possible that different escape strategies would work against each predator, but that's all really unlikely. That means (D) is the least likely to be affected by seasons.

Figuring it out: Learned behavior

Unlike reflexes and fixed action patterns, learned behavior is something that is not completely automatic. The animal needs to use its inborn mental abilities to somehow figure out what to do and how to do it. This can be anything from the simple trial and error learning of ants to the complex problem solving of humans.

It's important to understand the differences between instinctual and learned behavior for the SAT II, so we're going to explain it in a different way. A behavior is instinctual if the animal does it the very first time it experiences the appropriate stimulus. Learned behaviors, on the other hand, require that the animal first be able to pick up on some sort of regularity in its environment, and then the behavior is tuned to that specific regularity.

Getting used to it: Habituation

Habituation is the simplest kind of learned behavior. Suppose there is a certain stimulus that regularly triggers a reflex or fixed action pattern. If that stimulus is applied repeatedly then the animal will become less and less likely to respond. Think about poking a snail. Well, it won't take him long to learn that you're just poking him for fun and that you aren't going to smash him or eat him (we hope), and so he'll stop reacting, stop going back into his shell. In other words, he'll become habituated to the stimulus.

Dogs do this, too, of course, but their habituation is a lot more complicated. For example, a dog will probably fall for the old trick of just pretending to throw the ball, but after he's sprinted off for no reason a few times, the dog will (hopefully) stop reacting with such enthusiasm. He will become habituated to the throwing stimulus.

Speaking of canines, the classic tale of the boy who cried wolf is also a story of habituation. After the villagers got all worked up a few times, they stopped reacting to that dumb kid who kept sounding the wolf alarm. This also demonstrates the potential dangers of habituation. While it's good to learn to ignore a meaningless stimulus, next time that stimulus may really be telling you that a predator is coming to eat you, and if you ignore it you may end up as someone else's dinner.

Getting it eventually: Trial and error

When most animals have a simple task to perform that is not accomplished by a fixed-action pattern, they usually just try many variations on a basic behavioral theme until one works. A good example of this is when a dog is trying to carrying its stick through a doggy door that is too narrow. At first the stick gets hung up on the door, so the dog tries to vary its approach in different ways until finally, by luck, it gets the stick through the door. If the dog is really smart, he'll remember the successful strategy for next time, but he probably won't.

Making associations: Conditioning

Conditioning happens when an animal learns to associate an otherwise unimportant stimulus with a really important one. This is also called *association learning*, or sometimes *operant learning*. In the classic example, a Russian scientist named Pavlov rang a little bell every time he fed his dogs. Bells don't really have anything to do with food, but after a short while the dogs learned that feeding time always comes with the bell. Afterward, whenever the dogs heard a bell, they started drooling and looking for food. You may not like it, but you have been conditioned to pay attention to all sorts of stimuli like this. For example, when you're driving along in your car and you see a big red octagon, you stop. You have been conditioned to associate big red octagons (stop signs) with the possibility that there may be another car about to cross your path.

Copying off your neighbor: Mimicry

Mimicry is a more complicated kind of learning. One animal observes another animal (usually of the same species) performing a certain behavior. Without really knowing what the behavior is for, the observer tries to mimic the behavior. This can work out really well if the behavior is useful, as when carnivores are learning to catch prey by watching their parents, but other times it is totally useless. For example, some orangutans in southeast Asia will wash clothes in the river because they're mimicking the humans who are doing it, and they do it even though the orangutans have absolutely no use for clothes, let alone clean clothes.

Figuring it out: Insight learning

Insight learning is definitely the most complicated of them all, and is best explained by contrasting it with the other, dumber kinds of learning, such as trial and error. For example, suppose an animal needs to find its way from its little den to a source of water. Some animals find the water by wandering around trying to sniff it out until they finally stumble upon it. Then to get back, they just follow their own scent trail that they laid down on the way to the water source until they arrive back at their den. From then on, the animal will just follow that same exact path, no matter how much it winds around and takes the long route. The animal never notices or uses the shortcuts that would dramatically cut its travel time. An animal capable of insight learning, on the other hand, will understand what its goal is and will be on the lookout for ways to achieve the goal faster. An animal like this will notice the shortcuts and use them, and that's using insight.

Another example is when an animal discovers an unconventional way to achieve a goal. For example, if a banana is hung too high to reach, some chimpanzees are able to figure out how to stack up objects in their area in order to reach the banana. Of course, humans seem to be the best at this kind of insight learning — it is the basis of all the major fields of human endeavor from math and science to art and literature. There are no clear rules, so you just have to figure it out in your head using your intuition and insight.

To help with your learning, try these sample questions on learned behavior.

Questions 1–3 refer to the following:

(A) habituation

(B) trial and error

(C) conditioning

(D) mimicry

(E) insight

1. Learning to ignore a repeated stimulus.

2. Learning that involves repeating the behavior observed in another animal.

3. Learning in which one stimulus becomes linked to another stimulus so that the first stimulus triggers the behavior that is normally only triggered by the second stimulus.

For #1, the answer is (A). When an animal becomes habituated to a stimulus, it has learned to ignore it because it isn't being followed by anything important like food or a predator.

For #2, the answer is (D). Mimicry is like being a copycat.

For #3, the answer is (C). Conditioning happens when an important stimulus that normally triggers a specific reaction becomes linked to an unimportant stimulus. The unimportant stimulus then triggers the behavior that is normally triggered by the important one.

Finding the Right One: Reproduction

Chapters 8 and 9 discuss that there are two basic kinds of reproduction, sexual and asexual. Asexual reproduction results in the production of offspring that are genetically identical to the parent, while sexual reproduction involves the mixing of genes from two parents to produce an offspring with a unique combination. Most animals reproduce sexually, but a few can sometimes reproduce asexually.

Going alone: Asexual reproduction

Following are the three modes of asexual reproduction in animals:

- *Budding* only happens in simple animals like hydras. The hydra produces a small structure (a bud) that breaks off from the rest of the animal. The bud floats away and grows into a new hydra somewhere else. Pretty boring, isn't it.

- *Regeneration* is sort of an accidental reproduction. A few animals, such as starfish, can be cut in half, and the two halves will survive and re-grow their missing halves, which results in two whole animals. Starfish don't purposely cut themselves in half, nor could they. This sort of regeneration only happens naturally when a big predator fish bites the starfish in half but doesn't eat it. Even though it's unintentional, this still counts as reproduction because where there used to be only one starfish, now there's two.

- *Parthenogenesis* is a weird phenomena that happens to a female animal that normally does regular sexual reproduction. Under specific conditions, the female's eggs begin developing into offspring even though they have never been fertilized by a male. For example, lots of amphibians are able to reproduce by parthenogenesis. If for some reason there are no males around during the mating season, some females can lay their eggs and have them develop into offspring anyway, just to make sure the species keeps going.

Working with a partner: Sexual reproduction

As Chapter 9 details, sexual reproduction involves the mixing of genes from two parents. Each parent has a set of germ cells that go through meiosis to produce gametes, and the gametes are either sperm or eggs. The organs where the germ cells undergo meiosis to produce gametes are called the *gonads*. In males, the gonads are testes, and they produce sperm cells. In females, the gonads are ovaries and they produce eggs, also called *ova*. Some kinds of animals have gonads that are only active at particular times of the year (during mating season). Other animals, like humans, have gonads that are active all year round.

Finding a date: Courtship

As mentioned earlier in this chapter, courtship and mating in most animals are just particular kinds of fixed action patterns, and there are a few different kinds of behaviors you may see here. First, there's basic attraction between the mates. This tends to be the one most affected by the seasons because most animals only become reproductively capable at certain times of the year. During those times the female may produce a key stimulus — sights, sounds, smells, or whatever — that trigger mating-related behavior in the males. When the male picks up that signal, he immediately tracks down the source of the stimulus. On the other hand, the male may provide colors, sounds, or smells that attract the females, as in the colors and songs of lots of different male birds. For some animals, such as most insects, the story stops there. As soon as they find each other, they mate.

At this point, you may ask what makes one stimulus more attractive than another? Okay, even if you weren't asking, we're going to tell you anyway. First of all, animals are usually hard-wired to be on the lookout for the right sounds, sights, or smells that can lead them to potential mates of their own species. Then, from among the potential mates, some are more attractive than others because the quality of the stimulus indicates the quality of the genes. For example, if a male bird can produce an especially loud and complex song, then he must be pretty robust and intelligent guy who would make a great partner. That is, his genes are likely to produce some good, strong offspring.

Next comes the phase where the animals make their intentions known to each other. As I mentioned before, some skip this part and get right down to business. But for others, especially the predators, this is an important step in their relationship. Predators tend to be pretty dangerous animals with big teeth and sharp claws, so if a male just runs right at a potential mate, she may worry that he's attacking, and she'll either fight or run. Either way, the male loses out.

So, instead of triggering her attack behaviors, he needs to trigger her mating behaviors. For some leopards, this includes rolling over and acting like a kitten. Female leopards don't attack or run from kittens, so his apparent playfulness keeps her around long enough to get to know him. In some species of birds and mammals this phase also includes developing a pair bonding for cooperative parenting. They need to show each other that they will be good parents by building a nest or gathering food or displaying some other kind of strength or skill that can help in raising offspring.

Going all the way: Mating

Mating is the process by which a male and a female actually combine sperm and egg to produce a *zygote,* which is the first official cell of the offspring. There are two basic ways of mating. The first method is *external fertilization,* which is used by most aquatic invertebrates and by most fish and amphibians. In external fertilization, the female releases her eggs into the water, and then the male releases his sperm on top of the eggs so that they get fertilized. The eggs are then left to develop and hatch into larvae and, if all goes according to plan, the larvae will develop into adults. Since the eggs and the larvae are left to develop on their own, they are extremely vulnerable to predators. In fact, predators can be expected to eat almost all of the offspring before they develop into adults. To make sure that at least some of them survive, the parents produce a huge number of zygotes, sometimes many thousands.

The other kind of mating is called *internal fertilization,* and in this version the male injects sperm into the female to fertilize the eggs. After that, there are a few different possibilities, depending on what kind of animal we're talking about. Most female insects that engage in internal fertilization lay the eggs soon after mating, and then the process continues much like it did in external fertilization. Other animals, such as reptiles and birds, keep the eggs inside until they have developed for a while, and then lay large, shell-covered eggs in a safe place. Most of these animals also care for the eggs and for the eventual hatchlings to make sure they do okay. Mammals are famous for not laying any eggs at all (except for the platypus). Instead, they let the offspring develop for a long time inside the uterus and then give birth to live young. Most mammals try to take really good care of their young, especially the mammals that only produce one or two offspring at a time.

When the gonads of mammals are active, the males tend to produce large amounts of sperm and are able to impregnate many females (at least for species that aren't monogamous). Females, on the other hand, produce only one or a few eggs at a time and are generally impregnated by only one male. Each egg is called an *ovum* (plural: ova) and is surrounded by a bunch of supporting cells and a sort of nutrient jelly. The ovum and all the stuff around it is called a *follicle*. While the males are continuously producing ready-to-go sperm, females produce ready-to-go follicles only once during their reproductive cycle.

When a follicle is mature and ready to be fertilized, it emerges from the ovary and enters the fallopian tube (see Figure 15-2). This is called ***ovulation***, and it's when the female is most likely to be receptive to courtship from males. The length of the cycle varies a lot among mammal species. Some have a cycle that lasts one whole year, so they only ovulate at the beginning of the mating season. Other mammals have cycles that last less than a week and are almost always able to get pregnant. Humans produce one mature follicle every 28 days or so and are usually able to get pregnant for only the three or four days around ovulation.

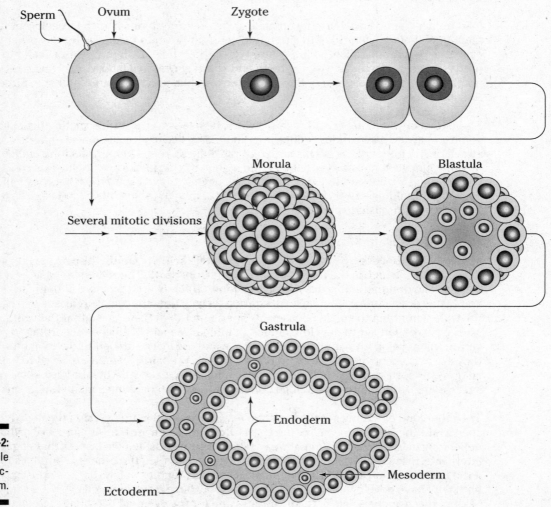

Figure 15-2:
Female
reproduc-
tive system.

Now try your luck with some questions about mating.

Which of the following is least likely to be a result of courtship behavior?

(A) activation of gametes production

(B) pair bonding

(C) fitness testing

(D) establishing territory

(E) avoiding violent confrontation

First notice that the question asks which is *least* likely to be a result of courtship behavior, which means that all of them *could* be caused by courtship behavior. It's best to eliminate the one's you know are very likely to result from courtship.

Pair bonding is a pretty standard reason for courtship, so (B) is out. Fitness testing is figuring out whether your potential mate has good genes, which is also a purpose of courtship. Good courtship usually means good genes, so cross out (C). If the female isn't sure what the male's intentions are, she may defend herself when he approaches. That could be dangerous for both of them, and courtship often helps to avoid such misunderstandings, so (E) is out also. That leaves (A) and (D). Of course, the whole point of engaging in courtship behavior is to combine gametes through mating, and most animals won't mate without going through the standard rituals, so many of them don't even bother producing gametes until courtship begins. On the other hand, when a male is engaging in courtship behavior he is not interested in chasing anyone off. In fact, he's specifically interested in getting his mate to stick around. Therefore, he is very unlikely to be simultaneously trying to establish territorial boundaries, which means the correct answer is (D).

Which of the following are forms of sexual reproduction?

   I. budding

  II. internal fertilization

 III. external fertilization

 IV. parthenogenesis

(A) II only

(B) I and II only

(C) II and III only

(D) II, III, and IV only

(E) I and IV only

Sexual reproduction involves the fertilization of an egg by a sperm, so the choices that include the word fertilization are most likely to be forms of sexual reproduction.

Budding is definitely asexual because it is where a piece of a simple animal pops off and floats away to start growing somewhere else. Cross out I and eliminate answer choices (B) and (E).

All of the remaining answer choices include II, so you don't even have to consider it; you know it is a form of sexual reproduction. (C) and (D) both include III, so look at IV first to see if you can rule it out.

Parthenogenesis happens with species who normally reproduce sexually, but parthenogenesis itself is actually a form of asexual reproduction. It is when the eggs develop into offspring even though they were never fertilized. You know that (D) is wrong. External reproduction (III) is a form of sexual reproduction, so the correct answer is (C).

Raising the kids: Animal development

Okay, so the animals have mated, the sperm and egg have combined to form a zygote, and so now what happens? Figure 15-3 shows the next stages of development of the offspring. Within minutes after fertilization, the zygote undergoes mitosis (see Chapter 3) to form two identical cells, which soon split into four identical cells, and then eight, and so on. After about 24 hours, there are many identical cells bunched together in a ball called a *morula*. Next, the cells of the morula move around to form a hollow ball called a *blastula*. Some cells from the walls of the blastula then move away from the sides and float around inside the ball, and when that happens the ball totally changes shape. It folds in on itself and forms something like a little tube. At this point, the embryo is called a *gastrula*.

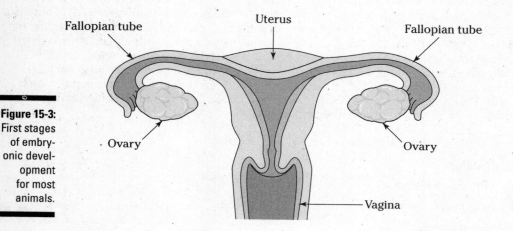

Figure 15-3:
First stages of embryonic development for most animals.

The layers that form as a result of this initial folding are the three main tissue layers in most animals (other than in the most simple animals like the sponges). The outermost part is called the *ectoderm*; the inner fold is called the *endoderm*; and the area that was inside the middle of the ball is called the *mesoderm*. These three layers develop into the main tissues in all animals. For example, the endoderm develops into the digestive and respiratory systems, the ectoderm develops into skin (or shell) and the nervous system, and the mesoderm develops into the muscular, skeletal, circulatory, and reproductive systems.

The cells of each layer continue dividing, and soon start to differentiate. That is, they start to become more like the various specialized cells that belong to all of the different organ systems discussed in Chapter 14. This is when the embryo starts to take on the shape of an animal. Over the subsequent days and weeks, the embryo develops functional organ systems and becomes a fetus, which eventually becomes a full-blown baby.

Some questions on the SAT II may focus exclusively on the human female's cycle, so the rest of this section will apply primarily to humans. Just to warn you, this description includes a lot of terminology and names of hormones. The names themselves aren't important for understanding the whole process, but there's a chance they may show up on a specific question.

First of all, human males produce a more or less continuous amount of testosterone throughout their adult lives, which means they also produce sperm more or less continuously. Females, on the other hand, go through what is called a menstrual cycle and they produce only one or two follicles each cycle. The menstrual cycle is divided into two main parts, the follicular phase and the luteal phase. During the follicular phase, the follicle (which is the ovum and the supporting cells) is developing and getting ready to be fertilized. At the same time, the uterus is growing and getting ready to support an embryo. The most important hormone for making this stage happen is follicle stimulating hormone (FSH) from the pituitary gland, though the whole process couldn't happen without the hormone estrogen, which is present in various levels throughout the whole menstrual cycle.

After the follicular phase has gone on for about 14 days, the follicle is ready to emerge from the ovary. This is called ovulation, and it is triggered by a different pituitary hormone called leutinizing hormone (LH). Now the woman has entered the luteal phase, during which the follicle enters the fallopian tube and travels to the uterus.

In the luteal phase, the cells that surrounded the ovum within the follicle, called the corpus luteum, start secreting another hormone, called progesterone. This hormone helps keep the uterus active and ready to support the embryo. If no fertilization happens, though, the corpus luteum eventually runs out of progesterone, and the uterus starts to degrade. Most of the uterine tissue, as well as the unfertilized ovum, are lost out through the vagina in a process called menstruation. Menstruation involves a decent amount of blood loss because the uterus had developed a big blood supply during the follicular phase. If no zygote needs to be supported, though, it isn't worth the effort to keep the uterus active.

But what happens if the ovum is fertilized? Fertilization happens in the fallopian tubes, and after about 24 hours, when the embryo is at the morula stage, it implants in the uterus, which means that the embryo connects itself to the inner lining. At the point of implantation, the cells surrounding the ovum start to form a placenta, which is the interface between the mother's blood supply and the developing embryo. Eventually, an umbilical cord will connect the fetus to the placenta. In the meantime, those cells that initially form the placenta also start to produce a hormone called *human chorionic gonadotropin.* This is a very important hormone because it stops the normal menstrual cycle and preserves the uterus — it is the way the embryo says, "I'm, here! Support me!" When that hormone is detected by the mother's body, she goes into pregnancy mode instead of beginning menstruation, and the embryo develops normally.

Now try some last sample questions on animal development.

Which of the following organs develop from the ectoderm?

(A) lungs

(B) skin

(C) heart

(D) intestine

(E) bones

Ecto is a prefix that comes up a lot in biology, and it means outside. Of the choices given the one that's the most on the outside is, of course, the skin. The other organ system that comes from the ectoderm is the nervous system. The answer is (B).

Which of the following is false concerning the menstrual cycle and pregnancy in human females?

(A) cells from the follicle form the placenta

(B) menstruation only happens if there is no fertilization

(C) fertilization happens during the follicular phase

(D) the uterus builds up a large blood supply during the follicular phase

(E) ovulation is caused by leutinizing hormone

The follicular phase is when the follicle is developing before ovulation. Ovulation is when the follicle emerges and enters the fallopian tube, and it marks the switch from the follicular phase to the luteal phase. Fertilization can't happen until the follicle with the ovum inside exits the ovary, so fertilization must happen in the luteal phase, so (C) is false (and the correct answer). All of the others are true.

Part V
Practice Makes Perfect

In this part . . .

Okay, now that you've got a handle on the basic biology information for the SAT II, it's time to try some practice tests. Each chapter in Parts II, III, and IV included a lot of sample SAT II questions, but now in Part V everything will be set up just like it is on the actual SAT II Biology E/M Test. The format, the directions, the balance of questions from the different subjects, and everything else are exactly the same as what you'll see on the real test. The only difference is that these aren't the actual questions you'll see (that would be cheating, right?). All you need now is a quiet, private hour at a clean desk or table so you can complete the test all in one sitting, just like on test day. You'll also need a pencil to mark your answers, and some sort of timer to keep yourself working within the official time constraints. You will have one hour to finish the exam.

After each test you'll find an answer key and a guide to calculating your official score. Then, in the chapters that come after each test, you'll find detailed explanations for the answers to all of the questions. These explanations go through the biology knowledge that's being tested in each question, plus they include little hints and strategies for zeroing in on the right answer even when you aren't sure about the biological facts. Ready? Well, once you're sure you've got everything set up, take a deep breath and dive in.

Chapter 16

Practice Test 1

· ·

*O*kay, you know your stuff. Now is your chance to shine. The following exam is an 80-question multiple-choice test. You have one hour to complete it. On the actual exam, you would chose whether you wish to take the E section or the M section. If you chose to take the E section answer the first 60 questions, then questions 61–80 in the E section. If you chose to take the M section answer the first 60 questions, then questions 61–80 in the M section.

To make the most of this practice exam, take the test under similar conditions to the actual test:

1. Find a place where you won't be distracted. (Preferably as far from your younger sibling as possible.)
2. If possible, take the practice test at approximately the same time of day as you will for your real SAT II.
3. Set an alarm for 60 minutes.
4. Mark your answers on the provided answer grid.
5. If you finish before time runs out, go back and check your answers.
6. When your 60 minutes are over, put your pencil down.

After you have finished, you can check your answers on the answer key at the end of this chapter. Use the scoring chart to find out your final score.

Read through all of the explanations in Chapter 17. You learn more by examining the answers to the question than you do by almost any other method.

Practice Test 1 Answer Sheet

1. Ⓐ Ⓑ Ⓒ Ⓓ Ⓔ	51. Ⓐ Ⓑ Ⓒ Ⓓ Ⓔ
2. Ⓐ Ⓑ Ⓒ Ⓓ Ⓔ	52. Ⓐ Ⓑ Ⓒ Ⓓ Ⓔ
3. Ⓐ Ⓑ Ⓒ Ⓓ Ⓔ	53. Ⓐ Ⓑ Ⓒ Ⓓ Ⓔ
4. Ⓐ Ⓑ Ⓒ Ⓓ Ⓔ	54. Ⓐ Ⓑ Ⓒ Ⓓ Ⓔ
5. Ⓐ Ⓑ Ⓒ Ⓓ Ⓔ	55. Ⓐ Ⓑ Ⓒ Ⓓ Ⓔ
6. Ⓐ Ⓑ Ⓒ Ⓓ Ⓔ	56. Ⓐ Ⓑ Ⓒ Ⓓ Ⓔ
7. Ⓐ Ⓑ Ⓒ Ⓓ Ⓔ	57. Ⓐ Ⓑ Ⓒ Ⓓ Ⓔ
8. Ⓐ Ⓑ Ⓒ Ⓓ Ⓔ	58. Ⓐ Ⓑ Ⓒ Ⓓ Ⓔ
9. Ⓐ Ⓑ Ⓒ Ⓓ Ⓔ	59. Ⓐ Ⓑ Ⓒ Ⓓ Ⓔ
10. Ⓐ Ⓑ Ⓒ Ⓓ Ⓔ	60. Ⓐ Ⓑ Ⓒ Ⓓ Ⓔ
11. Ⓐ Ⓑ Ⓒ Ⓓ Ⓔ	61. Ⓐ Ⓑ Ⓒ Ⓓ Ⓔ
12. Ⓐ Ⓑ Ⓒ Ⓓ Ⓔ	62. Ⓐ Ⓑ Ⓒ Ⓓ Ⓔ
13. Ⓐ Ⓑ Ⓒ Ⓓ Ⓔ	63. Ⓐ Ⓑ Ⓒ Ⓓ Ⓔ
14. Ⓐ Ⓑ Ⓒ Ⓓ Ⓔ	64. Ⓐ Ⓑ Ⓒ Ⓓ Ⓔ
15. Ⓐ Ⓑ Ⓒ Ⓓ Ⓔ	65. Ⓐ Ⓑ Ⓒ Ⓓ Ⓔ
16. Ⓐ Ⓑ Ⓒ Ⓓ Ⓔ	66. Ⓐ Ⓑ Ⓒ Ⓓ Ⓔ
17. Ⓐ Ⓑ Ⓒ Ⓓ Ⓔ	67. Ⓐ Ⓑ Ⓒ Ⓓ Ⓔ
18. Ⓐ Ⓑ Ⓒ Ⓓ Ⓔ	68. Ⓐ Ⓑ Ⓒ Ⓓ Ⓔ
19. Ⓐ Ⓑ Ⓒ Ⓓ Ⓔ	69. Ⓐ Ⓑ Ⓒ Ⓓ Ⓔ
20. Ⓐ Ⓑ Ⓒ Ⓓ Ⓔ	70. Ⓐ Ⓑ Ⓒ Ⓓ Ⓔ
21. Ⓐ Ⓑ Ⓒ Ⓓ Ⓔ	71. Ⓐ Ⓑ Ⓒ Ⓓ Ⓔ
22. Ⓐ Ⓑ Ⓒ Ⓓ Ⓔ	72. Ⓐ Ⓑ Ⓒ Ⓓ Ⓔ
23. Ⓐ Ⓑ Ⓒ Ⓓ Ⓔ	73. Ⓐ Ⓑ Ⓒ Ⓓ Ⓔ
24. Ⓐ Ⓑ Ⓒ Ⓓ Ⓔ	74. Ⓐ Ⓑ Ⓒ Ⓓ Ⓔ
25. Ⓐ Ⓑ Ⓒ Ⓓ Ⓔ	75. Ⓐ Ⓑ Ⓒ Ⓓ Ⓔ
26. Ⓐ Ⓑ Ⓒ Ⓓ Ⓔ	76. Ⓐ Ⓑ Ⓒ Ⓓ Ⓔ
27. Ⓐ Ⓑ Ⓒ Ⓓ Ⓔ	77. Ⓐ Ⓑ Ⓒ Ⓓ Ⓔ
28. Ⓐ Ⓑ Ⓒ Ⓓ Ⓔ	78. Ⓐ Ⓑ Ⓒ Ⓓ Ⓔ
29. Ⓐ Ⓑ Ⓒ Ⓓ Ⓔ	79. Ⓐ Ⓑ Ⓒ Ⓓ Ⓔ
30. Ⓐ Ⓑ Ⓒ Ⓓ Ⓔ	80. Ⓐ Ⓑ Ⓒ Ⓓ Ⓔ
31. Ⓐ Ⓑ Ⓒ Ⓓ Ⓔ	81. Ⓐ Ⓑ Ⓒ Ⓓ Ⓔ
32. Ⓐ Ⓑ Ⓒ Ⓓ Ⓔ	82. Ⓐ Ⓑ Ⓒ Ⓓ Ⓔ
33. Ⓐ Ⓑ Ⓒ Ⓓ Ⓔ	83. Ⓐ Ⓑ Ⓒ Ⓓ Ⓔ
34. Ⓐ Ⓑ Ⓒ Ⓓ Ⓔ	84. Ⓐ Ⓑ Ⓒ Ⓓ Ⓔ
35. Ⓐ Ⓑ Ⓒ Ⓓ Ⓔ	85. Ⓐ Ⓑ Ⓒ Ⓓ Ⓔ
36. Ⓐ Ⓑ Ⓒ Ⓓ Ⓔ	86. Ⓐ Ⓑ Ⓒ Ⓓ Ⓔ
37. Ⓐ Ⓑ Ⓒ Ⓓ Ⓔ	87. Ⓐ Ⓑ Ⓒ Ⓓ Ⓔ
38. Ⓐ Ⓑ Ⓒ Ⓓ Ⓔ	88. Ⓐ Ⓑ Ⓒ Ⓓ Ⓔ
39. Ⓐ Ⓑ Ⓒ Ⓓ Ⓔ	89. Ⓐ Ⓑ Ⓒ Ⓓ Ⓔ
40. Ⓐ Ⓑ Ⓒ Ⓓ Ⓔ	90. Ⓐ Ⓑ Ⓒ Ⓓ Ⓔ
41. Ⓐ Ⓑ Ⓒ Ⓓ Ⓔ	91. Ⓐ Ⓑ Ⓒ Ⓓ Ⓔ
42. Ⓐ Ⓑ Ⓒ Ⓓ Ⓔ	92. Ⓐ Ⓑ Ⓒ Ⓓ Ⓔ
43. Ⓐ Ⓑ Ⓒ Ⓓ Ⓔ	93. Ⓐ Ⓑ Ⓒ Ⓓ Ⓔ
44. Ⓐ Ⓑ Ⓒ Ⓓ Ⓔ	94. Ⓐ Ⓑ Ⓒ Ⓓ Ⓔ
45. Ⓐ Ⓑ Ⓒ Ⓓ Ⓔ	95. Ⓐ Ⓑ Ⓒ Ⓓ Ⓔ
46. Ⓐ Ⓑ Ⓒ Ⓓ Ⓔ	96. Ⓐ Ⓑ Ⓒ Ⓓ Ⓔ
47. Ⓐ Ⓑ Ⓒ Ⓓ Ⓔ	97. Ⓐ Ⓑ Ⓒ Ⓓ Ⓔ
48. Ⓐ Ⓑ Ⓒ Ⓓ Ⓔ	98. Ⓐ Ⓑ Ⓒ Ⓓ Ⓔ
49. Ⓐ Ⓑ Ⓒ Ⓓ Ⓔ	99. Ⓐ Ⓑ Ⓒ Ⓓ Ⓔ
50. Ⓐ Ⓑ Ⓒ Ⓓ Ⓔ	100. Ⓐ Ⓑ Ⓒ Ⓓ Ⓔ

BIOLOGY E/M TEST

FOR BOTH BIOLOGY-E AND BIOLOGY-M

ANSWER QUESTIONS 1–60

<u>Directions:</u> Each set of choices marked (A) – (E) below refers to the questions or statements immediately following it. Choose the lettered choice that best answers each question or matches each statement and fill in the corresponding oval on the answer sheet. You may use a lettered choice once, more than once, or not at all in each set.

Questions 1–4

(A) Gymnosperms

(B) Angiosperms

(C) Algae

(D) Tracheophytes

(E) Nontracheophytes

1. Plants that do not make use of xylem and phloem

2. Plants that often need help of animals in order to reproduce

3. Plant group that includes mosses and liverworts

4. Group composed of unicellular Protists

Questions 5–7

(A) Migration

(B) Diffusion

(C) Active Transport

(D) Phototropism

(E) Endocytosis

5. Spontaneous movement from an area of high concentration to an area of low concentration

6. Growth toward a source of light

7. Use of energy to move a substance against its concentration gradient

Questions 8–11

(A) Mitochondria

(B) Nucleus

(C) Chloroplast

(D) Flagella

(E) Rough Endoplasmic Reticulum

8. Structure found in some prokaryotic cells

9. Organelle where proteins are constructed

10. Organelle in which DNA is stored

11. Organelle in which the Krebs cycle occurs

Questions 12–15

(A) Fungi

(B) Animalia

(C) Plantae

(D) Monera

(E) Protista

12. Kingdom composed exclusively of decomposers

13. Kingdom most likely to contain a tertiary consumer

14. Kingdom that only contains photo-synthesizers

15. Kingdom that contains organisms that perform nitrogen-fixation

Go on to next page

> Directions: Each of the questions below is followed by five answers. Some groups of questions relate to a laboratory or experimental situation. For each question, select the best answer to the question and then fill in the corresponding oval on the answer sheet.

16. Which of the following biomes has the greatest diversity?

    (A) tundra

    (B) taiga

    (C) deciduous forest

    (D) ocean

    (E) freshwater

17. Which of the following are characteristics of the very first cells?

    I. heterotrophs

    II. prokaryotes

    III. autotrophs

    IV. eukaryotes

    (A) I and II only

    (B) I and III only

    (C) II and III only

    (D) II and IV only

    (E) III and IV only

18. A mammal's blood pH has dropped. This situation will be corrected by increased activity in the animal's

    (A) circulatory system

    (B) digestive system

    (C) nervous system

    (D) endocrine system

    (E) respiratory system

19. A plant that produces blue flowers reproduces with a plant of the same species that produces yellow flowers. Each of its offspring produces some yellow flowers and some blue flowers. This is an example of

    (A) co-dominance

    (B) incomplete dominance

    (C) recessive traits

    (D) partial dominance

    (E) genetic mutation

20. Which of the following is the best example of a conditioned behavior?

    (A) a bird begins building a nest at the beginning of spring

    (B) after watching their parents do the same, young chimpanzees begin using tools to rack open nuts

    (C) male cichlid fish perform courtship rituals with females and chase away other males

    (D) an antelope is chased by a lion at a certain watering hole and subsequently never returns to that watering hole

    (E) all of the above

Go on to next page

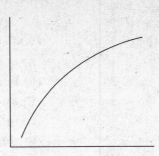

21. The graph above is most likely to depict which of the following?

(A) population undergoing exponential growth

(B) population undergoing directional selection

(C) population size approaching carrying capacity

(D) population undergoing stabilizing selection

(E) population size moving away from carrying capacity

22. Which of the following would be good evidence that two organisms are closely related genetically?

   I. They have very similar DNA

   II. They have very similar RNA

   III. They have very similar proteins

(A) I only

(B) II only

(C) III only

(D) I and II only

(E) I, II, and III

23. Which of the following are exocrine glands?

   I. sweat glands

   II. pituitary glands

   III. mammary glands

   IV. adrenal glands

(A) I and II only

(B) II and III only

(C) I and III only

(D) III and IV only

(E) II and IV only

24. Which of the following flower parts will attract pollinators?

(A) stamen

(B) nectar

(C) anthers

(D) petals

(E) sepals

25. The animals in a certain community are all endotherms. Which biome is this community most likely to be in?

(A) desert

(B) tundra

(C) ocean

(D) tropical rain forest

(E) taiga

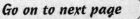 *Go on to next page*

26. A man and a woman both have type O blood. What is the probability that their children will also have type O blood?

    (A) 0%

    (B) 25%

    (C) 50%

    (D) 75%

    (E) 100%

27. Which of the following is not a role of the vertebrate nervous system?

    (A) muscle coordination

    (B) receiving incoming sensory stimuli

    (C) heartbeat and breathing modulation

    (D) conditioned learning

    (E) initiating sexual development

28. Forest fires are beneficial to certain gymnosperms because

    (A) fires cause the seeds in the cones to open

    (B) fires drive away herbivores that might eat the gymnosperm seedlings

    (C) fires aid in pollination

    (D) fires clear away dead brush to provide room for seedlings

    (E) both (A) and (D)

29. Which of the following is the correct sequence of human development?

    (A) zygote → gastrula → blastula → fetus → baby

    (B) blastula → gastrula → zygote → fetus → baby

    (C) gastrula → blastula → zygote → fetus → baby

    (D) zygote → blastula → gastrula → fetus → baby

    (E) blastula → zygote → gastrula → fetus → baby

30. Which of the following animal groups is exothermic?

    (A) aves

    (B) reptilia

    (C) carnivora

    (D) cetaceans

    (E) primates

31. Which color light would most likely produce the smallest amount of growth in a plant?

    (A) red

    (B) yellow

    (C) green

    (D) orange

    (E) white

Go on to next page

32. Suppose a vertebrate animal was unable to properly regulate its blood pH. Based on this information, which of the following brain structures is most likely to be damaged?

    (A) thalamus

    (B) hypothalamus

    (C) medulla

    (D) cerebellum

    (E) cerebrum

33. In humans, the brown eye gene (Br) is dominant and the blue eye gene (bl) is recessive. A man and a woman both have brown eyes, and they have a boy who has blue eyes. What is the genotype of the parents?

    (A) Br-Br and Br-Br

    (B) Br-bl and bl-bl

    (C) Br-bl and Br-bl

    (D) Br-bl and Br-Br

    (E) not enough information to determine

34. A baby goose hatches in captivity and follows its human handler around wherever he goes. This is an example of

    (A) imprinting

    (B) conditioning

    (C) habituation

    (D) instinct

    (E) trial and error

35. Which of the following is a purpose of the human liver?

    (A) break down toxic molecules in the blood stream

    (B) filter toxic molecules out of the blood stream

    (C) store sugar for times of famine

    (D) both (A) and (B)

    (E) both (A) and (C)

36. According to Darwin's theory of evolution by natural selection, which of the following is the unit of selection?

    (A) individual

    (B) population

    (C) community

    (D) immediate family

    (E) species

37. Which of the following biomes tends to have the greatest temperature swings?

    (A) tropical rain forest

    (B) temperate deciduous forest

    (C) taiga

    (D) desert

    (E) ocean

Go on to next page

38. Which of the following is not carried by the xylem?

    (A) minerals

    (B) water

    (C) ammonia

    (D) sugars

    (E) all of the above are carried by the xylem

39. A person at high elevation will breathe faster in order to get more O_2. Which of the following is a likely consequence of this increased breathing rate?

    (A) increased CO_2 level in blood

    (B) decreased pH of blood

    (C) increased pH of blood

    (D) decreased O_2 level in blood

    (E) decreased blood pressure

40. The human pancreas produces digestive fluid that is delivered to the small intestine. Which of the following polymers are pancreas cells likely to produce most?

    (A) glycogen

    (B) nucleic acids

    (C) proteins

    (D) cellulose

    (E) cholesterol

41. A blood vessel is carrying blood away from the heart. The walls of this blood vessel are lined with

    (A) skeletal muscle

    (B) smooth muscle

    (C) cardiac muscle

    (D) striated muscle

    (E) no muscle

42. Which of the following is not a function of the excretory system?

    (A) modifying blood pressure

    (B) modifying blood contents

    (C) filtering wastes from blood

    (D) controlling the exocrine glands

    (E) storing urine

Go on to next page

Questions 43–45

A deer suddenly finds itself being chased by a mountain lion.

43. Which of the following would be a reaction of the endocrine system?

(A) secretion of thyroid hormone

(B) secretion of epinephrine

(C) secretion of melatonin

(D) secretion of growth hormone

(E) secretion of testosterone

44. Which of the following would not be a reaction of the circulatory system?

(A) vasodilation in small intestine

(B) vasodilation in muscular system

(C) increased blood pressure

(D) vasodilation in respiratory system

(E) vasoconstriction in epidermis

45. Which of the following would be a reaction of the digestive system?

(A) increase activity of small intestine to digest more fuel

(B) store excess fuel as glycogen in liver

(C) increase enzyme production in pancreas

(D) secretion of insulin by the pancreas

(E) release stored glucose from the liver

Go on to next page

Questions 46–49

An experiment was conducted to test the effectiveness of antibiotics on bacteria growth. A culture of bacteria was placed on four different Petri dishes, each of which contained a high-nutrient growth medium. Small paper circles were soaked with antibiotics. Paper circles marked with an *A* were soaked in penicillin. Paper circles marked with a *B* were soaked in erythromycin. A single *A* circle was placed in Petri dish I, a single *B* circle was placed in Petri dish II, and Petri dish III received one *A* and one *B* circle. Petri dish IV was left without a paper circle. The bacteria were then allowed to grow for 24 hours. The diagrams below show the patterns of bacterial growth on each of the Petri dishes.

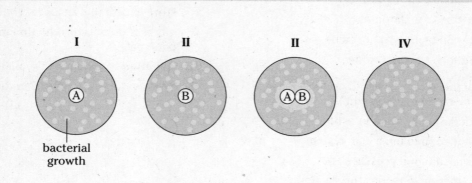

Go on to next page ⇒

46. Which of the dishes was the control group?

    (A) dish #1

    (B) dish #2

    (C) dish #3

    (D) dish #4

    (E) this experiment lacks a control group

47. Which of the following would have been a good control group?

    (A) A dish with bacteria and a paper circle soaked in a third antibiotic such as streptomycin

    (B) A dish with bacteria and a low-nutrient growth medium

    (C) A dish with bacteria and a paper circle soaked in bleach

    (D) A dish with no bacteria

    (E) A dish with bacteria and a plain paper circle that was not soaked in any antibiotic

48. Which of the following is the best explanation for the results?

    (A) erythromycin and penicillin have the same effect on this bacteria

    (B) the bacteria is immune to both penicillin and erythromycin

    (C) individual bacteria in the culture are immune to either penicillin or erythromycin, but never to both simultaneously

    (D) dishes #1 and #2 must have been contaminated

    (E) a genetic mutation must have occurred in the bacteria in dish #3

49. Which of the following would be a good follow-up test?

    (A) take some of the bacteria on dish #1 and grow it in a Petri dish with a "B" circle.

    (B) take some of the bacteria on dish #2 and grow it in a Petri dish with an "A" circle.

    (C) take some of the bacteria from dish #3 and grow it in a Petri dish with no paper circles

    (D) both (A) and (B)

    (E) all of the above

Go on to next page

Questions 50–52

A famous experiment called the Miller-Urey Experiment provided intriguing insights into the origins of life on earth. In order to simulate the conditions of the early earth, the experimenters placed H_2O, NH_3, CH_3, and H_2 in a sealed container and added energy through electric sparks. The result was the spontaneous formation of many sugars, amino acids, and other organic molecules. This was hailed as providing significant evidence in support of what has become the most popular view concerning the origins of life on earth.

50. The results of the Miller-Urey Experiment are intended to show that

    (A) under present-day conditions on earth, life regularly forms out of non-organic precursors

    (B) under present-day conditions on earth, the organic building blocks of organisms can readily form out of non-organic precursors

    (C) under the conditions of the early earth, life cannot form out of non-organic precursors

    (D) under the conditions of the early earth, life can readily form out of non-organic precursors

    (E) under the conditions of the early earth, the organic building blocks of organisms can readily form out of non-organic precursors

51. Which of the following assumptions made by the researchers is the least reliable?

    (A) electrical sparks can cause chemical reactions

    (B) the experimental conditions are similar to the conditions of the early earth

    (C) the first organisms were made out of organic molecules

    (D) the conditions of the early earth were significantly different than they are today

    (E) H_2O was present in the early earth

Go on to next page

52. Which of the following would be a good follow-up study to this single experiment?

    (A) continue the experiment to determine whether the products change over time

    (B) examine the products of the reactions to determine which of them appear in modern organisms

    (C) repeat the experiment several more times, modifying the environmental conditions each time

    (D) repeat the experiment several more times, using different energy sources each time

    (E) all of the above would be good follow-up studies

Go on to next page

Questions 53–56

An organism was isolated and sealed in a large container in a laboratory. The organism was given the basic nutrients it needed to survive. The concentrations of O_2 and CO_2 were monitored over the course of 24 hours. The graph below shows the results of the measurements.

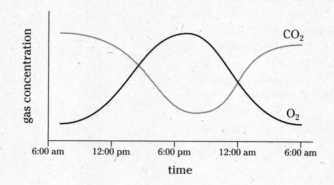

Go on to next page

53. According to the graph, what most likely happened at 6 pm?

    (A) the organism fell asleep

    (B) the organism died

    (C) the lights in the lab were turned off

    (D) the container began to leak

    (E) the organism reproduced

54. According to the information given, it can be inferred that this organism can perform which of the following processes?

    (A) photosynthesis

    (B) aerobic cellular respiration

    (C) fermentation

    (D) both (A) and (B)

    (E) both (B) and (C)

55. Which of the taxonomic following groups is this organism most likely a member of?

    (A) bryophyta

    (B) protozoa

    (C) porifera

    (D) cnidaria

    (E) mammalia

56. Which role would this organism most likely play in a typical ecosystem?

    (A) omnivore

    (B) decomposer

    (C) primary consumer

    (D) primary producer

    (E) secondary consumer

Go on to next page

Questions 57–60

Sickle-cell anemia is a genetic disease influenced by a single pair of alleles. The recessive allele (b), when homozygous, will produce the sickle-cell phenotype, which involves misshapen red blood cells. The dominant gene (B) produces normal red blood cells. In the family tree below, circles are males and squares are females. Shaded figures represent individuals with the sickle-cell phenotype.

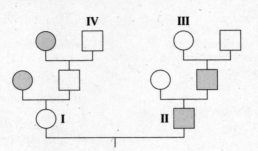

Go on to next page

57. What is the genotype of person I?

    (A) BB

    (B) Bb

    (C) bb

    (D) could be BB or Bb

    (E) could be Bb or bb

58. What are the chances that a child of individuals I and II would have the sickle cell phenotype?

    (A) 0%

    (B) 25%

    (C) 50%

    (D) 75%

    (E) 100%

59. What is the genotype of person III?

    (A) BB

    (B) Bb

    (C) bb

    (D) could be BB or Bb

    (E) could be Bb or bb

60. What is the genotype of person IV?

    (A) BB

    (B) Bb

    (C) bb

    (D) could be BB or Bb

    (E) could be Bb or bb

If you are taking the Biology-E test, continue with questions 61–80 on the next page.

If you are taking the Biology-M test, skip to questions 81–100 now.

Go on to next page

BIOLOGY-E SECTION

Directions: Each of the questions below is followed by five answers. Some groups of questions relate to a laboratory or experimental situation. For each question, select the best answer to the question and then fill in the corresponding oval on the answer sheet.

61. Which of the following groups of animals is endothermic?

    I. reptiles

    II. birds

    III. mammals

    IV. insects

    (A) I and III only

    (B) I and II only

    (C) II only

    (D) III only

    (E) II and III only

62. Which of the following kingdoms contains organisms that are autotrophs?

    I. Monera

    II. Protista

    III. Fungi

    IV. Plantae

    V. Animalia

    (A) I, III and IV only

    (B) IV only

    (C) II and IV only

    (D) I, II, and IV only

    (E) I, II, IV, and V only

63. Which of the following is not a condition for a population to be in Hardy-Weinberg equilibrium?

    (A) random mating

    (B) large population size

    (C) extensive immigration

    (D) no mutations

    (E) random reproductive success

64. Every year, the population of a certain species of animal will first rise far above its carrying capacity, and then fall far below it. This species is most likely to be a member of which of the following groups?

    (A) arthropoda

    (B) primates

    (C) carnivora

    (D) echinodermata

    (E) aves

65. Which of the following is an abiotic component of a niche?

    (A) predators

    (B) parasites

    (C) lake

    (D) seeds

    (E) shade trees

66. Over many generations, certain prey species of fish in ocean habitats have developed more streamlined bodies in order to outrun their predators. During the same period of time, the predators have also developed more streamlined bodies in order to continue catching the prey. This is an example of

    (A) analogous structures

    (B) co-evolution

    (C) stabilizing selection

    (D) mutualistic symbiosis

    (E) intraspecific competition

Go on to next page

67. Which of the following is most likely to be a founder species that could begin ecological succession?

    (A) cyanobacteria

    (B) lichen

    (C) small grasses

    (D) insects

    (E) mosses

68. Which of the following is not a serious weakness of the fossil record as evidence for various evolutionary hypotheses?

    (A) very few organisms fossilize after they die

    (B) fossils are often hard to find

    (C) geological processes may destroy fossils before scientists can examine them

    (D) almost no soft tissues ever fossilize

    (E) scientists can't be sure what is a fossil and what is normal rock formation

69. Which of the following statements is consistent with Darwinian evolution but not with Lamarckian evolution?

    (A) species can change over time to better fit their environmental conditions

    (B) individuals can acquire new characteristics over their lifetimes that can be passed on to their offspring

    (C) evolution can only act on populations, not on individuals

    (D) Some characteristics work better in a certain environment than do other characteristics

    (E) most members of a species are exactly the same

70. Which of the following is required for two populations of a single species to undergo speciation?

    (A) no regular interbreeding between populations

    (B) populations must experience different environmental conditions

    (C) there must be no mutations in either species

    (D) the populations must be roughly the same size

    (E) the populations must experience similar environmental conditions

71. Which of the following taxonomic groups primarily includes decomposers?

    I. annelida

    II. fungi

    III. protozoa

    IV. slime molds

    (A) I and II

    (B) II only

    (C) II, III and IV only

    (D) I, II, and IV only

    (E) I, II, III, and IV

72. Which of the following pairs may be considered homologous structures?

    (A) shark tails and dolphin tails

    (B) bat wings and bird wings

    (C) seal flippers and dolphin flippers

    (D) bat sonar and dolphin sonar

    (E) turtle beaks and bird beaks

Go on to next page

73. Which of the following is most likely to be an r-selected species?

    (A) bullfrog

    (B) elephant

    (C) human

    (D) giraffe

    (E) hippopotamus

74. Which of the following scenarios is most likely to result in directional selection?

    (A) a prey insect's environment always includes patches of brown dirt and patches of green grass

    (B) the temperature in the environment is very stable over long periods of time

    (C) females prefer males that are solid gray

    (D) females prefer the males with the loudest mating calls

    (E) females prefer the males with the best tail symmetry

75. Which of the following is not an ecological role of producers?

    (A) produce O_2

    (B) provide food and energy to consumers

    (C) produce glucose

    (D) produce N_2

    (E) consume CO_2

76. Which of the following populations is likely to experience the most dramatic evolutionary change over the generations?

    (A) a sexually reproducing population in a stable environment

    (B) an asexually reproducing population in a stable environment

    (C) a sexually reproducing species in a changing environment

    (D) an asexually reproducing species in a changing environment

    (E) a sexually reproducing species that is migrating away from a changing environment to a more stable one

Go on to next page

Questions 77–80

An ecologist is studying an ecosystem. The community in the ecosystem consists of hundreds of different populations including the following species: field mouse, bunch grass, red tail hawk, honey bee, mule deer, jackrabbit, sunflower, and gray wolf. One summer, the ecologist observes a disease spread through the wolf population that kills off 80% of the wolves.

77. Over the next few years, which of the following is least likely to be an ecological effect of the loss of wolves?

    (A) deer population will increase

    (B) grass population will decrease

    (C) remaining wolves will have an abundance of food

    (D) jackrabbit population will increase

    (E) hawk population will decrease

78. Which of the following is most likely to be a food chain in this ecosystem?

    (A) sunflower → jackrabbit → mule deer → wolf

    (B) grass → jackrabbit → hawk → wolf

    (C) grass → honey bee → mule deer → wolf

    (D) sunflower → honey bee

    (E) grass → mule deer → hawk → wolf

79. Over the next few years, which of the following will be least affected by the loss of wolves?

    (A) primary producers

    (B) decomposers

    (C) primary consumers

    (D) secondary consumers

    (E) omnivores

80. As a result of the loss of wolves, competition is most likely to increase between which two populations?

    (A) wolf and hawk

    (B) wolf and mule deer

    (C) mule deer and jackrabbit

    (D) jackrabbit and hawk

    (E) grass and sunflower

 IF YOU FINISH BEFORE TIME IS CALLED, YOU MAY CHECK YOUR WORK ON THE BIOLOGY-E TEST ONLY. DO NOT TURN TO ANY OTHER TEST IN THE BOOK.

BIOLOGY-M SECTION

This is the Biology-M section. Answer questions 81–100. Make sure you begin with question 81 on your answer sheet.

Directions: Each of the questions below is followed by five answers. Some groups of questions relate to a laboratory or experimental situation. For each question, select the best answer to the question and then fill in the corresponding oval on the answer sheet.

81. Which of the following situations would require use of a light microscope?

   (A) obtaining a high-resolution image of a mineral surface

   (B) determining the bonding structure of a molecule

   (C) observing cellular processes of a prokaryote

   (D) determining the structure of a cockroach antenna

   (E) determining the shape of a prokaryote

82. Which of the following can be used to distinguish prokaryotes from eukaryotes?

   (A) presence of cell membrane

   (B) presence of a flagellum

   (C) presence of ribosomes

   (D) presence of a cytoskeleton

   (E) presence of chloroplasts

83. Consider a situation in which there is a higher concentration of sodium in the extracellular fluid than in the cytoplasm of a certain cell. What method would the cell most likely use to move sodium from the cytoplasm to the extracellular fluid?

   (A) simple diffusion

   (B) passive diffusion

   (C) active transport

   (D) endocytosis

   (E) exocytosis

84. Which of the following is most likely to be able to diffuse through a cell membrane?

   (A) a cholesterol molecule

   (B) an amino acid

   (C) a carbohydrate

   (D) a nucleotide

   (E) an ion

85. A sperm cell only needs to carry genetic information and swim. Which three cell parts are most likely to be found in sperm cells?

   (A) mitochondria, chloroplast, flagellum

   (B) nucleus, ribosomes, mitochondria

   (C) nucleus, chloroplast, flagellum

   (D) nucleus, mitochondria, flagellum

   (E) nucleus, mitochondria, cilia

86. In which phase of mitosis do sister chromatids separate?

   (A) prophase

   (B) metaphase

   (C) anaphase

   (D) telophase

   (E) interphase

Go on to next page

87. Which of the following is not made from glucose?

    (A) cellulose

    (B) chitin

    (C) glycogen

    (D) starch

    (E) sucrose

88. Which of the following is a possible result of a point mutation on the DNA of a gene?

    (A) change in protein shape

    (B) change in protein amino acid sequence

    (C) change in protein function

    (D) no effect

    (E) all of the above

89. Trait X is a sex-linked trait, and the phenotype usually only shows up in males. Suppose a male with the X phenotype mates and produces offspring with a female that is not a carrier for the trait. What are the chances that their male offspring will show the phenotype for trait X?

    (A) 0%

    (B) 25%

    (C) 50%

    (D) 75%

    (E) 100%

90. Which three molecules go into constructing a single DNA nucleotide?

    (A) phosphate group, glucose sugar, nitrogen base

    (B) phosphate group, ribose sugar, nitrogen base

    (C) phosphate group, deoxyribose sugar, phosphate base

    (D) nitrogen group, deoxyribose sugar, nitrogen base

    (E) phosphate group, deoxyribose sugar, nitrogen base

91. Which of the following molecules is a source of energy for cells?

    (A) glucose

    (B) lipids

    (C) ATP

    (D) glycogen

    (E) all of the above

92. In aerobic cellular respiration, the role of NAD^+ is to

    (A) transfer electrons from glucose to the electron transport chain

    (B) transfer electrons from glucose to CO_2

    (C) transfer electrons from glucose to the Krebs cycle

    (D) transfer electrons from the electron transfer chain to O_2

    (E) transfer electrons from CO_2 to O_2

Go on to next page

93. Which of the following processes produces CO_2?

    I. aerobic cellular respiration

    II. photosynthesis

    III. fermentation

    IV. dehydration synthesis

    (A) I only

    (B) I and III only

    (C) III only

    (D) II and IV only

    (E) I and IV only

94. Which of the following processes does not produce ATP?

    I. light-dependent reactions

    II. Krebs cycle

    III. Calvin cycle

    IV. anaerobic cellular respiration

    (A) I and III only

    (B) II and III only

    (C) III only

    (D) IV only

    (E) I and II only

95. Which of the following best represents the inputs and outputs of the Krebs cycle?

    (A) glucose, 2 FAD^+ and 8 NAD^+ in; 6 CO_2, 2 FADH and 8 NADH out

    (B) 2 pyruvate, 2 FADH and 8 NADH in; 6 CO_2, 2 FAD^+ and 8 NAD^+ out

    (C) 2 pyruvate, 2 FAD^+ and 8 NAD^+ in; 6 CO_2, 2 FADH and 8 NADH out

    (D) glucose and 6 O_2 in; 6 CO_2 and 6 H_2O out

    (E) 1 pyruvate, 1 FAD^+ and 4 NAD^+ in; 3 CO_2, 1 FADH and 4 NADH out

Go on to next page

96. Which of the following stages of meiosis decreases a cell's chromosome number from diploid to haploid?

    (A) Anaphase II

    (B) Anaphase I

    (C) Metaphase II

    (D) Metaphase I

    (E) Telophase I.

97. Which of the following organic molecules typically includes nitrogen?

    I. amino acids

    II. carbohydrates

    III. lipids

    IV. nucleotides

    (A) I and III only

    (B) I and IV only

    (C) II, III and IV only

    (D) IV only

    (E) I, II, III, and IV

Go on to next page

Questions 98–100

A certain species of flowering plant has two alleles for the gene that controls flower color, the red gene (R) and the white gene (W). Below is a diagram of a test cross for this species, showing the phenotypes of the members of each generation. The F_2 generation resulted from a mating between one red member and white member of the F_1 generation.

P	red	white
F_1	15 red	17 white
F_2	18 red	16 white

Go on to next page

98. What were the genotypes of the two plants in the P generation?

    (A) R-W and R-W

    (B) R-R and R-W

    (C) W-W and R-W

    (D) R-R and W-W

    (E) R-W and W-R

99. Which of the following best describes the relationship between the two alleles?

    (A) W is dominant over R

    (B) W is recessive compared to R

    (C) R is dominant over W

    (D) the two alleles are codominant

    (E) the two alleles show incomplete dominance

100. If you were to breed a red and a white member of the F_2 generation, what chances does each offspring have of ending up with red flowers?

    (A) 0%

    (B) 25%

    (C) 50%

    (D) 75%

    (E) 100%

STOP

IF YOU FINISH BEFORE TIME IS CALLED, YOU MAY CHECK YOUR WORK ON THE BIOLOGY-M TEST ONLY. DO NOT TURN TO ANY OTHER TEST IN THE BOOK.

Now it's time to figure out your scores. The SAT uses an unusual scoring system. Every question that you answer correctly counts for one point (not too strange so far). Every wrong answer counts for 1/4 of a point (okay, that's a little odd). Questions that are left unanswered or that receive more than one answer are not counted at all. That means that if you skip a question, you won't get a point added to your raw score or a 1/4 point deducted from your raw score. The raw score is the total correct minus 1/4 of the total incorrect. This raw score is then converted into a scaled score.

Table 16-1 lists the correct answer to every question in the core section of the exam. Compare your answers to the correct answers, and for each question, put a mark in the "Right" column if your answer is correct, and put a check in the "Wrong" column if your answer is incorrect. Leave both spaces blank for any question you did not answer. Count up the total number of checks in each column and enter that number at the bottom.

Table 16-1	Answers to the Core Section		
Question Number	*Correct Answer*	*Right*	*Wrong*
1	E		
2	B		
3	E		
4	C		
5	B		
6	D		
7	C		
8	D		
9	E		
10	B		
11	A		
12	A		
13	B		
14	C		
15	D		
16	D		
17	A		
18	E		
19	A		
20	D		
21	C		
22	E		
23	C		
24	D		
25	B		
26	E		
27	E		
28	E		
29	D		
30	B		
31	C		

(continued)

Table 16-1 *(continued)*

Question Number	Correct Answer	Right	Wrong
32	B		
33	C		
34	A		
35	E		
36	A		
37	D		
38	D		
39	C		
40	C		
41	B		
42	D		
43	B		
44	A		
45	E		
46	D		
47	E		
48	C		
49	D		
50	E		
51	B		
52	E		
53	C		
54	D		
55	A		
56	D		
57	B		
58	C		
59	B		
60	D		
Totals:			

Table 16-2 lists the correct answers to all of the questions on the Biology-E section of the test. If you took the Biology-E section, then compare your answers to the answers given, and for each question, put a mark in the "Right" column if your answer is correct, and put a check in the "Wrong" column if your answer is incorrect. Leave both columns blank for any question you did not answer. Count up the total number of checks in each column and enter that number at the bottom.

Table 16-2	Answers to Biology-E Section		
Question Number	Correct Answer	Right	Wrong
61	E		
62	D		
63	C		
64	A		
65	C		
66	B		
67	B		
68	E		
69	C		
70	A		
71	D		
72	C		
73	A		
74	D		
75	D		
76	C		
77	E		
78	D		
79	B		
80	C		
Totals:			

Table 16-3 lists the correct answers to all of the questions on the Biology-M section of the test. If you took the Biology-M section, then compare your answers to the answers given, and for each question, put a mark in the "Right" column if your answer is correct, and put a check in the "Wrong" column if your answer is incorrect. Leave both columns blank for any question you did not answer. Count up the total number of checks in each column and enter that number at the bottom.

Table 16-3	Answers to Biology-M Section		
Question Number	Correct Answer	Right	Wrong
81	C		
82	E		
83	C		
84	A		
85	D		
86	C		
87	B		
88	E		
89	A		
90	E		
91	E		
92	A		
93	B		
94	C		
95	E		
96	E		
97	B		
98	B		
99	A		
100	C		
Totals:			

Add together your total number right from both the core section and the subject section of the test and write in on this line _____. This number is your "Total Correct" number.

Add together your total number wrong from both the core section and the subject section of the test and write it on this line _____. This number is your "Total Incorrect" number.

Multiply your "Total Incorrect" number by 0.25, and write the product on this line _____. This is your "Adjusted Incorrect" number.

Calculate your "Raw Score" using this formula:

(Total Correct) – (Adjusted Incorrect) = Raw Score

Round your Raw Score to the nearest whole number and enter the result on this line _____. This is your final Raw Score.

Table 16-4 shows you how to find your Scaled Score on the 200 to 800 scale used by the SAT people. The Scaled Score is the score that is sent to the colleges to which you are applying.

Table 16-4	Raw Scores and Their Associated Scaled Scores		
Raw Score	Scaled Score	Raw Score	Scaled Score
80	800	29	490
79	800	28	480
78	800	27	480
77	800	26	470
76	800	25	460
75	800	24	460
74	800	23	450
73	800	22	440
72	790	21	440
71	780	20	430
70	780	19	430
69	770	18	420
68	760	17	410
67	760	16	410
66	750	15	400
65	740	14	400
64	730	13	390
63	730	12	380
62	720	11	380

(continued)

Table 16-4 *(continued)*

Raw Score	Scaled Score	Raw Score	Scaled Score
61	710	10	370
60	710	9	360
59	700	8	360
58	690	7	350
57	690	6	340
56	680	5	340
55	670	4	330
54	670	3	330
53	660	2	320
52	650	1	310
51	640	0	300
50	630	−1	290
49	630	−2	280
48	620	−3	270
47	610	−4	270
46	610	−5	260
45	600	−6	250
44	600	−7	250
43	590	−8	240
42	590	−9	240
41	580	−10	240
40	570	−11	240
39	570	−12	230
38	560	−13	230
37	550	−14	230
36	550	−15	230
35	540	−16	230
34	530	−17	220
33	520	−18	220
32	510	−19	220
31	510	−20	220
30	500		

Chapter 17

Practice Test 1:
Answers and Explanations

∙∙

*T*he simple list of answers to every question on Practice Test #1 are listed at the end of Chapter 16. This chapter goes further by providing detailed explanations for every question in Practice Test #1, which will help to reinforce the biology contained in the previous chapters. In addition, these explanations will give you the inside story on the structure of SAT II-style questions and which strategies will help you answer the questions correctly, sometimes even when you aren't sure about the biological facts.

Not only do we explain which answer is correct, but also why the other answers are wrong. Remember that knowing which answers are wrong can sometimes be just as important as knowing which answer is correct because if you are able to eliminate a few options, you may end up pinpointing the right answer.

There are a few general things to watch out for. First of all, make sure you read the questions very carefully because sometimes the wording is kind of tricky. Some questions ask something like, "Which of the following is a function of proteins?" For questions like this, you can either look for the one you know is definitely a function of proteins, or you can eliminate the ones that you know are definitely not functions of proteins. Actually, you should probably use both strategies just to be sure you don't miss something. On the other hand, the question is just as likely to ask, "Which of the following is not a function of proteins?" Always look for words like "except,""not," or "false" because these call for the reverse strategy. In this case you should eliminate the options that you definitely know *are* functions of proteins, and then choose the one that probably is not.

Harder questions ask something like, "Which of the following is most likely to be true?" Notice the "mostly likely" phrase. With these, every answer *could* be true, but only one answer is the *most likely* to be true. Make sure you read each choice carefully before making your decision, and watch out for when you need to reverse the strategy, like if it says "least likely to be true" or "most likely to be false."

Questions 1–60: Core Section

1. **E.** You probably noticed right off the bat, but this question has a "not" in it. The correct answer is actually the answer that is not a xylem and phloem user.

Xylem and phloem are the circulatory tubes of the more advanced plants, such as trees, bushes, and flowers. These are all called tracheophytes, because "trache" means "tube," as in the "trachea" which is your windpipe. That eliminates option (D), and also means that whatever is the opposite of the tracheophytes is probably the correct answer. That means the plants that do *not* use xylem and phloem are the nontracheophytes. All this plant stuff is covered in Chapter 13.

2. **B.** The animals that help plants to reproduce are the pollinators such as bees, butterflies, and hummingbirds. Pollinators only visit plants that have flowers, and the only plants with flowers are the angiosperms.

3. **E.** Mosses and liverworts are the simplest kinds of plants, so they don't have any fancy circulatory systems, which means they are nontracheophytes. Mosses are just fuzzy patches on the rocks, trees, and ground of wet, forested areas. Mosses don't have any regular stems or leaves or anything, so you know they are pretty simple compared to the tracheophytes.

4. **C.** This one may have thrown you off because the first three were all about plants while this one is about Protists. Questions on the SAT II could ask about anything at any time, so don't assume that just because the last few have all been about plants, then the next one will be also.

   The only one of the choices that's in the Protista kingdom (rather than in Plantae) is the algae, so that's the one to choose. See Chapter 11 for more on algae and other Protists.

5. **B.** Spontaneous movement from high concentration to low concentration is diffusion. It is "spontaneous" because it doesn't require any energy to make it happen — it just goes naturally on its own unless there is a barrier (like a cell membrane) preventing it.

6. **D.** Even if you didn't remember the answer to this one from Chapter 13, you can give yourself a hint by noticing that only one of the answers has something about light in its name ("photo" refers to "light"). This isn't always guaranteed to land you on the right answer, but it can at least guide you to a likely contender.

   In this case, phototropism really is the right choice. "Tropism" refers to growth, so the word means growth toward light. None of the others have anything to do with growth or with light, so they can all be easily eliminated.

7. **C.** This question asks about the opposite of diffusion because now the cell is using energy to move something against its concentration gradient (from low concentration to high). That definitely won't happen spontaneously, so it requires active transport.

8. **D.** All of the choices except flagella are kinds of internal organelles, and organelles are found exclusively in eukaryotic cells. Flagella are tail-like structures found in lots of eukaryotes, but in many prokaryotes as well. So, flagella is the only choice that might be found in some prokaryotic cells. See Chapter 3 for more about the differences between prokaryotes and eukaryotes.

9. **E.** This is mostly just a memorization question from Chapter 3. Proteins are constructed using mRNA, tRNA, and amino acids, and the actual construction process happens on a ribosome (rRNA). Ribosomes are found on the rough endoplasmic reticulum, which appears rough because it has so many ribosomes stuck all over it.

10. **B.** Here is another memorization question from Chapter 3. The nucleus is where DNA is stored in eukaryotic cells. This is also important for the processes described in Chapter 7. DNA contains the genetic information, which needs to stay safe inside the nucleus.

11. **A.** You need to remember two different facts for this question. The Krebs cycle is the second stage of aerobic cellular respiration, and aerobic cellular respiration happens in the mitochondria.

12. **A.** All kingdoms except Plantae include at least a few decomposers, but the only one that contains *only* decomposers and nothing else is Fungi.

13. **B.** This question asks you to remember something from ecology (Chapter 12) and classification (Chapter 11).

   The information you need to know to answer some question may come from a combination of topics.

   Tertiary consumers are pretty high up in the food chain because they are carnivores that eat other carnivores. Fungi are all decomposers and plants are all primary producers, so they're both out of the running. Monera and Protista contain some organisms that consume other organisms, but since they're so small, none of them would really count as carnivores that eat other carnivores. Animalia, on the other hand, contains lots of obvious examples of tertiary consumers like sharks and hawks.

Even if you weren't sure about the other kingdoms, you can be sure that Animalia definitely contains tertiary consumers; so don't worry about the other options at all.

14. **C.** Protista and Monera contain some photosynthesizers, but they contain a lot of heterotrophs as well, such as decomposers. The only kingdom that contains exclusively photosynthesizers is Plantae.

As with the last question, even if you weren't sure about some of the other kingdoms, you can be sure that everyone in the Plantae kingdom can do photosynthesis, so you can ignore the other options.

15. **D.** This "nitrogen-fixation" thing has to do with the nitrogen cycle. Members of certain kinds of bacteria are the only organisms on earth than can convert the N_2 gas in the atmosphere into NO_3, a process called nitrogen fixation. Nobody else on earth can do that; and if they didn't do it, everyone would suffer from lack of a sufficient nitrogen source in our diets.

16. **D.** Biomes with the greatest diversity are the ones with the most water and the most stable temperatures.

Of the options provided, obviously both freshwater and ocean biomes have plenty of water, so all the others can be eliminated. The ocean in general stays at a more stable temperature than most freshwater habitats, and as a result, the oceans have more diversity. By the way, as explained in Chapter 12, the only terrestrial biome that has more diversity than the oceans is the tropical rain forest.

17. **A.** This question doesn't involve a straightforward fact to memorize from Chapter 3, so you're going to have to reason your way through it.

The very first cells would be the simplest possible cells. Prokaryotes are simpler than eukaryotes, so (D) and (E) are both wrong because they both include the eukaryotes option. To be an autotroph, an organism would have to perform photosynthesis, which is a pretty complicated process. Being a heterotroph is a lot simpler, especially if you just do fermentation. Some modern heterotrophs (like you, for example) use aerobic cellular respiration, which is also pretty complicated. You actually can rule out aerobic cellular respiration because it requires O_2. There wasn't any O_2 around that long ago, so the first cells couldn't have been doing aerobic cellular respiration. So, now you can be pretty sure that the first cells were heterotrophs, so options I and II are the right combination.

18. **E.** The simple route would be to assume that since this is a question about blood, the answer must be the circulatory system, but the SAT II usually doesn't let you go the simple route. Think about how speeding up the circulatory system may affect pH. Actually, there isn't any obvious way that would have any affect at all on pH, so maybe you should check some of the other options.

The nervous system is always monitoring and modifying the internal states of your body, so something like a pH imbalance isn't going to make it work any more or less than normal. The digestive system can't help. It just breaks down and absorbs whatever you eat. The endocrine system itself can't do anything about changing the internal environment. It can only turn other organs on or off in order to make them do something about it.

You may remember from Chapter 14 that the presence of CO_2 in the blood makes the pH of the blood go down, and if the animal needs to bring the pH back up, it needs to get rid of CO_2. CO_2 is exhaled through the respiratory system, so by increasing its breathing rate the animal can get rid of some extra CO_2, which should allow its blood pH to go back up to where it should be.

19. **A.** The offspring had completely yellow flowers and completely blue flowers on the same plants, so the two traits showed up independently and fully in the phenotypes of the offspring. This means that both alleles must be fully dominant, also known as co-dominant. If there were incomplete dominance, each flower would be some kind of blend of yellow and blue. A recessive trait wouldn't show up at all, and a genetic mutation is always an explanation you use when all else fails. Partial dominance is not a term used in classical genetics.

20. **D.** Conditioning occurs when an animal learns to perform an unusual behavior because of the expectation of some other event or stimulus. The deer wouldn't normally avoid a watering hole, but it now associates the presence of a predator at that particular water hole, so it has learned never to return to that valuable source of water. The chimpanzees are an example of mimicry (and perhaps some higher-level intuitive learning), and the other two are both basic instinctual behaviors. Chapter 15 explains animal behavior in more detail.

21. **C.** The graph depicts something increasing fast and then slowly reaching some sort of maximum. The only option that matches this depiction is a population approaching carrying capacity. In such a scenario, the population will grow pretty fast, but the closer it gets to the carrying capacity, the slower the rate of growth until it pretty much stops growing right around the carrying capacity. Exponential growth, on the other hand, just keeps getting bigger and bigger, faster and faster, so (A) is wrong. A graph showing a selection effect would show two bell curves shifted apart from each other in some way, so (B) and (D) are wrong also. A population moving away from carrying capacity would start out flat and then bend either upwards or downwards, so you can eliminate (E).

22. **E.** All three of the choices go together, so you have to either pick all of them or none of them. Picking none of them wasn't an option, so it must be all of them.

   Technically, for two organisms to be closely related means that they have very similar DNA sequences. As described in Chapter 7, the nucleotide sequence in the DNA determines the nucleotide sequence in the RNA, and the sequence in the RNA determines the amino acid sequence in the proteins. So, if two organisms are similar with regard to any one of the three, then they are almost certainly similar in the other two ways as well.

23. **C.** Exocrine glands secrete their substance out onto the surface of the body or into a space within the body. Sweat glands and mammary glands both do this, so they are both exocrine glands. The pituitary and adrenal glands both secrete their substances (hormones) into the blood stream, so they are both endocrine glands.

24. **D.** This one is probably pretty easy. Pollinators want to find flowers because flowers contain nectar, but the nectar itself is hard to see or smell. Flowering plants want the pollinators to find the nectar, so they need to advertise. The most obvious flower advertisement is the brightly colored petals. The stamen and anthers are part of the actual reproductive organs, which the pollinators aren't really interested in, and the sepals are just structural parts.

25. **B.** This question asks you to bring together some knowledge about biomes with knowledge about animals. Endotherms (warm-blooded animals) are able to maintain their body temperature even when it gets really cold outside. For ectotherms (cold-blooded animals), on the other hand, if the weather gets cold, their bodies get cold right along with it. This can become a serious problem if the outside temperature drops to freezing because any ectotherms caught outside will freeze to death.

   Of the choices given, this is mostly likely to happen in the tundra, where everything is completely frozen for much of the year, so any animals that live in the tundra are almost certainly endotherms, such as caribou, polar bears, penguins, and seals. You aren't too likely to see snakes or frogs on the tundra.

26. **E.** In the ABO blood type set of genes, the type-O allele is recessive. That means in order to have the type-O phenotype, you must have two type-O alleles because any type A- or B-alleles will dominate the type O. Since both parents have type-O blood, it must be that neither of them has an A or a B allele to pass on to their children. That means the chances their children will be type O is 100 percent.

27. **E.** Notice the "not" in this question. You are looking for something the vertebrate nervous system does *not* do.

    The nervous system usually controls things that are really fast and require some sort of information processing, while the endocrine (hormone) system controls things that happen over long time periods. The longer the time period, the more likely that it's the endocrine system handling it. The first four choices are all things that require quick actions and information processing, so they are the domain of the nervous system, so they are likely to be functions of the nervous system. Sexual development, on the other hand, is a multiyear process that just moves steadily forward, so this one is *not* a function of the nervous system, and therefore is the correct answer to the question.

28. **E.** Remember that gymnosperms are cone-producing plants like pine and fir trees. Forest fires, as long as they are not so intense that they turn the whole forest to ash, actually help gymnosperms to reproduce.

    Fires do drive away herbivores, but only temporarily. They will soon return to eat up little seedlings, so (B) can be crossed out. Gymnosperms rely on the wind to carry their pollen, so (C) is wrong also. The high heat of fires causes the seeds inside of cones to open up and be able to sprout, so (A) is right, but so also is (D). The seedlings need some room to get going, and if there's dead brush on the ground, the seedlings can't get any light. When the fire rushes through, it burns off most of the dead brush.

29. **D.** This is really just a memorization question. The fertilized egg is called a zygote, so that one definitely comes first. Therefore, you can eliminate (B), (C), and (E). The baby, obviously, comes last.

    All answers list baby last and fetus next to last, so all you need to know is which comes first, blastula or gastrula. It's blastula, then gastrula, so (D) is the correct answer.

30. **B.** Exothermic animals are cold-blooded, and this category includes all animals except birds and mammals. Aves is the taxonomic name for birds. Carnivores, cetaceans, and primates are all kinds of mammals. Reptiles, on the other hand, are definitely not birds or mammals, and definitely are cold-blooded.

31. **C.** Plant leaves appear green because that is the only color that bounces off the leaves and comes into your eyes. Since green light bounces off of the leaves, the leaves cannot use it to energize photosynthesis. This means that if a plant is getting only green light, then it won't be able to grow very well at all. The best light for plants is the more red to yellow light, and white light contains all of the colors.

32. **B.** The part of the brain that monitors all of the automatic functions of the body is the hypothalamus, so if it is damaged, the animal will have a hard time monitoring and regulating things like blood pH, as well as blood pressure and body temperature.

    The thalamus, which is located above the hypothalamus, relays most of the sensory information (such as vision and hearing) to other parts of the brain. The medulla drives some automatic functions such as heart rate and breathing, but it doesn't keep track of how it's all going and it can't really decide to modify anything like the hypothalamus can. The cerebellum is important for coordinating movements, and the cerebrum is used for higher brain functions such as perception and memory

33. **C.** Both parents have the brown eye phenotype, so you know they both have at least one brown eye allele; but that means their genotypes could be either Br-Br or Br-bl. The child has blue eyes, so its genotype must bl-bl, which means that each parent must have passed on a blue eye allele. From this you can conclude that both parents must have the Br-bl genotype.

    You can draw out a Punnet square to confirm that this will work out, but this is time consuming, so only draw a square if the problem is too difficult to determine without it.

34. **A.** Geese certainly don't have a hard-wired instinct to follow humans, so (D) can be crossed out. Conditioning requires some kind of specific training, and nothing like that was mentioned in the question, so (B) is wrong also. The question also never mentioned any repeated rounds of trial and error, so cross out (E) as well. When they first hatch, geese will look at whatever animal is around and assume it is their mother. They pick out some distinguishing characteristic and latch onto that as the main characteristic of "mom." This is an example of imprinting.

35. **E.** The liver is a multi-functional organ. It breaks down toxic molecules, so (A) is true, but it does not filter them out of the blood, so (B) is false. Filtering is the job of the kidneys. The liver also stores glucose in the form of glycogen, so (C) is true also. That means the correct answer is (E).

36. **A.** Natural selection is all about how gene frequencies change in a population over time, but nature can't select individual genes. It can only select which individual organisms are well suited to the environment and which are not. The fit individuals survive and reproduce, while the unfit ones die off. Evolution is covered in more detail in Chapter 10.

37 **D.** You may remember from Chapter 12 that the drier a biome is, the greater temperature swings it will have. The desert is the driest biome of all, and luckily the desert happens to be one of the choices.

38. **D.** Xylem is the part of a plant's circulatory system that carries stuff that has been soaked up by the roots, and it sends that stuff from the roots to the leaves. Minerals, water, and ammonia are all things found in soil and are absorbed by the roots. Sugar, on the other hand, is produced in the leaves and sent out to the rest of the plant through the phloem.

39. **C.** If you breathe faster, you will not only take in more O_2, you will also release extra CO_2. That will make the O_2 level in the blood increase and the CO_2 level decrease, so (A) and (D) are wrong. From the information given, there isn't any way to be sure what will happen to the blood pressure, so (E) is probably wrong too. If the amount of CO_2 in the blood decreases, then the pH of the blood will increase.

40. **C.** This sounds like a strange question. What does the first part about digestive fluid have to do with polymers? As you can see from looking at the choices, polymers are those organic molecule chains from Chapter 5. Now remember from Chapter 14 that digestive fluid contains a lot of enzymes that will break down food in the small intestine. Enzymes are made of proteins, so the pancreas is likely to be building a lot more proteins than anything else.

41. **B.** First of all, if a blood vessel is lined with any muscle at all it will be smooth muscle, so (A), (C), and (D) can be crossed out right away. If a blood vessel is carrying blood away from the heart, then it must be an artery, and arteries are sure to be lined with some smooth muscle.

42. **D.** There's that "not" again, so remember how to approach this question; eliminate things you know are functions of the excretory system.

Chapter 14 describes how the excretory system includes the kidneys and bladder. The kidneys regulate the contents of the blood by removing wastes and regulating the amount of ions and water in the blood. This, in turn, will modify blood pressure, so (A), (B) and (C) are all functions of the excretory system. The function of the bladder, of course, is to store urine, so (E) is also included. The exocrine glands, on the other hand, are not part of the kidney-bladder system at all, so they are definitely not regulated by the excretory system (despite their similar-sounding names). That means the correct answer is (D).

43. **B.** In the situation described, the deer will be experiencing the fight-or-flight response, which gets the animal ready for serious action. Any general growth or maintenance systems are shut down, and extra resources are diverted to the areas that will help the animal deal with the immediate life-threatening situation. The hormone we associate with this response is adrenaline, and the official name for adrenaline is epinephrine.

44. **A.** This one's got a "not," so you need to look for the one that doesn't belong. During the fight or flight response, the heart starts pounding really hard and really fast, so blood pressure would certainly increase, so cross out (C).

    Chapter 14 explained how vasodilation in the circulatory system is the opening up of blood vessels to allow greater blood flow, while vasoconstriction is the narrowing of blood vessels to restrict blood flow. The respiratory and muscular systems would definitely need more blood during the fight or flight response because their performance goes way up, so cross out (B) and (D) also.

    How about the epidermis? This one isn't as intuitive as the others, but blood flow to the skin is restricted during fight or flight, so (E) is out, too. In general, the digestive system is not immediately necessary, so there shouldn't be any vasodilation there, so that's the one that would not be a reaction of the circulatory system.

45. **E.** Not every organ of the digestive system goes completely dormant during fight or flight. During normal times, the liver stores a lot of carbohydrate fuel (glucose). During fight or flight, the heart, lungs, and muscles all need that stored fuel, so the liver will release it. That means (E) is the correct answer. All of the other choices are things that happen when the animal has time to relax and digest its previous meal.

46. **D.** The rest of the questions in the core section all pertain to a complicated scenario or experiment, so some of the explanations will start to get a little long.

    The control group for this experiment would be a dish that does not contain the experimental variable, which is the presence of antibiotics.

    Dish #4 does not contain any antibiotics at all so it is the control group. They will be able to compare the other dishes to this one in order to determine whether the antibiotics have any affect on the bacteria.

47. **E.** The researchers wanted to see how bacteria grow in the presence of different antibiotics versus how they grow under regular circumstances. Dishes with a third antibiotic or with bleach or with a low-nutrient growth medium would be extensions of the current experiment because they would introduce new experimental variables that weren't present before, so (A), (B), and (C) are out. A dish with no bacteria would not introduce any new experimental variables, but it would eliminate the very thing they wanted to study, so (D) is out as well. The researchers probably know what an empty Petri dish looks like.

    A dish with a plain paper circle would be a good control group because it isolates and removes the experimental variable even better than dish #4. This way, they could make sure that the presence of paper (instead of the antibiotic *on* the paper) doesn't somehow affect bacterial growth.

48. **C.** The question asks for the best explanation, which means that the statements in all five choices are consistent with the results and you need to find the one that is the *best* explanation for what happened overall.

    According to the results, the growth in dishes #1 and #2 looked pretty much the same as the control group, so you could conclude from them that erythromycin and penicillin didn't affect the total amount of bacterial growth. That is, the culture contains bacteria that seem to be immune to these antibiotics. Putting the antibiotics together, however, definitely stopped bacterial growth, so the antibiotics aren't completely ineffective.

    The best explanation is that the culture must contain at least two kinds of bacteria: one immune to penicillin and one immune to erythromycin. In dish #1, the bacteria immune to penicillin grew like crazy and filled the whole dish. In dish #2, the bacteria immune to erythromycin was able to take over. In dish #3, however, both kinds of bacteria were stopped, so the area around the paper circles was clear of bacteria.

49. **D.** The explanation from the last question theorizes that the bacteria that grew in dish #1 is immune to penicillin but not to erythromycin. That means the bacteria from the middle of dish #1 should be vulnerable to erythromycin; and if the researchers transfer it to a dish with a "B" circle, they can test that prediction, so (A) would be a good follow-up study. The situation is the same in dish #2, but with the antibiotics reversed, so (B) would be a good follow-up as well. Taking bacteria from anywhere and growing it in a dish with no circles would pretty much be just like the control group, so the researchers wouldn't expect the results of that follow-up to be very interesting. That means (D) is the correct answer.

50. **E.** This experiment had lots of implications for the origins of life, but the actual experiment itself had a much simpler and focused purpose. No life was produced in the Miller-Urey Experiment, so they can't conclude anything about life itself from their results, so (A), (C) and (D) can be crossed out. The experiment definitely was not simulating the conditions of present-day earth, so (B) is wrong also. The only thing this experiment shows is that basic organic molecules are easy to make under the conditions of the early earth, so the correct answer is (E). See Chapter 10 for more details on the early earth and the origins of life.

When you are asked to evaluate experiments, make sure you choose an answer choice that does not go beyond the scope of the experiment. You probably won't be asked to apply an SAT II experiment to a broad concept of life.

51. **B.** This is kind of a tough one. The answer to the last question said that organic molecules are easy to make under the conditions of the early earth. Did the researchers get in a time machine and travel back to the early earth to conduct the experiment? Well, they never mentioned that in their research report, so probably not. To be careful scientists, (and the SAT II will always be careful!) all they can really say is that organic molecules are easy to form under the conditions they cooked up in the laboratory, so the correct answer is (B). The first answer is easily testable, so it isn't a problematic assumption. The last three are all untestable assumptions, but they're much safer assumptions than the very specific idea that the exact conditions of the early earth were just like the conditions in the Miller-Urey Experiment.

52. **E.** The correct answer is (E) because all of these would be good follow-up studies. Since they don't really know if their experimental conditions exactly match the conditions of early earth, they should vary the experimental variables to cover lots of different possible scenarios. They should also make sure that present-day organisms contain the same kinds of organic molecules as were made in the experiment. If not, then the implications for the origins of life are diminished. The same thing goes for letting the experiment go for a while to see if the organic products change into something totally different after a while.

53. **C.** According to the graph, during the first few hours, the organism was taking CO_2 out of the air and was releasing O_2, but something happened at 6 pm to stop it. The only process that does this is photosynthesis, and absence of light will certainly stop photosynthesis, so the correct answer is (C). You can support this choice with the idea that 6 pm is right about time for people to turn off the lights and head home for the evening. See, some common sense really can help out on the SAT II.

54. **D.** From #53, you know that the organism must at least do photosynthesis. After 6 pm, the organism did the reverse of photosynthesis by taking in O_2 and releasing CO_2. The process that accomplishes this is aerobic cellular respiration, so the organism must be able to do that as well. Maybe it also can do fermentation, but there's no clear evidence of that from the information given.

Avoid answer choices that make you assume things about an experiment that are backed by the details of the experiment.

55. **A.** The organism must be in a taxonomic category that includes things that can do photosynthesis. Protozoans are heterotrophic Protists, so none of them do photosynthesis. Porifera, Cnidaria and Mammalia are all types of animals, and no animals ever do photosynthesis. Bryophyta, on the other hand, is a category of nonvascular plants.

56. **D.** If this organism can do photosynthesis then it must be a primary producer, so the correct answer is (D).

57. **B.** According to the example, in order to have the phenotype for sickle-cell anemia, a person must have two recessive alleles. That is, the genotype must be bb. If you do not have that phenotype, then your genotype could be either BB or Bb. Person I has a parent that has sickle-cell anemia, so you know that parent's genotype must be bb and they must have passed on the b allele. However, person I does not have sickle-cell anemia, so he must have the dominant B as his other allele, so his genotype must be Bb. That means the correct answer is, coincidentally, (B).

58. **C.** To find out the chances, first you have to know the genotypes of the two parents and then you have to put them into a Punnet square. From the last question, you know that person I's genotype is Bb. Person II has sickle-cell anemia, so she must have the bb genotype.

You'll probably need to draw a Punnet square (see Chapter 8) for this problem.

If you run these through a Punnet square, you'll find that half the possible allele combinations from these two parents are bb, which means their children have a 50% chance of having the sickle-cell anemia phenotype.

59. **B.** Person III does not have sickle-cell anemia, so at least one of his genes must be the dominant B allele. His daughter does have sickle-cell anemia, which means that she must have received a recessive b allele from each parent, so person III must have had one b allele to give. This means that person III's genotype must be Bb.

60. **D.** Person IV is more ambiguous. We know that she must have at least one dominant B allele because she does not have sickle-cell anemia, but what allele is her other gene: B or b? Her daughter received a B gene from person IV, so that doesn't help at all. The fact is, you just can't tell from the information given; her genotype could be either BB or Bb, so the correct answer is (D).

Biology-E Section

61. **E.** Endothermic means warm-blooded, and only birds and mammals are warm-blooded. Insects and reptiles are both cold-blooded. See Chapter 11 for more information on endotherms and ectotherms.

62. **D.** Autotrophs are organisms that can make their own glucose through photosynthesis. The only kingdoms that don't have any members that can do photosynthesis are Animalia and Fungi.

63. **C.** Hardy-Weinberg equilibrium is a fairly artificial situation in which no evolution is occurring at all. In other words, the proportions of all the alleles in the population would stay the same over the generations. For this to work, the population needs to be large and well mixed, with no genes entering or exiting the population. Any immigration at all would bring in new genes and would throw off the allele proportions, and that can't happen if the population is going to stay in Hardy-Weinberg equilibrium.

64. **A.** This species produces a lot of offspring every year, causing the population to go way over the carrying capacity. Since they go so far over carrying capacity, most of the individuals die from starvation or get eaten by predators, both of which will bring the population way back down.

What species follow this pattern? This usually doesn't happen in larger animals like primates and carnivorous mammals. Birds tend not to do this either, at least not as dramatically as described in the example. You may have no idea whether echinoderms do this or not, but you probably know that arthropoda includes insects, and there's lots of species of insects that have a huge population boom every spring, only to pretty much disappear in a few weeks. That fits the pattern in the example, so the correct answer is (A).

65. **C.** This one is pretty straightforward. An abiotic component is not alive, and the only non-living item among the choices is the lake, so the correct answer is (C).

66. **B.** This is an example of two sets of organisms that interact with each other in such a way as to drive each other's evolution in a specific direction. In this case, the predator and the prey have driven each other to evolve more and more streamlined bodies. This is called co-evolution because they evolve together.

Analogous structures is when two unrelated species end up with similar structures. Both of the species in the example are kinds of fish, so these are homologous structures (See Chapter 10). Stabilizing selection is when all of the members of a population are coming closer to the average over the generations. This isn't happening because the animals in the example are becoming more extreme over time. Mutualistic symbiosis is when two species are physically connected all the time, which (luckily for the prey) is not happening here. "Intra" means "within," so intraspecific competition is competition within a species. The example has to do with interaction *between* two species.

67. **B.** A founder species has to be able to live where there is no other organic material of any kind. Very few species can do that. First of all, it needs to be an autotroph, so (D) can be crossed out because insects are heterotrophs. Plants need some kind of dirt with at least some organic content to survive, so (C) and (E) can be crossed out, too. Cyanobacteria and lichen could both possibly survive there, but only lichen will break down inorganic rocks to provide dirt for some plants to move in, which would lead to ecological succession, so it is the only possible founder species on the choices.

68. **E.** Notice that this question has a "not." The first four options definitely are problems for the fossil record. As for the last choice, geologists and paleontologists know what regular rocks and sediment look like, so they can usually tell the difference between a fossil and normal rock formation. Sometimes they need to do some really detailed tests to be sure, but that's pretty rare.

69. **C.** You need to find which statement satisfies both criteria in the question at the same time. It needs to be both consistent with Darwinian evolutionary theory and, at the same time, it needs to be incompatible with Lamarck's theory, both of which are discussed in Chapter 11.

Options (A) and (D) are consistent with both theories, so they can be ruled out. Option (E) isn't considered true by either theory, so it can be crossed out also. Lamarck thought that organisms could acquire new characteristics during their lifetimes to better cope with their environment, and that they could pass down those acquired traits to their offspring. That means Lamarck thought that evolution acted on individual organisms rather than on whole populations. Darwin thought the exact opposite. Option (B) is consistent with Lamarck's ideas, but not with Darwin's, so it's not the answer. The only one that satisfies both criteria is (C).

70. **A.** As long as two populations are reproductively isolated from each other (no interbreeding), then they will automatically start to diverge over the generations. There will always be mutations, so (C) is automatically wrong. The other choices may affect the rate at which the populations diverge, but none of those conditions are *required* for them to diverge. Chapter 11 contains more details on speciation.

71. **D.** Annelida includes earthworms, which eat dirt, so they are decomposers. Fungi are all 100-percent decomposers, so they're on board also. Slime molds are the kinds of Protists that are most like fungi, so they're decomposers, too. Protozoans consume other living cells, so they are more like primary consumers than decomposers, so they're the only ones not included. That means the correct answer is (D).

72. **C.** Sometimes two different species will have some anatomical structure that is similar. If the species share some distant ancestor that also had that structure, then the structures are homologous. If they do not share an ancestor that had the structure, then the structures must have evolved independently in the two species. Those are called analogous structures.

Among the choices given, the only pair that demonstrates homologous structures is the flippers on seals and dolphins. The limbs of all mammals are homologous because there was a very, very distant ancestor of all mammals that had similar sorts of limbs. All of the other choices are analogous structures.

73. **A.** An r-selected species is one that produces a lot of offspring and then lets them fend for themselves, which means that most of them will die. Larger animals, on the other hand, tend to produce just a few offspring and then try to take good care of them.

The last four options are all large mammals, so they would not be r-selected species, which leads you right to the bullfrog. In fact, most of the amphibians are r-selected species.

74. **D.** Directional selection happens when the most extreme version of a trait results in the most reproductive success. This means the answer will say something about the biggest, brightest, smartest, or some other kind of "-est". The only choice that fits that description is the selection in favor of the loudest males.

75. **D.** Here's another "not" question, so eliminate what roles you know the producers do play.

Producers absorb CO_2 and H_2O to make food, mainly in the form of glucose, and they also produce O_2. Some of the food ends up going toward supporting the consumers. This means that the only thing on the list that they don't do is produce N_2.

76. **C.** Sexually reproducing species produce more variety in each generation, so they tend to evolve faster; so (B) and (D) can be crossed out. If a species is in a stable environment, then it probably isn't experiencing as many new problems as one living in a changing environment. New problems can provide new selection pressures that speed up evolution, so the correct answer is (C).

77. **E.** The question asks which is *least* likely to happen. That means that all of the answers are things that could happen, but based on the information given in the example, some choices are more likely than others.

If a secondary consumer, like a wolf, decreased in numbers, then any primary consumers that were the wolves' prey would increase in numbers because fewer of them are being eaten. That means the deer and jackrabbit populations are very likely to increase, so (A) and (D) can be crossed out. This also means that whatever wolves are still alive will have plenty of prey, so (C) can be crossed out also. Now, if the populations of primary consumers go up, then they will eat a lot more of the producers, so the grass population could very easily go down, so (B) is out. As for the hawk population, it isn't so clear what could happen. They could very easily increase in numbers because any competition they got from the wolves would pretty much be gone, leaving all those jackrabbits for the hawks. Based on the information in the example, there isn't any specific reason to think that the hawk population will decrease, so that is the least likely to happen.

78. **D.** Remember that a food chain must go from primary producer → primary consumer (herbivore) → secondary consumer (carnivore) → tertiary consumer (if any). Answers (A) and (C) have mule deer acting as secondary consumers, so they must be wrong. Answers (B) and (E) have wolves eating hawks, but wolves tend to be exclusively secondary consumers. The only one that doesn't violate the food chain order in some way is the shortest one, with the nectar from the sunflower (primary producer) going to the bee (primary consumer).

If you were tempted by an answer in which the wolves were eating hawks (a wolf certainly could eat a hawk if it really wanted to), then there is still a strategy you can use to get this one right. There is something about the structure of the answer choices that rules some of the wrong answers. Two choices, (B) and (E), have wolves eating hawks. If that would make an okay food chain, then (B) and (E) would both be correct, and this question doesn't allow for multiple answers, so you can eliminate them both. You'll come across a lot of questions that have this feature, and if you aren't sure which is the correct choice, some little trick of logic like this might help you jump to the right one.

79. **B.** Like in question #77, this one asks which is *least* likely to happen. All of the trophic levels are likely to be affected by the loss of wolves, but the decomposers sort of sit outside the normal scheme of things. Decomposers don't care if you're a producer, consumer, or whatever. As long as it's dead, they consume it. So, as long as the whole community of plants and animals doesn't start to disappear, the decomposers will do just fine.

80. **C.** Unlike the others, this one asks which is *most* likely to happen. If two populations are in competition, then their competition will intensify if their populations increase or if the resources they compete for are harder to find. As you found in #77, the mule deer and jackrabbit populations are both likely to increase as a result of the loss of wolves, and they share some food sources, so their competition is likely to intensify.

The jackrabbit and hawk in choice (D) are in a predator-prey relationship, not competition, so that one can't be right. All of the other choices include at least one population that will decrease as a result of the loss of the wolves, so none of them will have increased competition either.

Biology-M Section

81. **C.** Electron microscopes are good for seeing fine detail at high magnifications, but they can only view objects that stay perfectly still.

All of the choices are objects that can easily be made to stay frozen, except the cellular processes of a prokaryote. If you want to see them, you have to let them be active and do their thing, and only a light microscope can capture that.

82. **E.** Eukaryotes are bigger than prokaryotes, and eukaryotes have internal organelles while prokaryotes do not. Of the choices, the only one that is an internal organelle is the chloroplasts, so that's the only one of the choices that can be used to pick out the eukaryotes.

83. **C.** The cell wants to move sodium from low concentration to high concentration, which is going against the concentration gradient; so the cell is going to need to use energy to make it happen. That means using active transport. Diffusion goes from high concentration to low, which is the exact opposite of the example, and endocytosis and exocytosis aren't used to move ions.

84. **A.** Cell membranes are resistant to anything that has a charge on it. In other words, they are resistant to hydrophilic things like ions and carbohydrates. Hydrophobic things, which do not have a charge, can diffuse right through the membrane. Cholesterol is a kind of lipid, and lipids are hydrophobic, so cholesterol can diffuse through no problem.

85. **D.** Genetic information is in the DNA, and DNA is kept in the nucleus, so the sperm will have one of those. Some cells swim using cilia, but sperm use a flagellum, so it's got to have that also. Swimming takes lots of energy, so the sperm will also need mitochondria to break down fuel and produce ATP. So, the correct answer is (D) because it includes only a nucleus, mitochondria and a flagellum.

86. **C.** This is pretty much just a memorization question from Chapter 3. Sister chromatids separate during anaphase.

87. **B.** You're probably noticing them just fine by now, but this is another "not" question, and you know what that means. Four of the choices are made from glucose; one is not. You need to find the one that's not.

Glucose is an amazingly versatile molecule, and can be used to make a lot of different polymers. Cellulose is the strongest glucose polymer and is used in plant cell walls, so cross out (A). Glycogen and starch are long polymers used to store glucose, so cross out (C) and (D) also. Sucrose is a disaccharide made from glucose and fructose, so (E) is also gone. Chitin is used in insect exoskeletons and fungi cell walls, and is made from something called an amino sugar, so it's the one that is *not* made of glucose.

88. **E.** This is kind of a hard one, but you can reason it out. Genes contain information for how to build proteins. Specifically, they tell the cell what sequence the amino acids should be in. If the DNA changes in some way, the amino acid sequence of the protein is also likely to change in some way.

What other consequences might this have? Well, as explained in Chapter 5, the amino acid sequence is important for making the protein fold up into its proper 3-D shape, so if the amino acid sequence changes, the 3-D shape might end up being altered as well. Of course, the shape of a protein is vitally important for making the protein work correctly, so if the shape changes, the function could change as well.

Answers (A), (B), and (C) are all correct, so it looks like this is an "all of the above" answer, but (D) seems to contradict what's been said so far about all these changes that will happen to the proteins. Remember from Chapter 7 that sometimes you can get a silent mutation in which a single nucleotide is changed, but it doesn't affect the amino acid sequence of the protein. This means that it is entirely possible that the point mutation will have no effect at all, so it really is "all of the above."

89. **A.** A sex-linked trait comes from a gene on the X chromosome. Boys are XY, so if they get an X chromosome that has the gene for the sex-linked trait, they do not have a backup X to mask the effect of the gene, so they end up with the trait. A man who has sex-linked phenotype will not pass it on to his male children because his sons will get his Y chromosome, not his X chromosome, and if the mother doesn't have the sex-linked gene at all, then she can't pass it on either. So, there is no chance that this couple will have a son with the trait.

Create a Punnet square to confirm your reasoning, like the one below.

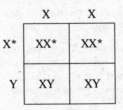

90. **E.** This is another memorization question. As you saw in Chapter 4, a DNA nucleotide has a phosphate group, a nitrogen base, and a deoxyribose sugar.

Aside from the basic memorization, there is something to watch out for in these DNA and RNA questions. Remember that DNA stands for *deoxyribonucleic acid.* That means the sugar it uses for its nucleotides is deoxyribose. RNA, on the other hand, stands for "ribonucleic acid," which means its nucleotides use regular ribose sugar.

91. **E.** This is a tricky question because "energy source" is such a broad category. Consider all types of energy sources.

When a cell is about to perform some action, such as pumping an ion against a concentration gradient, the cell uses ATP for energy. Cells store energy in ATP by breaking down glucose or lipid molecules through aerobic cellular respiration in the mitochondria, so these could be considered energy sources as well. When it isn't needed as a fuel at the moment, glucose is stored as a polymer called glycogen, so that too can be considered an energy source. The answer, then, is "all of the above."

92. **A.** As you saw in Chapter 6, aerobic cellular respiration has three main stages. The first two (glycolysis and the Krebs cycle) oxidize glucose. In other words, they pull electrons off of the glucose molecule, and this breaks the glucose down to CO_2. The electrons are sent to the electron transport chain where most of the ATP gets made. The thing that carries the electrons to the electron transport chain is NAD⁺, which means the correct answer is (A).

CO_2 is what's left over when electrons are removed from glucose, so (B) is wrong. The electrons are going to stage three — the electron transport chain — and not to the Krebs cycle, so (C) is also wrong. Electrons are eventually transferred to O_2 to make H_2O at the end of the electron transport chain, but NAD^+ plays no role in that, so (D) is wrong, too. Answer (E) is just weird, so it's definitely wrong.

93. **B.** Two kinds of processes break down glucose to produce CO_2: regular aerobic cellular respiration and fermentation. You can remember that fermentation produces CO_2 because it is the process used in production of beer and champagne, both of which are bubbly carbonated beverages. Glucose breakdown and photosynthesis are all covered in Chapter 6.

Once you know that choice I is right, you can eliminate answers (C), (D), and (E) because they don't contain I. Now all you have to do is consider III to know whether your answer is (A) or (B). You don't even need to consider II and IV.

Since fermentation also breaks down CO_2, you know the answer is (B). Just to confirm, photosynthesis *consumes* CO_2, so you know that choice II must be wrong. Dehydration synthesis was covered in Chapter 5, and is the process of building polymers. "Dehydration" means loss of water, so this reaction is called "dehydration synthesis" because a water molecule is produced. No CO_2 there, so IV can be eliminated also.

94. **C.** All right, here's one more "not" question. It asks which process does not produce ATP, and any process that involves the breakdown of glucose will make at least a little bit of ATP, so the Krebs cycle and anaerobic cellular respiration can be crossed out.

Photosynthesis consists of two main stages. In the first stage, the light-dependent reactions, light energy is used to make ATP (and to make NADPH), so this one can be crossed out as well. The second stage, the light-independent reactions — also called the Calvin cycle — uses the energy from ATP to build sugar molecules, so this is the only one that doesn't produce any ATP at all. Plus, it is the only one left after eliminating choices I, II, and IV.

95. **E.** Chapter 4 explains what happens in the Krebs cycle, which is the second stage in aerobic cellular respiration. The first stage, glycolysis, produces two pyruvate molecules, which then get broken down to CO_2 in the Krebs cycle. This has already eliminated (A) and (E) because they have glucose as an input.

Even if you can't remember all the stuff about NAD^+ and FAD^+, there is a way to jump to the correct answer here. Remember that the Krebs cycle can only handle one pyruvate at a time. Answers (B) and (C) show 2 pyruvates entering the Krebs cycle, so they both must be wrong. That leaves only answer (E), which just happens to be correct.

96. **E.** A cell that is diploid has all of the homologous pairs of chromosomes. Regular somatic cells are all diploid, and so are germ cells before they go through meiosis.

The homologous pairs separate during anaphase I, but at the end of this stage there is still only a single cell that has all of the chromosomes, so even though (B) may have been tempting, it is actually wrong. Only after telophase I do we have two separate cells, each with only one member of every homologous pair.

97. **B.** This is another memorization question from Chapter 5, so you can refer back there to find diagrams of these molecular structures. Remember that lipids are mainly just carbon and hydrogen (that's what makes them hydrophobic), so they aren't likely to have any nitrogen, so choice III can be crossed out.

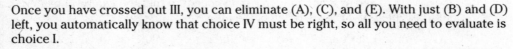

Once you have crossed out III, you can eliminate (A), (C), and (E). With just (B) and (D) left, you automatically know that choice IV must be right, so all you need to evaluate is choice I.

Every amino acid has an NH_2 on one end in order to form a peptide bond with another amino acid, so they definitely all have nitrogen. Nucleotides all have three parts, one of which is a nitrogen base, so they obviously have nitrogen as well. This means that choices I and IV are the winners.

Just to make sure you're right, glance at choice II. Carbohydrates always follow the same basic molecule formula, $C_nH_{2n}O_n$, so there isn't any room for nitrogen in there either, so you can also cross out choice II.

98. **B.** For genetic questions like this, you should try a few possible Punnet squares (see Chapter 8) to see which one best fits the information in the example. Before that, though, notice that the phenotype of the male parent is red and the phenotype of the female parent is white, so you know that the male parent must have at least one red allele and the female parent must have at least one white allele. That means (C) can't be correct.

Now, for the other possible genotypes, you can put them each into a Punnet square (like the ones below) and see if the results can produce what you see in the F_1 generation, in which approximately half the plants produce white flowers and the other half produces red flowers.

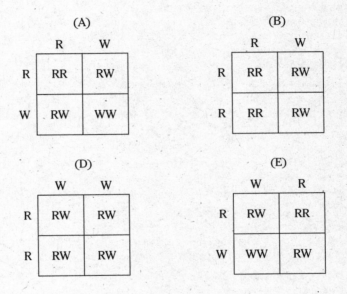

The results for (A) show that if the white allele were dominant, then 75 percent of the offspring in F1 would be white, and that doesn't match the given results. Same thing goes if the red allele is dominant, because then 75 percent of the offspring would be red, so (A) is definitely wrong. As added support, notice that (A) and (E) produce the same results (just in different orders), and they can't both be right, so they must both be wrong. Now, the Punnet square for (D) results in all offspring having the exact same genotype, and that doesn't match the results at all, so (D) is wrong, too. The Punnet square for (B) produces half of the offspring with one phenotype and half with another, so even though you haven't decided yet which allele is dominant, this is mostly likely to represent the genotypes of the parents.

If you are running out of time at this late point in the test, you don't have to draw all four Punnet squares. You can use one square and cross out or erase to change the combinations for each answer choice.

99. **A.** Given that answer (B) in the last question gets the parents' genotypes right, you can tell that the white allele must be dominant over the red allele. If it were the other way around, then all of the offspring would be red because they all have at least one red allele. You also know that the alleles aren't codominant because every offspring has either all red flowers or all white flowers. Codominant alleles would produce individual plants that had both white flowers and red flowers at the same time. If the alleles were incompletely dominant, then the heterozygous plants (with the R-W genotype) would end up with pink flowers, which would be a blending of the two alleles.

100. **C.** The F2 generation is pretty much just like the F1 generation because it resulted from the mating of one plant with the R-R genotype and one with the R-W genotype. Since the W allele is dominant, this would result in 50 percent white and 50 percent red offspring every time, as shown in the Punnet square for option (B) in question #98.

Now that you have thoroughly examined the explanations for Practice Test #1, give yourself a long break and your brain a rest. Try Practice Test #2 on another day when you are more refreshed.

Chapter 18

Practice Test 2

. . . .

*O*kay, you know your stuff. Now is your chance to shine. The following exam is an 80-question multiple-choice test. You have one hour to complete it. On the actual exam, you would chose whether you wish to take the Biology-E section or the Biology-M section. If you chose to take the Biology-E section answer the first 60 questions, then questions 61–80 in the Biology-E section. If you chose to take the Biology-M section answer the first 60 questions, then questions 61–80 in the Biology-M section.

To make the most of this practice exam, take the test under the following similar conditions to the actual test:

1. Find a place where you won't be distracted. (Preferably as far from your younger sibling as possible.)

2. If possible, take the practice test at approximately the same time of day as you will for your real SAT II.

3. Set an alarm for 60 minutes.

4. Mark your answers on the provided answer grid.

5. If you finish before time runs out, go back and check your answers.

6. When your 60 minutes are over, put your pencil down.

After you have finished, you can check your answers on the answer key at the end of this chapter. Use the scoring chart to find out your final score.

Read through all of the explanations in Chapter 19. You learn more by examining the answers to the question than you do by almost any other method.

Practice Test 2 Answer Sheet

1. Ⓐ Ⓑ Ⓒ Ⓓ Ⓔ	51. Ⓐ Ⓑ Ⓒ Ⓓ Ⓔ
2. Ⓐ Ⓑ Ⓒ Ⓓ Ⓔ	52. Ⓐ Ⓑ Ⓒ Ⓓ Ⓔ
3. Ⓐ Ⓑ Ⓒ Ⓓ Ⓔ	53. Ⓐ Ⓑ Ⓒ Ⓓ Ⓔ
4. Ⓐ Ⓑ Ⓒ Ⓓ Ⓔ	54. Ⓐ Ⓑ Ⓒ Ⓓ Ⓔ
5. Ⓐ Ⓑ Ⓒ Ⓓ Ⓔ	55. Ⓐ Ⓑ Ⓒ Ⓓ Ⓔ
6. Ⓐ Ⓑ Ⓒ Ⓓ Ⓔ	56. Ⓐ Ⓑ Ⓒ Ⓓ Ⓔ
7. Ⓐ Ⓑ Ⓒ Ⓓ Ⓔ	57. Ⓐ Ⓑ Ⓒ Ⓓ Ⓔ
8. Ⓐ Ⓑ Ⓒ Ⓓ Ⓔ	58. Ⓐ Ⓑ Ⓒ Ⓓ Ⓔ
9. Ⓐ Ⓑ Ⓒ Ⓓ Ⓔ	59. Ⓐ Ⓑ Ⓒ Ⓓ Ⓔ
10. Ⓐ Ⓑ Ⓒ Ⓓ Ⓔ	60. Ⓐ Ⓑ Ⓒ Ⓓ Ⓔ
11. Ⓐ Ⓑ Ⓒ Ⓓ Ⓔ	61. Ⓐ Ⓑ Ⓒ Ⓓ Ⓔ
12. Ⓐ Ⓑ Ⓒ Ⓓ Ⓔ	62. Ⓐ Ⓑ Ⓒ Ⓓ Ⓔ
13. Ⓐ Ⓑ Ⓒ Ⓓ Ⓔ	63. Ⓐ Ⓑ Ⓒ Ⓓ Ⓔ
14. Ⓐ Ⓑ Ⓒ Ⓓ Ⓔ	64. Ⓐ Ⓑ Ⓒ Ⓓ Ⓔ
15. Ⓐ Ⓑ Ⓒ Ⓓ Ⓔ	65. Ⓐ Ⓑ Ⓒ Ⓓ Ⓔ
16. Ⓐ Ⓑ Ⓒ Ⓓ Ⓔ	66. Ⓐ Ⓑ Ⓒ Ⓓ Ⓔ
17. Ⓐ Ⓑ Ⓒ Ⓓ Ⓔ	67. Ⓐ Ⓑ Ⓒ Ⓓ Ⓔ
18. Ⓐ Ⓑ Ⓒ Ⓓ Ⓔ	68. Ⓐ Ⓑ Ⓒ Ⓓ Ⓔ
19. Ⓐ Ⓑ Ⓒ Ⓓ Ⓔ	69. Ⓐ Ⓑ Ⓒ Ⓓ Ⓔ
20. Ⓐ Ⓑ Ⓒ Ⓓ Ⓔ	70. Ⓐ Ⓑ Ⓒ Ⓓ Ⓔ
21. Ⓐ Ⓑ Ⓒ Ⓓ Ⓔ	71. Ⓐ Ⓑ Ⓒ Ⓓ Ⓔ
22. Ⓐ Ⓑ Ⓒ Ⓓ Ⓔ	72. Ⓐ Ⓑ Ⓒ Ⓓ Ⓔ
23. Ⓐ Ⓑ Ⓒ Ⓓ Ⓔ	73. Ⓐ Ⓑ Ⓒ Ⓓ Ⓔ
24. Ⓐ Ⓑ Ⓒ Ⓓ Ⓔ	74. Ⓐ Ⓑ Ⓒ Ⓓ Ⓔ
25. Ⓐ Ⓑ Ⓒ Ⓓ Ⓔ	75. Ⓐ Ⓑ Ⓒ Ⓓ Ⓔ
26. Ⓐ Ⓑ Ⓒ Ⓓ Ⓔ	76. Ⓐ Ⓑ Ⓒ Ⓓ Ⓔ
27. Ⓐ Ⓑ Ⓒ Ⓓ Ⓔ	77. Ⓐ Ⓑ Ⓒ Ⓓ Ⓔ
28. Ⓐ Ⓑ Ⓒ Ⓓ Ⓔ	78. Ⓐ Ⓑ Ⓒ Ⓓ Ⓔ
29. Ⓐ Ⓑ Ⓒ Ⓓ Ⓔ	79. Ⓐ Ⓑ Ⓒ Ⓓ Ⓔ
30. Ⓐ Ⓑ Ⓒ Ⓓ Ⓔ	80. Ⓐ Ⓑ Ⓒ Ⓓ Ⓔ
31. Ⓐ Ⓑ Ⓒ Ⓓ Ⓔ	81. Ⓐ Ⓑ Ⓒ Ⓓ Ⓔ
32. Ⓐ Ⓑ Ⓒ Ⓓ Ⓔ	82. Ⓐ Ⓑ Ⓒ Ⓓ Ⓔ
33. Ⓐ Ⓑ Ⓒ Ⓓ Ⓔ	83. Ⓐ Ⓑ Ⓒ Ⓓ Ⓔ
34. Ⓐ Ⓑ Ⓒ Ⓓ Ⓔ	84. Ⓐ Ⓑ Ⓒ Ⓓ Ⓔ
35. Ⓐ Ⓑ Ⓒ Ⓓ Ⓔ	85. Ⓐ Ⓑ Ⓒ Ⓓ Ⓔ
36. Ⓐ Ⓑ Ⓒ Ⓓ Ⓔ	86. Ⓐ Ⓑ Ⓒ Ⓓ Ⓔ
37. Ⓐ Ⓑ Ⓒ Ⓓ Ⓔ	87. Ⓐ Ⓑ Ⓒ Ⓓ Ⓔ
38. Ⓐ Ⓑ Ⓒ Ⓓ Ⓔ	88. Ⓐ Ⓑ Ⓒ Ⓓ Ⓔ
39. Ⓐ Ⓑ Ⓒ Ⓓ Ⓔ	89. Ⓐ Ⓑ Ⓒ Ⓓ Ⓔ
40. Ⓐ Ⓑ Ⓒ Ⓓ Ⓔ	90. Ⓐ Ⓑ Ⓒ Ⓓ Ⓔ
41. Ⓐ Ⓑ Ⓒ Ⓓ Ⓔ	91. Ⓐ Ⓑ Ⓒ Ⓓ Ⓔ
42. Ⓐ Ⓑ Ⓒ Ⓓ Ⓔ	92. Ⓐ Ⓑ Ⓒ Ⓓ Ⓔ
43. Ⓐ Ⓑ Ⓒ Ⓓ Ⓔ	93. Ⓐ Ⓑ Ⓒ Ⓓ Ⓔ
44. Ⓐ Ⓑ Ⓒ Ⓓ Ⓔ	94. Ⓐ Ⓑ Ⓒ Ⓓ Ⓔ
45. Ⓐ Ⓑ Ⓒ Ⓓ Ⓔ	95. Ⓐ Ⓑ Ⓒ Ⓓ Ⓔ
46. Ⓐ Ⓑ Ⓒ Ⓓ Ⓔ	96. Ⓐ Ⓑ Ⓒ Ⓓ Ⓔ
47. Ⓐ Ⓑ Ⓒ Ⓓ Ⓔ	97. Ⓐ Ⓑ Ⓒ Ⓓ Ⓔ
48. Ⓐ Ⓑ Ⓒ Ⓓ Ⓔ	98. Ⓐ Ⓑ Ⓒ Ⓓ Ⓔ
49. Ⓐ Ⓑ Ⓒ Ⓓ Ⓔ	99. Ⓐ Ⓑ Ⓒ Ⓓ Ⓔ
50. Ⓐ Ⓑ Ⓒ Ⓓ Ⓔ	100. Ⓐ Ⓑ Ⓒ Ⓓ Ⓔ

BIOLOGY E/M TEST

FOR BOTH BIOLOGY-E AND BIOLOGY-M

ANSWER QUESTIONS 1-60

<u>Directions:</u> Each set of choices marked (A)–(E) below refers to the questions or statements immediately following it. Choose the lettered choice that best answers each question or matches each statement and fill in the corresponding oval on the answer sheet. You may use a lettered choice once, more than once, or not at all in each set.

Questions 1–4

    (A) bird wings and bat wings

    (B) prokaryotes and eukaryotes

    (C) mitochondria and chloroplasts

    (D) horse limbs and dog limbs

    (E) gills and lungs

1. analogous structures

2. result of convergent evolution

3. distinguished by presence or absence of organelles

4. receive pulmonary circulation

Questions 5–7

    (A) carbohydrates

    (B) proteins

    (C) minerals

    (D) lipids

    (E) DNA

5. genes are constructed of this type of molecule

6. Cell membranes are made of this type of molecule

7. plant cell walls are made of this type of molecule

Questions 8–10

    (A) Monera

    (B) Protista

    (C) Fungi

    (D) Plantae

    (E) Animalia

8. kingdom that contains endothermic organisms

9. kingdom that contains no multicellular organisms

10. kingdom that most closely resembles the first organisms on earth

Questions 11–13

    (A) digestive system

    (B) muscular system

    (C) skeletal system

    (D) cardiovascular system

    (E) respiratory system

11. inhibited by the sympathetic nervous system

12. responsible for regulating pH of blood

13. responsible for storage of certain minerals

Go on to next page

Questions 14–16

    (A) gamete

    (B) homozygous

    (C) heterozygous

    (D) haploid

    (E) diploid

14. cell type that results from mitosis

15. cell with two identical alleles for a particular trait

16. cell type that results from the first division of meiosis

---

Directions: Each of the questions below is followed by five answers. Some groups of questions relate to a laboratory or experimental situation. For each question, select the best answer to the question and then fill in the corresponding bubble on the answer sheet.

---

17. Which of the following characteristics is least likely to belong to a plant that lives in the desert?

    (A) spines

    (B) large leaves

    (C) wide root system

    (D) flowers

    (E) small leaves

18. Most hormones must attach to receptors on the outside of cells because they cannot penetrate the cell membrane. Some hormones, such as testosterone, are exceptions. Hormones such as testosterone are derived from which of the following kind of organic molecule?

    (A) cholesterol

    (B) protein

    (C) nucleic acid

    (D) amino acid

    (E) carbohydrate

19. A species of migrating birds tries to fly as fast as it can to the northern breeding grounds in order to stake out the best territory for attracting mates. This is an example of

    (A) intraspecific competition

    (B) interspecific competition

    (C) directional selection

    (D) stabilizing selection

    (E) mutualistic symbiosis

20. Which of the following hormones is most likely to be released after a meal?

    (A) adrenocorticotropic hormone

    (B) thyroid hormone

    (C) growth hormone

    (D) insulin

    (E) epinephrine

Go on to next page

21. Aerobic cellular respiration is least dependent on which of the following organ systems?

    (A) excretory system

    (B) circulatory system

    (C) respiratory system

    (D) digestive system

    (E) skeletal system

22. Trait Q is a sex-linked trait, the gene for which is located on the X chromosome. A man and a woman are planning on having children, and the woman is a carrier for Q, while the man does not have the Q phenotype. What are the chances that one of their sons could have trait Q?

    (A) 0%

    (B) 25%

    (C) 50%

    (D) 75%

    (E) 100%

23. Which of the following is not a biotic component of an animal's niche?

    (A) availability of mates

    (B) presence of parasites

    (C) number of predators

    (D) density of competitors

    (E) size of a different population of the same species

24. Which of the following is monitored by the hypothalamus?

    (A) body temperature

    (B) blood pH

    (C) blood pressure

    (D) blood salinity

    (E) all of the above

Go on to next page

Questions 25–27 refer to the following diagram

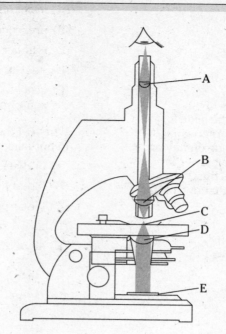

25. objective lens

26. specimen

27. light source

Go on to next page

28. Which of the following is not a characteristic of the tropical rain forest?

    (A) high species diversity

    (B) located near the equator

    (C) large temperature fluctuations occur regularly

    (D) high species density

    (E) high yearly rainfall

29. Which of the following processes is least likely to be controlled by the nervous system?

    (A) finger movements

    (B) epinephrine release

    (C) basal metabolic rate

    (D) vasoconstriction

    (E) vasodilation

30. Which of the following would not be a characteristic of a monocot?

    (A) parallel leaf veins

    (B) fibrous roots

    (C) interaction with pollinators

    (D) production of nectar

    (E) reproduction without the use of seeds

31. Which of the following best describes the direct purpose of crossing over during meiosis?

    (A) to promote mutations in order to increase diversity in the next generation

    (B) to shuffle the combinations of genes that end up in the gametes

    (C) to strengthen the gene pool

    (D) to allow genes from other species to enter a population's gene pool

    (E) to separate homologous chromosomes

32. Which of the following is the best explanation for why most nocturnal animals are endothermic?

    (A) exothermic animals tend to hunt by sight, which doesn't work as well at night

    (B) endothermic animals tend to have superior vision

    (C) endothermic animals can keep themselves warm during the colder nighttime hours

    (D) the primary food for exothermic animals tends to be available during the day

    (E) the predators of endothermic animals are more likely to be active during the day

33. Which of the following hormones is least likely to be secreted during the fight or flight response?

    (A) cortisol

    (B) growth hormone

    (C) adrenocorticotropic hormone

    (D) epinephrine

    (E) glucagon

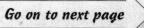*Go on to next page*

34. Which of the following statements about Darwinian evolution is false?

    (A) organisms tend to be perfectly adapted to their environments

    (B) factors in the environment help determine which characteristics are preserved in a population

    (C) variations in a population arise from random mutations

    (D) if there is no variation in the population, evolution cannot occur

    (E) individual organisms are the primary unit of selection

35. Which of the following is least likely to occur inside a neuron during an action potential?

    (A) membrane potential rises

    (B) neurotransmitter is reabsorbed

    (C) sodium channels are open

    (D) sodium-potassium pump is operating

    (E) sodium ions are flowing into the axon

36. Which of the following is considered evidence in favor of the theory that all life on earth has descended from a single common ancestor?

    I. all living things have the same number of chromosomes

    II. all life on earth is based on the same basic biochemistry

    III. all living things are made of eukaryotic cells

    (A) I and II only

    (B) II and III only

    (C) I and III only

    (D) I only

    (E) II only

37. Which of the following is arranged in the correct taxonomic sequence?

    (A) kingdom → phylum → order → genus

    (B) kingdom → phylum → order → class

    (C) kingdom → order → class → species

    (D) phylum → order → class → genus

    (E) kingdom → phylum → family → class

38. Which of the following methods is most reliable for determining relatedness?

    (A) anatomical similarity

    (B) dietary similarity

    (C) niche similarity

    (D) chromosomal similarity

    (E) behavioral similarity

Go on to next page

Questions 39–41

Consider the following experimental situations designed to test plant growth under different conditions.

    I. plant is upright, light source is coming from the left

    II. plant is upright, light source is coming from the right

    III. plant is upright, light source is coming from above

    IV. plant is upright, light source is arranged so as to come from all directions equally

    V. plant is tilted to the left and light source is arranged so as to come from all directions equally

The following diagram depicts three of the plants that resulted from this experiment.

39. Which of the following experimental situations is (are) most likely to result in the growth seen in plant #2?

    (A) I only

    (B) II only

    (C) IV and V only

    (D) I and V only

    (E) II and V only

40. Which of the following experimental situations is (are) most likely to result in the growth seen in plant #1?

    (A) III only

    (B) III, IV, and V only

    (C) III and IV only

    (D) IV only

    (E) IV and V only

41. Experimental situation V is designed to test which phenomenon?

    (A) transpiration

    (B) photoperiodism

    (C) phototropism

    (D) gravitropism

    (E) gravattraction

Go on to next page

Questions 42–45

A certain species of animal has two alleles for height. The "H" allele codes for the tall phenotype, while the "h" allele codes for the short phenotype. Below is a short family tree showing some of the genotypes and phenotypes.

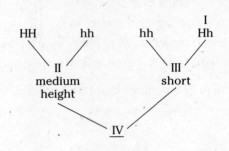

42. Which of the following best describes the relationship between these two alleles?

    (A) H dominant, h recessive

    (B) H recessive, h dominant

    (C) codominance

    (D) incomplete dominance

    (E) not enough information to determine

43. What is the phenotype of animal I?

    (A) short

    (B) medium

    (C) tall

    (D) none of the above

    (E) not enough information to determine

44. What are the chances of animal IV winding up with medium height?

    (A) 0%

    (B) 25%

    (C) 50%

    (D) 75%

    (E) 100%

45. Suppose this animal is an herbivore that feeds on the leaves of trees. If the trees are getting taller over many years, which of the following will most likely occur?

    I. directional selection

    II. H allele will increase in frequency

    III. h allele will decrease in frequency

    IV. stabilizing selection

    (A) I and II only

    (B) II and III only

    (C) II and IV only

    (D) I, II, and III only

    (E) II, III, and IV only

Go on to next page

Questions 46–49 refer to the following diagram

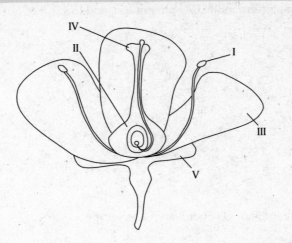

46. Which of the following part(s) contain(s) gametes?

    (A) I only
    (B) II only
    (C) I and II only
    (D) I and IV only
    (E) V only

47. Which of the following develops into fruit?

    (A) I only
    (B) II only
    (C) I and II only
    (D) IV only
    (E) V only

48. Which of the following attracts pollinators?

    (A) I and III only
    (B) III and V only
    (C) III only
    (D) III and IV only
    (E) I, III, and IV only

49. Which of the following is most likely to be found on a gymnosperm?

    (A) I only
    (B) I and II only
    (C) III and IV only
    (D) V only
    (E) none of the above

Go on to next page

Questions 50–51

Consider the following family tree in which information about the blood type of each family member is shown. Capital letters indicate a phenotype, and lowercase letters indicate a genotype.

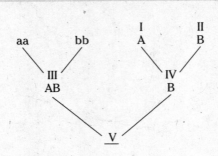

50. Which of the following individuals could have a genotype of "ao"?

    (A) III and V only

    (B) III only

    (C) I and V only

    (D) I only

    (E) V only

51. Which of the following is a possible genotype of person V?

    (A) ao

    (B) bo

    (C) ab

    (D) bb

    (E) all of the above

Go on to next page

Questions 52–55

A behavioral scientist is studying the behavior of a certain species of rodents that normally lives in habitats with both open grassy areas and areas with fairly dense bushes. The scientist prepares a large, controlled living area for the rodents by placing lots of bushes and small trees on one side of the habitat, leaving the other half covered only by short grass. Next, she makes sure there are no other animals in the area, and then distributes food (seeds) equally over the entire habitat. She then releases the rodents into the area and tracks their movements. The following graph represents some of the data the scientist collected.

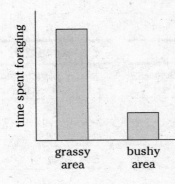

52. Which of the following hypotheses is best supported by the information provided?

(A) some rodents established territories in the bushy area and forced all others into the grassy area

(B) the rodents had no preference for either area

(C) the rodents are less likely to face competition in the grassy area

(D) the rodents are adapted to always feed in grassy areas

(E) it is easier for the rodents to find the seeds in the grassy area

53. Suppose the scientist suspended a model of a hawk above the controlled habitat. Which of the following behavioral changes would be most likely?

(A) proportions of time spent in each area would be unaffected

(B) proportions of time spent in each area would even out

(C) proportions of time spent in each area would reverse

(D) more rodents would move into the grassy area

(E) rodents would bunch closer together

54. Suppose the scientist placed twice as much food in the bushy area as compared to the grassy area. Which of the following behavioral changes would be most likely?

(A) proportions of time spent in each area would be unaffected

(B) proportions of time spent in each area would even out

(C) proportions of time spent in each area would reverse

(D) more rodents would move into the grassy area

(E) rodents would spread out

55. The behavior of the rodents in the experiment is most likely an example of

(A) insight learning

(B) instinctual behavior

(C) a reflex

(D) conditioned behavior

(E) imprinting

Go on to next page

Questions 56–60

A set of experiments was conducted to test the activity of an enzyme under various aqueous conditions. When the enzyme is working, the aqueous solution will begin to turn blue. The amount of blue color in the solution can be measured using a spectrophotometer, and is measured in units of "percent transmittance." Each experiment involved five beakers, with one specific environmental parameter being varied between beakers. Experiment #1 varied the salt concentration. Experiment #2 varied the pH. Experiment #3 varied the temperature. The researchers were able to compare reaction rates under the various conditions by measuring the percent transmittance of the solution in each beaker after 10 minutes of reaction time. Below are three tables listing the results of the three experiments, along with five graphs.

Experiment #1

salt concentration (g / L)	%transmittance after 10 min.
0.1	52
0.2	48
0.3	52
0.4	54
0.5	47

Experiment #2

pH	%transmittance after 10 min
4	9
5	27
6	48
7	66
8	82

Experiment #3

temp (°C)	% transmittance after 10 min.
15	95
25	82
35	60
45	31
55	8

I

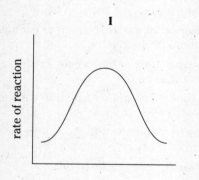

II

III

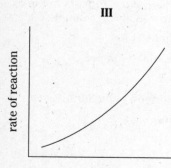

IV

V

Go on to next page

56. Which of the following statements is supported by the experimental evidence?

    (A) the reaction rate is unaffected by salt concentration

    (B) the reaction rate decreases as temperature increases

    (C) the reaction rate decreases as salt concentration increases

    (D) the reaction rate is unaffected by pH

    (E) the reaction rate increases as pH increases

57. Which graph most closely represents the results of experiment #1?

    (A) I

    (B) II

    (C) III

    (D) IV

    (E) V

58. Which graph most closely represents the results of experiment #2?

    (A) I

    (B) II

    (C) III

    (D) IV

    (E) V

59. Which graph most closely represents the results of experiment #3?

    (A) I

    (B) II

    (C) III

    (D) IV

    (E) V

60. Which of the following would be a good control group for the above experiments?

    (A) a reaction solution with no salt

    (B) a reaction solution similar to experimental solution, but with no enzyme

    (C) a reaction solution with a pH of 0

    (D) a reaction solution with a temperature of 0°C

    (E) all of the above would be good control groups

If you are taking the Biology-E test, continue with questions 61–80.

If you are taking the Biology-M test, go to question 81 now.

Go on to next page

BIOLOGY-E SECTION

<u>Directions</u>: Each of the questions below is followed by five answers. Some groups of questions relate to a laboratory or experimental situation. For each question, select the best answer to the question and then fill in the corresponding bubble on the answer sheet.

61. Which of the following is most likely to occur when a desert biome slowly turns into a tundra?

    (A) convergent evolution

    (B) directional selection

    (C) stabilizing selection

    (D) destabilizing selection

    (E) co-evolution

62. Which part of the ocean biome is least likely to contain primary producers?

    (A) intertidal zone

    (B) pelagic zone

    (C) photic zone

    (D) aphotic zone

    (E) all of the above are likely to contain primary producers

63. Which of the following relationships is most likely to result in co-evolution?

    (A) flower and pollinator

    (B) predator and prey

    (C) parasite and host

    (D) all of the above

    (E) none of the above

64. A species that begins ecological succession is called a

    (A) decomposer

    (B) pioneer species

    (C) primary producer

    (D) primary consumer

    (E) helper species

65. A gazelle and zebra are feeding on the same grassy field. This is an example of

    (A) intraspecific competition

    (B) interspecific competition

    (C) directional selection

    (D) stabilizing selection

    (E) mutualistic symbiosis

66. Some species of whales still have very small, nonfunctional hip bones left over from their terrestrial ancestors. The hip bone in whales provides an example of

    (A) stabilizing selection

    (B) disruptive selection

    (C) co-evolution

    (D) Lamarckian evolution

    (E) a vestigial structure

67. A certain habitat has the following characteristics. Average daily high temperature of -5° C. Low species diversity and density. Low yearly rainfall. In which of the following biomes is this habitat located?

    (A) temperate deciduous forest

    (B) taiga

    (C) desert

    (D) savanna

    (E) tropical rain forest

Go on to next page

68. Which of the following is true of both Lamarckian evolution and Darwinian evolution?

    (A) an individual may acquire an adaptive trait during its own lifetime and pass that trait on to its offspring

    (B) populations change over time to be better adapted to their environments

    (C) random mutations are the source of variation within a population

    (D) fitness depends on the number of viable offspring produced

    (E) competition prevents evolution from occurring

69. Which of the following is most likely to result in speciation?

    (A) a population is divided into clans that regularly exchange members

    (B) a population is decimated by a large storm

    (C) a population of squirrels is divided by a large river

    (D) a virus enters the population that only affects 34% of the individuals

    (E) a new predator is introduced into the community

70. Suppose that all of the populations in a certain community are very near carrying capacity. This situation is called a(n)

    (A) biome

    (B) ecosystem

    (C) biosphere

    (D) mutualistic symbiosis

    (E) climax community

71. Which of the following groups does not have an exoskeleton?

    (A) mollusks

    (B) crustaceans

    (C) arthropods

    (D) insects

    (E) echinoderms

72. Which of the following is arranged correctly in order from largest to smallest?

    (A) community → population → territory → organism

    (B) population → ecosystem → territory → organism

    (C) biome → ecosystem → organism → territory

    (D) population → community → territory → home range

    (E) biome → population → ecosystem → organism

73. Which of the following is not a distinguishing characteristic of mammals?

    (A) bear live young

    (B) mammary glands

    (C) endoskeleton

    (D) hair or fur

    (E) all of the above are distinguishing characteristics of mammals

74. A certain community has only about 8% as many lions as grazing herbivores. Which of the following best explains why this is?

    (A) a disease spread through the lion population, killing off a large number of individuals

    (B) the lions are dying off because the gazelle have become so fast that the lions can no longer catch them

    (C) the habitat is shrinking

    (D) the lions have just recently entered the community

    (E) most of the nutrients and energy in the grazing herbivores are lost before the lions can get them

Go on to next page

Questions 75–76 refer to the following graph.

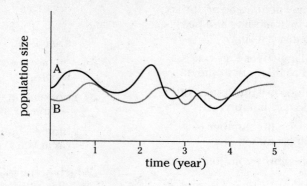

75. The above graph could represent which of the following?

    (A) predator–prey relationship

    (B) parasitism

    (C) mutualistic symbiosis

    (D) flower–pollinator interaction

    (E) all of the above

76. Which of the following phenomena is most likely to result from the interaction depicted above?

    (A) disruptive selection

    (B) Hardy-Weinberg equilibrium

    (C) co-evolution

    (D) speciation

    (E) reproductive isolation

Go on to next page

Questions 77–80

An ecologist records the abundance of five different species in a community. The bar graph below represents his findings.

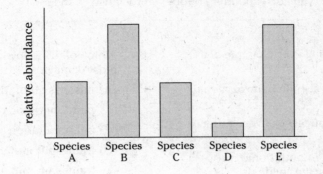

77. Based on the information in the graph, which of the following is most likely to be a food chain in this community? The arrows indicate the flow of nutrients and energy.

    (A) A → E → C

    (B) D → C → A

    (C) D → E → A

    (D) B → C → A

    (E) B → C → D

78. Based on the information in the graph, species C is most likely to be which of the following?

    (A) primary consumer

    (B) primary producer

    (C) secondary consumer

    (D) decomposer

    (E) tertiary consumer

79. Suppose this community is located in the tundra. Which of the following is least likely to be species A?

    (A) rabbit

    (B) caribou

    (C) squirrel

    (D) snake

    (E) bird

80. If species D were to go extinct, which of the following is least likely to occur in the next year?

    (A) species A will increase

    (B) species E will increase

    (C) direct competition between B and E will decrease

    (D) species B will decrease

    (E) direct competition between A and C will increase

IF YOU FINISH BEFORE TIME IS CALLED, YOU MAY CHECK YOUR WORK ON THE ENTIRE BIOLOGY-E TEST ONLY.

BIOLOGY-M SECTION

81. Which of the following is an example of a recessive trait?

    (A) the trait is only seen in heterozygous individuals

    (B) the trait only appears in every other generation

    (C) the trait is seen in both homozygous and heterozygous individuals

    (D) the trait is only seen in homozygous individuals

    (E) the trait is never seen in any individuals

82. Which of the following is an appropriate way to distinguish between prokaryotes and eukaryotes?

    (A) one always has a cell wall, the other does not

    (B) one always has flagella, the other does not

    (C) one contains DNA, the other does not

    (D) one has a nucleus, the other does not

    (E) one performs photosynthesis, the other does not

83. Which of the following mutations would be most damaging?

    (A) missense mutation on DNA

    (B) point mutation on mRNA

    (C) point mutation on DNA

    (D) frameshift mutation on mRNA

    (E) frameshift mutation on DNA

84. Which of the following is most likely to be moved across a cell membrane via endocytosis?

    (A) an ion

    (B) a virus

    (C) a sugar

    (D) O_2

    (E) CO_2

Go on to next page

85. If an individual possesses two different alleles for a certain trait, that person is said to be

    (A) recessive

    (B) dominant

    (C) homozygous

    (D) heterozygous

    (E) haploid

86. Some white blood cells called *leukocytes* engulf and destroy viruses. Which of the following organelles are the leukocytes likely to have in unusual abundance?

    (A) chloroplasts

    (B) endoplasmic reticulum

    (C) mitochondria

    (D) nucleus

    (E) lysosomes

87. Which of the following is arranged in the correct sequence?

    (A) translation → transcription → protein product

    (B) protein product → transcription → translation

    (C) transcription → protein product → translation

    (D) transcription → translation → protein product

    (E) translation → protein product → transcription

88. The monomers of polymers are linked together in a process known as

    (A) hydrolysis

    (B) dehydration synthesis

    (C) translation

    (D) hydrolation

    (E) dehydrolysis

89. Gregor Mendel is best known for studying

    (A) genetics of lab rats

    (B) evolution of finches

    (C) genetics of pea plants

    (D) evolution of pea plants

    (E) DNA structure

Go on to next page

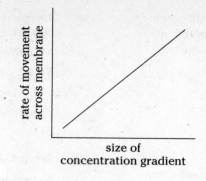

90. The above graph most likely depicts which of the following?

    (A) endocytosis

    (B) mitosis

    (C) active transport

    (D) simple diffusion

    (E) facilitated diffusion

91. Which of the following is a real difference between sexual and asexual reproduction?

    (A) sexual reproduction always uses chromosomes, while asexual reproduction never involves chromosomes

    (B) sexual reproduction tends to result in greater diversity than asexual reproduction

    (C) sexual reproduction involves replication of DNA while asexual reproduction does not

    (D) asexual reproduction involves cell division while sexual reproduction does not

    (E) asexual reproduction involves the joining of two haploid cells while sexual reproduction does not

92. Which of the following processes involves an electron transport chain?

    I. aerobic cellular respiration

    II. fermentation

    III. lactic acid production

    IV. photosynthesis

    (A) I only

    (B) I and II only

    (C) I, II, and III only

    (D) II and III only

    (E) I and IV only

Go on to next page

93. The dominant allele for a certain trait is represented by T, while the recessive allele is represented by t. A man whose genotype is TT marries a woman who has the dominant phenotype. What are the chances that one of their children will also have the dominant phenotype?

    (A) 25%

    (B) 50%

    (C) 75%

    (D) 100%

    (E) cannot determine from the information given

94. Which of the following is false about chromosomes?

    (A) they are matched up in homologous pairs during meiosis

    (B) they are not matched up in homologous pairs during mitosis

    (C) they can be found throughout the cell

    (D) they are involved in the process known as crossing over

    (E) they are composed mainly of DNA

95. Which of the following is false about carbon?

    (A) it is one of the rarest elements on earth

    (B) it is the basis for all organic molecules

    (C) it can form four covalent bonds

    (D) it is necessary for life as it is known on earth

    (E) it can form covalent bonds with a wide variety of elements

96. Which of the following occurs in the nucleus of a cell?

    I. replication

    II. transcription

    III. translation

    IV. protein synthesis

    (A) I only

    (B) II only

    (C) II and III only

    (D) I and II only

    (E) III and IV only

Go on to next page

Questions 97–100

A student has prepared an experiment using yeast and algae. Into six different bottles, the student placed equal amounts of a solution containing basic nutrients plus a small amount of glucose. In three of the bottles she placed an equal amount of yeast, while in the three other bottles, she placed an equivalent amount of algae. She then placed a balloon over each bottle to catch any gasses that might emerge. After the balloons were in place, she set the bottles into different environments as shown below.

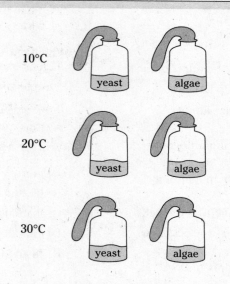

97. Which of the following graphs will best represent the sizes of the balloons in the different temperatures?

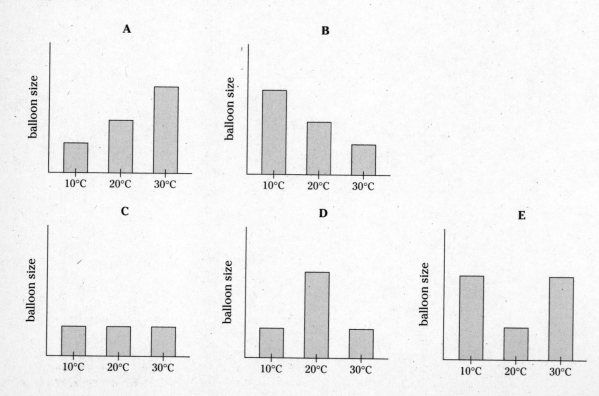

98. Which of the following is most likely to fill the balloons covering the yeast bottles?

    (A) CO_2

    (B) O_2

    (C) NH_3

    (D) H_2O

    (E) N_2

99. Which bottle would most likely be able to sustain metabolic activity the longest?

    (A) yeast at 2°C

    (B) algae at 30°C

    (C) algae at 10°C

    (D) yeast at 30°C

    (E) yeast at 10°C

100. Which of the following would be the best control group for this experiment?

    (A) bottles with nutrient solution, yeast or algae, and no balloons

    (B) empty bottles with balloons

    (C) empty bottles with no balloons

    (D) bottles with nutrient solution and balloon but no yeast or algae

    (E) bottles with nutrient solution but no balloons, yeast or algae

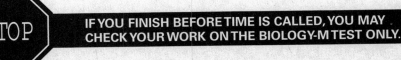

STOP IF YOU FINISH BEFORE TIME IS CALLED, YOU MAY CHECK YOUR WORK ON THE BIOLOGY-M TEST ONLY.

Table 18-1	Answers to the Core Section		
Question Number	Correct Answer	Right	Wrong
1	A		
2	A		
3	B		
4	E		
5	E		
6	D		
7	A		
8	E		
9	A		
10	A		
11	A		
12	E		
13	C		
14	E		
15	B		
16	D		
17	B		
18	A		
19	A		
20	D		
21	E		
22	C		
23	E		
24	E		
25	B		
26	C		
27	E		
28	C		
29	C		
30	E		
31	B		

Question Number	Correct Answer	Right	Wrong
32	C		
33	B		
34	A		
35	B		
36	E		
37	A		
38	D		
39	E		
40	C		
41	D		
42	D		
43	B		
44	C		
45	D		
46	C		
47	B		
48	C		
49	E		
50	C		
51	E		
52	E		
53	C		
54	B		
55	B		
56	A		
57	D		
58	B		
59	E		
60	B		
Totals:			

Table 18-2 lists the correct answers to all of the questions on the Biology-E section of the test. If you took the Biology-E section, then compare your answers to the answers given, and for each question, put a mark in the "Right" column if your answer is correct, and put a check in the "Wrong" column if your answer is incorrect. Leave both columns blank for any question you did not answer. Count up the total number of checks in each column and enter that number at the bottom.

Table 18-2	Answers to Biology-E Section		
Question Number	Correct Answer	Right	Wrong
61	B		
62	D		
63	D		
64	B		
65	B		
66	E		
67	C		
68	B		
69	C		
70	E		
71	E		
72	A		
73	C		
74	E		
75	E		
76	C		
77	E		
78	A		
79	D		
80	B		
Totals:			

Table 18-3 lists the correct answers to all of the questions on the Biology-M section of the test. If you took the Biology-M section, then compare your answers to the answers given, and for each question, put a mark in the "Right" column if your answer is correct, and put a check in the "Wrong" column if your answer is incorrect. Leave both columns blank for any question you did not answer. Count up the total number of checks in each column and enter that number at the bottom.

Table 18-3	Answers to Biology-M Section		
Question Number	*Correct Answer*	*Right*	*Wrong*
81	D		
82	D		
83	E		
84	B		
85	D		
86	E		
87	D		
88	B		
89	C		
90	D		
91	B		
92	E		
93	D		
94	C		
95	A		
96	D		
97	A		
98	A		
99	C		
100	D		
Totals:			

Add together your total number right from both the core section and the subject section of the test and write in on this line _____. This number is your "Total Correct" number.

Add together your total number wrong from both the core section and the subject section of the test and write it on this line _____. This number is your "Total Incorrect" number.

Divide your "Total Incorrect" number by 4, and write the quotient on this line _____. This is your "Adjusted Incorrect" number.

Calculate your "Raw Score" using this formula:

(Total Correct) – (Adjusted Incorrect) = Raw Score

Round your Raw Score to the nearest whole number and enter the result on this line _____. This is your final Raw Score.

Table 18-4 shows you how to find your Scaled Score on the 200 to 800 scale used by the SAT people. The Scaled Score is the score that is sent to the colleges to which you are applying.

Table 18-4	Raw Scores and Their Associated Scaled Scores		
Raw Score	Scaled Score	Raw Score	Scaled Score
80	800	29	490
79	800	28	480
78	800	27	480
77	800	26	470
76	800	25	460
75	800	24	460
74	800	23	450
73	800	22	440
72	790	21	440
71	780	20	430
70	780	19	430
69	770	18	420
68	760	17	410
67	760	16	410
66	750	15	400
65	740	14	400
64	730	13	390
63	730	12	380
62	720	11	380
61	710	10	370
60	710	9	360
59	700	8	360
58	690	7	350
57	690	6	340
56	680	5	340
55	670	4	330
54	670	3	330
53	660	2	320

(continued)

Table 18-4 *(continued)*

Raw Score	Scaled Score	Raw Score	Scaled Score
52	650	1	310
51	640	0	300
50	630	-1	290
49	630	-2	280
48	620	-3	270
47	610	-4	270
46	610	-5	260
45	600	-6	250
44	600	-7	250
43	590	-8	240
42	590	-9	240
41	580	-10	240
40	570	-11	240
39	570	-12	230
38	560	-13	230
37	550	-14	230
36	550	-15	230
35	540	-16	230
34	530	-17	220
33	520	-18	220
32	510	-19	220
31	510	-20	220
30	500		

Chapter 19

Practice Test 2: Answers and Explanations

• •

The simple letter answers to every question on Practice Test 2 are listed at the end of Chapter 18. This chapter goes further by providing detailed explanations for every question in Practice Test 2, which will help to reinforce the biology contained in the previous chapters. In addition, these explanations will give you the inside story on the structure of SAT II–style questions and which strategies will help you answer the questions correctly, sometimes even when you aren't sure about the biological facts.

Not only do we explain which answer is correct, but also why the other answers are wrong. Remember that knowing which answers are wrong can sometimes be just as important as knowing which answer is correct because if you are able to eliminate a few options, you may end up pinpointing the right answer.

There are a few general things to watch out for. First of all, make sure you read the questions very carefully because sometimes the wording is kind of tricky. Some questions ask something like, "Which of the following is a function of proteins?" For questions like this, you can either look for the one you know is definitely a function of proteins, or you can eliminate the ones that you know are definitely not functions of proteins. Actually, you should probably use both strategies just to be sure you don't miss something. On the other hand, the question is just as likely to ask, "Which of the following is not a function of proteins?" Always look for words like "not" or "false" because these call for the reverse strategy. In this case you should eliminate the options that you definitely know *are* functions of proteins, and then choose the one that probably is not.

Harder questions ask something like, "Which of the following is most likely to be true?" Notice the "mostly likely" phrase. With these, every answer *could* be true, but only one answer is the *most likely* to be true. Make sure you read each choice carefully before making your decision, still watch out for when you need to reverse the strategy, like if it says "least likely to be true" or "most likely to be false."

Questions 1–60: Core Section

1. **A.** An analogous structure is one that's similar between the two species but that evolved independently. Answers (B) and (C) include things that are not similar structures, so you can cross them out right away. Gills and lungs are a little trickier because they serve a similar function (gas exchange), but they do it in very different ways and are structurally very different, so (E) isn't a candidate either. The horse and dog limbs are good candidate structures, but all mammals have that same basic limb structure, we know that feature evolved way before the horses and the dogs diverged, which means they aren't *analogous* structures, but rather *homologous* structures. On the other hand, birds and bats each developed wings long after their family lineages diverged tens of millions of years ago. That means they must have evolved wings independently, which makes them analogous structures. See Chapter 10 for more on analogous and homologous structures.

2. **A.** Yep, this one is (A) also. Remember that with these classification questions at the beginning of the exam, some answers can get used more than once while others may not get used at all.

   So, convergent evolution is when two different lineages evolve a similar solution to a similar problem. Birds and bats fit this scenario because they both faced the problem of how to stay aloft in the air, and they both developed wings. In fact, all *analogous* structures are the result of convergent evolution.

3. **B.** If you know a little about the vocabulary words involved here, then there's only one possible answer. Organelles are the little compartments inside of a cell, such as the nucleus, mitochondria, chloroplast, lysosome, and so on. All eukaryotic cells have organelles and all prokaryotic cells lack organelles, so the answer must be (B). See Chapter 3 for more on cell structures.

4. **E.** Pulmonary circulation is the part that delivers blood through the gas exchange organs, which would be gills or lungs. This is covered in Chapter 14 on animal organs.

5. **E.** Genes are what carries the genetic information, which is encoded in DNA. Hopefully that was an easy one. If not, you may want to go back to Chapter 5 and brush up on your organic molecules.

6. **D.** Cell membranes are meant to be water resistant in order to keep the internal water in, and the external water out. Lipids make good cell membranes because they're hydrophobic, which means they resist mixing with water. If you want to get specific about it, you can say the cell membrane is made of "phospholipids." See Chapter 3 for more miscellaneous facts about cell membranes.

7. **A.** This one may be a little harder. Maybe you remembered that plant cell walls are made of cellulose, but do you remember what cellulose is made of? As covered in Chapter 5, cellulose is a very strong polymer of *glucose* molecules, which means that cellulose is a kind of carbohydrate. If you've ever used the Atkins diet, then you know that you need to avoid vegetables because they're full of carbs.

8. **E.** Endothermic organisms are ones that can generate enough body heat to keep themselves warm, also known as being "warm blooded." Only birds and mammals can do this, and they both obviously belong to the animal kingdom.

9. **A.** Both Protista and Monera contain unicellular organisms, but Protista also contains *some* multicellular organisms. That means the only one that doesn't contain any multicellular members at all is Monera. Actually, that's how the kingdom got it's name because "mono" means "single."

10. **A.** The first organisms on earth were the simplest, and the Monerans (which are prokaryotic bacteria cells) are the simplest organisms around today. That means the Monerans are most similar to the very first organisms. After all, it's strange enough to think that living bacteria cells could emerge out of the primordial ooze, so just think how crazy it would be to get whole banana trees or water buffalo as the first things to spring to life. The early earth and the emergence of life is covered in Chapter 10 on evolution.

11. **A.** These three questions are all covered in Chapter 14 on animal organ systems. The sympathetic nervous system is responsible for getting the body ready for serious action, as in some sort of emergency situation. In such a situation, immediate survival becomes the main priority, so the muscles, heart, and lungs all become more active and receive more blood. The digestive system, on the other hand, can just sit tight for awhile until the emergency is over, so the sympathetic nervous system *inhibits* digestive activity.

12. **E.** You may think that the cardiovascular system would be responsible for anything having to do with blood, but in fact, it's the respiratory system that regulates the pH of the blood. The pH of blood needs to be very closely regulated, and if the pH needs to go down, then breathing slows down. If pH needs to go up, then breathing gets faster and deeper.

13. **C.** You may be able to guess at this one because the skeletal system is the most solid of all the organ systems, and things made of minerals tend to be solid. Well, if you guessed that way you'd be right because both calcium and phosphorus are stored in the bones of the skeletal system.

14. **E.** Mitosis is the asexual reproduction of a single cell by splitting in two, which is covered in Chapter 3. Only cells with chromosomes go through mitosis, and the result is two cells that are genetically identical to the original single cell. Typically, the original single cell is diploid, meaning it has two alleles for every trait, or, to put it another way, the cell has two sets of chromosomes. Anyway, the answer is (E). This stuff about haploid and diploid cells is covered in Chapter 9.

15. **B.** Here you've got a cell with two identical alleles for a particular trait. This means the cell is diploid, but it also means that it is homozygous for that trait. This is where you need to fall back on the specific direction to "choose the one that *best* answers the question."

    The question specifically mentions that the cell has "two identical alleles for a particular trait." If they wanted to point you to the diploid answer, they could just say it has two alleles for every trait, which tells you nothing about being homozygous or heterozygous. That extra bit of information about the "identical alleles for a particular trait" points you very specifically toward the idea that the cell is homozygous, so that's the best choice. See Chapter 9 for more on what it means to be homozygous vs. heterozygous.

16. **D.** The process of meiosis is the production of gametes. This involves the conversion of diploid cells with two alleles (genes) for every trait into haploid cells with only one allele for every trait. The actual reduction from diploid to haploid occurs at the end of the first division of meiosis, so the answer is (D). The full details are too long to go into here, but you can look back into Chapter 9 to see how it all works.

17. **B.** Notice that you are looking for the *least* likely characteristic of a desert plant, so you can eliminate the ones you know are pretty common in the desert. If you live in a desert with areas of natural vegetation, then this one may be pretty easy for you.

    Even if you don't, you probably know that cactus is usually found in the desert, and every cactus has spines, so you can at least cross out (A) immediately. Okay, now remember from Chapter 12 that the most important characteristic of a desert is that it's really dry and, therefore, usually really sunny. That means the desert plants are likely to 1) get more than enough sunlight, and 2) run a serious risk of dehydration. This means they'll probably have wide root systems to catch as much rainfall as possible, so cross out (C). It also means that they'll be able to get by with small leaves that minimize water loss, so cross out (E) also. Small leaves can still capture plenty of desert sunlight, while big leaves would lose too much water through transpiration (see Chapter 13), so the least likely characteristic is big leaves. In fact, every single large-leaf plant that you ever find around desert cities is transplanted from another biome.

18. **A.** As discussed in Chapter 3, cell membranes are hydrophobic, which means they are water resistant. It also means that other hydrophobic things will be able to pass right through the membrane, which is what testosterone is doing in the example. Chapter 5 talks about which molecules are hydrophobic and which are hydrophilic, and in there it says that lipids are the class of molecules that are mostly hydrophobic. Cholesterol is a lipid, and none of the other choices are lipids, so (A) must be the right answer.

19. **A.** When the birds are trying to beat each other to the best territories, they are competing with other members of their own species, which is called intraspecific competition.

    The *intra* prefix means "within," while the *inter* prefix means "without," as in "outside of." That means *inter*specific competition would occur between members of *different* species.

    The other species of nesting birds that may be heading to the same summer breeding grounds, so cross out (B). Answers (C) and (D) are wrong because we don't see any actual selection going on in the example itself. So far, the birds are all just racing north. Mutualistic symbiosis is a completely different thing that happens when two different species work together and help each other survive, so (E) was way off.

20. **D.** As you digest your food right after a meal, you begin absorbing the nutrients into your blood stream. Once in the blood, the nutrients have to be taken away and put into storage somewhere. Insulin is the hormone that helps your cells take most of the sugar that you eat out of your blood and into storage, so the correct answer is (D). Maybe you know someone with diabetes, which occurs when someone has serious insulin problems that make them unable to put their sugars into storage properly. What about the wrong ones? Well, answers (A) and (E) are wrong because they're both associated with the fight or flight response, which is the exact opposite of the relaxing and digesting that's normally supposed to happen right after a meal. Growth hormone is sometimes released when you are relaxing, but mostly just when you are in a deep sleep, which may happen after a Thanksgiving-style meal, but not after most regular meals. Thyroid hormone is release more or less continuously to keep your metabolic rate from ever dropping too low, so it isn't affected by mealtimes.

21. **E.** The question asks for which organ system aerobic cellular respiration is *least* dependent on, which means that it could be at least *slightly* dependent upon all of them, so weigh them all carefully.

    As you'll find in Chapter 6, aerobic cellular respiration needs two main things, glucose and O_2. The digestive system obtains the glucose (plus a bunch of other nutrients) from food, and the respiratory system gets O_2 from the air (plus it gets rid of CO_2). That leaves the skeletal and excretory systems. Neither of these has anything *directly* to contribute to aerobic cellular respiration, so you need to look for *indirect* contributions to break the tie. The excretory system, specifically the kidneys, are directly responsible for maintenance of the blood contents, and if the kidneys shut down, the blood deteriorates very quickly because so many toxins aren't getting filtered out. That's why people with kidney failure need to be put on regular dialysis to clean their blood. The skeletal system's contribution is the bone marrow, which produces blood cells, but cells last more than just a few days, so that's not as immediate of an issue as cleaning the blood. That means that aerobic cellular respiration is *least* dependent on the skeletal system.

22. **C.** For these questions it's always good to draw out a quick Punnet square, and Figure 19-1 shows the right way to set it up for this question.

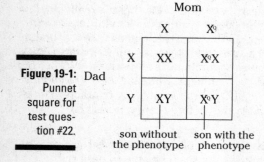

Figure 19-1: Punnet square for test question #22.

    Trait Q is sex linked and on the X chromosome. Boys get one of mom's X chromosomes, along with dad's only Y chromosome. Girls, on the other hand would get dad's X chromosome. So, if dad passes down a Y, then the child has a 50% chance of getting the X chromosome that lacks the gene for trait Q, and a 50% chance of getting the X chromosome that does have the gene for trait Q. If he gets the one from mom with the Q gene, then he will end up with the Q phenotype because the Y chromosome doesn't have a comparable allele that could act as an anti-Q gene the way mom's other chromosome does for her. So, any one of their sons has a 50% chance of getting the phenotype.

23. **E.** First of all, it turns out that the "biotic" part of this question was an unnecessary little thing that was there just to get you to have to think a little harder about this question. The "biotic components" include all the living things, and all of the choices involve living

things, so what's going on? Well, take a look at the other part of the question. A niche is the place that an organism occupies in an ecosystem, and it includes everything that the organism interacts with or that somehow directly affects the organism. Mates, parasites, predators, and competitors are things that the animal directly interacts with. On the other hand, a different population of the same species is, by definition, something that is separated from the animal in question, so that other population does not directly interact with the animal and therefore is not part of the animal's niche. This stuff about niches is in Chapter 12 on ecology.

24. **E.** The hypothalamus is the part of the brain that keeps track of autonomic functions. Those are the things that are vital for keeping you alive but that you don't have to actually think about. Among the things that get taken care of without your conscious awareness are body temperature and status of the blood stream, including pH, pressure, and salinity. So the answer is all of the above.

In a way, the addition of that "all of the above" option makes things a little trickier. However, you can twist the test's little ploy and use it to your advantage because you don't need to recognize every answer. If you are very sure that at least two of the answers are correct, then go for "all of the above." On the other hand, if you're sure that at least one of them is wrong, then stay away from "all of the above."

25. **B.** The microscope questions mainly just require some memorization. That's not to say that the names don't make sense, it's just that you need to remember where they all fit in on the actual microscope. The *objective* lens is the one closest to the *object* that you want to view. The *ocular* lens is the one closest to your eye as you look down into the microscope (*ocular* refers to "eyes").

26. **C.** The specimen is the object that you're looking at, so it should go right underneath the objective lens.

27. **E.** The light source has to shine up through the lenses toward your eye, so it comes from the very bottom.

28. **C.** Notice that the question is asking for the one that is *not* a feature, so you can cross out all those that are. Tropical rain forests are, well, really rainy, so obviously cross out (E). It's also known for having the highest species density and diversity of all terrestrial biomes, so cross out (A) and (D). The tropics are the area of the globe around the equator, so cross out (B) as well. As for (C), the more water that's around, the less the temperature changes from day to night or from season to season. The TRF certainly has a lot of water, so it must have a pretty stable temperature (which it does), so that's the right answer. Biome info is in Chapter 12.

29. **C.** The nervous system handles stuff that needs to be controlled on a second by second basis, or that requires very precise fine-tuning. This one turns out to be kind of a hard question, because for most of the choices, it isn't immediately obvious if they are the sort of things that require nervous system (NS) control.

Finger movements are the only really obvious ones, and they are definitely under NS control, so cross out (A). Epinephrine is part of the fight or flight response, and if you face a serious emergency situation, you need to trigger epinephrine release immediately, so that one's also under NS control (specifically the sympathetic system), so cross out (B) also. You may not know if vasodilation or vasoconstriction are under NS control (they are), but it makes sense that whatever controls one must control the other, and you can't choose them both, so you have to rule them both out. That leaves basal metabolic rate, which is something that just always continues at a steady pace no matter what. That certainly doesn't sound like something that needs the kind of attention the NS can give, so that's the one to choose. Animal organ systems like this are covered in Chapter 14.

30. **E.** Monocots and dicots are both subcategories within the angiosperm kind of plants. All angiosperms produce flowers, which attract pollinators and give back nectar, so cross out (C) and (D). It also turns out that all monocots have fibrous roots and parallel leaf veins, so

(A) and (B) should be crossed out, too. But even if you didn't remember that, you can still tell that the right answer is (E). Angiosperms (including monocots) and gymnosperms are the two kinds of seed-bearing plants, so the monocots must use seeds to reproduce. Also, the grasses and grains are all monocots, which includes wheat, barley, and corn. The parts of these plants we most commonly eat are the seeds! Plant stuff is covered in Chapter 13.

31. **B.** Crossing over is when homologous chromosomes exchange parts. They swap a few alleles in order to increase the number of allele combinations that can end up in the gametes. See Chapter 9 for a full diagram and description of how this works. You may be able to shoot right for this answer, but we'll also show how to eliminate the wrong ones. First you can eliminate choice (D) because different species almost never exchange genes — that's what makes them different species, so that one cannot be right. Now, the purpose of crossing over is definitely *not* to create mutations. In fact, cells do just about everything they can to avoid mutations because most of the time mutations have really bad results, so cross out (A) also. Answer (E) is also out because separation of homologous chromosomes is a separate step that happens *after* crossing over. As for strengthening the gene pool, crossing over generates greater diversity, which in turn can end up increasing overall fitness of the population, but that's a pretty indirect effect and the question asks for the *most* direct effect. The *direct* purpose is to shuffle the combination of genes (alleles) that end up in the gametes.

32. **C.** Nocturnal animals sleep all day and are only active at night. The two main differences between day and night are the difference in light and the difference in temperature. There's a hint in the question, because "endothermic" animals are quite literally heated from the inside, and this makes them able to maintain a constant body temperature. Exothermic animals, on the other hand, have a body temperature that's always the same as the outside temperature. That means the answer may have something to do with temperature rather than light. The only one that involves temperature is (C), and it turns out to be the right answer. Exothermic animals get too cold to stay active in the middle of the night, while the endotherms can stay nice and warm in their fur. As always, you can either work toward the correct answer or eliminate the wrong ones. You can eliminate (A) and (B) because they pretty much the same thing, and they can't both be right, so they should both be eliminated. (D) and (E) describe situations that could apply just as easily to endothermic or exothermic animals, so neither of them can explain the phenomenon either.

33. **B.** Okay, this one contains a bunch of hormone names that are really hard to remember, but that only makes it look harder than it really is. Remember that the fight or flight response is a reaction to an emergency situation, and so the body prepares for immediate, life saving action. This means that everything that has to do with O_2 delivery and muscle action will start working faster, while everything that has to do with long-term growth, maintenance, and healing goes inactive for a while. Luckily, growth hormone stands out from the others because its name tells you what it does, and since growth is a long term project, growth hormone is unlikely to be secreted during the fight-or-flight response, so you could go for that one even if you don't know what the others are.

34. **A.** First notice that the question is asking for the *false* answer, so you can start by crossing out the ones you know are true.

Chapter 10 talks about Darwinian evolution, and in there it explains how answers (B) through (E) are all important parts of evolutionary theory. As for (A), no legitimate theory would claim that an organism could ever be perfectly adapted to its environment. In fact, nobody is even sure what it would take to be perfectly adapted, because it seems like there would always be room for improvement.

35. **B.** An action potential is the electrical signal sent down the axon of a neuron (see Chapter 14). The process includes a lot of miscellaneous details that are hard to keep straight, especially during test time. Sometimes this kind of SAT II question is just hard and that's it, but just as often they contain little shortcuts that can get you to the right answer.

For this question, you don't need to remember all those details about ions and channels and pumps because if you remember that neurotransmitters are only used in the synapse between neurons instead of inside neurons, then you can jump right to (B). The question asks what happens *inside* a neuron, not what happens around the synapse. Plus, the re-absorption of neurotransmitter is not triggered by an action potential anyway.

36. **E.** Probably the most obvious one to eliminate is III, because the whole kingdom Monera is made of prokaryotic cells, not eukaryotic cells, so any answer that includes III must be wrong — cross out (B) and (C). Now, if all living things had the same number of chromosomes, then that would be good evidence that all life is related, but in fact, different species tend to have very different numbers of chromosomes and some don't even have any chromosomes at all. That leaves just II, so the correct answer must be (E). Even if you weren't sure about II, there wasn't a "none of the above" option, so at least one of them had to be right. If you want to refresh your memory, Chapter 10 covers evidence in favor of common ancestry.

37. **A.** The taxonomic levels are: kingdom, phylum, class, order, family, genus, species. This question is a little weird because each of the choices you're given actually skips some of the levels, but if you remember the sequence, you should be able to see the one that gets it right is (A).

You may want to write down the list of taxonomic levels on your test booklet as soon as you start so that you have it ready in case you hit a question like this.

38. **D.** The question asks for the one that is *most* reliable, which means that more than one of them may be at least *somewhat* reliable, so be sure to read all the choices carefully before answering. Answers (B), (C), and (E) may give you some initial clues about relatedness, but there's just way too many examples of totally unrelated species sharing these kinds of similarities. Just consider bees and hummingbirds. They have similar diets, niches, and behaviors, but they are about as unrelated as animals can get. Anatomical similarity is considered pretty reliable, especially when they start measuring something like the sizes of the bumps on the teeth of mice, but check out (D) before choosing this one. Ultimately, relatedness is based on genetic similarity, and the genes are located in the chromosomes, so chromosomal similarity is actually the most reliable of the choices.

39. **E.** All this stuff about plants is covered in Chapter 13. Plant #2 in the diagram is growing toward the right side. If it is growing toward it's light source, then situation II is a possibility because in that one, the light is coming in from the right. In situation I, the light is coming from the left, so the plant would have to be growing away from the light source, which is not very likely. In the other situations, the light is either coming from directly overhead or from all directions equally, and as long as everything else is normal, both lighting schemes will cause the plant to just grow upward normally. In situation V, however, everything is not normal because the plant is tilted to the left. Plants tend to grow away from the pull of gravity, which in this case would mean bending to the right to counteract the fact that the whole flower pot is tilted left. That means plant #2 could have come from either situation II or situation V, so the answer is (E).

40. **C.** Plant #1 is growing straight up. Situation III is the most obvious choice because this is just a normal situation where the plant grows upward toward the light and away from the pull of gravity. In situation IV, the plant can't grow *toward* the light because the light is coming from every direction at once. The direction away from the pull of gravity, however, is still straight up, so that's the way the plant goes.

41. **D.** The plant in that situation is growing away from the force of gravity, which is called gravitropism. The plant cannot be growing toward the light source, which would be phototropism, because the light is coming from every direction at once. Testing transpiration or photoperiodism would need a very different experimental setup, and "gravattraction" is not a word used in biology.

42. **D.** This genetics stuff is all in Chapter 8. Based on the information given, you can know the genotype of person II for sure. One of animal II's parents can only provide an H allele, while the other parent can only provide h, so the offspring will definitely be Hh. It says that the phenotype animal II ends up having is medium height, which must be what happens when you have both tall and short alleles. This means that neither gene is strictly dominant or recessive, so (A) and (B) are definitely wrong. Whenever you see a blending of two genes like this, it's called incomplete dominance, so the correct answer is (D). Codominance is when you see both alleles expressed fully and equally, which isn't really possible when you're dealing with body size, so that's definitely wrong.

43. **B.** Once you answer the last one, the answer to this one should be easy. Animal I is heterozygous (Hh), so it will end up with medium height.

44. **C.** Time to set up another Punnet square (see Figure 19-2). One parent is animal II, who we decided had the Hh genotype. The other parent is animal III who, in order to be short, must have two h alleles, so their genotype is hh.

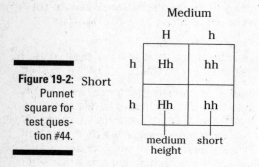

Figure 19-2: Punnet square for test question #44.

In order to have medium height, its genotype has to be Hh. As you can see, two of the four possible gene combinations result in Hh, so the chances of an offspring getting the medium-height phenotype is 50%.

45. **D.** If the trees are getting taller, one thing that could happen is the animals that are shorter won't be able to reach the leaves, and could suffer from malnutrition. That means that the short animals with the hh genotype will be really bad off, and the medium sized ones with the Hh genotype may even have a hard time. Animals with the h allele, therefore, are less likely to survive and reproduce, which would decrease the frequency of the h allele in the population. On the other hand, animals with the HH genotype will not have much of a problem, which will allow the H allele to increase in frequency over the generations, so choices II and III seem like winners. So what about choices IV and V? Well, as the H allele increases in frequency, there will be more offspring born the HH genotype and fewer with the Hh or hh genotypes. That means that there will be more and more tall individuals and fewer and fewer short individuals, and that's called directional selection, so choice I should be included also, which leads to (D). The evolutionary stuff is covered in Chapter 10.

46. **C.** Gametes are the cells that need to be combined to produce offspring in sexual reproduction — one from the male and one from the female. Remember from Chapter 14 that the male gametes are called pollen, and the female ones are called ova. The pollen is on the anthers, which is part I, and the ova are inside the ovary, which is part II.

47. **B.** The ovary develops into the fruit, while the ova inside develop into seeds.

48. **C.** Sometimes the smell of a flower can attract pollinators, but nothing in the diagram is pointing to the flower's smell, so forget about that one. Other than smell, the only thing that actually attracts pollinators are the petals, which are labeled as part III. You may think that nectar would be a possible answer to this question, but the nectar doesn't really *attract* the pollinators, it just rewards them for stopping by. As for the pollen, that's something that most pollinators don't even notice — the plant just sneaks it in there.

49. **E.** Okay, sort of a trick question here, because gymnosperms are the kinds of plants that reproduce using cones rather than flowers. None of the flower parts would be caught dead on a gymnosperm, so the answer is none of the above.

50. **C.** Blood types are covered in Chapter 7 on genetics, and when it comes to blood types, anybody with the b gene or B type blood cannot have a genotype of ao, so II, III, and IV are all out of the running. That means answers (A) and (B) can both be crossed out. You also know that the o allele is recessive, so person I, with blood type A could be either aa or ao. Since person I's child has blood type B, person I could not possibly have passed on an a allele, so he must have the ao genotype and passed down the o allele. That means person I should be included, which eliminates answer (E). That leaves (C) and (D). It turns out that person V could also be ao, for reasons explained in #51, so the answer is (C).

51. **E.** You definitely need to draw out a Punnet square (see Figure 19-3) for this one because it is sort of complicated. Okay, the parents you're looking at are persons III and IV. Person III has blood type AB, so they must have the genotype ab. Person IV has blood type B, so they could be bb or bo. Which is it? Well, person I is one of IV's parents and you know from the last question that person I passed on the o allele to person IV. So person IV must have the bo genotype. So, finally here's the Punnet square for Persons III and IV.

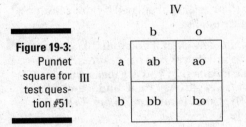

Figure 19-3:
Punnet
square for
test ques-
tion #51.

As you can see, every one of the answer choices shows up in the Punnet square, so the answer is all of the above. As before, as long as you were sure that more than one of the choices was right, then head straight for "all of the above" on these kinds of questions.

52. **E.** The graph shows the rodents spending more foraging time in the grassy area than the bushy area even though the food they are gathering is spread equally throughout the habitat. This means they have a strong preference for the grassy area, so (B) is definitely wrong.

Now, the question asks which conclusion is best supported by the information provided. This means that you're looking for a conclusion that only involves factors that are present in the example as given.

Answer (A) *may* be accurately describing what actually happened, but the example doesn't say anything about territorial behavior, so maybe that's happening and maybe it's not. You just can't be sure based on the information given, so try considering the others before going with that one. The example also said that the researcher cleared out all the other animals before putting in the rodent species, so there couldn't have been any competitors, so cross out (C). Answer (D) says that they are adapted to *always* be in the grassy area, but according to the graph the rodents still spend at least a little time in the bushy area, so that one's wrong too. Answer (E) presents a hypothesis that is consistent with the results in the bar graph, and doesn't include anything but foraging behavior, so that one turns out to be the best supported of the choices.

53. **C.** Hawks are likely to be a natural predator of this species, so if they see a hawk, the rodents are likely to try to hide in the bushes while they forage. Even though it may be harder to find seeds in there, at least they're at less risk of getting picked off by the hawk. This means that the results would most likely reverse with the rodents spending almost all of their time in the bushy area.

54. **B.** Here the rodents have more incentive to go into the bushes than in the original situation, but finding more seeds isn't as big a deal as hiding from a predator. This means that the bar graph would not completely reverse like in the last question, but it would probably even out.

55. **B.** Even though it is easier to talk about their behavior if we describe the rodents as checking out the scene and deciding what to do, they really aren't as smart as that. Plus, these are the sorts of basic behaviors that they need to have right away in order to survive in the wild, so they can't take time to *learn* to do things like "hide from hawks" or "measure the difference in food distribution in your habitat." This means it must all be instinctual behavior on the part of the rodents. Specific information about animal behavior is covered in Chapter 15.

56. **A.** Okay, these are the hardest questions on the test because there's so much to keep track of. The SAT II can ask some particularly nasty questions about complicated experimental situations, and they can even expect you to know a little about laboratory equipment and how it works.

The idea in this example is that the faster the enzyme works, the bluer it's solution will be after 10 minutes of enzyme action. The amount of blueness is measured in a slightly tricky way. A spectrophotometer shines a light through a solution in a test tube and then tells you how much of the light made it through (rather than getting absorbed by the solution). The darker the solution, the less light that makes it through.

Now, the units used in the example is *percent transmittance*. Even if you didn't know anything about spectrophotometers, you may be able to tell that this is a measure of the percentage of light that makes it through. Basically, this means that you are measuring how transparent the solution is. A high number means it is very transparent, and a low number means it is nearly opaque. Figure 19-4 shows what the tubes from experiment #3 would look like, based on the table provided in the example.

Figure 19-4:
Appearance of the test tubes that resulted from experiment #3.

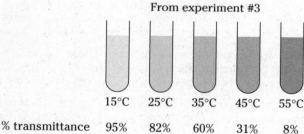

From experiment #3

	15°C	25°C	35°C	45°C	55°C
% transmittance	95%	82%	60%	31%	8%

Okay, so now focus on question #56. This one at least you could get even if you were totally confused by all the other details. You can see in the table for experiment #1 that the results were all really similar no matter what the salt concentration was. That means (A) has a good chance of being right, so the safe choice would be to pick that.

57. **D.** Once you've figured out that changing the salt concentration had no effect on enzyme activity, you can figure out which graph reflects these results. The one that doesn't increase or decrease at all is the one to choose.

58. **B.** Okay, now you can follow one of two strategies. If you understand the details of the experiment and the results, then you can go in search of the right answer. If you are still a little foggy on how it all works, then you can at least narrow down the possible choices through the elimination strategy.

We'll start with the elimination strategy. You can see that the numbers for % transmittance went up steadily as the pH went up, so graph I, which goes up and then down, can safely be crossed out. Also, graph IV, which just goes straight across is no good for experiment #2.

That leaves II, III, and V. Graphs III and V both go up, so one reasonable way of guessing would be to choose the odd one out, which is graph II, and in this case it would get you the right answer.

Okay, now for the direct route. According to the table, as pH goes up, so does percentage transmittance. Since greater % transmittance means less blue color, then it must also mean that there was *less* enzyme activity. The graph that represents enzyme activity decreasing as the experimental variable increases is graph II.

59. **E.** The results for experiment #3 were the opposite of experiment #2, so you should find a graph that goes up instead of down. Both graphs III and V go up, but in different ways. Graph III turns out to be wrong because the % transmission stays low for a while and then shoots up really fast all of a sudden, and according to the table, that didn't really happen in experiment #3. So, the best choice is graph V which just goes up steadily.

60. **B.** The thing that the experimenters were testing was the activity of the enzyme, so a good control group would need to exclude the enzyme. Only option (B) actually does that, so it's the correct answer. The others just change various experimental parameters in a different ways.

Biology-E Section

61. **B.** The main thing that's going to happen whenever a biome turns into a tundra is that it would gradually get colder and colder over many decades or centuries (see Chapter 12 for more on biomes). This would give some of the species in the area time to adapt to the changes by way of evolution by natural selection, which is covered in Chapter 10. All of the choices are something that *could* happen under these circumstances, but you need to choose the one that is *most likely*, based on the information given. If some important feature of the ecosystem is changing in a specific direction, like getting progressively wetter, drier, hotter, colder, and so on, then it will likely result in a lot of directional selection in favor of animals that are better and better and handling the change.

62. **D.** Primary producers, covered in Chapter 12 on ecology, are organisms that perform photosynthesis, so they need light. That means if any of the ocean zones has very little light, then that's where primary producers are least likely to be found. As the name suggests, the aphotic zone gets almost no light at all, so that's the correct answer.

63. **D.** Co-evolution occurs between two species that spend a long time interacting in a very direct and dramatic way. With flowers and pollinators, the flowers will evolve better ways to take advantage of the pollinators, and the pollinators will evolve better ways to locate and consume the nectar. Predators become better hunters while prey become better escapers. Parasites get better at evading the defenses of the host, causing the host to evolve even better means of defense. That lands you on "all of the above."

64. **B.** Ecological succession is when an area starts with no living organisms at all and eventually works it's way back to a thriving climax community. See Chapter 12 for more on how that works. Pioneers are the sorts of things that try to establish a new home where nobody is currently living, so the pioneer species are the ones to start a new ecosystem. Instead of traveling in covered wagons, these pioneers usually just get carried by the wind.

65. **B.** In the example, there are two different species trying to eat the same food source. That means they are in direct competition (unless there's just tons and tons of grass available, which is not mentioned in the question). The prefix "inter" means "between," so this is an example of *inter*specific competition. As for (C) and (D), there *may* be some kind of long-term selection going on over the generations, but the question just asks about what is going on right now as these animals graze on the savannah. See Chapter 12 for more info.

66. **E.** When an organism has some sort of non-functional thing that used to have a function in the organism's distant ancestors, that's called a vestigial structure. See Chapter 10 on evolution for more details on this kind of thing.

67. **C.** This one's a little bit tricky because it could succeed in misdirecting you. The fact that the average temperature is so low, you may immediately think it's going to be the tundra, but that's not one of the options. If you look back over the characteristics, the next feature of this biome to really stand out should be the low yearly rainfall, which points right at the desert. Even though the most famous deserts are usually really hot, the thing that really matters is the dryness, so some deserts are actually really cold.

68. **B.** As discussed in Chapter 10, Darwinian and Lamarckian evolution are different in a lot of important ways, but they do have a few things in common. Answer (A) describes the main feature of Lamarckian evolution, which is an idea that's completely rejected by Darwin, so cross that one out. Answers (C) and (D) are only true of Darwinian evolution because Lamarckian evolution doesn't involve any randomness or reproductive fitness. Answer (E) is false of both theories, so cross it out, too. Now, both theories agree that species change over time to be better adapted to their environments, so go for (B). In fact, that's the exact thing that they're both trying to explain!

69. **C.** Speciation is covered in Chapter 10 on evolution. This happens when a single population, which is made of just one species, splits and evolves into two distinct species. Normally, populations tend to evolve together as a unit because they continue to mix their genes together through interbreeding. So, in order for a new species to evolve from an old population, the two must not be able to interbreed anymore. The only one of the choices that could split the population into two parts whose members can't come in contact with each other for breeding is the large river. All the others will certainly affect the population in some dramatic way, but they aren't as likely to split the population in half.

70. **E.** Carrying capacity is the maximum number of individuals that an ecological area can support. If all of the populations in a community are at carrying capacity, then the area is completely maxed out and the community is very stable. This is called a climax community, which is covered in Chapter 12 on ecology.

71. **E.** An exoskeleton is basically a shell. Some of these creatures you may easily recognize as having a shell, like insects, and maybe even crustaceans and mollusks, so you can cross them out if you're pretty sure about them. Arthropods may be harder to remember, and what the heck are echinoderms? Chapter 11 on taxonomy covers these kinds of animals, and it turns out that arthropods are a big category (a phylum, actually) that includes both insects and mollusks, so arthropods have an exoskeleton. That leaves just the echinoderms as the one to pick. These guys are the starfish and sea urchins, which, believe it or not, actually have an *endo*skeleton.

72. **A.** This is another list that you should write down on the test booklet as soon as you start, just like the taxonomic levels from question #37. Chapter 12 on ecology explains the relative sizes of the different ecological levels, and (A) is the one that gets it right. A single organism is certainly the smallest level, so it's in the right spot there at the end. Now starting at the beginning, a community is a group of populations, and a territory is an area occupied by an individual member of a population, which is always going to be at least slightly larger than the individual organism itself.

73. **C.** Notice that the question is asking for the one that it *not* a characteristic of animals, so you can cross out all the ones you know that are. Mammary glands, of course, are characteristic of mammals, as are the bearing of live young and having fur, so cross out all of those. While it's true that mammals all have an endoskeleton, so do a lot of other animals like fish and reptiles, so that's not a *distinguishing* characteristic of mammals, so that's the one to pick.

74. **E.** This sort of thing is almost always true in a regular ecosystem (see the trophic levels in Chapter 12). The higher up the food chain you go, the fewer animals you see, and the drop-off between levels is usually pretty huge, as it is in this example. The first four choices all describe situations that need more support from the given information to be good explanations. They require some outside thing like a disease or a new predator or habitat loss. As for answer (E), the herbivores always burn off a lot of energy as they run around and live their lives, sometimes for many years, before they finally get caught by a predator, and that energy is lost forever. The carnivore only gets the nutrients and energy that happen to be inside the herbivore when the lion eats it, plus the lion spends a lot of energy chasing the herbivore down and killing it, so there's not really much left to support a big predator population.

75. **E.** Whenever two populations dramatically affect each other, their population sizes tend to rise and fall together, with just a little bit of time lag between them. Each of the choices involves a kind of close interaction where the two populations involved would certainly affect each other pretty dramatically, so it must be all of the above.

76. **C.** Whenever you have two species in a close relationship like this, you are likely to see co-evolution happening.

77. **E.** As discussed in Chapter 12 on ecology, any ecosystem you come across is likely to show the following sort of pattern with its trophic levels: the primary producers are going to be the biggest group, with primary consumers (herbivores) coming next, and then secondary consumers (carnivores) being the smallest group. So, with that in mind, you need to find the choice that starts with one of the most common species, which would be either species B or species E. Next comes a medium species, such as species A or C, and then the smallest one, species D.

78. **A.** Based on the information discussed for #77, species C must be a primary consumer, also called an herbivore.

79. **D.** The tundra is really cold, so only species that can survive such conditions will be living there. Exothermic (cold-blooded) animals like reptiles cannot handle such serious cold, so the snake is the least likely.

80. **B.** For this one, you need to think about what sort of impact of the loss of species D will have on the other species. Also, it asks which one is the *least* likely, so you can start by crossing out the ones that are *most* likely to happen. The herbivores will probably be happy because they aren't being hunted anymore, so their populations are likely to increase, so cross out answer (A). If the herbivores increase, then they will be able to eat more plants, which means the populations of primary producers will decrease, so cross out answer (D) as well. Now, if there's more of both species A and species C, then competition between those two will increase, and if there's less of species B and E, then competition between them will decrease, so answers (C) and (E) can also be eliminated. That leaves answer (B). Species E will NOT increase because there are more herbivores around to eat it.

Biology-M Section

81. **D.** As discussed in Chapter 8, a trait is recessive if it is produced by a recessive allele. A recessive allele can only do its thing when it is not matched with a dominant allele. That is, there must be two recessive alleles, which is also known as being homozygous recessive, so recessive traits can only be seen in a certain kind of homozygous situation.

82. **D.** The basic differences between prokaryotes and eukaryotes are covered back in Chapter 3. The most obvious difference is that eukaryotes have tiny internal compartments (called organelles), while prokaryotes do not. The nucleus is a kind of organelle, so that means all eukaryotes have a nucleus and all prokaryotes do not, which makes this a great way to distinguish between them. All cells contain DNA, so (C) was clearly wrong. As for (A), (B), and (E) all those things can be found here and there among both eukaryotes and prokaryotes.

83. **E.** The question asks which would be the *most* damaging because, in fact, all of the choices would be at least slightly damaging.

    What makes a mutation bad? Well, the more it screws up the protein that it's supposed to make, the more damage it can do. As discussed in Chapter 7, a missense mutation would only result in changing one amino acid in the resulting protein, which is a pretty small change, and it's possible that it won't make any real difference at all. A point mutation is when one nucleotide gets changed, which could also end up being no big deal. A frameshift mutation, on the other hand, completely changes the amino acid sequence of the protein that gets made, so this has the most damage potential. That narrows it down to (D) and (E). Now, it would be more damaging to have any of these mutations happen on the DNA because the DNA is permanent, while the RNA strands are just temporary copies of the DNA that will soon get broken down and recycled anyway.

84. **B.** Endocytosis is covered in Chapter 3, and it's usually reserved for really big stuff like proteins or small cells. The ion, the sugar molecule, and the two gas molecules are all really small, so they would most likely enter through channels or pumps, or maybe by simple diffusion. The virus, however, is too big to go through any of those routes, so it gets taken in by endocytosis. You may have been thrown off a little by the idea that the cell is bringing in a dangerous virus on purpose. Well, it turns out that the virus is able to trick the cell into reacting as though the virus is actually a good thing that the cell should bring inside. Yep, viruses don't play fair.

85. **D.** This is a basic genetics question, and that stuff is covered in Chapter 8. Everyone has two alleles for every trait. If the two alleles you have are exactly the same, then you are homozygous for that trait. If, on the other hand, the two alleles you have are different, then you are heterozygous for that trait.

86. **E.** Okay, so you're looking for the organelle that would be most directly involved with the "ingest and destroy mission" of the leukocytes. If you need a quick review, all these organelles are covered in Chapter 3. Chloroplasts are pretty unlikely to be around at all because these are blood cells, not plant cells doing photosynthesis, so cross off (A) immediately. As for (D), all eukaryotic cells have a nucleus, and there's no need for more than one, so cross that off too. Extra mitochondria would only be needed if leukocytes needed more ATP (energy) than other cells, but other kinds of cells are just as active and hardworking as the leukocytes, so that can't be the one either. More endoplasmic reticulum? Again, other cells need to make a lot of lipids and proteins too, so there's no reason to think that leukocytes need an unusual abundance of endoplasmic reticulum. Lysosomes are the organelles that contain enzymes for breaking down proteins, nucleic acids, carbohydrates, and lipids. Now *that* sounds like something a leukocyte needs a lot of in order to break down and destroy invading viruses.

87. **D.** Transcription is when you go from DNA to mRNA, and then translation is when you go from mRNA to protein. This stuff is covered in Chapter 7.

88. **B.** This is pretty much just a memorization question from Chapter 5. A water molecule always comes out every time two monomers link together. Since the process is synthesizing (just a fancy word for "making") a polymer and the process loses a water molecule, it is called dehydration synthesis.

89. **C.** Mendel was the famous monk from the 1800's that studied pea plants in his monastery at about the same time Darwin was developing his theory of evolution. While Darwin focused on evolutionary change, Mendel focused on how traits get passed down from parent to offspring, which is genetics.

90. **D.** The graph displays information about movement across a cell membrane, and mitosis has nothing to do with that, so cross off (B) right away. Endocytosis and active transport are not influenced in any simple way by the concentration gradient, so you can cross them off too. That narrows it down to the two kinds of diffusion. Simple diffusion goes right through the membrane itself, which can happen all over the place. Facilitated diffusion,

on the other hand, is when the stuff diffuses through a channel. There's only so many channels, so there's a maximum rate at which stuff can get through, like when everyone tries to exit a crowded theater at once. Since the graph never levels off at a maximum rate (see Figure 19-5), it must not be facilitated diffusion, so the correct answer is simple diffusion. See Chapter 3 for descriptions of the different ways to get across a membrane, and for a graph of facilitated diffusion.

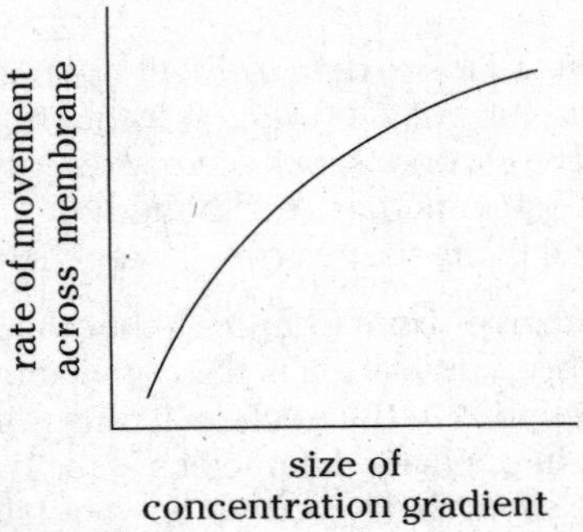

Figure 19-5:
Graph of facilitated diffusion vs. size of concentration gradient.

(graph: vertical axis labeled "rate of movement across membrane", horizontal axis labeled "size of concentration gradient")

91. **B.** As discussed in Chapter 9, sexual reproduction is when a single individual produces a genetic copy of itself, while sexual reproduction produces an offspring that is a genetic *mixture* of two parents. Since it produces a genetic mixture instead of just an exact copy, sexual reproduction results in greater diversity than asexual reproduction, so the correct answer is (B). The problem with answer (A) is its second part. There are lots of occasions when asexual reproduction involves chromosomes. In fact, every time a cell goes through mitosis, it is undergoing a kind of asexual reproduction. Answers (C) and (D) are wrong because they include things that happen in both kinds of reproduction. Answer (E) gets it backward. The haploid cells are involved in *sexual* reproduction, not asexual.

92. **E.** Everything about aerobic cellular respiration and photosynthesis and all that stuff is covered in Chapter 6. The third step of aerobic cellular respiration is called "the electron transport chain," so choice I is definitely in. The light reactions of photosynthesis also include an electron transport chain for making ATP, so IV should be included, too. Only one of the answers includes IV, so if you knew this about photosynthesis, you're home free. If you didn't, then here's another way to narrow down the choices. Fermentation and lactic acid production are very quick, simple processes, while electron transport chains are pretty complicated and slow, so choices II and III are both eliminated, which knocks out answers (C) and (D).

93. **D.** You may want to draw up a Punnet square for this one and see what happens when you fill it in. The dad's side is easy because the question just tells you his genotype is TT. Since the T allele is dominant, and this is the only allele that the father can pass down, then there is automatically a 100% chance that their kids will have the dominant phenotype. As you can see in Figure 19-6, even if mom gives the kids a recessive allele, it will be masked by the dominant allele from dad.

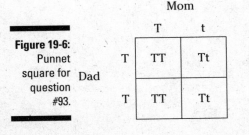

Figure 19-6:
Punnet square for question #93.

Mom

	T	t
T	TT	Tt
T	TT	Tt

Dad

94. **C.** This question contains a lot of miscellaneous information about what's happening to the chromosomes in a bunch of different situations. Although it's confusing to figure out which is the false one, you can zero in on the answer if you take a moment to consider the things you know about chromosomes. Chromosomes are where the genes are located, and the genes are made of DNA. DNA is too important to let it loose to float around anywhere in the cell, so DNA needs to be kept safe inside the nucleus. That means answer (C) is the false one. Flip back to Chapters 3 and 7 for a review of some of this stuff about DNA and the nucleus.

95. **A.** Here's another "look for the false one" question. All these details about the nature of carbon are covered in Chapter 4 on chemistry, and it turns out that (B) through (E) are all true. As for answer (A), you may not know how rare carbon is, but there are a lot of elements that you almost never hear of, like thallium and beryllium, that are a bound to be a lot rarer than carbon since carbon is the main element in all living tissues everywhere on earth.

96. **D.** Since the question asks about the nucleus, remember from Chapter 3 that the most important thing about the nucleus is that it holds the DNA. Replication is the copying of DNA in preparation for reproduction, so that definitely happens in the nucleus. Transcription is copying short segments of DNA into RNA, so that happens in the nucleus also. Translation and protein synthesis (which are pretty much the same thing) both happen outside the nucleus, out in the cytoplasm or in the rough endoplasmic reticulum, so keep them out.

97. **A.** In general, as temperature increases, chemical reactions go faster, and this includes the metabolic activity of organisms. As the temperature increases, the activity of the organism increases as well, and if they produce any gasses at all (which they most likely will) then the higher the temperature, the more gas they'll release.

    Graph (A) shows a steady increase in average balloon size as temperature increases, just like you should expect.

98. **A.** Algae are protists that perform photosynthesis, while yeast are unicellular fungus that perform cellular respiration. The gas released from cellular respiration, whether it's aerobic cellular respiration or fermentation, is CO_2.

99. **C.** First of all, the colder the temperature, the slower the metabolism, so an organism at lower temperature is likely to last longer in this situation than one at a higher temperature. That narrows it down to (C) and (E). Now, the yeast can only do cellular respiration until it runs out of O_2 or it runs out of sugar. Algae, on the other hand, can do both cellular respiration and photosynthesis, so after it produces a bunch of sugar and O_2, it can run those through cellular respiration to produce CO_2 and H_2O. Then it can run those through photosynthesis to start it all over again. Eventually it would build up too many waste molecules to continue, but it could go on like that for a long time.

100. **D.** A control group should preserve as many of the experimental conditions as possible while eliminating the experimental variable. In this case, the experimental variable is the activity of the algae or the yeast, so those should be absent. In the situation described in (D), the student would be able to see if the size of the balloon changed at all even when no living things were placed inside. If so, then that could affect the way she interprets her results.

Part VI
The Part of Tens

The 5th Wave   By Rich Tennant

BIOCAFETERIAOLOGIST

TODAYS
MACARONI + CHEE
MEAT LOAF SAND
NAVY BEANS & R
SCALLOPED POTATO
TER KUG

"I'll have the cheese sandwich with the interesting mold on the bread, and the manicotti with the fungal growth, and that really really old dish of vanilla bread pudding."

In this part . . .

Part VI gives you a chance to remind yourself what happened in the main biology chapters, and it can also serve as a quick review just before you go into the test. Each chapter in Part VI includes a list of ten items under a certain topic that are almost guaranteed to show up on the SAT II Biology E/M Test. Of course, not everything that will show up can be covered in these lists, but they at least give a good review of the most important facts.

Chapter 20

Ten Crucial Categories

One of the things that can come up a lot on the SAT II is stuff about specific kinds of organisms. Sometimes they just ask something basic, such as, "Which of the following is a member of the kingdom Protista?" For that kind of information, you just have to remember them in whatever way works best for you — flash cards, writing it out a bunch of times, saying out loud, putting to music, and so on. You'll probably only see a few of those kinds of questions on the exam, but even the questions that ask about genetics or ecology or metabolism can use specific kinds of organisms as examples, and it can really help if you know roughly what sort of organism they're talking about and what its basic characteristics are.

This information and a whole lot more is contained in Chapter 11 on taxonomy, but this chapter lists ten of the most likely categories of organisms that could show up on the SAT II. Some, like the monocots and dicots, are lumped together because you really can't talk about one without mentioning the other.

Monera: The Bacteria

Eubacteria and Archaebacteria are the two main kinds of bacteria, which all fit under the kingdom Monera. The Monerans are all prokaryotes, which means they are unicellular and they don't have any organelles inside at all. Eubacteria are the most familiar ones that live around us all the time. When they reproduce too much they can cause problems for us, such as the bacteria that cause food poisoning and stuff like that. Archaebacteria, on the other hand, are the crazy extreme bacteria that live in places humans never really go. Thermoacidophiles can't get enough of those super hot temperatures and low pH. These ones aren't likely to make you sick because the boiling acid would probably get you first. Halophiles like to live where it's really salty, like the Great Salt Lake in Utah or the Dead Sea in the Middle East. People sometimes swim in these places, but they can't spend too much time there without suffering some weird dehydration effects.

Protists

Members of the Protista kingdom are all made of eukaryotic cells, so their cells all have a nucleus and other organelles. Protists are pretty simple organisms that are usually unicellular and always live in the water. Protozoans are the highly mobile single-celled Protists that swim around hunting for bacteria cells. They are able to swim using little cilia or larger tail-like things called flagella. Algae are the Protists that can do photosynthesis, and while a lot of them are also unicellular, some of them are big multicellular things like seaweed, kelp, and the stringy green stuff you find in some lakes and rivers. The plankton in the ocean is made of unicellular algae and protozoans.

Fungi

Fungi is the kingdom of the full-time decomposers. All of the fungi are eukaryotes, and they all have cell walls made of chitin. The cells of a fungus line up in strands called hyphae, and the molds are the ones that form very loosely packed hyphae that look kind of fuzzy while the mushrooms are the kind that form pretty densely packed hyphae. In order to reproduce, fungi grow a fruiting body that releases spores into the air or water. The mushrooms you see growing above ground are the fruiting bodies of underground fungi.

Plants: Gymnosperms

Gymnosperms, including pines, firs, and junipers, are the plants that use cones as their reproductive parts. The male cone produces huge amounts of pollen that gets blown by the wind in huge clouds. Some of that pollen is bound to land on a female cone, where it can fertilize the eggs. The eggs turn into seeds and the cone drops off. Many species of gymnosperms need a quick brushfire to come through and singe the cones in order to open them up. Once they're open, then the seeds can sprout. Gymnosperms tend to be the dominant tree type in the taiga biome.

Plants: Angiosperms

Angiosperms are the ones that have flowers as their reproductive parts. That means they're all in a mutualistic symbiosis with at least one animal pollinator species, such as a bee, butterfly, hummingbird, or sometimes even a bat. The flower uses its petals and its scent to attract pollinators who come flying in to drink some of the nectar the flower is producing. As it comes in to get the nectar, the pollinator brushes past the anthers of the flower and gets some pollen stuck on its body. When the pollinator goes to the next flower, some of the pollen it's carrying can get rubbed off on the flower's stamen. The pollen can then go down to the ovary and fertilize the eggs (also called the ova). The eggs then develop into seeds.

Plants: Monocots and Dicots

Monocots and Dicots are the two kinds of angiosperms. Monocots are the grasses and grains, while dicots are all the other flowering plants, such as all the other trees and bushes and most of the things you may grow in a vegetable garden. The primary difference between monocots and dicots is how they sprout. Monocots sprout with one baby leaf (called a cotyledon), and then form long, blade-shaped adult leaves. Dicots sprout from the seed with two cotyledons, and tend to develop more distinct stems or trunks, with adult leaves hanging onto the branches. When they produce seeds, monocots usually allow them to be spread in the wind, and while many dicots also use the wind to spread their seeds, a lot of them use some kind of fruit. The fruit are used to attract animals who eat the fruit and eventually deposit the seeds some distance away from the parent plant.

Animals: Arthropods

Arthropods are the animals that have exoskeletons and can walk or fly around. Their exoskeletons aren't just solid, rigid shells like the mollusks. Instead, the arthropod exoskeleton has jointed appendages for the legs and/or wings. We know that this kind of exoskeleton works really well because the arthropod class is gigantic. It includes 1) the crustaceans, which are the walking or swimming shellfish like crabs, lobsters, and shrimp; 2) the arachnids such as spiders and scorpions; and 3) the insects, which is the biggest group of arthropods. There are many millions of different insect species, from bees to beetles to butterflies to ants to termites to dragonflies. These things are everywhere, and sometimes in gigantic numbers.

Animals: Annelids

The Annelids are the segmented worms. Some, like earthworms, are harmless decomposers that munch on soil all day. Others, like the leeches, are nasty parasites that want to suck your blood. You aren't likely to see many details about this phylum on the SAT II, but they may show up in a couple of examples, so keep an eye out for these squishy critters.

Animals: Chordates

Chordates are the animals with some sort of endoskeleton, especially a spine. In fact, the name for this group comes from the fact that they all have some sort of distinct spinal cord. The Chordate phylum includes fish, amphibians, reptiles, birds and mammals. The fish, amphibians and reptiles are all exothermic animals, which means that they don't generate enough body heat to keep themselves warm during cold weather. The birds and mammals, on the other hand, are endothermic — the only ones on the planet. Endothermic (warm blooded) animals have really fast metabolisms and can generate a lot of body heat to keep themselves warm and active even when it gets really cold outside. Birds and mammals are also most likely to have lots of insulation, as in feathers or fur.

Animals: Mammals

Mammals are the chordates that are most likely to show up on the SAT II. The main thing to remember is that mammals have a few very specific distinguishing characteristics. The one that gives them their name is the fact that they have mammary glands that can provide sustenance to offspring. Another distinguishing characteristic is that all mammals (except the freaky platypus) give birth to full-fledged babies instead of eggs. All other chordates (with a few rare exceptions) lay eggs of some kind that develop for a while outside of the mother and then hatch into babies. Another thing about mammals is that they almost all have a lot of fur or hair to keep them warm. No other animals have anything like the fur you find on mammals. The only mammals that no longer have any real fur are some of the fully aquatic kinds like seals, dolphins and whales.

Chapter 21

Ten Key Components of Cells

The various cell parts are another thing that comes up a lot on the SAT II, both in the direct questions like, "Cell membranes are constructed of," and as examples in questions about other things. This chapter covers the ten most important cell parts, from the basic membrane and cytoplasm that all cells have, to the specialized structures such as cell walls, cilia, and flagella, to the most important organelles. It's important here to remember the basic differences between prokaryotic and eukaryotic cells. The prokaryotic cells (also called bacteria or Monerans) have a regular cell membrane and cytoplasm and stuff, but they don't have any organelles. Eukaryotic cells, on the other hand, all have at least a few organelles in addition to a membrane and cytoplasm.

Cytoplasm

This is the watery interior of the cell. There's a lot of stuff dissolved in the cytoplasm, such as minerals like sodium and potassium, along with some gasses like CO_2 or O_2. There's also a whole lot of stuff floating around inside like individual sugar molecules, amino acids, and nucleotides, as well as some big things like enzymes. If you're talking about a prokaryotic bacteria cell, then there's also a big DNA chain floating around. If, on the other hand, you're dealing with a eukaryotic cell, then the various organelles will be suspended in the cytoplasm.

Membrane

The main purpose of the membrane is to protect the cytoplasm from whatever may be outside. Usually it's some other kind of water solution on the outside, and usually it's a different kind of water solution from the cytoplasm, which is why the membrane needs to keep the cytoplasm contained and protected. The membrane is made of phospholipids which are, of course, a kind of lipid. Lipids are very hydrophobic, which means they do not like to be in contact with water, and this allows them to act as a good water-resistant barrier for the cell. Remember also that each phospholipid has not just a lipid part, but also a phosphate part. The phosphate part is hydrophilic so it can touch water with no problems, and the phosphates on the phospholipids line the inner and outer surfaces of the cell membrane.

Channels and Pumps

The membrane can't be an *absolute* barrier to hydrophilic stuff, because then the cell couldn't import and export minerals, sugars, and lots of other important molecules. Channels are tiny tunnels in the membrane that allow specific hydrophobic things to diffuse through. For example, most cells have a channel that's reserved for just sodium (Na^+), while a different channel is reserved only for chloride (Cl^-). When a channel is open, the ion or the molecule diffuses through to the other side. Diffusion is when something moves from an area of high concentration to an area of low concentration, and sometimes this means the thing will diffuse in, while other times it means the thing will move out. In order for you to know which will happen, you need to be told which side of the membrane has a higher concentration. By the way, diffusion through a channel like this is called facilitated diffusion. Pumps, on the other hand, use ATP energy to force ions or molecules across the membrane no matter what the situation is with the concentration gradient.

Cell Wall

Cell walls are tough shells around the cell membrane of certain kinds of cells. Lots of bacteria and protists have cell walls, but not all. All of the fungi have cell walls made of a fairly soft material called chitin. Almost all plant cells have cell walls made of cellulose, which is a very tough polymer fiber made from glucose molecules. Cellulose in their cell walls is what makes plants able to stand up straight and also why it can be really hard to digest them. In fact, no animal can digest cellulose. They can chew it up pretty well and get some nutrients out of the plant, but they don't have the right enzymes to break the cellulose all the way down to individual glucose molecules. Herbivores that feed almost entirely on cellulose get help from symbiotic bacteria that break down the cellulose for the animal.

Flagella and Cilia

These are the structures that swimming cells use to move around. Lots of unicellular bacteria and protists can swim around, and a few animal cells can also. Flagella are long, whip-like tails that propel the cell in one direction. The ones you are most likely to have seen pictures of are the little sperm cells frantically whipping their flagella as they race toward the egg. Cilia are a lot smaller, but the cell will have a whole lot more of them, perhaps even hundreds covering the whole surface of the cell. By wiggling its cilia in just the right ways, the cell can move in any direction it wants.

Organelle: Nucleus

Just like all the organelles, the nucleus is found only in eukaryotic cells. The nucleus is where the DNA is stored, and kept safe. Under normal circumstances, DNA never comes out of the nucleus because it needs to stay protected from the enzymes that are lurking outside in the cytoplasm. RNA, on the other hand, needs to enter and exit the nucleus all the time because it needs to carry the DNA's genetic information from the nucleus out to where the proteins are made. Luckily, there's a bunch of little holes in the membrane of the nucleus called nuclear pores that let the RNA pass through.

Organelle: Mitochondria

The mitochondria is the main power generator of eukaryotic cells. It accepts various fuels like sugars, fats, and proteins, and it burns them in the process of aerobic cellular respiration. The energy that's released from this fuel use is trapped in ATP molecules which the cell can then use to power whatever cell processes it needs to perform, such as active transport, DNA copying, protein building, and so on. The mitochondria requires O_2 along with the fuel as an input and it releases CO_2 and H_2O as wastes. As for its basic structure, the mitochondria has a regular outer membrane, plus an inner membrane. The area inside the inner membrane is called the matrix, and the space between the membranes is called the intermembrane space. Another miscellaneous fact the SAT II may spring on you is that the mitochondria has its own DNA and can reproduce separately inside the cell.

Organelle: Chloroplast

The chloroplasts are found only in eukaryotic cells, and only the ones that perform photosynthesis. Photosynthesis is when the plant or the algae absorbs light energy in order to power the production of organic molecules, especially glucose. The glucose is made from H_2O and CO_2, and the process kicks out O_2 as a waste product. As with the mitochondria, chloroplasts also have their own DNA and can reproduce separately inside the cell. Organisms that have chloroplasts are always the primary producers in any ecosystem because they're the ones manufacturing the basic food for everyone else.

Organelle: Lysosome

Lysosomes contain digestive enzymes, and they act as the recycling stations in a eukaryotic cell. Whenever a cell needs to break down little bits and pieces of old proteins and nucleic acids, it can send them to the lysosomes where they get chopped up into their component parts and recycled back into the cell. The cell can then use those building blocks to build new proteins and nucleic acids. Special cells of the immune system called leukocytes use lysosomes to destroy invading viruses, bacteria, and fungi.

Organelle: Endoplasmic Reticulum

The endoplasmic reticulum is the industrial factory of the cell. The whole thing is made of folded up layers of membrane and is separated into two sections, the smooth endoplasmic reticulum (the SER) and the rough endoplasmic reticulum (the RER). The SER manufactures whatever kinds of lipids the cell may need, especially phospholipids for the cell membrane. The rough endoplasmic reticulum gets its name because it has little ribosomes attached all over it. The ribosomes are where new proteins are manufactured from individual amino acids.

Chapter 22

Ten Significant Cell Processes

All living things are made of cells, so the processes that go on inside of cells are what make life really go. If you understand the basic cell processes, then you're already a long way toward understanding everything else in biology. The SAT II will ask a lot of questions about cell processes in both the Biology E/M core and the Biology-M section, especially in the questions where you need to interpret experimental results. This chapter covers the ten most important cell processes that you will encounter in your adventures with the SAT II.

Aerobic Cellular Respiration

Aerobic cellular respiration is the process where an organism breaks down fuel (usually glucose) using O_2, and it happens inside the mitochondria of eukaryotic cells. The official inputs and outputs of the whole thing are: $6\ O_2 + 1\ C_6H_{12}O_6 \rightarrow 6\ CO_2 + 6\ H_2O + \textbf{energy}$. The energy that comes out is trapped in a bunch of ATP molecules. The ATPs can then be used by the cell to do whatever the cell needs to do, such as active transport, DNA copying, protein building, and so on. The three steps of aerobic cellular respiration are glycolysis, the Krebs cycle, and the electron transport chain. Most of the consumers in an ecosystem (including humans) rely on aerobic cellular respiration to get their energy.

Anaerobic Cellular Respiration: Fermentation and Lactic Acid Production

Anaerobic cellular respiration is the process where an organism breaks down fuel (usually glucose) *without* using O_2. No mitochondria needed here. The glucose only gets broken down a little bit and only 2 ATPs get produced, but the process is really fast and it doesn't need any outside air. There are two kinds of anaerobic cellular respiration. The first kind is done by yeast and they break the glucose down to ethyl alcohol and CO_2 in a process called *fermentation*. The other kind, *lactic acid production,* is done by the muscle cells of animals when they break the glucose down to lactic acid, which causes a burning sensation. Muscles only do this for quick bursts, like in jumping or sprinting.

Photosynthesis

Photosynthesis is the process where plants and algae use light energy to power the production of organic molecules, especially glucose. The official inputs and outputs of the whole thing are: $6\ CO_2 + 6\ H_2O + \textbf{light energy} \rightarrow 6\ O_2 + 1\ C_6H_{12}O_6$. Photosynthesis is divided into two big stages. The first stage is called the light-dependent reactions, and is where light energy is absorbed by chlorophyll. This causes some electrons from the H_2O molecules to go through an electron transport chain to produce ATP. This also causes the oxygen atoms from the water molecules to be released as O_2. The next step is sometimes called the light-independent reactions, and sometimes also called the Calvin cycle. This is where the ATPs from the first stage are used to power the production of glucose from CO_2 molecules taken out of the air and H_2O molecules taken from the soil.

DNA Replication

DNA replication is the copying of DNA in preparation for cell division. DNA is made of two parallel polymers of nucleotides that are wrapped around each other in that famous double-helix structure. There are four nucleotides, A, T, G, and C, and they are arranged in a very specific sequence on the two strands. It turns out that when the two strands line up together, A and T always need to be across from each other, and C and G also need to always be across from each other. In order to make a full copy of this double-stranded DNA, the cell first separates the two strands, and then adds in new nucleotides to each strand following those same nucleotide matching rules of A-T and C-G. The result is *two* double-stranded DNAs, each with the same sequences of nucleotides on their two strands. This is a big deal because the sequence of nucleotides encodes the all-important genetic information, and every cell that gets made needs to have that info.

Transcription

The genetic information encoded in the DNA tells the cell how to make each of the different proteins that the cell might need. The proteins get made out in the cytoplasm or in the rough endoplasmic reticulum, but the DNA needs to stay in the nucleus, so the cell makes an RNA copy of a gene, called a messenger RNA (mRNA), and sends the mRNA out to where the protein will be made. *Transcription* is the process of constructing an mRNA from a gene on the DNA, and the process involves the matching up of nucleotides just like in DNA replication. The only difference is that RNA uses U as the nucleotide to match up with A (instead of having T match up with A).

Translation

Translation is the construction of a protein based on the information encoded in an mRNA. This construction process happens on a ribosome that's either floating around in the cytoplasm or is stuck on the rough endoplasmic reticulum. In order for a protein to work right, it's amino acids need to be placed in just the right sequence, and this "sequence information" is what's encoded in the mRNA. Every set of three nucleotides on the mRNA is called a codon, and each different codon represents a different amino acid. This way, the sequence of codons on the mRNA can tell the cell what the sequence of amino acids in the protein is supposed to be. Another kind of RNA, called tRNA, helps to match up the codons with the proper amino acids.

Mitosis

Mitosis is the asexual reproduction of a single eukaryotic cell, and is sometimes just called cell division. When the cell divides, it needs to send full copies of the DNA to each new cell, and it does so by copying and sorting the chromosomes. Chromosomes are huge bundles of DNA, and all of them get copied through DNA replication. The first stage of mitosis is called *prophase,* and this is where the copied chromosomes start to get organized. Next is *metaphase* where the chromosomes all line up in the middle of the cell. *Anaphase* is when the two copies of each chromosome (called sister chromatids) split apart and move to either side of the cell. Last is *telophase,* where the cell physically splits in two, with one full set of chromosomes in each half.

Meiosis

Meiosis is the production of gametes in preparation for sexual reproduction, and it looks like a variation on mitosis, but with some new things happening with the chromosomes. Each chromosome has a partner with similar genes, and together they make up a homologous pair of chromosomes. A cell with both members of every homologous pair is called a diploid cell. Meiosis will produce four haploid cells that have only one chromosome of each homologous pair.

First the chromosomes all get copied, and then the cell goes through two rounds of division. Prophase I is just like the prophase of mitosis. Metaphase I is when the homologous pairs line up in the middle of the cell, and anaphase I is when the homologous pairs move to opposite sides of the cell. Telophase I splits the cell in two, with each half containing one chromosome from each homologous pair. The cells are now haploid, but we're not done yet. Each cell then goes into metaphase II, where the chromosomes all line up again in the middle of each cell. Then in anaphase II, the sister chromatids of each chromosome split apart and move to opposite sides of the cells, and telophase II splits the cells in half. The result is four haploid cells called gametes, which are the sperm or egg that will be used in sexual reproduction.

Endocytosis and Exocytosis

Endocytosis and exocytosis are how cells move big stuff in and out when the stuff won't fit through a channel or a pump. This includes big polymers like proteins and nucleic acids, and sometimes even small cells or viruses. *Endocytosis* is when the cell takes in one of these things. The cell forms an indentation in its membrane, and the stuff that's coming in settles into that indentation. Then the indentation forms into a deep pocket in the membrane and the sides close off above the pocket. The whole thing then pinches off from the rest of the membrane and forms a free-floating bubble inside the cell called a vesicle. *Exocytosis* happens when some big stuff is put into a vesicle and sent out to the cell membrane. The vesicle's membrane merges with the cell membrane, and the stuff in the vesicle gets dumped outside.

Neuron signaling

Neurons are the special cells in animals that send control signals back and forth really fast. They receive signals through their dendrites and send signals out through their axons. The electrical signal (called an action potential) travels down the axon until it hits the end. When it gets to the end of the axon, the action potential causes neurotransmitter molecules to be released into the synapse, which is the space between this axon and the cell it is sending a signal to. The neurotransmitters float across the synapse and attach to receptors on the next cell, which causes that cell to be activated or inhibited, depending on the neurotransmitter.

Chapter 23

Ten Momentous Molecules

*A*ll living things are made of cells, and all cells are made of a specific set of molecules, which means that these molecules get a lot of attention on the SAT II. They may ask something about molecules directly, such as "Glucose contains which of the following elements?" On the other hand, they may just use molecules as examples in questions about other things, in which case it could be useful to know something about the molecules they mention. This chapter covers the ten molecules that will show up most often on the SAT II.

H_2O

The water molecule is one of the most important in all of biology. The cytoplasm inside of every cell is a special kind of water solution, and a lot of cellular processes involve the use of or production of water. For example, aerobic cellular respiration produces H_2O as a by-product, while photosynthesis uses H_2O as an ingredient. Dehydration synthesis is the reaction that links together the monomers that go into making a polymer, and this process also releases H_2O as a by-product. Another thing about water that could easily come up is what it will mix with. Hydrophilic substances, such as minerals and sugars, are ones that can easily mix with water. Hydrophobic things, like fats and oils, cannot mix with water.

O_2

Oxygen gas is a really important molecule, but it shows up at only two specific places in all of biology. First of all, O_2 is a necessary ingredient for aerobic cellular respiration because right at the end it is combined with H atoms to produce H_2O. The other place you find O_2, is when it is produced right at the beginning of photosynthesis. This way the producers, like plants and algae, that are doing photosynthesis are providing glucose and O_2 for the consumers. The consumers then turn around and provide CO_2 and H_2O to the producers.

CO_2

Carbon dioxide is an important ingredient in photosynthesis because it is used to build glucose molecules. CO_2 is also a waste product of aerobic cellular respiration which breaks those glucose molecules back down to CO_2 and H_2O. Burning of fossil fuels such as coal and oil releases a lot of excess CO_2 into the atmosphere, which leads to an increase in the greenhouse effect.

Glucose and the Polysaccharides

Glucose is one of the central molecules in all of biology, and it's chemical formula is $C_6H_{12}O_6$. Glucose is the main product of photosynthesis and the main fuel for cellular respiration. Aside from being used as a fuel, glucose molecules can also be hooked together to form a few different kinds of polymers called polysaccharides. For example, if an animal wants to store glucose, it can link a bunch of them together in a polymer called glycogen. For plants, the glucose storage polymer is called starch. Another important glucose polymer is cellulose, which is the material that's used to make plant cell walls.

Amino Acids

Amino acids are the molecules that are used to make proteins, so the amino acids need to be able to be linked together in big long polymers. In order for this to work, every amino acid has the same basic structure on either end so that any amino acid can be attached to any other in the same basic way. The bond that forms between two amino acids is called a peptide bond, and since they can all form peptide bonds in the same way, the amino acids can be strung together in any sequence you want. There are 20 different amino acids, and what makes them all different is the kind of thing they have attached to the middle of the amino acid. Some have just a few carbon and hydrogen atoms while others have big ring structures that include nitrogen or sulfur. Some of these things can make the amino acid very hydrophilic and others can make the amino acid very hydrophobic.

Proteins

Proteins are the main structural elements and work horses of an organism. All proteins are made from the same 20 amino acids, and each kind of protein differs only in its actual sequence of amino acids. The amino acids sequence determines the function of the protein, so if the sequence gets messed up somehow, the protein might not work right anymore. Possible functions for proteins include: enzymes, channels, active transport pumps, hormones, receptors, and structural elements such as hair, muscle, and skin.

Nucleotides

Nucleotides are molecules that can be strung together to make nucleic acid polymers such as DNA and RNA. Each nucleotide has three parts: the ribose (or deoxyribose) sugar, a phosphate group, and a nitrogen base. The only thing that makes one kind of nucleotide different than another is its nitrogen base. There are four different nitrogen bases that get used in DNA nucleotides: adenine (A), thymine (T), cytosine (C), and guanine (G). RNA nucleotides use the same nitrogen bases except that RNA uses uracil (U) instead of thymine.

DNA

Deoxyribonucleic acid consists of two parallel polymers made of nucleotides. The sequence of nucleotides in DNA encodes the all-important genetic information that tells an organism how to construct all of its proteins properly. The DNA of prokaryotic bacteria cells is just one big loop that floats around in the cytoplasm. In eukaryotic cells, the DNA is coiled up into chromosomes and is contained inside the nucleus.

RNA

Ribonucleic acid is also a polymer of nucleotides, but there are a few key differences between RNA and DNA. RNA nucleotides use a ribose sugar instead of the deoxyribose used in DNA nucleotides; RNA is single-stranded instead of double-stranded; and RNA includes uracil instead of thymine. The main role for RNA is to carry the genetic information from the DNA in the nucleus out to the ribosomes where the proteins are made. The cell can then use the information on the RNA to produce a protein, which is a process called translation.

Phospholipids

Phospholipids are the kind of lipid used to make cell membranes. All lipids are hydrophobic, so they make a good water-resistant barrier for cells. Phospholipids are especially good because they include small, hydrophilic phosphate groups that can touch water more easily than the lipid part of the molecules can. The phospholipids arrange themselves in a double layer, with the lipid "tail" sections facing each other in the interior of the membrane, and with the phosphate "head" sections facing either the watery cytoplasm on the inside or the watery extracellular fluid on the outside.

Index

Notes

Notes

BUSINESS, CAREERS & PERSONAL FINANCE

Grant Writing For Dummies
0-7645-5307-0

Home Buying For Dummies
0-7645-5331-3 *†

Also available:

- Accounting For Dummies †
  0-7645-5314-3
- Business Plans Kit For Dummies †
  0-7645-5365-8
- Cover Letters For Dummies
  0-7645-5224-4
- Frugal Living For Dummies
  0-7645-5403-4
- Leadership For Dummies
  0-7645-5176-0
- Managing For Dummies
  0-7645-1771-6

- Marketing For Dummies
  0-7645-5600-2
- Personal Finance For Dummies *
  0-7645-2590-5
- Project Management For Dummies
  0-7645-5283-X
- Resumes For Dummies †
  0-7645-5471-9
- Selling For Dummies
  0-7645-5363-1
- Small Business Kit For Dummies *†
  0-7645-5093-4

HOME & BUSINESS COMPUTER BASICS

Windows XP For Dummies
0-7645-4074-2

Excel 2003 All-in-One Desk Reference For Dummies
0-7645-3758-X

Also available:

- ACT! 6 For Dummies
  0-7645-2645-6
- iLife '04 All-in-One Desk Reference
  For Dummies
  0-7645-7347-0
- iPAQ For Dummies
  0-7645-6769-1
- Mac OS X Panther Timesaving
  Techniques For Dummies
  0-7645-5812-9
- Macs For Dummies
  0-7645-5656-8
- Microsoft Money 2004 For Dummies
  0-7645-4195-1

- Office 2003 All-in-One Desk Reference
  For Dummies
  0-7645-3883-7
- Outlook 2003 For Dummies
  0-7645-3759-8
- PCs For Dummies
  0-7645-4074-2
- TiVo For Dummies
  0-7645-6923-6
- Upgrading and Fixing PCs For Dummies
  0-7645-1665-5
- Windows XP Timesaving Techniques
  For Dummies
  0-7645-3748-2

FOOD, HOME, GARDEN, HOBBIES, MUSIC & PETS

Feng Shui For Dummies
0-7645-5295-3

Poker For Dummies
0-7645-5232-5

Also available:

- Bass Guitar For Dummies
  0-7645-2487-9
- Diabetes Cookbook For Dummies
  0-7645-5230-9
- Gardening For Dummies *
  0-7645-5130-2
- Guitar For Dummies
  0-7645-5106-X
- Holiday Decorating For Dummies
  0-7645-2570-0
- Home Improvement All-in-One
  For Dummies
  0-7645-5680-0

- Knitting For Dummies
  0-7645-5395-X
- Piano For Dummies
  0-7645-5105-1
- Puppies For Dummies
  0-7645-5255-4
- Scrapbooking For Dummies
  0-7645-7208-3
- Senior Dogs For Dummies
  0-7645-5818-8
- Singing For Dummies
  0-7645-2475-5
- 30-Minute Meals For Dummies
  0-7645-2589-1

INTERNET & DIGITAL MEDIA

Digital Photography For Dummies
0-7645-1664-7

Starting an eBay Business For Dummies
0-7645-6924-4

Also available:

- 2005 Online Shopping Directory
  For Dummies
  0-7645-7495-7
- CD & DVD Recording For Dummies
  0-7645-5956-7
- eBay For Dummies
  0-7645-5654-1
- Fighting Spam For Dummies
  0-7645-5965-6
- Genealogy Online For Dummies
  0-7645-5964-8
- Google For Dummies
  0-7645-4420-9

- Home Recording For Musicians
  For Dummies
  0-7645-1634-5
- The Internet For Dummies
  0-7645-4173-0
- iPod & iTunes For Dummies
  0-7645-7772-7
- Preventing Identity Theft For Dummies
  0-7645-7336-5
- Pro Tools All-in-One Desk Reference
  For Dummies
  0-7645-5714-9
- Roxio Easy Media Creator For Dummies
  0-7645-7131-1

* Separate Canadian edition also available

† Separate U.K. edition also available

SPORTS, FITNESS, PARENTING, RELIGION & SPIRITUALITY

0-7645-5146-9   0-7645-5418-2

Also available:
- Adoption For Dummies
  0-7645-5488-3
- Basketball For Dummies
  0-7645-5248-1
- The Bible For Dummies
  0-7645-5296-1
- Buddhism For Dummies
  0-7645-5359-3
- Catholicism For Dummies
  0-7645-5391-7
- Hockey For Dummies
  0-7645-5228-7

- Judaism For Dummies
  0-7645-5299-6
- Martial Arts For Dummies
  0-7645-5358-5
- Pilates For Dummies
  0-7645-5397-6
- Religion For Dummies
  0-7645-5264-3
- Teaching Kids to Read For Dummies
  0-7645-4043-2
- Weight Training For Dummies
  0-7645-5168-X
- Yoga For Dummies
  0-7645-5117-5

TRAVEL

0-7645-5438-7   0-7645-5453-0

Also available:
- Alaska For Dummies
  0-7645-1761-9
- Arizona For Dummies
  0-7645-6938-4
- Cancún and the Yucatán For Dummies
  0-7645-2437-2
- Cruise Vacations For Dummies
  0-7645-6941-4
- Europe For Dummies
  0-7645-5456-5
- Ireland For Dummies
  0-7645-5455-7

- Las Vegas For Dummies
  0-7645-5448-4
- London For Dummies
  0-7645-4277-X
- New York City For Dummies
  0-7645-6945-7
- Paris For Dummies
  0-7645-5494-8
- RV Vacations For Dummies
  0-7645-5443-3
- Walt Disney World & Orlando For Dummies
  0-7645-6943-0

GRAPHICS, DESIGN & WEB DEVELOPMENT

0-7645-4345-8   0-7645-5589-8

Also available:
- Adobe Acrobat 6 PDF For Dummies
  0-7645-3760-1
- Building a Web Site For Dummies
  0-7645-7144-3
- Dreamweaver MX 2004 For Dummies
  0-7645-4342-3
- FrontPage 2003 For Dummies
  0-7645-3882-9
- HTML 4 For Dummies
  0-7645-1995-6
- Illustrator CS For Dummies
  0-7645-4084-X

- Macromedia Flash MX 2004 For Dummies
  0-7645-4358-X
- Photoshop 7 All-in-One Desk Reference For Dummies
  0-7645-1667-1
- Photoshop CS Timesaving Techniques For Dummies
  0-7645-6782-9
- PHP 5 For Dummies
  0-7645-4166-8
- PowerPoint 2003 For Dummies
  0-7645-3908-6
- QuarkXPress 6 For Dummies
  0-7645-2593-X

NETWORKING, SECURITY, PROGRAMMING & DATABASES

0-7645-6852-3   0-7645-5784-X

Also available:
- A+ Certification For Dummies
  0-7645-4187-0
- Access 2003 All-in-One Desk Reference For Dummies
  0-7645-3988-4
- Beginning Programming For Dummies
  0-7645-4997-9
- C For Dummies
  0-7645-7068-4
- Firewalls For Dummies
  0-7645-4048-3
- Home Networking For Dummies
  0-7645-42796

- Network Security For Dummies
  0-7645-1679-5
- Networking For Dummies
  0-7645-1677-9
- TCP/IP For Dummies
  0-7645-1760-0
- VBA For Dummies
  0-7645-3989-2
- Wireless All In-One Desk Reference For Dummies
  0-7645-7496-5
- Wireless Home Networking For Dummies
  0-7645-3910-8

HEALTH & SELF-HELP

0-7645-6820-5 *†

0-7645-2566-2

Also available:
- Alzheimer's For Dummies
  0-7645-3899-3
- Asthma For Dummies
  0-7645-4233-8
- Controlling Cholesterol For Dummies
  0-7645-5440-9
- Depression For Dummies
  0-7645-3900-0
- Dieting For Dummies
  0-7645-4149-8
- Fertility For Dummies
  0-7645-2549-2
- Fibromyalgia For Dummies
  0-7645-5441-7

- Improving Your Memory For Dummies
  0-7645-5435-2
- Pregnancy For Dummies †
  0-7645-4483-7
- Quitting Smoking For Dummies
  0-7645-2629-4
- Relationships For Dummies
  0-7645-5384-4
- Thyroid For Dummies
  0-7645-5385-2

EDUCATION, HISTORY, REFERENCE & TEST PREPARATION

0-7645-5194-9

0-7645-4186-2

Also available:
- Algebra For Dummies
  0-7645-5325-9
- British History For Dummies
  0-7645-7021-8
- Calculus For Dummies
  0-7645-2498-4
- English Grammar For Dummies
  0-7645-5322-4
- Forensics For Dummies
  0-7645-5580-4
- The GMAT For Dummies
  0-7645-5251-1
- Inglés Para Dummies
  0-7645-5427-1

- Italian For Dummies
  0-7645-5196-5
- Latin For Dummies
  0-7645-5431-X
- Lewis & Clark For Dummies
  0-7645-2545-X
- Research Papers For Dummies
  0-7645-5426-3
- The SAT I For Dummies
  0-7645-7193-1
- Science Fair Projects For Dummies
  0-7645-5460-3
- U.S. History For Dummies
  0-7645-5249-X

Get smart @ dummies.com®
- **Find a full list of Dummies titles**
- **Look into loads of FREE on-site articles**
- **Sign up for FREE eTips e-mailed to you weekly**
- **See what other products carry the Dummies name**
- **Shop directly from the Dummies bookstore**
- **Enter to win new prizes every month!**

* Separate Canadian edition also available
† Separate U.K. edition also available

Available wherever books are sold. For more information or to order direct: U.S. customers visit www.dummies.com or call 1-877-762-2974.
U.K. customers visit www.wileyeurope.com or call 0800 243407. Canadian customers visit www.wiley.ca or call 1-800-567-4797.